For anyone striving to be good, keeping the candle lit.

Edited by Belinda Busteed Burum
Design by Lisa Andrews

ISBN# 978-0-578-93195-1
stonebalancer.com

YOU ARE LOVED

CREATIVE AND SPIRITUAL ADVENTURES

A Memoir

ALEX COOK

CONTENTS

INTRODUCTION

For as long as I can remember I've felt an impulse to tell other people about my life. As I learned things, as I found beauty, fought battles, and was surprised by life, it felt natural to talk about it. And unnatural not to. When I found that I loved making pictures, writing songs, and telling stories, the impulse to share found a natural outlet.

As experience got more difficult and there was more pain, mistakes, and confusion, the impulse to share didn't diminish. By some beautiful, intuitive certainty, I knew it was safe to share my inner wilderness life. Actually, it felt safer than not sharing it. And as time went on, I felt a sureness that each time I revealed something about my own path, it might help someone feel less alone or afraid.

Anyone striving to bring their inspiration into the world encounters resistance and fear. In this book I reveal the path I traced, facing those enemies. This has often felt like a life-or-death struggle, with my purpose and meaning hanging in the balance. I thank God for the spiritual tools I've found and learned to practice over these many years.

This book was written for you, the one working to bring your own dream into the world. You probably face skepticism and indifference to your pure idea, maybe even in your own thoughts. This book will show you, in stories of my very human life, that you are not alone in your fear and confusion. Nor are you alone in your soaring inspiration, and desire to make something wonderful.

Living a creative life can be very difficult. I certainly had some knock-down, drag-out battles to fight. I was helped on by spiritual texts, and a few books of other creatives. I know this book will reach some people right where they are, in the midst of their own battles. It will bring recognition, comfort, inspiration, and a fighting spirit.

It is indispensably powerful to remember our certain, un-erasable experiences of goodness, breakthrough, and glory. Each time I have an experience of goodness beyond what I'd previously known, it expands my understanding. My willingness to hope for greater goodness grows. The same thing happens when I hear of someone else's experience. If it could happen to them, it could happen to me! So, when I look back on the times my prayers have been answered, when I recall the deep, life-transforming effects of God, beauty, and holiness, I want to set them down for the record and say unequivocally, "This happened!"

As an artist, one hopes to create something that will be universal. The best way I know to do that is to have faith that we all are humans, having our very real human experiences. The deeper and more honest I am in my expressing, the greater is my right to hope that others will relate to it. As different as the trappings of our lives are, and as unsimilar the specifics, I have an abiding faith that in the very intimate places, we can relate to one another. These stories are the experiences of a white, college-educated man, beginning around 1992. My privileged position allowed me to feel free and safe in situations where some others almost certainly would not have. Because I am an artist, many of the stories are about the struggles and victories of a person navigating that life. Because for most of my adult life I have been a Christian—a Christian Scientist to be specific—these stories are seen through that lens. Despite all those inescapable specifics, I remain confident that everyone can relate to fear, and everyone can relate to love.

As it relates to religion and spirituality, word choice can mean the difference between reaching one person and losing another. When I say I am a Christian Scientist, I may lose people who don't consider themselves religious. Heck, I may even lose some other Christians. But, if I describe the same spiritual phenomena with different language, I might just as likely draw those same people to me. I've done my best to be honest about my close relationship with the Bible and the Christian Science textbook, *Science and Health with Key to the Scriptures*, while at the same time, focusing not on dogma and jargon, but on living spiritual principles that people of any spiritual background can observe.

The stories are told in a generally chronological order. It was natural to order them this way because each breakthrough depends upon the understanding revealed in previous stories. That said, because one story may take place over a series of days or weeks, and others over years, there is overlap in the chronology. A shorter story may have taken place within the timeline of a longer one. Rest assured that as you progress through the stories time is passing though they are not filled with specific dates.

There is no good art without pure, unstinting honesty. These stories are honest. With all my heart I hope you will find them interesting and useful.

Alex Cook, April 2021

DANCING

What is God like?

As a young person I had the idea that God is good, and really big, but I got the feeling that He is also kind of stiff and stern.

One evening in the spring of 1992 I was sitting upstairs in my room doing homework. I was a senior in high school, used to getting good grades. I sat there at my desk dutifully engaged with textbooks and worksheets. My family was elsewhere in the house—my mom probably in the kitchen cleaning up after dinner, dad in his office, reading the mail, my sister Cecily in her room doing whatever she was doing. A normal night at home for the Cook family.

Somewhere in the placid hours of the evening, after dark, I was interrupted from my US History (or whatever it was). A feeling arrived in me as clearly as if it were a new worksheet in my pile. It said: *Put on your Walkman and walk down the street.*

It wasn't words. Just a feeling that that's what should happen. I didn't think too much about it, but it felt good. So, without much fanfare, I put on a sweatshirt, threw my little yellow Sony cassette Walkman in my pocket, put the headphones in my ears and walked downstairs and out the front door.

As I ambled down the street, away from our house I had an easy breezy feeling, doing something I wouldn't normally do. On any given night I would finish my homework, watch tv, talk on the phone—normal suburban teenager stuff. Tonight, somehow, I found myself walking down our leafy, quiet street in the fresh spring air.

Churning in my pocket was the little cassette Walkman. Inside was a tape I'd borrowed from my sister. I didn't know the band. The music was bouncy and new to my ears.

About 100 yards down the street, past just a couple houses, I came to a rocky outcropping that overlooked the street. I'd never really noticed it before. I climbed up a small hill among the trees and crawled to the top of the little cliff. It poked out of the abbreviated woods between two houses, about 15 feet above the street.

Looking out on the empty, lamp-washed asphalt, I began to notice the music in my ears. It was good! I began to sway with the groove. It was REALLY good. I could feel it in my body. It was bouncing in my ears with new colors and electric waves. Then, like the most natural thing that ever happened, I danced. Despite the fact that I had never in my life spent a single thought on dancing, like there was nothing between me and that music, I felt it in my whole soul and body and danced. There were no moves, just freedom. Just me and the music, the brisk night air and my little neighborhood, a distant 15 feet below.

Five minutes earlier I had been sitting, pencil in hand, undisturbed in my quiet upstairs room. The comfortable routine was in place. The gentle hum of the dishwasher running in the kitchen.

Like little Lucy Pevensie I'd walked through the wardrobe and into another universe. I spent no time boggling at the fact that I was dancing. I just danced. The most comforting, freeing, expanding, enlightening feeling. I was alone, and so fulfilled. My normally shy demeanor was dust, and my body moved broadly, expressively, confidently, joyfully.

Each song was new to me. I'd never heard any of it before. Just like this night. New. Everything was new. In the silence between songs, I waited hungrily for the next one to fill my ears. They came, each one like a startling new friend at the coolest party I never dreamed of being invited to. Everything was new and yes.

Finally, the album came to its end. I stood there, eyes wide, sweating, the sound of the Walkman's gears grinding in my ears. I watched my breath turning to steam, pouring out of my mouth. My whole body was steaming, flushed and humid inside my clothes. With a happy exhale I clambered down the little hill through the woods and out onto the sidewalk. A minivan hissed by. Everything was normal down here in the street. Down here it was as if the world hadn't changed at all. But it had.

I walked the two minutes back to the house, wiped off my muddy sneakers, and quietly stepped inside. Up the brown carpeted stairs into my room where my papers lay unfinished on the desk, the lamp still shining down on them.

I never mentioned this to anyone until years later.

I did, in the following months and years, make a secret habit of heading out in the deep of night to some schoolyard or ballfield, with my cassette Walkman singing all kinds of wonderful songs, to dance. I learned that life can be good enough to justify itself without any proof for anyone. It can be free and joyful in intimate solitude. It can be me and the sky, the music and the grass, the weather and the air. I learned that I can dance to funk music or classical, heavy metal or the gentlest voice. I might dance like explosions, kicks, or karate. I might be a lion or a squirrel or a butterfly. I might get right down in the grass like a dog off leash, or cuddle with the earth itself. I might do my best at an Irish Riverdance, the Moscow ballet, or scuttle around like a lobster at the bottom of the sea. I saw there is nothing embarrassing, no movement too strange, or even strange at all, if it's honest.

So, what is God like? God is the one who interrupts homework on a quiet Tuesday night and says "Put on your Walkman and walk down the street."

LOVE ARRIVES

I was raised in a well-off suburban home, in a religious family, going to Sunday School. At the age of 12, on the heels of my 13-year-old sister, I quit the Sunday School part. It felt lame and forced, and I didn't feel engaged by it at all.

In my last year of high school I began to go for walks. It started over the winter. I would leave school with my backpack on, Walkman playing in my ears, and explore the snowy streets of my little hometown, Wellesley, Massachusetts. How free to walk and walk, alone and feeling. My music, my loneliness, the wooded streets, finding new places, secret paths from yard to yard. I found I had a prowling hunger for walking. After ambling for hours each afternoon, I would find myself on the road home, with the deep blue evening lowering around me.

Later that year, when the weather got warm, I would take myself out for walks late at night. The summer air moving in the tree tops, the street lamps illuminating the asphalt in pools, my new understanding that I am a person with feelings.

On one of these late-night walks I began to feel Love. I had no explanation. I just began to feel Love. Not for anyone in particular, but for everyone and all. I began to understand that all the people in the world are connected and precious, and not just to me, but to Love itself. It was true in my bones and made me feel strong and capable. I found that I loved Love. There was nothing about it that wasn't good. It was beautiful and made me know that, along with everyone else, I am part of something unbelievably valuable.

Love was in the evening air. It was in the dark forest. I saw it resting gently over the head of a friend while she slept. Love was in the illuminated windows on a cold afternoon. It was in the music that blasted in my ears from my headphones. It was in the dinner my mom made.

At one point it dawned on me—this must be God. After all those years in Sunday School, not really knowing why it was important, I got it. It was *so* important. It was the most important thing. But it wasn't important because they told me. It was important because I felt it. I would do anything for my beautiful Love.

Because it was mine, I began to follow it with all my heart. It was real and I knew it. *God is real, and I know it.* Love is a powerful force, stitched into me, my life, this life. I wasn't ashamed or embarrassed about it. Because it was mine, I didn't need anyone to tell me about it. With a great desire I wanted to explore it, learn about it. It made me strong. I wasn't afraid of talking to girls anymore. I loved them. I knew they were God's creations and there was nothing to fear from them. I found it easy to see through peoples' bad behavior. I knew it wasn't them. They were just afraid. I knew that I was free to love them.

I went to college. I joined my friends in convoluted, college-y philoso-phizing, but I never wondered if Love was an absolutely present force, a fact. I talked to my friends about it, perhaps too much. I learned that one person at college referred to me as "The Love Guy." I was a bit embarrassed, but happy about the label.

The feeling continued. One night I sat at my desk drawing. I felt a pas-sionate, intoxicating love as I drew people. I felt a deep, flowing compassion for them. Later, one summer afternoon, when I was driving home from somewhere, I passed by a schoolyard where two young girls were swinging on the swings. In that moment, the veil was not there, and I saw innocence in its primary colors. It wasn't because they were young. It was because they were God's voice. They were the holy creation. Innocence without explanation.

On another late night when I was out walking, I made my way beyond what I knew, through a neighborhood I'd not explored before. Mist rose from the grass and surrounded the tidy suburban homes. Mist curled around the wet trunks of trees. The houses, the short, cropped grass, the trees, the swelling mist, came together like a perfect poem. They spoke to each other. They were real. I could not believe in boredom. I couldn't believe in meaninglessness. Every leaf, every blade of grass, every brick, was just where it was supposed to be. And love swelled in me like a wave. It grew and grew and until I cried. I longed to run home to make a painting, to draw perfect lines to reflect back what I was seeing. It was too good. It was so good it nearly hurt.

I felt the enormity of Beauty. Its vastness was all-towering. If this small corner, this random selection of trees and 1960's era suburban houses below the misty night sky could reveal this deluge of perfection, then what of the rest of the world? What of more romantic places? Beauty is *everywhere*. Love is every-where. I felt I would fall apart. Love would take me apart with its vastness, its genuine eternity.

I walked home, filled with tears, filled with joy. I shook my head, the space inside me expanding like a helium balloon to hold the night sky, the stars, the swirling mist. Almost in pain, I longed to make art that would sing this song. To say something back to it. To be part of it. I was agitated, nearly suffering from the sight of so much Beauty.

But, I objected, pain isn't the outcome of Beauty and Love! What was it? For some months I wondered. Why did this open door of Beauty, of Love, with its declarations of infinity, cause me this nearly frantic reaction?

I watched my feelings. I listened with my honest heart. I began to under-stand. It was the feeling of being mortal, crying out, screaming, "Love will kill me! Eternity is too big for me! I have to give back! I have to say what I think about it! I must say who I am and make it mine!"

God was opening His quilted robes to my peering eyes and His eternity was doing its work. It was seeping into me, coursing through my being, revealing smallness and fear that couldn't come along on this journey of Love. I began to see that this frantic feeling was no part of Love. I would never have ownership of eternity. I would never be big enough to make a contribution to its galleries. It would give and I would receive. Beauty and Love would be the tower, the wind, the sky, the all. And I would receive their gifts and give their gifts, all in Love's time. Never in mine.

Love will ever be a wave, far too large to oppose. Beyond our control, never to be bartered with. Only to ride, and praise its motion. When Love is revealed, it changes us. We are never the same. We fear less. We desire goodness more. We can never go back!

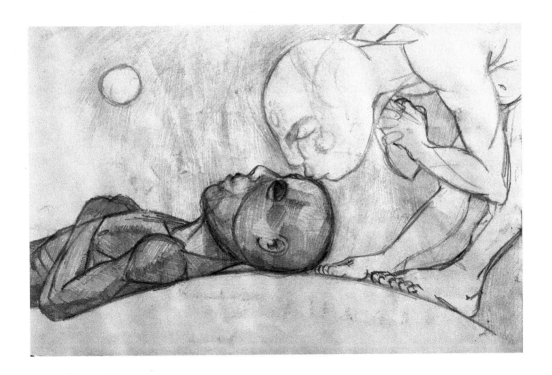

PICKING UP THE GUITAR

Sunday afternoon, late August, and the melancholy drop in the stomach that school will be starting again soon. But for now, the air is warm and there is *nothing* to do. This Sunday afternoon may as well stretch on for weeks because all that is coming is another warm Monday morning, still summer.

In those long summery days, it's hard to say what happened. I didn't know to notice or to watch. An hour slipped into another hour. I might be listening to music in my room, playing with sticks in the yard, drawing a picture.

I did not yet think of myself as an artist, a musician, an athlete, or any of the words that have come to describe me. I had those inclinations, which came out now and then in unconvincing ways. I was just myself, a kid.

On that afternoon I was in my room, upstairs. I wasn't doing much. Sort of bouncing from one thing to another, not bored. At one point I sat on my bed. The house was quiet and still. As I sat there, mostly thoughtless, I felt a very clear feeling to go down into the basement and get my mom's old acoustic guitar and bring it up to my room. I did.

I had never thought about this guitar. Or any guitars, to be honest. I was much more into video games and basketball practice. I loved to listen to music. I had never thought about playing music. I didn't know anything about guitars. I didn't know anyone who played the guitar. Mom had, but only in old stories. I had never seen her strum a chord. So, when the idea came to pick up this old guitar, it was not a familiar notion.

I opened the old cardboard case and pulled it out. It was a classical guitar with nylon strings. It lit no rock-and-roll fire in me. In fact, my thought was so far from the idea of making music that I just felt a kind of wonder. "What can you do with this thing?" I didn't know how to hold it or what to do with my hands. I put it where it felt most natural, which was lying flat across my lap. For some time, like a traveler, I explored sounds I could make with the strings. It was like a foreign landscape. So much unknown, so much to investigate. It was hard to imagine how people made music with this object. I couldn't fathom it.

I had no illusions that I would ever be able to play the guitar, so I just laid it there and played around. It was fun to try to make good sounds come out of it.

I did keep that guitar in my room though. And I did keep trying to make good sounds come out of it. Days turned to weeks and weeks turned to months and I was becoming more and more entranced with the pure, clear sounds that could come from the strings.

For two years I played that guitar, laying it flat on my lap. Because I knew there was no way I would ever be able to actually play the guitar, I never tried to hold it the way I saw musicians holding it—upright against their body, their wrist amazingly going under the neck with fingers curling around from underneath to make chords. I continued to play it flat, pressing my fingers on the neck from above like a piano.

I fell in love with the sad, compassionate sound of the E minor chord. I would sit and strum, listening to its soft message.

One day I realized I loved the feelings I could make with this old guitar so much I was going to actually play it. And if I did, I knew I would have to give up my flat-on-the-lap way of playing.

It was a hard pill to swallow. I would have to learn everything all over again, this time holding the guitar the real way. It was painful and slow, but there was no way around it.

I took guitar lessons for about six months. It was boring. I never did the scales or the homework. But I did keep strumming chords. I kept listening to the music I loved and tried to figure out how they were doing it. I taught myself to play *The Thieving Magpie* overture by Gioachino Rossini. I'd heard my dad playing it on the living room stereo and the melody was too cool to not try. I played it horribly and unrecognizably, but it was mine to do. In a total ignorance of accepted musical approaches, the guitar was as much mine as my own backyard.

I began writing pieces of guitar music. I had no musical knowledge or theory. I just copied the sounds I heard in myself. I found combinations of notes on the guitar neck that were interesting to me. They were far beyond my ability to play well. This was great because it revealed a path to follow to get better.

As my fingers got more facile with transitions, jumping from chord to chord, I began to try writing songs. They were horrible. I felt embarrassed by them. Still, I practiced them and got good at playing them. I wanted badly to write songs that felt real. I tried and tried and tried. They were forced and lame. I never showed them to anyone. They weren't worth it. Still, now that the component parts were there in my hands, the desire to write songs emerged as a pillar of fire.

For a year I pushed and stumbled, each time facing the limping ideas that I had created. I wondered, "What makes a good song?" "What do I *do*?!" I thought of all the artists I loved and felt that there was a club of people who can and another, larger, club that can't. It was clear that I was in the second category. Still, the pillar of fire burned against the barrier. I filled my notebook with words and musical ideas that I didn't like.

One afternoon I put some words on top of a new chord progression I'd come up with. I played and sang. It was ok. In fact, I might even go so far as to say that it wasn't embarrassing. I sang it again. It *wasn't embarrassing!* There it was on the page. I'd written a song I didn't feel embarrassed about. There was something real about it.

From that moment, I never again wondered if I could write songs. It just happened. I knew that I could. I ceased pursuing "good songs" and began trying to express what I was seeing and feeling. Little by little I could see my feelings making their way out onto the pages of my notebooks. I began to make choices of words, and what to sing about that said what I meant. My sad, compassionate words found their home with the E minor chord I loved.

This was the stumbling foundation of what has become (so far) a 30-year love affair with creating songs. Little did I know that these first tender explorations would turn into creating music that would one day have an effect in the lives of others. I didn't know it would pay my bills, or that it would cause people to cry when they hear it, or dance, or laugh. I didn't know people would tell me they had been healed by these combinations of words and music. And I certainly had no idea of the riches of heart and soul that would fill my life.

AN ANGEL

In the first months of my freshman year of college, I happily fell in with a gang of new friends. We all were nervous and excited, full of questions, telling everyone else about their hometown. Fresh from our high school homes, we all longed to belong in some new way.

This gang of folks, John, Chad, Chuck, Gwen, Jessie, and myself, somehow landed together. Soon it was the regular thing to meet up in Chuck's dorm room, which became known as "The Pad." Everyone was relieved to have somewhere to go and someone to hang out with. Our hearts pounded slightly less nervously.

As the weeks progressed, it wasn't hard to see that in spite of the haphazard, arbitrary way this group had fallen together, some substantial friendships were forming. John and I hit it off great and laughed all the time. It was clear Chuck was head over heels in love with Gwen. Chad and Jessie began to come along with John and me. What lay in the hearts, beneath the surface, began to assert itself. The people were sorting themselves out.

Weeks passed and we settled in to our new lives. Uncertainties turned into rhythms; nervousness evolved into a little more confidence. We began to see less of Chuck and Gwen as they spent more and more time alone.

One evening in November I was on the balcony, just down the hall from The Pad. Even in November, the Savannah evening air is balmy and gentle. The dorm, a repurposed Holiday Inn, whirred with the energy of the 300 kids it housed. In the distance, a terrible guttural scream ripped the twilight. I looked down the hall, but all the doors were closed. I couldn't tell where it had come from. I noticed a few other kids on the balcony trying to figure it out too. Frankly, with hundreds of 18-year-olds all piled on top of each other, there was whooping and yelling just about every night. I didn't think much of it.

But, very soon, John and Jessie were racing down to my room, banging on the door. The fear in their eyes spoke before the words hit me. Chuck had slit his wrists and was being rushed to the hospital. I ran out the door with them and someone drove us to the emergency room.

I'd never encountered anything like this. To me, this kind of thing was only in movies. It was far beyond what I'd been prepared for—way over my head and more than I knew how to respond to. I couldn't begin to imagine the reality of it. What was Chuck feeling? Why would he do something like that?

John, Chad, Jessie, myself, and some other of Chuck's friends congregated in the waiting room. Everyone was miserable. We drew close together, with nothing to say. Fear and shock closed everyone's mouths. The waiting room was stale, the air hard to breathe. Inwardly I shook my head in wonder. "What's happening?" I boggled. A room full of 18-year-old kids, eyes as wide as they could be, trying to be strong and in control. Longing to know what to do.

Wanting only to feel some solidness, I tried to calm myself down. I thought of my parents. They were solid. I thought of my dad telling me about the power of being grateful even when things are bad—or maybe especially when things are bad. I remembered a phrase that got thrown around in our house. "Be grateful for the doorknob." It came from a story he told from his own time in college. He'd sat in his dorm room overcome with depression over some problem. He'd been working on being grateful, no matter what. As the story goes, he thought to himself, "What on earth can I be grateful for? Everything is going wrong." Peering hopelessly around the room his eyes landed on the knob of the door. Then, humbly, "If there were no doorknob, I couldn't get out of this room. I'm grateful for that doorknob." The story had always moved me. Thinking of my dad, so cheerful and together in all the time I'd known him, reduced to such humility.

In my family, when things were looking bleak, you would be encouraged to be grateful for the doorknob. In short, look for the good, no matter what. Sitting with these near strangers in the waiting room of the hospital introduced a new kind of seriousness, beyond anything my 18 years had yet brought me. I decided to try to be grateful for the doorknob. To see some goodness in that weary waiting room.

I gazed slowly around the worried faces surrounding me. A messy pile of torn, exhausted magazines splayed out on a well-worn coffee table. I imagined months of worried faces, thoughtlessly leafing through the pages, distracted and distraught. I noticed our friend Jessie gently checking in with one of Chuck's friends. She was sitting on the arm of the chair one of the other girls was sitting in. She was listening to the girl tell a story about Chuck. I continued watching. Simply, and without fanfare Jessie made her way around the room, checking in with each of Chuck's friends. In a simple, 18-year-old way she made sure everyone had what they needed, seeing how people were doing. As I watched her care for her peers, natural as a forest brook, I adored her.

In my humble position, ready to be grateful for the doorknob, she became an angel before my very eyes. Though it was just her, this goofy, slightly defiant college freshman, she was surrounded by a Love that was not hers personally. Her love was God's love. They were not different. I witnessed God's love glowing patiently through that waiting room. All the purity and affection of Love itself was in that room caring for each one of those kids fearing for their friend. It was my friend Jessie, but it was also the actual angel of God Himself. I watched her and was comforted. My attention was lifted away from violence and fear. In their place, a Love untouched by those things. Goodness itself was there in the room with us. It didn't come from Jessie—but she embodied it.

That night when I went back to the dorm I was invigorated. Love had been there with us, unimpressed by the screams, the blood, the fear. It had moved Jessie around the room, as she laid her hands on the shoulders of Chuck's friends, looking in their eyes, listening to their fear. It had opened my eyes to the holiness of God, moving with certainty and grace among those humbled, surprised children. I thought of Jessie, this girl I'd known only these several weeks. In that waiting room she'd been an angel—the impulse to comfort those in need.

Deep in the night, sitting at my desk I thought of that angel, ministering to us kids, and drew it as faithfully as I could. I made no effort to draw Jessie. It was the angel I wanted to commemorate. She had long wings, gentle hands, and a look of serene care on her face. She had a halo around her head, making it clear that she was God's messenger, moving among us. As I drew, I knew I would give it to Jessie and tell her what I saw: *I saw your care. I saw your love. I knew it was Love greater than just you. It was the real thing.*

Some weeks later, Chuck was back in school. Everyone breathed a sigh of relief. And, entirely to my surprise, Jessie and I began to have a warm romance.

ANOTHER ANGEL, ANNOUNCING A JOURNEY

As a teenager, I rode my bike around Wellesley. The streets and yards spread out around me like a garden. In every direction I saw a beckoning path. Under bridges, the shores of lakes, tiny forests between homes. Independence brought with it a luminescent desire to explore. My imagination was easily seduced by curving roads, wending away through the swaying trees and off into the wilderness. I began to ride my bicycle to places I had only gone in a car. There was a sign on route 16, the main street in town that said "Uxbridge 26 miles." I didn't know where Uxbridge was or why it was on that sign, but I began to imagine riding out that way on some sunny afternoon. I never imagined arriving in Uxbridge—I only wanted to go. A dream was born.

I never rode to Uxbridge. It never crossed my mind that I *could* do it. That dream slept in me for years. I wasn't any kind of adventurer. No sir. I was wrapped up in school, suburban sports, my friends.

It's the coincidence of the dream and the doing that makes wonderful things happen. The trembling moment when you first allow that this fantasy you've had is something that you could actually do. The moment of stepping out of well-worn tracks into blustering winds of action and consequences. We don't know what will happen.

At the end of my first year of college down in Savannah, Georgia I had just turned 19. The summer and the future were taking me back to Massachusetts. Jessie, now my girlfriend of 6 months, was 1000 miles away, in Wisconsin, a state I had heard of. After months of happy romance all the elements of normal life were tossed into the air. They dangled there as if in suspended animation, with not a peep as to what the future would hold. On the drive back to Massachusetts I was dreaming about how to be with her.

I sat in the back seat of my family's tan Nissan Stanza as we hurtled north on Interstate 95. "Angel Dust" by Faith No More growled in my Walkman. Dad was driving, mom snoozing in the passenger seat. The hours of passing trees and the solitude of being inside my headphones put me in a nebulous haze, musing and listening. I wasn't thinking about very much when, like a warm glow, an idea arrived as if it had walked in the door. It was simple and obvious: "I don't want to spend the money to fly to Wisconsin, so…I'll ride my bike." Just like that. Without questions and what-if's, the idea lay sparkling in my lap, shining like a fact. My mind's ears pricked up like a dog's. The haze evaporated. I shook myself. I felt as if some golden, living thing had entered the car—a life-shifting thought, as real as a person. I prodded and probed the idea to see if it was real. I remember looking around to see if my parents were feeling its presence. It was so thunderous, so utterly breathtaking, I could hardly imagine it was only inside me. They drove on, unaware. Over the next five minutes I sat with it, soaking it in. Enthusiasm swept over me like a wave. A pure joy, a radiant love for being alive. "Oh my God!" I thought again and again. "I can *do* that!" From that moment I knew it would happen.

For the next few weeks the plan walked around in my thoughts, settling into the cracks. I was full of romantic images of sleeping under bridges, drinking from rivers, and eating apples off trees.

I told a friend about my idea and she was all excited to help with the planning. "What planning?" I asked her, annoyed.

I hated the planning. My parents suggested and coaxed. I just wanted to get on my bike and sleep under the stars. The road was calling and all they wanted to do was make lists and buy toiletries. Charting and mapping, schedules and phone calls were detestable. Didn't they know that adventure was about spontaneity? It was only with much firm suggesting that I agreed to even take a tent. I felt the poetry seeping out of my precious trip like air from a balloon. Planning was like homework on a Saturday. All they wanted to do was worry.

In a perfect world, once the idea was in place the voyage would flow forward like a movie. What more was there than to begin? I would swashbuckle fearlessly through the landscape, feeling no pain or doubt. I would sleep in the hands of the grass and wear the blessing of the stars at night. Yes, yes, that is certainly how it would be. But without those lists, forced upon me like unwanted, aching saddlebags on a stubborn mule, I would have landed hard on that poetic road, tentless and freezing. My teeth would have rotted in my mouth and I would have been hopelessly lost at the first uncertainty. Oh Lord, get my head out of the stars and plant my feet back on the ground.

I'd saved up a thousand dollars from summer jobs over the years. It was my natural inclination to live frugally. I planned to eat PB&J, apples and carrots every day and every night. I would sleep in my tent. I didn't expect to make much of a dent in my savings.

Two or three weeks after the idea waltzed up in the backseat, the trip began. I would ride the whole way on U.S. 20, "the Old Post Road" interstate before there were interstates. It stretches from Boston to Portland, Oregon, a straight shot the whole way. I would get off in Chicago. Simple.

As the date of departure arrived, I was harried and annoyed. Surrounded by well-wishers and safety-wishers. Like a girl on her first nervous date, I wished they would forget all about it. I was scared and irritable. Honestly, under the scrutiny and self-consciousness of the hour I was only going because that was the plan. The decision had been made, written in blood on the calendar. Then came the uncertainty and terror of really doing it. The morning of departure was a far cry from the bliss of the angelic announcement.

****

15

On the first day I rode about 30 miles before stopping for lunch. I slowed down, looking for a place to take a break. As I pedaled, I saw a woman gardening in her front yard. She was about 35, kneeling in the flowerbeds below the front windows. It came to me to approach her and begin a conversation. I wondered at myself. Who knows what we are when we're in a situation beyond our previous experience? I checked myself to see if the idea was really mine. Most of me is shy and this kind of idea was entirely new. I felt like there was a stranger inside me telling me to approach this lady. I had only been away from home for three or four hours, but already there was a new yearning in me that I didn't recognize—to be connected. To see that my warm body and beating heart still included me in the world even though I was away from everything I knew. I dismounted and approached the woman, walking up the front path. I blurted out, "Hi," to her turned back as she unsuspectingly pulled weeds from the dirt. She whipped around, startled half to death. Apologizing, and startled myself, I haltingly told her my situation. As an excuse to be having the conversation at all, I mentioned that I wanted to call my parents. Soon we were talking amiably. Yes, I could use her phone.

She led me into the house, asking questions. I was struck by how comfortable she was having a complete stranger in her home. We talked about my biking, begun just hours before, and I soon felt comfortable myself. I could smell the smells of an unfamiliar family. Sunlight wandered in the sliding glass door and the window over the sink. The kitchen counter was wiped clean, but cereal bowls remained from that morning's breakfast. How had I come to be in this house? I imagined that I'd wandered onto the set of some private movie, the documentary of someone else's life. Then, to my amazement, she was making me a couple of sandwiches, and poured me a glass of milk. My brain fell over backwards from surprise, but my body sidled up to the counter and dug in. I bubbled and chirped to her about my new trip. My heart sang inside me. We chatted, she doing dishes as I gobbled up sandwiches. I learned that she was a nurse at a nearby hospital. Hardly surprising. I thought, "I bet everyone on her ward gets better fast." She told me she would be leaving soon to pick up her son from school and go to work. I silently admired her for fitting me in like she had. She was a woman with a schedule, but not too busy to take in a wayward cyclist. Then, before I could excuse myself so as to not get in her way, she invited me to swim in the backyard pool. "Well…yes!" I thought, thinking it was too good to be true, but concertedly not looking the gift horse in the mouth.

She went back out to the front to do her weeding and I found the pool in the back. It was an above ground pool, big, cool and wet in the hot, lazy grass. Splashing around in the water, I exclaimed to myself, "Just look where in the world I am! How did I get here?!" The wildness of what was happening crawled all over me. Yesterday I was in my own house. Everything was normal.

Now I'm in this pool, in a town I've never heard of, in the backyard of this lady I don't know. Anyone can be on the *other* side of this house, standing on the sidewalk, but somehow, on this strange new day, my life has taken me out of what anyone can do and put me in this little situation that only I can be in. A few minutes later the woman came out the sliding glass door and said she had to go to work, but I could stay and rest as long as I liked. I could even go inside and watch TV. The rubber bands in my brain snapped with finality and fell limply to the floor. People don't do this do they?

I quickly jumped out of the pool so I could get her name and address before she left. I thanked her a thousand times, stammering with surprise and gratitude. She drove away and I sat in her dry den watching half of some old sitcom on TV. It was strange to be in this unfamiliar house, alone. All around me were the artifacts of human life—of real, specific human lives. Framed photos of her family crowded the end tables. In the shelves were her books. As I sat on the worn sofa I could feel the hundreds of nights spent there—friends, falling asleep, intimacies. I felt as though I could hear the conversations that had been spoken through the years. The life of this family was spread out before me like treasures in an attic. I imagined I was from the future, visiting a museum of the 1990's.

Another angel. I sat with a pool-wet head on the tired sofa in her TV room, considering, learning again what an angel is. In one sense this day was normal. I hadn't walked through any glowing time vortex or been sucked into a black hole. I hadn't witnessed the shining arm of God descend from the sky to land me in this living room. But I had witnessed this stunning openness. On this first day of my first foray into the wide-open world, I'd conspicuously been shown a broad, joyous generosity, the likes of which had never before crossed my mind. Somehow I had slipped into a wonder-place where there is more possibility than I'd known. The voice inside had nudged me to have a conversation with her. A deep sense of comfort stole over me like a bed sheet.

After a short rest I felt a healthy desire to be back on my two wheels. I closed and locked the door behind me and walked out the path with my bicycle.

My experience with this woman colored the way I saw the whole rest of the trip. She had showed me something some people don't even believe exists—openness and generosity between strangers. It was the first time I had ever *been* a stranger. No one had ever mentioned to me that people invite total strangers into their houses. I wondered if anyone at home knew that there were people who do that. Or was this lady the only one? Was this ordinary? Does everyone do this? Considering the broad world, I realized I really didn't know. The roof had been blown off the top of my thinking and the wild blue air was rushing all around in there. It was all so deeply good. It turned out that even away from the life I knew, I was cared for. But more than that, there was a message here. Even before I got a foot in the door of this trip, the trip itself was trying to show me something. It was *speaking* to me. Life was saying—"This is something to notice." *There is more good than you know.* It was far beyond all the warnings, fears, and everything I'd been told before. From that point forward, the trip wore a sheen of hope. It began to glow with a sense that out here, in the new, wild land, things can happen that couldn't have happened before.

****

The next afternoon the roads were empty and the sun beat down. The land was huge and unrelenting before me. My thighs burned from straining and pushing over hill after hill. They beckoned me on into the distance only to reveal endless expanses. The landscape fanned out around me as if I was a microbe in a frying pan. After a few hours of pushing in that dusty heat I was discouraged and beaten. In every direction there was only distance. Every distance was mute, silent company.

I'd not known it, but hiding inside my innocent desire to set out on this voyage, was a hungry, growling, gluttony to be done with it already. Entirely apart from my conscious self, I longed to be going a million times faster than I was. Every moment of the slow pace of actual cycling was a torment. I couldn't stand to encounter the real distances I faced. With each revolution of the pedals sending me a pitiful six feet towards my goal, I felt the towering, unforgiving distance that lay ahead. I was so small. I couldn't stand it. Impatience ate me up, scraping and clawing at my thoughts.

In my desperation a new idea emerged—a shocking, mad glimmer of hope, like a flag flapping wildly in the gale. I imagined myself, almost as if I were someone else, getting off my bike. I would stand at the side of the road and… hitchhike. I didn't know if hitchhiking worked. I'd certainly never been in a car with anyone who picked up a hitchhiker. We'd passed some sometimes when I was a kid, but never broken stride. As I imagined sticking out my thumb, I felt the indignant clamor of the countless voices of propriety in my mind. Their eyes were wide as dinner plates, horrified that I'd even consider doing such a thing. Their great disdain for hitchhikers and anyone at all who didn't have a nice car, a nice job, good schooling and good grades. I felt their horror at my thought, and wondered if I might be disowned by my family, my wealthy suburban hometown.

I got off my bike and raised my thumb. I begged in my heart for some relief—some speed. I'd planned to ride this thousand miles to Wisconsin in 20 days. 50 miles a day—simple. But I could scarcely see to the end of one day, let alone 20 days of grueling labor in the too-calm country silence. A thought dawned—there is no short cut. I have to live every moment of this. There is no fast forward.

Putting out my thumb I could feel a new door opening. Every voice of authority I had ever known had told me never to hitchhike. They looked down on hitchhikers. They scorned them. But I was so tired and overwhelmed it seemed the only thing *to* do. My heart longed for it. I wasn't afraid something bad would happen. I was nervous, but only because I was defying my mother, my father, and every trusted voice I had known. In fact, I was disobeying everybody's mother. My thoughts buzzed. I half wondered if the cars going by would laugh at me. "Hah! Look at that poor fool! He actually thinks someone is going to pick him up!" It felt quite possible that hitchhiking was just a dream that I had made up—it didn't even exist in the world. I'd be exposed. Once I put up my thumb, the whole world can see. I raised my thumb and watched.

Miraculously, after a short wait, a pickup truck pulled over and slowed to a halt on the gravelly shoulder. I threw my bike in the back and jumped up onto the vinyl bench seat. Hitchhiking was real. My guts flew like birds in my belly. I got a ride for eight miles and watched the distance go by in a blissful flash.

This, like the nurse in her home the day before, was bright lightning in the landscape of my understanding. I'd not known it—in fact, I'd been counseled against it—but the gem was unveiled. The rough outlines of a new understanding came slowly into view—people are somehow connected. Strangers. There is some kind of humble, human network out there that can be called upon and will respond. In my desperation on the side of the road I am, unbelievably, not alone. A common goodness in another person will respond to the common goodness in me. It had been revealed two times in two days. It had something to do with being on this trip. Something to do with stepping outside of what's expected, normal, safe. I didn't know how it worked, but I saw it. A small corner of glory was uncovered.

****

A couple of days later, now 60 miles into New York State, the June evening was cooling, the sun simmering behind the trees. I found myself deep into the afternoon's miles somehow without food, or a place to sleep. In these tiny towns I'd come across no grocery stores. They offered no campgrounds or grassy fields for a tent. I strained to think of what to do when every inch of space was either the road, someone's yard, or a cornfield. I pushed on slowly as the sun disappeared behind the horizon, my saddlebags swaying heavily. I had in mind that maybe I could camp in somebody's yard, but I didn't know how it could come to be. In just these few days I'd come to understand that there could be solutions in places where I didn't see them. My eyes scanned the landscape, peering hard to see past the surface and into some possibility. Silent, dark-windowed houses passed by offering no relief.

Then, a simple sign of life called me to it. A woman working quietly in her yard. The evening darkness crowded around her as she coiled a garden hose at the side of the house. With plain, pressing need prevailing in my mind, I was drawn to her unthreatening presence. I walked slowly up the driveway in the dark, hoping. I stepped as gently as I could, hating the thought of scaring her as I had that wonderful nurse. Emerging from the darkness into the wash of the driveway lamp, I introduced myself. Again, I asked to use the phone. She graciously led me inside and introduced me to her boyfriend. When they learned about my trip, they invited me to stay for supper and to camp in their back yard.

They were a couple in their mid-20's—Eva a nursing student and Walt, a mailman. Blessedly, the night bloomed with hospitality and warmth. Their home was industrious, as if imbued with a feeling of concentration and willingness to work for happiness. In stark contrast to the sagging blue darkness outside, the home felt bright beyond the power of the electric lights. On the walls were homemade cards and posters, notes to themselves and each other. A smiley face drawn in purple marker with the words "Stay Positive!". We looked at a map and I asked them exactly where we were. Eva pointed out Sloansville, New York.

Walt and Eva were free spirits, living in the country, honest and thrifty. They grew their own food when they could and even got a good amount of meat from fresh roadkill. I could hear most of the folks at home cringing at that idea, but sitting with them in their home, I didn't. In fact, we ate a succulent venison dinner from just such a deer. Who was I, a mere three days from Wellesley, eating deer? Deep in the night, stars of exhaustion were bursting around my eyes. Walt turned out the lights and we said goodnight. I walked out to my tent, and they retired to the inner reaches of their home.

In the morning I went in the house to thank Walt and Eva. They were just serving a big breakfast of scrambled eggs. We sat and ate, chit-chatting in the kitchen. I calculated to myself that I was about 200 miles from my home. When I left after breakfast, they gave me a can of tuna and some bread to last me until I could get to a grocery store. I accepted it gratefully, feeling the beginnings of nervousness for the road. Soon I would be out on my own again, pushing over the exacting hills of infinite New York. Judging from our previous night's conversation Walt presented me with a list of books he thought I would like, philosophies and poetry.

In that new morning I saw hills the likes of which I had never dreamed. They were enormous and steep, it's true, but the really unbearable part was that there was nothing else in sight anywhere. They stretched on as far as the eye could see. They were reminiscent of the rolling undulations a second grader might draw—endlessly up and down with seemingly vertical sides. Between, in the valleys, I was swallowed up, bullied and belittled, by the swelling, towering hills. Looking up to the crest from the hollow it was easy to imagine that it was the edge of the world. Each rise might be the last. I traversed 25 miles in three hours, at each hilltop expecting to look out on oblivion.

At about midday I took a break at a dusty old pit stop in a baking valley. The sun beat down. Cold water from a faucet on the side of a garage quenched my searing thirst. I ate my lunch in the shade of a tree. The valley was hot and silent with no hint that there was anything else on earth but the heat and the steaming land. How could I be this far from anything? Sitting on the surface of silence, I noticed the chirping crickets and puffy white clouds rolling lazily above. It was like a big trick—the hills, the sky, the breeze—they all whispered, "There is no such thing as a city. There is no such thing as California, or Boston. There is only *right here*." It was easy to believe. Everything was so quiet, soft and forgotten like a silently falling leaf. It was hard even to imagine that the rest of the world was anything but a rumor. I sat eating my sandwich, trusting that somewhere over this sea of hills there were cities, stores, and things I remembered.

Refreshed, I began up the next hill. I started like a lumbering truck grinding through its gears, slowly gaining momentum. As I neared the top, I routinely shifted. A horrible crunching sound ripped from my shifter as if I had crushed an enormous beetle. The pedals locked and the bike lost all momentum. I leapt awkwardly from the pedals so as to not topple over with the bicycle. As I fell on the asphalt shoulder, the bike lost all will and crashed to the ground. We each lay crumpled in the road as if struck by lightning. The shifter was jammed up and broken, utterly killed. I tried lamely to fix it, ignorantly probing its insides with my Swiss army knife. But who am I kidding? I don't go rushing into hospitals demanding a scalpel, why would I imagine that on the side of the road I could repair the broken lungs of my bike? After a few minutes of pounding on its chest I gave up and the line went flat.

Stupefied, I stood up on the side of that hill, and assessed my situation. I'm on a thousand-mile bike trip and in one foul instant, there is no bike. I boggled at my predicament. Then I began to feel really, really stupid. Who on earth did I think I was? What a fool! Without a functioning bike my presence here was absurd. What was I even doing? Why am I here at all?!

Out of ideas I walked back down the hill (that's how bad it was—my bike couldn't even coast anymore) to a nearby payphone and called my parents—no answer. I called Walt and Eva—no answer. Never had I been so without a clue of what to do. Intuitively I tried to put my thoughts together slowly and carefully, as if I was walking a mental balance beam. I could feel that if I let go of calm thinking I would lose it. I asked myself as if I was my own father, "What do I have? What do I need?" I struggled to comprehend.

I walked back down to the garage at the bottom of the hill. I held a foolish hope that someone there could make the repair. They couldn't fix it, but I found a ride six miles back to a bike store tucked away in the hills. It would take me way off my route. I found it almost impossible to countenance the thought of *adding* miles to my day. Inwardly I stamped my foot like a spoiled child. I could feel myself yearning over the hills to the west, lamely wishing in that direction. Still, I took the ride in the man's shiny green pickup and we talked about its newly rebuilt engine.

Three hours later the bike was fixed. I was glad to be back up to speed, but the idea of backtracking was more than I could bear. Wisconsin was too far away. Just to think it sent me tumbling. I could barely handle the day's activities one at a time, let alone 15 more days of hard problems balanced on the needle of my hurried ambition. The fresh glow of riding had rubbed to a raw ache. In the face of this insurmountable distance, the day felt wasted. Lifelessly I pushed through the six miles, passing the place where the shifter had crunched like a knife through lettuce, and forced my way through the heat and dust. This afternoon, these fields, and this truck exhaust are all there is and there is nothing I can do about it.

I labored under a desperate, grabbing desire to be covering more territory than I was. I was gripped by an unquenchable nervousness to have more distance behind me than in front. Driven by this madness, I spent much of the afternoon walking my bike up the hills with my thumb out. There were too many damn hills. Reason had departed. Rules and sense were slowly tipping away while a hot wind blew my kite-self around. The impatience, the longing, pulled me along like a marionette. The lurching start and stop of walking and riding was mindless and makeshift. It was all I could think of to do.

I didn't get any rides. Not until the very end of the day. I trudged up a long incline with my thumb leveled to the traffic and my other hand guiding my leaden bicycle. Like a ghost, a car pulled over ahead of me. Instantly the softest wave of relief washed over me. After hours of the gaunt highway growling, there was sign of life.

It was not a beat-up pickup like I had come to expect. This was a cream-colored sedan, looking too fancy to be this far out in the country. At the wheel was a woman of about 40 or 45 asking if I needed a ride. Like a man lost in the desert I coughed a glorious "yes," to the water she offered. The woman asked what was wrong with my bicycle. "Oh, nothing," I responded. She stiffened. My heart sank. *That was why she had stopped.* She thought I was hitching because my bike was busted. I thought to myself, *Well, you should have been there four hours ago.* I think she must have read the desperation on my face because after a short pause she told me she supposed she could hardly turn me down now, after having stopped. She smiled at me as she made the decision. So, as I took the wheels off my bike in that dusty orange evening, I breathed a sigh of relief—saved, yet again.

In the clean smelling interior of the car she asked me why I was out here in the middle of nowhere with my bike and all my belongings. When I told her that I was biking from Boston to Chicago by myself she was shocked, almost offended. She demanded, "Does your mother know you're doing this?!" I assured her she did. She said, "Well, I'm not doing this for you, I'm doing this for your mother!"

Over the next 20 miles or so she decided that not only would I ride with her, but that I was going to sleep at her house that night and that she would drive me back to Route 20 in the morning. And just like that, water flowed from a stone. I lay back in the passenger seat, exhausted and newly hopeful. We rode together, talking, she trying to understand why I would do what I was doing, and I, hardly hearing, glorying in my salvation. I soon found out that she had two sons my age and a husband. She was a little nervous to have me appear before them, some stranger she had accidentally picked up, but she was strong in her conviction that she had to protect me.

I felt a pang of nerves as we veered off the road that had defined me since I'd left home. We emerged into the rest of the world where life exists in three dimensions and doesn't revolve on a single westward line. About 50 miles later we pulled into a wide driveway at her home in suburban Syracuse. A basketball hoop stood at the far end, the very symbol of the presence of suburban sons. She had driven a long day, returning from a visit to her sister in Massachusetts. It seemed vaguely unfair that she had come farther than I had, crossing the same state line, all in a single day.

As we stepped into the kitchen through the back door, I felt like I was walking into my own home. The room was clean, well lit, and decorated. The rest of the house was the same, bearing the mark of a comfortable upper-middle-class family. I might be walking into my own life, a disembodied specter.

The family went on with their business as if I wasn't there. The woman (who began to feel more and more like the mother of one of my friends) fed me hot dogs and potato salad at the immaculate Formica counter in the kitchen. Later I called home, incredulous to report my safety, and the wonders of the unfolding day. I could hardly keep up with all that had happened. The breakdown of that morning felt like ancient history, seen through the cloudy lens of a dimming past. The world had been built, burned to the ground, and rebuilt all in a day. That night I slept in a bed of mythological comfort. I felt a million miles from my own bed. Lying down, safe, the hardships of the day seemed thin and frail in comparison to the luxury of this cool, calm rest. This bed had appeared, fallen from the sky in a great wilderness.

The next day I rode and hitched, alternately joyful at the wild freedom, and ruled by manic impatience. Mile after mile, I got pulled along, slave to the pounding drum.

****

As evening threatened, I looked for a place to sleep. Between hitching and pedaling I'd made it over 100 miles in a single day. Once unthinkably distant, Buffalo crouched just over the horizon. As I rode I began to fear that I'd blundered too far into its urban sprawl. I meandered around the nearby neighborhoods, scanning yards, over fences, and the spaces in between. I couldn't find a spot of woods, or a single secluded moment of land. Again, I was running on empty. Exhausted. No ideas. What would happen? The daily pressure and worry were catching up with me. All the uncertainty. In the first few days it had only come in small spurts, but that pressure had grown and descended like a vulture. The problem of finding a place for the night brought with it a deluge of inner threats and loneliness. I was so alone, so far from home. I was scared. I couldn't think right. Waves of terror washed through me. My eyes grew wide in a growing panic without reason. I had to make this trip work myself. I was a fool. It was too much for me.

I aimlessly rode around, my eyes probing frantically for a safe place. I tried asking to use the phone to make a connection. No great solutions appeared, though I did get some good advice from my dad when I got through on a call. He told me to calm down and let the answer come. In my frantic mind, no solution existed. His voice on the phone was the one contact I had with sanity. With only the trust in my dad's advice leading me, I decided to quit my search and calm my head before doing anything else. I didn't see how this was going to solve the problem, but it was better than any idea I had. All I could think was, "Yell! Scream! Die of terror!"

I rolled past a schoolyard and pulled in to watch a Little League baseball game. Anything to put my mind elsewhere. Initially it seemed almost impossible to tear my thoughts away from the maddening and terrible question of where to camp for the night. How could I sit and pretend that nothing was wrong while the light fades from the day and I am left alone in a black night? But as I thought about it, if I was going to be lost, I knew it would be better to do it calmly than to let this fear walk all over me. I sat and watched the boys run around the bases. Just to sit still brought some peace. I didn't know what was going to happen, but I wouldn't run around anymore, ruled by panic. I was an empty cup, open to any conversation, any idea. I watched the game, lost and humble, waiting.

After a while I felt better. I was able to sit and take in the scene, no longer lunging at shadows. Still, the game ended and the field emptied—and nothing happened. The baseball lights went off and the dark sky came on. Evening ended and night was blue black. With no goal, and no thought in my mind, I slowly biked back onto the street. Somehow, blessedly, the pressure had lifted from my mind. The terror no longer choked me like a cloud of poison gas. Instead, I felt nonplussed, as if stars should swing around my head in cartoon circles. Around a corner I saw a house with a light on. I went to the door. It was answered by a thirtysomething man who looked like he probably was a father. Very soon after we began speaking, like the glory of the Lord, he invited me to stay the night in his house.

He was all smiles. When his wife and 7-year-old daughter came home he met them outside to tell them that I was there and not to be surprised. His wife was as sunny as he and seemed happy to have me there. She heated up some leftovers and again I had dinner at an unfamiliar table. I was like one whose tears are dried after long hours of weeping. Relief. A hesitant smile. The storm weathered.

Over the next hour, new wheels began to turn. After dinner I called Jessie and told her what was going on. I mentioned that the trip was wearing me down. I think she must have heard the desperation in my voice because she soon suggested what was, to me, unthinkable. She asked, "What if you took the bus from Buffalo to Chicago and I could pick you up at the station?" My mind stuttered. I could be there the next night! All those hills. All that towering, deafening, terrifying distance. But, the trip! *I was supposed to do it.* I was supposed to ride all the way. But my heart broke through. In one magical moment my proud dreams of being tough shriveled up like dead leaves. I realized, "Oh my God! I *can* do that! I'm not bound to the plan. I can be where I want to be right now!" The wall toppled over, revealing the simple truth that I could be there if I wanted to be. The answer was there, as plain as an object on a table. All I had to do was pick it up. As if it were a Christmas gift, I decided to take the bus. Humbled to my bones, gratitude engulfed me like warm water. The stubborn, selfish cords that had tied me to the road snapped and left me free. I'd wanted so badly to prove myself—to be tough. But I wasn't. The evening's monstrous desperation made it clear—I didn't care about being tough. I am free not only to adventure, but also to be kind to myself.

I was swept up in a new wave of excitement. When he heard the news, so was my host. We found out from Greyhound that I needed a cardboard box to pack my bike for the bus. I didn't know where I'd get that, but I put that on the back burner while I went inside to buy my bus ticket.

The new night was abuzz with activity. Things that mattered were happening. My heart was lit up like a birthday cake. After 20 minutes on the phone with Greyhound I walked back out to the garage. There, in the garage, door open to the night, surrounded in a golden halo, he was constructing a bike box. Like a fire on the cement floor he burned with a blue flame of life, of giving, of saying yes. I have, forever emblazoned in my mind, the image of this man, kneeling over this half-built box, working in the illumined garage on a hot, black, June night. He was *creating* something to help me, a kid he had never dreamed of two hours before.

The next morning he drove me the 20 miles to the bus station on his way to work. He wished me well and I poured out millions of thanks. That man is a hero to me. He never once resisted, like I was interrupting his life. He leaped into action taking it upon himself to use his own creativity to help me. For a short time he lived his life for the sake of mine. Life was lived that night.

Thirteen hours later I was in Chicago at the journey's end. Jessie met me at the gate with a radiant face and open arms. In the swarming crowd her presence shone to me, the warm, glowing fruit of familiarity. For the first time in a thousand miles, I relaxed.

I didn't get to say that I had ridden from Boston to Chicago. I had to own up to the fact that I just didn't want to. I couldn't do it. But gems of life were unearthed. I saw people be more generous than anyone had ever told me could happen in real life. I saw myself, not as the master of my own life. Instead, I was humbled, laboring, pushed around, protected and loved. I saw my needs met through listening, not force. I felt the fountain of life, that there is Love waiting, outside of what you know. And I got a great big fistful of adventure, the wide, beautiful land, my life, and what is possible.

RECONCILING GOD AND ART

Through my late teens and early twenties, images were coming to me. They were different than the pictures I had made before, copying album covers and comic books, portraits of rock stars. These new images were mine. I felt the dewy amazement of finding a world within myself, and beginning down the path of expressing it. I became interested in my own feelings, and who I might be. I made pictures about my own life, my longings, wonder, fury, love. Before long I was entirely engaged in the work of taking what was on my insides and putting it on paper.

The further I explored down the path of self-expression, the more freedom I found. It was glorious. Whatever was happening, be it good or bad, beautiful or heart-breaking, it could become art. I found that my ability to express my feelings rendered me strong, and largely unafraid of feelings. Even if I felt terrible, I could make it beautiful and give it meaning by turning it into art. It was deeply satisfying to create pictures that really expressed what I was feeling. I could do it. It was powerful.

The more I expressed, the deeper I wanted to go into expression. After some time, I found this desire pushing me to be bolder than I had been before. My desire to express was growing wild. Hungry to create, I wanted to explore everything, tell the truth about everything I saw and felt. I wanted to be an honest voice about what I was finding in myself and in the world. In art, nothing and no one could stop me from telling the truth.

Moving into my second year of college, I was living in this passion to express. Nothing was off limits. I felt strong in my desire to be honest, to make pictures that told the truth and expressed love and beauty. My expressive parameters expanded. I felt at home expressing my feelings about relationships, sex, existence, mortality, fear—all the things I was deeply interested in.

At the same time, I was also deeply interested in simply being good. Something in me told me to be the best I could be. In addition to making powerful art, I wanted to be moral. I wanted to be loving and kind.

As time went on, I began to feel like I had two distinct impulses going on in me. They seemed irreconcilable. The one, art, was wild freedom. I knew its value simply by the feeling it gave me. It was alive beyond anything I'd ever heard about. I knew I was on a strong, interesting, vital path. My pictures, and the expressive exploring I did to create them, told me, in very clear terms, that this was life-filled and worth doing.

At the same time, I had working in me a latent, basic love of good, decency, and in a way, God. I had learned about God in Sunday School. There were things about this God that I knew were right, beyond question. He simply was GOOD. He was RIGHT. He was just and fair and made the rules. That was about all I knew about Him. His goodness was undisputable. The Ten Commandments loomed large, the towering definition of rightness. All the laws of life were in God. But, from what I had heard, He didn't have much place in him for the kind of wild expression I was in love with. Now that I'd felt the joy of being so honest about my experiences, moving fearlessly into subjects that were taboo, this God felt a bit stiff. How did He relate to my expressing? How did my art relate to Him?

I paid attention to these feelings. The differences between these two worlds of thinking became clearer and clearer. On the one hand, the joy of art was my experience, my daily love. On the other, I'd learned about this good God from the adults in my life, my parents, and Sunday School teachers. I began to worry. Was my art-making wrong? Was it even sinful? Did I go too far? Or - was this God too small? Had I been taught incorrectly? Was the Bible (about which I knew almost nothing) wrong?

I couldn't see a way that these two worlds could exist together. It seemed one or the other was right, not both. An impenetrable wall divided the them, the two sides of my heart. Over a period of months, I waited and watched. I didn't know anything to do besides continue in my love and respect for both. I hoped I would understand more and maybe see some kind of change I could make to alleviate the tension.

During this time too, I was thinking a lot about Love. Just from feeling Love, and paying attention to it, my understanding that God *is* Love was growing in beautiful, comforting gulps. More and more I didn't just *know* that "God is love," I *felt* it. Almost daily I felt that God loves us. I felt love for the people around me. The students in my dorm. The people halfway around the world hurt in an earthquake. I felt the holiness of Love.

As my understanding of God transformed from something I had been told about to something that I knew and felt from experience, things began to shift. More and more I understood that Love had no argument with my art. Love was moving my art, causing my love of honesty, inviting my explorations. And despite all seeming, God's creativity is not at odds with His unshakable commandments. His towering laws, which I intuitively loved, but knew I didn't understand, were not at odds with His flowing, bending, and limitless creativity. Over these months, in a slowly ascending sunrise, I caught it—God is not stiff. Oh no. God is alive like nothing else. Rather than being threatened by my wild expressions, God is their source. *He* is the wild one. He is color and feeling and beauty. There was a crack in the wall. It grew and grew until finally the whole wall burst and the two worlds were one.

As this happened, interesting shifts occurred. Before the change, I'd felt my expressive explorations were apart from God, that I was doing the exploring on my own. My interests had been diverse, but largely focused on my emotions and personal experiences. After the wall came down, I understood more that God was there with me as I explored. Little by little these explorations became less about my personal feelings. They became more about my interest in the universe, existence, spirituality, and love. With the goodness of God included in my art-making, it felt a little silly to make pictures about my own petty narrative. As I progressed, I found that the wildness and freedom I loved continued unabated. I felt strong and unopposed in my ideas. They were fluent and relatively continuous. But things became naturally less personal, less about the tempestuous ups and downs of my own little life. My attention was drawn to other concepts that were just as fascinating. The change came, not by a chastisement from a God who opposed me, but by irresistible warmth and fascination emanating from the fountain of good ideas.

Understanding that exploring didn't put me in danger of separating myself from God made it natural to respect God right there in my wild, creative dance. And with God, the Adorable One, right there in thought, my attention was naturally drawn to Him.

In following years I have come to see that this reconciliation of seemingly opposed ideas is a pattern in the action of God. Because God is one, as God is revealed and clarified in human thought, division disappears. In my more limited understanding, I had felt God and art opposed each other and were irreconcilable. My limited view of each of them hid their larger natures. My picture of God was far too small, limited, and humanly dictated. My understanding of art was far too unspiritual. I thought I was a creator, making things with my own imagination. In fact, God is much bigger than a set of laws, and art is a creation *of* God, not of limited personal minds. Ultimately, the single, unified nature of God will lift every veil from our eyes and we will see that all ideas are reconciled, harmonized, and work together according to God's nature.

WHEN DAD DIED

Senior year of college. I was a star of the ultimate frisbee team, I had a pretty girlfriend, and my academics were good. Glory days.

Our team was playing in a tournament at Princeton University. After day one of the tournament we were piled high in the childhood home of one of the guys on the team. It had been a good day, hard play, and an easy-breezy night with the fellas. Somebody made an enormous pot of pasta, we watched a movie, and everyone felt good.

Around midnight as we were getting ready to sack out in preparation for another big day at the tournament, my buddy Nate came into the room with the cordless phone. I had a call.

That seemed strange. Who would call me here? Who even knew I was here? I got a buzzing feeling.

I picked up the phone. It was my sister. "Alex, our dad died."

The buzzing exploded in me. Buzzing, buzzing, buzzing, buzzing. What should I think? What should I do? I paced around the kitchen in this unfamiliar house. "This is where I am," I thought. "In this kitchen right here."

I paced, placing my feet in the square tiles on the floor. Listening to my sister, making plans to come home in the morning. We hung up.

Reaching out for something to hold on to I began to repeat some words I had learned in Christian Science Sunday School. "There is no life, truth, intelligence, nor substance in matter. All is infinite Mind and its infinite manifestation, for God is All-in-all. Spirit is immortal Truth; matter is mortal error. Spirit is the real and eternal; matter is the unreal and temporal. Spirit is God, and man is His image and likeness. Therefore, man is not material; he is spiritual." It's something we repeated each week at the end of Sunday School. The words felt like nothing, but I said them anyway. I let them repeat in my mouth and in my thoughts. I paced through the kitchen and let these words pace through my awareness.

I stood there on the tile floor, my mind still buzzing like it had been taken offline. Then, like a picture was being drawn for me, a teacher drawing a diagram so I could understand, I realized I had a very specific choice before me.

1) I could let go, lose my mind, and come unhinged.

2) I could go home and do what I could to help my mother and sister.

It was as clear as that. One or the other. Not both.

And frankly, the decision was not hard. I knew the right thing was to be useful and constructive. The buzzing stopped. It was a relief to be out of the daze, back into making decisions, living.

I walked back to the room where my friends were lounging around. I had to pack up and find a ride back to Boston in the morning. I quietly told a few of them what had happened. They melted with repetitions of "Oh my God" and one "Oh dear Jesus." That last one surprised me and remained in my thoughts. I was the only one on the team who really professed anything like religion.

They all, beautifully, wore their hearts on their sleeves. They gushed over me, telling me how sorry they were, asking what they could do to help. We made plans to drive up to New England in the morning. Three of my teammates would drive me up and drop me in Hartford, Connecticut where my sister would pick me up. I slept.

In the morning we packed the car silently while the rest of the team was blearily getting ready to play the second day of the tournament. Everyone had a softness about them—a quietness—a reverence.

Nate was driving his old Jeep. I sat in the shotgun seat while Josh and Jen sat in the back. I could feel every moment passing, feel the fact that each moment was new and I didn't know what would happen. What happens when your father dies? I was learning. This is what happens.

I could feel the intensity of their care for me. They wanted to be there. They wanted with all their hearts to make a difference for me. I felt like a balloon, getting blown by the wind—untethered from everything that had been taken for granted the day before.

The car started and we drove silently out into the morning. I was trying to concentrate on the good things that I could see. I'd been taught this as a child. What was happening right now that was good? Mostly I was humbly thinking of these people sitting in the car with me. They were not my closest friends. Yet their passion to help me was burning like a torch. There was Love.

Then, as I sat there in the seat, I felt someone take my right hand. It was Jen in the back seat. She took my hand in her own, and held it in the space between the seat and the door. She silently took my hand and held it for a long time. It dawned in my heart in the plainest way—Love is here. Love is here. I could feel that this was the real love of God, carrying my inexperienced heart from here to there. Yes, these were my not-close friends who I honestly barely knew. But in the same breath, they were the feather-soft agents of God's immortal Love, right here on earth.

As Jen held my hand, I sat in the amazing sunlight of gratitude. We drove to Hartford.

Many hours later, after meeting in Connecticut, my sister and I arrived home. The house was dark. My stunned mother, in her new role, was dutifully getting things done. Making arrangements with the funeral parlor, getting papers in order.

We went to the funeral home together, the three of us, as if wrapped in gauze. It was slow, quiet, boring. I tried to help my mom in all the ways I could think of.

That night I slept on the couch in the living room. Something felt different. I didn't want to sleep in my bed upstairs. As I slept, I had a dream.

In my dream I was sleeping, right where I really was sleeping, on the couch in the living room. I awoke to the familiar sound of the garage door opening and closing. It banged shut. Then footsteps in the basement. The day-in, day-out sound of footfalls coming up the wooden stairs. The creak of the door at the top of the stairs, the sound of someone coming into the house. I sat up on the couch and there, like the most beautiful creature, was my portly father, as if home from work. I stood up. He walked silently to me and gave me a strong, firm hug. In that moment I was a son with a father.

When I woke up in the morning, simply put, another day stretched out ahead. I had done all I could do to help with things and as the day stretched on, I was antsy. A few days earlier there had been a thrashing wind storm that had broken tree limbs all over town. Seeking only something to do to keep from sitting around ruminating, I took my mom's old branch saw and walked down to Boulder Brook Reservation, at the dead end of our street—a place I had spent countless days of my youth. My plan was to clear trails, to put myself to use.

I walked down our quiet street to the reservation. A boulder at the edge of the woods marked a trail that I had run, played, and walked on for years. I and my neighborhood friends had built forts of tree branches in these woods. On these wooded paths I had walked hand in hand with girlfriends, and then walked alone to ease my heart after those relationships had ended.

The path was littered with branches and fallen trees, strewn across the ground by the storm. I threw myself into the work of sawing, rolling, and lifting logs to clear the path. It felt healthy to be doing something—not sitting in that dark, sad house.

For some hours I worked. Between the branches and logs, thoughts of life and existence passed through my mind. What does it mean now? Where am I? Who am I? It felt big and airy. I didn't try too hard to think of anything or figure it out.

Then, gently, and sort of gradually, but with no regard for time, a thought arrived in me. It took shape and clarity. It said, "Nothing has changed." It was unsolicited. I didn't think of it. It just arrived—"Nothing has changed."

The idea gained clarity as if someone was turned the focus knob on a camera. "Nothing has changed." It was sitting inside me as if its meaning had been carved from stone. Usually when a new idea comes to me I consider it, look at it from all sides, exploring it. This was different. The voice that spoke it, its arrival, was absolute, complete. Though it was a new idea to me, it was as if I had known it forever. It required no convincing. It simply was fact. I looked at it and felt it. It came with a total (even unsurprising) certainty that it was so. It didn't even make sense to question it. Instead, I sat with it and began to feel what it meant.

If nothing has changed, it means my dad isn't dead. It means he is continuing to live and be his caring, cheerful, serious self. I thought of him, somewhere, continuing to think his thoughts, looking around corners, learning something in this new phase of his life. Then I continued. If nothing has changed, it also means that death is not really a thing. It means that all the fear that seems so big is actually small—really, it's nothing. I felt eternal Love. Eternal Love was everywhere. Life is timeless. Love is timeless. Everything is safe and cared for. *Life is so much bigger than you have dreamed.* It is safe, and good, and Love is in charge. I worked some more on the paths, basking, feeling happy, free.

I never again felt a moment of loss about my dad's passing. I couldn't. I knew that he was living, just fine. I knew that the reality of life is an enormous Love, far too big to be shaken.

For the next few weeks all I could speak about was this Love. So much so, in fact that some of my friends were disconcerted. One very close friend chastised me for not taking my father's passing seriously. She told me I was being dishonest and rude. I tried to explain to her what had happened. My words were happy and certain. I wasn't afraid of her misunderstanding of my behavior. I knew it was just a misunderstanding. I also wasn't tempted to wonder if I was wrong. This was, by far, the most convincing thing I had ever felt in my life.

During these weeks my life was imbued with a feeling of eternity. I felt a great love for my life, my friends, my situation. As time went on life went back to normal, but that experience in the woods, feeling the fact that nothing had changed, remains in me, a pillar of certainty. I can never go back to believing in death. It is impossible to believe that life ends. It changed my life forever, showing me how little I know, how much amazing goodness there is to understand.

COMING BACK TO CHURCH

I grew up going to a Christian Science Sunday School. My parents were faithful members and served the church dutifully and joyfully.

At the age of 12 I was a skeptic and wondered what I was supposed to be getting from it. My sister led the way the year before so my parents didn't put up much of a fuss when I said that I, too, wanted to quit going. I hadn't known it would be so easy!

I went into high school interested in philosophy and spirituality. I wanted to explore it all, read books, think and think. Without realizing it, I also felt protective of the ideas of Christian Science.

Like everyone else I knew, I came to have a disdain for organized religion. I didn't know anyone who was religious. No one seemed to have a use for it or any connection to it.

As I've said, in my late teens, and by no virtue of my own, I met God. He came to me and showed Himself in nature, beauty, and most of all, feelings of love. It was real and convincing—better than I had ever imagined.

After that I went confidently into my own spirituality, feeling a strong connection to Love that I knew was real. I happily called it "God" and had a full, innocent trust in it.

At the age of 23, I was engaged in my love of Love to the best of my ability. But my practice of it was undisciplined, ignorant, and naive. My holy texts were John Lennon songs and *The Power of Myth* by Joseph Campbell—a fine place to start, but not strong enough to be any more than that. At that time I was in a stagnant, lame, romantic relationship. Our feelings were often hurt, it was chasing its own tail, sticky and swampy.

One evening as I was hemming and hawing with myself about it, an idea broke through. It said with authority, "You know what you need is Principle, and you know where you will find it." The words were clear and unsparing. I did know. It was at the Christian Science Church. In the context of Christian Science teachings, the word "Principle" with a capital P is a synonym for God, specifically God as lawgiver, provider of constancy, certainty, and clarity. I did need Principle. I could do and be better than I was. But I couldn't do it on my own. This thought cut right through all the gossamer, self-centered hopes that had kept me ruminating about the relationship.

It was a humble moment. For these many years, I'd imagined myself a successful spiritual thinker. I'd had my prayers answered! I knew God! I envisioned myself as independent and inspired, entirely capable of having my relationship with this beautiful Love on my own. I'd mentally put church aside, a crutch for those who couldn't do it independently. I'd swallowed the popular college-y idea that organized religion is useless, even dangerous. It was uncool.

It was old. It was unoriginal. I didn't know anyone who went to church. Not a single one! And despite all that, the idea landed, as clear and plain as glass. It evaporated my previous thoughts and it alone remained. In my honesty, I knew it was right. Considering it I felt clean, free, and true. All the oozy cogitating was gone and, in its place a shocking, spartan clarity. I would go to church.

In a way it was anticlimactic. My thought shifted, and I went about my night. I knew I would go to church the next Sunday, and that was it.

Saturday night rolled around and I set my alarm clock on a weekend for the first time in years. I looked up the address of the Christian Science church in Northampton where I was living. Amazingly, it was only a few blocks away from my apartment. I'd never noticed.

I didn't tell any of my friends about it. I didn't know anyone who would have more than a shrugging tolerance for the thought. It felt like an idea from another planet, so unthinkable in my daily conversations. To wake up early on a Sunday morning, get dressed and walk to church was truly an independent thing to do. It was a moment of enormous solitude. I walked down the street, crossed through the parking lot of the police station, and there it was, less than a half a mile from my place. Walking through that parking lot I wondered who I was. What is this I'm doing?

I had no intentions. Just to follow the idea that had broken in and told me the truth. Love was revealing to me my limitations so that I could grow out of them.

I didn't know it at the time, but that first visit back to church after 12 years away set my whole life in a new direction. Little did I know at that point how much I needed Principle, God as lawgiver, guide, and parent. In the coming years, as life got tangled, and the wilderness grew deeper and darker, the structure of regular church attendance was a faithful, unchanging rock to me. In my undisciplined, self-centered spirituality, I could never have known how church would draw me out from the rudderless, well-meaning humanism of the college crowd, and plant me deep in the expectation of practical spirituality.

I could never have guessed that taking those utterly independent steps across the parking lot on that Sunday morning would set me on a path of such enormous learning. At that point I thought it was simply about attending services. I saw only the surface, and how it would affect me. But then, naturally, the church is a living being, filled with real people, hopes, plans, and needs. It begins to make demands and provide opportunities.

On that Sunday morning I wandered into the church and submitted myself to the sermon. I listened and felt the good, clean feeling of listening to a healthy authority. I knew my need. I longed for clarity, cleanness, discipline, rules. The books, the Bible and Science and Health by Mary Baker Eddy, were familiar in a hazy, general way, but the texts themselves were largely unknown to me. I listened, opening to the healthy cleanliness, the unwavering morality.

The room was quiet and old. It was, outwardly, totally familiar—the very same feeling as being at church when I was a kid. And at the same time, it was entirely new. I was no longer 12 years old. In the intervening 12 years I had met God, Himself. I was a different person. And with my new understanding, everything was new.

In the coming years I would wrestle, hard, with what it means to be part of a church. Does it need me? Is there anyone here like me? *Is* it uncool?

Each question, each worry or fear, was answered, summarily dealt with by sincere effort and prayer. Each time, God planted me further into understanding my place in church. And my relationship with church came to mimic my relationship with God—demanding and generous. It calls on me to give in ways I never would have guessed, and it metes out blessings in ways far beyond what I ever could have imagined.

RELATIONSHIPS WITH IDEAS

As an artist in all the great infinity of ideas, how do you know what to make?

From the outside it appears that an artist is free. He can choose to paint whatever he likes. I thought this. As I'd studied, learning the techniques of drawing and painting, I'd scattered my fire, making portraits, landscapes, cartoons, imaginations.

But then, when learning technique recedes, and the desire to express comes to the fore, there must be ideas. How do you get them?

I learned that I am not free. I do not choose. I listen and receive. And, thank God, because when I listen, what I receive is what I love best. In fact, it often defines what I love. I learn what I love from the ideas I receive. They are often better than what I had previously known I loved. They show me my own nature.

I began, as many artists do, with the idea of expressing myself. This is fine, but isn't good enough. The notion of expressing yourself is a closed circuit, where all the information is already known. You feel happy, you make a happy painting. You feel miserable, you make a miserable painting. The happiness and the misery are known to you. There are no surprises. You are yourself, so you can never be surprised by expressing yourself.

In order to be alive, to create something real, the artist himself must be surprised in the making of it. Every time it must be or contain some new conception. The creation itself has to be a new moment—an openness to learning, to an influx.

As a student in art school I gloried in images and poetry. They came fast and furious. I learned and learned. As I watched myself making pictures, seeing that they did, in fact, contain some real actual life, I wondered, how does this work? Sometimes, as I thought about the future, casting out into the unknown, blank life of an adult artist, I feared, "What if I run out of ideas?" With fear I wondered, what if I get my degree in art, make this commitment to being an artist, and then, for whatever reason, I just run out of good ideas? Can that happen? What happens then?

For a few years this fear came and went, sometimes descending like a harpy, only to be chased away by my excitement for the next project. But once I graduated from college, the weight of the endless unknown placed itself squarely before my eyes. As if it were a gruesome accident, I couldn't look away. I felt hypnotized by its towering, impossible implications. I would, in fact, need ideas... forever. I would need a constant flow of ideas for the rest of my life.

The characterizing fear of those first few years out of school was the aggressive, unrelenting arm-twisting to finish it all now. Like a gnawing animal it scraped away, ever reminding me that I might run out of ideas at any moment. Like a farmer under threat of drought, I ached to pile up ideas for years to come, so if they ever did run out, I'd have a stockpile to draw upon. Even while I worked, with a continuing interest and natural flow of ideas, I lived with a burden of fear that they would dry up.

One day I rode in the back seat of a friend's convertible, watching the landscape go by. My friends were speaking in the front seat, but the wind was loud and I couldn't hear. I gave up and looked at the mountains in the distance. A broad landscape of swaying grass swept the foreground. In that moment, by the wonderful grace of God and the willingness that comes from need, a realization visited me. Somehow, in a way they hadn't before, my thought of God and my fear that my ideas would run out, landed in the same mental room, right next to each other. With no thought—and great ease—I understood that God is infinite and the source of my ideas. They would never end. The fear evaporated and didn't exist anymore. I wondered how I could have been afraid for so long.

In retrospect it's clear to me that I had been harboring the notion that I am the source of my artistic ideas. I was laboring under the thought that I am a creator and that I somehow manufacture ideas. If that were true, it would really be a burden to keep coming up with ideas. What had happened was that the presumption that I was a creator was exposed to the greater understanding that God is infinite and the source of ideas. It was as if the barrier that had separated the two views had been removed and the real one destroyed the false.

From that point I continued on, never again worrying that my ideas could run out. They would continue, and be infinite, like God.

In my love of beauty, my desire to create, I had open eyes. I was looking and feeling. Ideas and images simply arrived. A figure in a meaningful pose. A landscape. A way to render a subject to create a particular emotional outcome. Unquestioning, I would put them down in sketchbooks, exploring. It became a natural process—an idea arrives, I lay it out in my sketchbook and explore it. As I explore, the idea evolves and there is something new to try. With every step there is new information, exploring, labor, surprise, delight.

I feel a deep, affectionate love for my images. I spend my time with them. They give me their gifts. The particular kind of images that are compelling to me tend to tell stories and operate as symbols. But when they arrive, it's just the image. It has no explanation. I only know that the image gives me a wonder-feeling, or a love-feeling, or a this-is-real-feeling. As I put the images down in the sketchbook, I meet them. The better ones, the ones that stick around, feel bigger than I can understand at first blush. I give it a first try, learn, and try again with a different angle. I use what I learned from the previous try. I wonder to myself, why is this image so compelling to me?

As the exploration continues, I try out multiple paintings of an image. The image becomes clearer to me as I learn about it. I learn what it means, what it is telling me. I realize I am learning about my own life and self as I work. There is a source, God, who is telling me amazing things about my most intimate and personal being, in this language of images. I make my art in the faith that if it is compelling to me, it will be compelling to someone else too. I begin to understand that God speaks in ways that my Sunday School teachers, my parents, and others who spoke to me as a child, didn't mention. This God speaks as much in wild, windy pictures and deep untold symbols as in commandments. He speaks *directly* to me.

I came to understand that it is never my job to make something up. It is my job to listen and receive. Then I work and explore. I came to think of the creative process as walking through an orchard. My thoughts are the fruits and I pick the ones that are ripe. Walking in the orchard is following fascination, moving with intuition and feeling. Then, when the fruit is harvested I work, make the paintings, and learn from the labor. I never say. I always listen. The images teach.

One day a new image arrived. It was a man, lying on his back, eyes closed, silent. When I first drew it in my sketchbook, I shuddered with how beautiful I thought it was. I had no idea why. Like many of my images, it wasn't beautiful in a "pretty mountains" sort of way. It was beautiful in its meaning. I gazed at the drawing and felt a stunning gravity.

I explored. I made drawings of him. Then paintings. I placed him below the horizon in landscape paintings. He dreamed interactions between other figures. He levitated in the air over a farm scene. Soon he was in almost every painting

I made. Over months and then years he was there, in painting after painting, continuing to exude a gravity that fed me like a spring of wonderful water.

First, I learned that he was the dreamer. He could lie there at the bottom of a painting and dream the scene above him. The worlds belonged to him, and changed as his thoughts changed. Then I noticed that because he was sleeping, he was unprotected, totally exposed. I realized he had no way to protect himself, but then, in these paintings there was also no need for protection. He, amazingly, was absolutely safe. I came to see that he exerted no will. He was entirely un-aggressive, and yet somehow lived in rich relation to the landscapes, figures, colors and patterns that surrounded him. I called him the "lying down guy."

I found that he could fly in the sky and exert a different feeling than when he was at the bottom of a canvas. A few times I tried painting him with his eyes open and it had a glaring, fearful effect. I placed him below a tree and it felt as though the tree grew from his being. He was in paintings with cityscapes and cars, forests and grain elevators, and in each case it created a relationship of new feeling.

I came to honestly love him. He was a mystery and yet as real to me as anything. I learned from him at least as much as from any of my human friends. After making pictures of him for a couple of years I began to reflect on this new kind of element in my life—a true, enduring relationship with an image. I'd not been told about this, and yet, here it was. I feel actual love. I look forward to spending my time with him. I learn from him. I give my time, my labor. I bend to the needs of the paintings. I will do whatever is needed to bring out his message.

This was like a bolt of lightning—and didn't fit with what I thought a relationship, a friendship, is. Don't friends need to be… people? But here, I have a friend and it is not a person. It is an idea. From this friendship I am being made stronger, more sensitive. My life is richer for it. I feel actual real love because of it. Yet, this relationship is not with a person.

As I let the idea unfold in me further, I came to an understanding that made me thank God. It was this: *All my friendships are with ideas. There is not a difference between my friendship with this idea and my friendship with a person.* My people-friends are ideas too. I asked myself if it was true. I compared my relationships with people and my relationships with ideas. They both provided me with joy and learning. They both had give and take. They both felt alive, interesting, demanding. I am simply surrounded by ideas. My interaction with ideas is what creates my life, gives me joy, and causes me to progress.

So, the gift of the man lying on his back is a spiritual gift from the Infinite Good just as are my many friendships with people. They all are surprising to me. They all cause me to grow, force me to get better, show me my need of God, show me God's glory, color, fascination. I accepted that it was true. Everything that I relate to is an idea. Whether it's a person, a tree, a cloud, or a painting, there is one category—they're all holy ideas.

After a couple of years I thought it was time to move on from the lying down guy. I became impatient. I imagined a ceremonious final painting that would send him respectfully off and usher in a new phase. I rolled out a huge paper, 7 feet long, 3 feet across, to do it right. Then, sort of like a roast, I had the great idea to kind of make fun of him. I dressed him up in bright red clown pants and surrounded him with gaudy, unlikely colors. I made myself laugh, ribbing him with my control over him, all the while loving him with a warm, friendly affection. I left the studio that night with a happy feeling of completion, excited for the next idea.

But, with absolute disregard for my presumed schedule, and as though my "final painting" had never happened, the next ideas I had were simply new explorations of the "lying down guy." And they kept coming. For more months, and even another year. I was a bit stunned, even abashed. What I

thought didn't matter. My pride weakly objected, but the reality of the situation was deeply good. There was a source of wise, interesting, expansive ideas giving to me generously, and I didn't even have the power to influence it. My place was to shut up, receive the gifts, and work.

Finally, and very much without ceremony, the era of the "lying down guy" came to a close and new images came into view. But I had a new standard for my relationship with my images. I now saw that while they were gifts to me, which I then give to others, I do not control them. If this relationship is going to reach its heights, I am a servant to them. It is their source, God, who knows their message, their purpose, and their means of doing their work in the world. These things are revealed as I walk the path. It is my place to listen, receive, and act as I am guided.

BIKING TO SAVANNAH, A SECOND CHANCE

I felt I had a score to settle with bike trips. The first one had bent me over its knee. I'd learned its lessons and wanted to put them into practice.

With a deep, soul feeling, I decided to ride from Boston down to Savannah, Georgia where I'd done my first year of college. The hope of growing into this adventure, of mastering what had mastered me, called to me. With the suffering of the previous summer ringing in my heart, I vowed to myself to be patient, to ride within my ability. Where I'd been blindsided by my impatience, this time I would be calm. The route allowed me to visit a handful of friends along the way in New York City, Washington, DC, and North Carolina. I wouldn't be entirely alone. I would be disciplined and patient, but also, wise. With a certainty not my own, I knew there was a rule of this new trip—if I started it, I had to finish it. This time I wouldn't take the bus.

In the last trip I'd felt a pulsating sensation of the unknown becoming real before my very eyes. In my almost total ignorance, every new development was a revelation. This time I couldn't claim ignorance. This time, if I failed it was on me. I'd made the choice to do it. I was responsible for it. On the day I set out, inspiration was nowhere in sight. I didn't feel any desire to leave... or to stay. I was only doing it because I'd made the plan.

Within the first 20 minutes, still pedaling in entirely familiar territory, fear screamed (as if on cue), "What the hell am I doing?!" Even more, "My legs are tired already!" And, "I am never going to make it, I can't even ride 15 miles." Terror piercing me, I longed to quit, right then and there. "I can't make it. I've taken on too much. I'm too scared!" But it couldn't be the truth. This time I had to make it.

That moment was ugly. Miserable. Its arguments were compelling, reasonable even. 1000 miles? What did that even mean? I'd failed the last time. I was a flea in the face of 1000 actual miles. I contemplated turning myself right around and pedaling back home. Round trip: 8 miles. All the fear could be over.

The moments I took making this decision were spent in a spiritual hall of naked living. It was a terrifying suggestion to think of turning back when this trip had been my plan for months. The thought of quitting was just as awful as riding 1000 miles to Savannah. I was trapped. Still, the thought of turning back slyly offered ease and comfort, not to mention an end to the terror of this moment. But it came with such a disgusting feeling of defeat that my stomach turned. To think of turning around, arriving back at my house, held a feeling of crushing sadness, my total demoralization. To return home would be the death of my heart. In pure honesty, surveying my feelings, I knew I'd be more miserable to go home than to push on into the hardness. In the desolation of that moment all I could see was the physical pain and my duty to finish. But I knew it would be better than walking in the front door of the house, knowing I wasn't supposed to be there. My destiny was to go, however it came out. I got on the bike and pushed.

I could not see what was ahead. I pedaled because the bike was beneath me. I pushed onward in the crucible of fear. I hated the thought of going back, and feared the uncertainty and darkness that lay ahead.

I turned west onto Route 20 and something shifted. I wasn't going back. I knew I wasn't going to turn around. Somehow that meant the whole trip was going to happen. A feeling of destiny swelled in my heart. I would leave again, into a great unknown. I would follow the soul-path come what may. As that understanding became real, the fears, the cruel, stabbing voices, like a miracle, melted away. They seeped out like water from a broken cup. What minutes earlier had pressed me to the quick, evaporated like a ghost at the dawn of day. Then as if the fears had never been, the trip dawned anew in my thoughts. It could become anything. I trembled. In a flash it transformed from a terrifying burden to a wide, open sky. I drank in the hope.

Amazingly, the rules of the adventure change each time there is a new one. My last foray had been resolved, gloriously, by realizing that my value didn't diminish even if I took the bus. This time it would be unacceptable to finish that way, and I knew it. It was simply that this adventure was about finishing. It was *about* the long view. The adventure talks as I move, letting me in on the new rules.

As clear as a bell, fears are like gates. Once we're past them they're gone. I was almost embarrassed for those fears, so empty when the curtain was drawn. Where had they gone? For the next many miles I was filled with a bubbly, joyful freedom. I sang and felt it deeply. The road, uncertain as it was, was solid beneath me. I had my integrity, my soul. I was visited by that angel that comes from taking responsibility for your life, taking your honest chances, and forging into the unknown.

During the first trip I'd seen the first inklings of navigation by intuition. I'd seen my problems solved by an invisible bond between strangers. I'd seen it reveal a deep, almost unbelievable love, right here in the mundane world. I wanted to practice it, test it. I wanted to understand better how my tools worked. I knew this adventure would be a social one. I would continue to look to strangers in an agile, not-expecting-anything sort of way.

****

In the first five days I rode through familiar Northampton, Massachusetts and then past Hartford, Connecticut. A day or so later, cruising through a thick forest, I happily spotted the yellow and blue "Welcome to New York" sign. It had been a long day and I was ready to set up camp. Finally, the forest broke and a rusty hill town opened around me. The cracked asphalt road wound around rocky ridges and crags. Small disheveled houses were built up the hillsides like a pile of boxes. Doors were shut and shades drawn. A pall of coldness hung over the neighborhood like a bad mood. It was getting to be evening and exhaustion pulsed in my muscles. I searched. Surely there was a field or schoolyard, somewhere I could create a little ring of safety. But each time I did find an empty lot it snarled to me, "No!" Instead of grass only broken glass. Everything seemed repellent.

As I'd learned to do, I tried listening in my heart and thoughts. I looked out to the houses, longing for a welcoming feeling. But nothing came. I felt deaf to intuition.

I left the main road and searched around broken streets and remote neighborhoods. The day's 60 miles yawned in my legs and arms. Every nook and acre of this little turn-off told me no. After rejecting multiple scary houses and a wrecked bus with tall grass growing all around it, I exhaustedly got back on the highway.

The sky was darkening over my scared self as I passed through dusty intersections, chain link fences, garages, and gravelly lots. In the last moments of daylight I was desolate. Running on fumes, as the dark blue sky turned to black, I rolled into Carmel, New York. A lake, stores, a church. I asked around and got a few directions that twisted weakly and drooped like string. "Take a left at the blah blah, go two or three lights down, take a right, (or is it a left?), and go behind the old blah blah building… oh, do you know where the blah blah store is?" At this point even my frustration wilted. If I had to search through the night, I would. I would fall down in some plot of woods at the side of the road and wake up in the morning. It would be ok. The time would pass. I settled into a kind of autopilot. My eyes glazed over and my body pedaled without thought.

In the deep blackness I saw a small neighborhood sparkling through the trees. Its lights reminded me of home. Longingly, I felt like Scrooge gazing in on the ghost of Christmas present. I turned off the main road and made my way up the hill onto its curling streets. There were three houses with lights on. I chose the one with children's toys in the front yard. As usual, I yearned for human connection, a conversation. I rang the bell.

The door opened and I knew I'd chosen the right place. A mustached man greeted me, and yes, I could use the phone. His name was Gerard. He was confident and assured as he invited me in. His three daughters peered from hiding places in the next room and behind their father's legs. The kitchen was warm, washed with bright yellow light. I met Jayne, Gerard's wife, and soon we were chatting warmly. In no time Jayne was digging through the fridge and soon after, I was munching on a ham and cheese sandwich. A hot shower washed the evening's fear away. And again, I was incredulous at the beauty of generosity. It sparkled like the warm lights through the trees.

Gerard invited me to rest in their den while he and Jayne put the girls to bed. I overheard the parents and daughters praying together upstairs. I rejoiced to hear it. In the privacy of their home they reach out to God, and teach their beloved children the same. It's not for show. It's their real hopes.

When he came back, Gerard and I talked for a long time on religion and family, his job in New York City, and my trip. I mentioned how good it made me feel to hear his daughters praying before they went to bed. Family is existing. The den was warm and wooden, and I loved to be there, just talking and enjoying the fatherly presence of this man.

When it was time for bed Gerard led me by flashlight to a small stand of trees down a stone path from the house. He bid me good night left the flashlight with me in case I needed to get up in the night. Lying down to sleep, a deep calm lay down with me. Around my head fizzy bubbles of exhaustion and gratitude popped and jumped like freshly poured soda. Where there had been fear, now there was none. I lay thinking, praying. I drank in the fact that I live in a world where we are able and inclined to help each other. I nestled in my tent, falling backwards into sleep.

****

As miles unfolded, each day was filled with pushing over hills, meeting people, improvisation. Each night found its solution. I slept in backyards, an unfinished construction site, even a dorm room at a small college.

Nine days into the trip, with about 400 miles behind me, I'd crossed from New Jersey into Pennsylvania. Evening was in full swing and again I ached for a place to stay. The day had been long and exhausting. With all the farmland around I didn't know where I could set up to camp. After these many days, approaching people felt more and more normal.

I rolled up to a house on a hill. It gave me a safe feeling. I knocked on the door. As easy as can be, the friendly couple soon offered dinner and a bed for the night. This was the first time I had ever been offered a bed. I soon learned it was the bed of their son, away at boarding school. I drank in the goodness of God. What is holier to a parent than the bed of their child? I adored their trust as I laid my things in his room. His pillow where his cheek lays at night. The plaid wallpaper. That night I felt like the son of these two people who are not my parents. Amazingly, their names were Steve and Ann, the same as my parents.

The next morning Steve and Ann had me up around 7:30. There were pancakes in the kitchen and we sat around the table like a real family. I knew they'd made the pancakes specially because I was there. It felt like Christmas morning, all the faces at the table shining. I was moved that they weren't nervous to wake me up for breakfast before Steve left for work. They wanted to include me. For this short time, I was one of them.

After breakfast Steve drove off in his truck, Ann stayed home, and I set out into the dewy morning. The cornfields were shining green and yellow in warm morning sun. Sun rays streamed across them, illuminating the undulating hills. Riding in and out of the immense shadows of shifting clouds I felt the cool chill of early morning. Emerging back into the sun I was bathed in warmth. The sky above was a bright blue song.

A mile down the road the morning spoke to me in a little voice and said, "Don't be in such a hurry! It's sunny and warm and where are you going that's better than this?" The green crops were waving on the hills. The low sun rang through dew droplets on the blades and stalks, spraying the morning with sparkles like a disco ball. I listened in a tiny way and pulled over to the side to listen better. Standing on the gravelly shoulder I closed my eyes and opened my inner listening. As I threw myself deeper and deeper into the journey, I was filled with deeper feelings. Something good was happening. Something inside me, beyond my control. Since the night I was saved from fear by Gerard and Jayne I had begun to feel a new depth of awe at what was happening to me. The care that I found in the wide-open world. It was relentless, consistent, and so real. Listening on the side of the road, I felt a cloud of *goodness* around me. *Harmony.* The trip was gaining momentum, expanding, learning who it was. It was like a sculpture that I, and the world around me, were carving, revealing. What had been only a faltering dream was now fully engaged. Some 400 miles in, its invisible treasures were in my hands and in the hills around me. At home it would require something really out of the ordinary to amaze me; now I found myself brought to the brink of grateful tears almost daily. My basic needs were being met, regularly, simply by people being kind. The interactions were loving, intimate, close. Day after day I witnessed people really *getting* along. In mundane neighborhoods, unexceptional houses, regular people, there was this tender generosity—a brightness, like angel halos. The individual instances of care, spread out over these 400 miles, separated by about 60 miles each day, began to form a chain of sparkling gems. A string of love-pearls.

That morning the growing soul-journey came out to greet me in the sun on the side of the road. It showed me itself, saying, "Look what you're doing. You're far from your home, and you're deeply into the meat of your life. You are cared for." I sat there in the sun feeling it.

****

A few days later I rolled into Washington DC. After a week with friends, visiting museums and drinking in the connection, I headed south again.

Some days later, between visits with friends at Duke University and Wake Forest University, I arrived in Greensboro, NC. It had been a short day's ride and was only mid-afternoon. I followed signs to the University of North Carolina at Greensboro with high hopes for a place to sleep. The campus was clean and new, bright like a freshly completed housing tract. I biked around slowly, keeping my eyes open.

After just a little while I saw a young man on a bike and felt that I should talk to him. He was tall and had shaggy blond hair. He seemed my age, but made me think of a 1950's muscle man. He struck me like a humble, backwoods Adonis. I asked him straight off if he knew a place where I could camp for the night. He quickly said that I could stay with him if I wanted, but that he had to hurry off and go do something. He said, "Why don't you just come with me right now and then we'll bike down to my house together?" Overjoyed, I accepted. This young man gave off a cheerful, bright satisfaction. We rode the short distance back into town. The thing he had to do was visit a contingent of homeless people in a nearby public park. Soon they were laughing as he shared food from his backpack. This person seemed so *good* as to be almost confusing. I felt as though I had wandered into the life of a young saint. I wound around a small area of the quaint downtown for half an hour while he sat and joked around with his homeless friends.

When they were done we rode about a mile to his house. He invited me in and showed me where to put my things. The house was clean and tidy, not a regular college guy apartment. His name was Jacob and he was 19 years old. I was surprised to learn that he was younger than me. He seemed more confident, more assured than anyone my age that I knew. We spent the rest of the night talking and had a great old time. I was amazed and frankly baffled by his purity and goodness. He just didn't seem beset by the limitations and self-consciousness that were accepted as normal by virtually everyone I knew. He cooked dinner and told me his life's story.

He had been out on his own for several years and had had problems with his parents. Jacob was as devout a Christian as I'd ever met and he lived it. Just in the few hours I had known him I had already seen Jacob give of himself so freely. It all fit together—his diligence in spending time with the homeless folks downtown, his swift willingness to help me, and the purity and honesty that he exuded. After dinner he showed me drawings and sculptures he had made, pulling them out of a closet. I opened my little book of paintings. I felt a brotherly closeness as we shared. We were two boys, sharing whatever wisdom and soul we'd found.

Jacob seemed like a person undistracted by ambitions of greatness, dead set on doing good *right now.* I could tell he was genuinely happy to have me there, but he seemed not in the least impressed by my journey. I had begun to expect everyone to be impressed. That made me wonder even more about the life of amazing Jacob.

Later, he said he had to go to bed to be up and out early in the morning. I had my own room and a soft warm bed with white knit blankets. The nights outside were getting cold as October unfolded. The journey continued its gentle care for me. This time, more than a shower and a warm meal, a vision of life lived for the sake of goodness and love. Here was a model, right before my very eyes, of a life committed to those virtues—all this from a boy-man younger than myself.

The next morning I woke up alone in the clean white house. I came out of my room and found a note on the kitchen counter.

Alex,
Please feel free to take what you might need from the cabinet. I'm more than happy to help you out. If you wish, leave any prayer requests that I could pray about at my daily devotional time. Alex, I wish you the best.
Truly, Jacob

I took the note and placed it between the pages of my journal. I left Jacob a note of my own, and rolled my bike out the sliding glass door.

****

From Greensboro I went on to visit another friend at Wake Forest University in Winston-Salem. Upon leaving there, I looked at the distance between Winston-Salem and Savannah. I expected it to take six or seven days. One straight shot. The distance ahead seemed unthinkably big, and longer than I wanted to face. A week in virtual solitude. I wondered if my heart would crumble under the loneliness. Seven days of wilderness. Would I disappear? As I considered the distance, I was grasping for an anchor, a north star, an assurance. How will I know I haven't fallen off the earth?

The challenge came instantly. As I pushed out into the miles, my mind bubbled and danced with temptations of hitching and speeding along. The same pressure I'd felt the summer before, jumping over myself to be at my destination faster than I could get there. It felt almost impossible to not long for instant arrival. It required consistent exercise— a rigorous discipline to put my mind back on what was happening now.

I was better prepared this time. I understood that this impatience was a trick. It wasn't the real path. I conscientiously took breaks, enjoyed the surroundings, and read my book. It was simply a matter of putting my hard-won knowledge to use. When I did, I felt like I'd come back to school in the next grade. I was bigger than the bully.

I had to arrive in Savannah on my bike. This was the law. It was time to dig in and push through. There was nothing else to do.

****

The Carolinas were hot, dry, and endless. Mile after mile and day after day I made progress, pushing through impatience and exhaustion.

A few days later I entered Camden, South Carolina in the darkening evening. One turn off the highway and I was on a tiny residential street. The houses were small and dilapidated. Spanish moss dripping from the trees. My eyes scanned the houses for signs of hospitality, but before I found anything, the street dead-ended into a thick, towering jungle. Vines crisscrossed from the telephone poles and trees, an impassible tangle. But, peering through the mess I saw a wonder. There in the house-sized bramble that ended the pavement was an ancient barn, sagging in the overgrowth, set in the dark thicket like a hiding cat.

It was too perfect. Without a second thought I rolled my bike up to the uneven door and hefted the whole thing inside. All my belongings went up through the door and into the darkness. The little barn swallowed my bike like a gaping mouth. I pulled myself up into the door and followed into the darkness. It was pitch black inside so I employed my little flashlight, a tool that was happy to get some use after going relatively unneeded for most of the trip. The small space was half full with boxes and crates. A slightly acrid musty smell rose from the floor and everything I touched. The wood floor was messily covered with old straw. I kneeled down and pulled together as much of it as I could. Feeling awfully biblical I laid my sleeping bag down over the pile.

I lay down and began the single worst night of sleep of the whole trip. It soon became clear that this spot was so perfect that plenty of other animals thought so too. All night from behind the boxes there came shifting, scratching sounds. At the first one I shot bolt upright in my bag. Was it a family of needle-toothed wolverines? I tried to ignore it, but I couldn't. I lay there twisting and tossing all night. I sang, prayed, I even counted sheep, but there was no sleep to be had.

Like a consolation prize, I finally drifted off in the dim glow of dawn. About four hours later I blearily awoke. A hot bar of light streamed through the door, illuminating the messy barn. It was mid-morning. The sweat and nerves of barn sleep were on me like a hangover. The barn creaked and steamed in the hot Carolina morning. Whatever it was that had spent the night scratching and clawing behind the boxes was now silent. Like it was my job, I packed up and prepared to move one day closer to Savannah.

As I stepped out into the light and lowered my bike onto the ground I was greeted by voices. I looked up and saw a group of people walking towards me. Then they were upon me and they weren't happy. It was a middle-aged woman and her two sons. They asked me who the hell I thought I was and what I was doing. This was their barn, and what kind of business did I have on their property? She told me I was lucky her boy didn't come out and beat me up right now.

Taken aback, I apologized and gathered my head together. I told them I was just passing through and I would be out of their hair as soon as this conversation stopped. They seemed to want to yell at me more, but there wasn't much to say. Unless they really were going to beat me up. As Bike and I rolled away, the woman explained venomously that all the vines around the door were poison oak. She said it like she hoped I had rolled in it.

Walking out to the road I passed a group of teenagers sitting on a front porch. They called me over and asked who I was and what I was doing. They had a more relaxed feel than the folks I'd so recently offended. Though there was a similar incredulity in their voices. Two guys and two girls sat on the steps smoking cigarettes. One of them had an old sports car pulled up on the grass of the front yard. I told them I was biking from Boston to Savannah. As if he was putting together the clues of a mystery, one of the guys said, "Oh, you don't have the money for the bus?" Over the next few minutes I tried to explain that I was doing it for fun and adventure. Their faces remained blank, like they were waiting for the real answer. It was like trying to describe color to someone who hasn't seen color. "Why don't you just take your car?" they asked.

"I don't have a car."

"Oh, so it *is* about money."

"No, I just don't own a car." And it went on like that. I began to see that this trip was just so far outside of what they considered worthwhile (or even considered) that my explanations didn't make sense. It just didn't fit with what they understood. We bid cordial, confused adieus, all of us feeling a bit stymied by the exchange. Rolling away I went over the conversation again: We speak the same language, and still we truly couldn't understand each other. Our cultural differences were too wide.

****

The vast majority of my interactions with strangers, whether it was on a bike trip or hitchhiking, were emphatically positive. I found that I could trust these folks who were opening their lives to me. Perhaps even more transformative though, was that *they trusted me*. They didn't suspect me of some ulterior motive. They weren't afraid of me. They invited me into their intimate spaces. I know that it had everything to do with the fact that I actively, consciously brought Love with me as I traveled. I was honest with them. I treasured them and expected our interactions to be holy. I treasured my own innocence, and the innocence of the interactions.

These wonders, as much as anything else, taught me to believe in God. These small, improvised relationships revealed a pre-existing Love that cared for me over and over again. My whole concept of reality was changed by it.

It was troubling to think of my women friends, or black friends not feeling safe to travel as I did. Later, when I did hitchhike with women friends several times, they expressed that they would never hitchhike without a man with them. I couldn't argue. Looking at the world, why would they? I thought of being brought into home after home, car after car, with couples, families, and individuals. Would a young black man my age be able to have an experience similar to mine? Would he be asked to eat with them at their tables and invited to sleep in their children's beds?

It would be easy to say that most of this boils down to gender and race. And naturally, from outward appearances, that's part of it. At the same time, I knew it was my thoughts, and the way I thought about others, that influenced my experience. Not every 21-year-old in my demographic group would have the experience I was having. While taking in the outward realities that were at play, I had to look beyond them as well. I had to believe the holiness of my own experience.

It leaves me with an awe for the power of trusting others. And at the same time, I am witness to the tragedy of not trusting others based on appearances. I feel a great awe for the quality of innocence. And I recognize the travesty of innocence disregarded. When people trusted me and treated me well, it changed my life. What resilience when people are not trusted and still find a way to bring their best to the table. Through this trust my eyes were opened, not only to the passing kindness of a few particular humans, but to a glowing, eternal Love. These people, as they trusted me, set me off into the world a different man, more alive to be and do good. I'm left with a great desire to give the same gift.

****

After a long, hot day, I found myself in Orangeburg, South Carolina. The evening was a dusty, sweaty, orange heat wave. The day's 60 miles behind me, I was teetering and exhausted. I decided this would be the night's resting spot. I rode slowly down the wide highway towards the city center. Jersey barriers and orange cones lined the road, marking places torn by construction, exuding rejection. "Move along, move along, nowhere to stop here."

Like me, the town was tired. Buildings drooped under decades of use and neglect. Scanning for gentle campsites, I was nervous and repelled. Staring back at me were dirty cinderblock buildings, broken sidewalks, and wide, spent fields of dirt and weeds. Windows peered out on every inch of land. There was nowhere to be safe from eyes that would fear me, camped in their town. As always, comes the perennial question, what do I do? I didn't have it in me to go all the way through the city and move on.

Up on the left, like a shining anomaly, was a modern-looking glass building that I found out was a hospital. With its reflecting mirror panes and black steel bars it seemed like a visitor from space. A little silly, I thought, "Hospitals have rooms. I'll ask if they have any open beds." I felt a bit ridiculous to even try, but I'd been seeing, again and again, that policy and regulations don't always rule. Sometimes one person is willing to say yes and find a way. So I went in through the front door into the fiercely air-conditioned lobby. Mustering my courage, I proposed my question at the front desk. Unphased, the woman let me know there was nothing they could do for me. And then fired back with what seemed to me to be an equally farcical notion—to ask at the fire station downtown. She gave me directions and I walked back out into the dusty sauna.

At this point, even I felt like the path I was on was worthless. How in the world is the fire department going to find me a place to stay for the night? Was she joking? But I had no other ideas. To be honest, I was actually getting used to this process. No idea what to do, but move ahead anyway. So, without faith in my trajectory I followed the directions to the fire department. I was blank-eyed and burnt, simply seeking help and someone to talk to.

For a while I rode around in circles in the parking lot at the station, peering in the open garage door. I was nervous to go in and ask. It was going to sound so stupid. "What? How in the world would I know where you should stay for the night? This is a fire station not a motel! Who the hell do you think you are? Go sleep in somebody's rickety old poison-oak barn!" Still, after a few more minutes I walked in the wide garage door, past the big red engine. I spoke to the first guy I saw, explaining my situation. We stood there on the cold cement floor in a scene unaccounted for by policy or protocol. When he invited me to come in and sit in the fireman's lounge, I didn't know what to expect. I rejoiced that he hadn't sneered and booted me out the door. He went off into the inner recesses of the station to speak to someone.

A few firemen and women sat watching TV in the lounge. I plopped myself down on the couch, an alien in the inner sanctum. We began to chat and soon I wasn't an alien anymore. Then, to my glorious surprise, they directed my attention to a huge, steaming pot of butter beans and hamhocks bubbling on the stove. I gratefully ate my fill, reveling in my tourist's dream of authentic Southern cooking. Almost instantly, my worries for the night's situation evaporated. How can I worry when I'm waist deep in butter beans? Also, with all this (Southern) hospitality I began to fantasize that I might be invited to *sleep in the fire station*. Maybe an alarm would go off in the night and we could all leap into action and slide down the silvery pole!

After an hour's time I almost assumed that the first guy I spoke to had forgotten all about me. He had mentioned that he was going to speak to someone on my behalf, but it had been so long I hardly dared hope. Maybe they would just usher me back onto the street. Maybe they were fattening me up with butter beans so they could cook me in the oven and eat me themselves. Who knew? Just as I was really beginning to wonder what had happened to him, he returned. Through the window I noticed a police car pulled up outside. I was introduced to the Orangeburg chief of police who had come over special just to talk to me. I was a little worried by the big scary car and being "talked to" by the chief of police, but I held my ground and told him who I was and what I was doing. Vagrancy charges flashed through my mind. I thought of the kids that morning who simply didn't understand my trip. The adult version would be, "We don't like your kind around here, boy." It had been a long night in that barn. How long would it feel in the city jail?

In retrospect, again, I have to consider race in this interaction. I was worried, but not scared. I knew whatever happened, I'd be ok. I'd felt safe to throw myself on the mercy of the town's public safety institutions. I didn't once worry that I'd be judged or responded to negatively based on my appearance.

The portly, mustached chief told me to get all my stuff and get in the car because they had a place for me to stay. No more information. I did what he said, entirely in the dark. As far as I could tell there were two possibilities. The first option was they were taking me to a bed somewhere. If so, *what was it?* If the police get you a place to stay, it's not going to be in the weeds behind the 7-Eleven. But what *would* it be? The second option was jail. It seemed possible too. I said grateful good-byes to the TV watchers and hamhock eaters in the lounge and went outside. Waiting with my things out by the police cruiser I felt like a child waiting either to be punished or taken to Disneyland. Why hadn't they told me where we were going? When he came out we packed my bike into the back seat of the car. I felt a little bad that my faithful bicycle had to sit in the back behind the grate like a criminal, but there was no other way. I whispered sweet comforts to her as we drove, consoling her hurt.

Finally, I got up the courage to ask him where we were going. We were halfway across town before I understood that somehow they had procured me a *free motel room* on the edge of town. I was utterly flabbergasted. He went on. The police had a deal with this particular motel for just such circumstances. Incredible. Incredible! I felt a little sheepish and ashamed to be sitting here in a car with this man, this police man, when my normal approach was to camp so as to avoid the police. Oops.

Making small talk I asked what kind of town Orangeburg is and what there is to do. Half joking, he replied, "Well, put it this way: the first thing you want to do when you get up tomorrow morning is get yourself out of town."

He dropped me off and checked me in at a little motel on the south side of town. It was beautiful. How could it not be? A sign out front said "Motel" in big black letters. Paint flecked off the old walls. Soon I was in my own personal palace. A shower, a bed, and the decadent, sugary frosting on the fabulous cake—cable TV. I took a shower and watched days of dust and dirt swirl wonderfully down the drain. I made PB & J sandwiches and lay on my back on my vast queen-sized bed. That night I slept in the fabulous luxury of that two-star motel, yet again agog at the table furnished in the wilderness.

****

The next day I muscled my way through another 60 miles. I reflected, feeling deep down in my soul how far this trip had come. I remembered the gates of fear that had stopped me in my tracks just five miles out the door. Now the journey was almost finished. I was wielding the sword. I was growing, daily handling the miles, the fear, the solitude, the joy. Daily I wrestled with the impatience that had so handily bested me before. Mostly I managed it, keeping my deal with myself. Sometimes it pushed me around, filling me with that headlong desire. Through it all, with each revolution of the pedals, I was closer to the unthinkable end.

That afternoon as the sun began to sink, I passed through Hampton, SC. Tall trees silhouetted darkly against the pale evening. These long, solitary days since heading out from Winston-Salem had been working on me. It'd been nearly a week since I'd seen a familiar face. When nightfall came, I didn't want to be camping, or outside, or alone. I kept looking for places where I might find a friendly human connection. I rode out of Hampton back out into the silent, lonely land. The road led me through the warm evening until I came to "Patrick Henry Academy," sitting on a low hill. The one-story school building sat back on its tired brown grass lawn. A U.S. flag flipped lazily in the breeze.

Beyond the school, I could see only fields and trees to the horizon. I turned into the driveway in front of the building to see what I could find. Like the previous night at the hospital, I went into the school feeling embarrassed but open. It seemed so unlikely that they would ever let me sleep in this school for the night, but there I was, asking.

I strode into the office and presented my request to the unsuspecting secretary. She was surprisingly calm to be met with this out-of-the-blue question in the lazy silence of the late afternoon. She told me no, there were no beds at the school, but she knew of something that might be helpful. "There's a teacher you might talk to," she intimated. It just happened that he was still there, working in his classroom. She directed me to him through the dark, quiet hallways, introduced us, and left.

I knew what I was doing was weird. I wondered, *how do you react when a stranger shows up in your workplace and asks if he can stay the night with you?* I stood in his classroom with paper cutouts and maps on the walls. His name was Alan. I explained the situation. Immediately, and with joyful ease, he invited me to stay the night at his house. It seemed like he had been expecting me.

Here begins one of the greatest nights of this trip. Before anything else, Alan needed to drive out to his cotton fields to see how the crop was doing. We hopped in the car and motored out to the cotton. He owned a few acres that his friend had given him. The evening was velvet, dripping peach syrup in the sky. An unspeakable peace hung over those fields in the waning light. As the sun set, we cruised slowly through the cotton fields. Alan was 48 years old, a second-grade teacher. He told me about coaching the kids on the school soccer team. He hadn't known anything about soccer, but there was no one else to do it and he was willing to learn. He said they all learned soccer together, and he taught them how to play as if they were "out for blood." He smiled with a joyous spark as he said it. I hung my arm out in the warm evening breeze. The cotton rustled in the beautiful night air as the fields became too dark to see.

Alan's house was cluttered and full of ideas. Projects everywhere. Lights strung across the room on wires. The old, wooden floors were crooked from one side of the room to the other. Half-finished paintings leaned up all over the house. An old guitar rested against the bookshelf. I felt no sense that he was an adult and I was a kid. For dinner we walked out into the neighborhood and around a few grassy corners to a barbecue restaurant. On the way, the night was ink black and sparkled with orange porch lights and hanging magnolia leaves.

As the hours passed, I began to feel that Alan was my long-lost brother from another generation. The amazing thing, I suppose, is when a friendship leaps into action without any effort or trying. This was more than a bed, a shower, and a meal, glorious as those things were. This was a friend. The puzzle pieces fit and made a new picture. We laughed late into the night. He was a bristling, bouncing ball of ideas, tucked away in sleepy rural South Carolina. By the direction of Providence, I had happened into this joyful night with him. We shared ideas about art and beauty. We sang "Swing Low, Sweet Chariot" and "Down by the Riverside" in harmony. He was in the choir at his church. This man was a bastion of fascination, so deeply interested in life, unencumbered by ambition. At four that afternoon neither of us had dreamed of the other. Yet, like a marionette on strings, I'd wandered unknowingly into Patrick Henry Academy, and the doors opened as if it was the most normal thing in the world. Sublimity was ruling with its immaculate hand.

Right before we retired to our rooms, we had a midnight snack—for each of us, a bowl of cereal and a slice of pecan pie. This was my kind of guy. When we finished, we brushed our teeth, and this I will always remember: I finished quickly and he went on brushing for minutes. He brushed and brushed. It went on far longer than I ever dreamed anyone could brush their teeth. When he was done, I asked him, "How can you brush your teeth for so long? And why?" Alan said, "Well, I brush my teeth until I think they're clean. Sometimes it takes 30 seconds, sometimes 5 minutes. How could I stop before my teeth felt clean?"

Alan had to be at school early in the morning but he said I was welcome to sleep in and go whenever I chose. I was reminded of the angel nurse I met on the first day of the first bike trip. Now, my last night on the road, it happened again. Beautiful strangers, confident that all would be well. The gates of trust.

****

When I woke up mid-morning, I was alone in the house. I packed up and got out quickly into the dry, waiting day. I was tingling and jumpy with excitement. Today was the day. 55 miles to Savannah. My stomach was full of butterflies, pride and wonder. What would happen next? Soon I would be among friends, with a roof over my head, and I will have done this thing. It was impossible to think of having done it. It was too big.

Getting out on the road, the voice of my body, with its, "I'm tired," was obsolete. My legs seemed irrelevant as I pedaled the two miles back to the quiet highway. With the completion of the adventure waiting a few hours away, the power of the trip did the riding for me. The impending arrival took up all my attention. Fatigue had no place to be.

A couple of hours down the road, my energy exploded as I passed a sign, "Savannah—15." 15 miles is nothing! I've done that a thousand times. 15 miles? That's like, soon. I became a motor. The rustling trees blew in a shady green blur. After 45 miles of gentle trees and marshes, I emerged again into the world of pawnshops and cement lots. Fast food and dollar stores. But behind them all was the thick reign of the jungle. This asphalt road, a wide highway back into civilization like a spangled rhinestone belt through the dirty wilderness. Far off, the top of the bridge over the Savannah River poked out from behind the trees. My heart leapt. I had known this bridge for the year I lived there. I had seen it every day—from the other side.

The 15 miles collapsed in what felt like minutes. Soon the bridge rose up in front of me, a great tower of cables and steel. I pushed up the long incline, pumping my legs, my heart pounding.

The bridge leveled out and I was at the highest point of its arch. The historic buildings and ancient trees of Savannah laid out before me like toys.

Pedaling hard and fast, I involuntarily threw my fists into the air. The joy was too much. A guy in a car coming the other way threw his fist in the air out the window and yelled some celebration to me. Oh my God.

Coming down the bridge, I reveled like I never had. I danced a little bike seat butt dance. I felt and felt and felt, the moment washing over me. I was so proud I could burst. *I* did it. No one else. And, I found, occupying the exact same space in myself, I was grateful to the point of weeping. This could *never* have happened without all the gifts I received, entirely outside my control. Generosity had watched over these days and nights. I felt them together—pure, heart-shining pride and abject, humble-as-dust gratitude, occupying the same space. They were the same. They couldn't be separated.

I cruised down the remainder of the bridge and curled off onto the ramp. Down and down and down and then… I was gently riding through the quaint streets of Savannah, Georgia. The momentum from the bridge slowly wore off and like a train finally stops after miles of slowing, with one last chug, I came to a halt. With awe I internalized that these cobbled streets were connected mile after mile, inch after inch, all the way back to Massachusetts.

It was 2:30. I wound around town feeling like a ghost. Was I really here? Could they see me? For me it was an unthinkably magnificent day. To the city around me, just another weekday. People went about their business. Shop doors opened and closed, jangling with bells. Men and women in suits filed in and out of the bank. In the parks birds chirped and squirrels raced from tree to tree. I sat on a bench and drank it in.

A few hours later my pals gave me a hero's welcome. That night we went to Ryan's Steakhouse for the all-you-can-eat buffet. We (or more likely it was just me) ate ourselves into oblivion.

The score had been settled. I'd returned to the vision of a 1000-mile bike trip, and held my own. Life had laid out the challenge and stirred my heart. I looked back on those beginning miles, remembering the poisonous fear that had stopped me in my tracks. In those moments I wasn't able to see *any* goodness in the trip. Now, having traveled every mile, navigated each problem, and savored each heart-opening moment, I could no longer believe fear the way I had before. Fear had showed its cards. It had poured it on thick to keep me from my path. But, having passed through it, I could see with ease that it didn't know what it was talking about. It had felt so real, but it was an empty threat. I would have missed the pile of riches that was waiting in every mile of the journey. The views, the fields, the wind in the trees. The morning air, arriving in new cities, the poetry of each night's accommodations. More importantly, I saw, time after time, the sparkling, strong, resilient web of spiritual love that exists between strangers. I could never doubt it again. I would go forward every day with an unshakeable understanding that no matter what other darkness we may see, this love is there. And the final treasure, towering in its staggering value, was the opportunity, again and again, to reach out in my need and longing, for guidance and help. I learned to practice it through every day and night. Every day, many times each day, fear descended—uncertainty, embarrassment, and exhaustion again and again. And, with practice, in one way or another, the simple need to keep living burned through the fear. I was amazed to find I felt such an ease with strangers. Almost by the day I could feel shyness leaving me in discernable chunks. With clock-like consistency the invisible next steps became visible. Arriving in Savannah was just the symbol. It represented a full victory over fear, with every step detailed and accomplished.

Looking back, I believe the trip was guided by God. In fact, this love I felt, so far from home, would never again let me believe that God doesn't exist. How can you doubt what you have seen, time after time? Stitched through 1100 miles, the soulful presence of a great, kind hand. So many times I was lost, without ideas. Following only the moment's next hope, I was led through each of them, into blessed experiences—better than just ok. I could never have planned those glories—or even dreamed them up. I rolled into town after town, feeling unsure and lost, but simply because it was all I could think of, I did it. This shows me a wonderful thing—God does not become present in my life by a matter of the right words, church attendance, or hours spent praying. My ability to see and feel the love of God grows as I live my great desire to do good and resist fear. I must submit to the idea of being led rather than leading. And move as the inspiration comes. God has better ideas than I do. Then inspirations and actions come out of me that I never knew or suspected I could do. I am put in situations that require me to grow. Adventure, by its very nature must bring us closer to God. It is always moving towards that openness, that willingness, showing us more. If it's not challenging us, it's not really an adventure. In fact, to have adventures, to radically follow our love and excitement, is the most efficient prayer of all. It is the prayer of action, relying on God.

HITCHING TO SKIDMORE

By the time I got to my senior year of college I was feeling confident. With my bike trips behind me, countless experiences with strangers and navigating the unknown, I felt more capable than I ever had. I'd learned to listen to trust the guidance of intuition. And, in addition to bike trips, I'd started hitchhiking and traveled thousands more miles in the cars of strangers, hearing their intimate stories, discerning that my listening could be a comfort. I was at home on the road and made a point of getting out and doing it frequently.

During the hundreds of rides I'd hitched over the years I learned the rules of the road. To keep myself and others safe I used my intuition like I always had. But I also made sure that I did it legally, not flouting the law or law enforcement. My approach to hitchhiking was so dependent upon innocence, I didn't want anything to darken its lightness.

It was February. I'd made plans to meet some friends at Skidmore College in Saratoga Springs, New York, 130 miles from my home in Northampton, Massachusetts. We'd meet on Saturday evening in Saratoga Springs, leaving me a full day to hitchhike there.

Setting out to hitchhike 130 miles, there's no way to know how long it's going to take. Could be 5 hours, could be 12 hours. Who knows? I set out on Saturday mid-morning.

I walked the mile or so from my home to the onramp of I-91. I stuck out my thumb and quickly got a ride down to I-90 where I would need to catch a ride going west. Now, here's a technical tidbit about hitchhiking—it's one thing to catch a ride on the side of a rural two-lane highway. It's one thing to get a lift on the ramp of the interstate. But it's a different kind of thing when you're at the crossroads of two interstates. The cars are going fast and don't have pedestrians in their minds. It's harder to get rides. I knew that going into it and hoped for the best. The ideal outcome would have been if the person who first picked me up on 91 happened to also be going west on I-90, but that wasn't how it turned out. So, I got out of the car and was standing at the side of a massive six-lane approach to the toll gate of I-90.

Still, I was confident. In recent months hitching had been going so well that I usually could get to wherever I was going just a little bit before a bus that left at the same time. It was really quite dependable.

I took myself over to the guardrail, set down my pack and took out the cardboard sign I had made at home the night before. "ALBANY," it said, in black Sharpie. I turned to the passing cars and held up my sign.

It was a sunny, snowy February day. Not freezing, but I was glad to have my heavy coat. Cars passed carelessly by.

In my several years of hitchhiking I had come to notice that it can be an emotional rollercoaster. Get this: what you're doing is the public equivalent of systematically asking every girl at the middle school dance for a spin. You're really putting yourself out there. Every person who sees you makes a choice to pull over and give you a ride or not. The vast majority don't. Basically, through a certain lens, there's a lot of rejection going on. Over the years I had felt it, shaken it off, felt it some more, shaken it off again, and so on. But hitchhiking is different from the middle school dance metaphor in that these days there's a dark stigma attached to hitchhikers. We are taught that anyone who would hitchhike is dirty, dangerous, poor, disgusting. So, when you put your thumb out you are putting yourself out there to have people think those thoughts about you. It's something you have to deal with. Over the years I'd learned that I had to be so clear about my own value that these cruel labels, floating around in our collective thoughts, couldn't find a landing place on me. I got used to the feeling of being so exposed. In fact, despite the insults and judgments that might pour forth, there was something wildly energizing about it. Like an actor in an improv show, I felt an amazing power buoying me up as I stepped out of anonymity and into the spotlight on the side of the road. I learned to bring a lot of energy to my hitchhiking adventures, pouring in my enjoyment of it, my love of the people who picked me up and a certainty of my own innocent motives. This was the way I found to defend myself from the potentially scary feeling of being so exposed to the eyes and judgments of passers-by.

Even knowing all this, every time I would get out there was a new experience. It's so very alive to be exposed like that. You don't know what's going to happen. With my thumb raised, naked to the world, asking for something— every second is an opportunity to take the rejection personally.

During these years I had my hitchhiking mojo working. I was used to picking up rides quickly. Within 20 minutes or so. (One very special time, in fact, as I got out of one car, I stuck out my thumb and another car pulled over almost before I could get my bags out of the first car.) So, I was used to standing there, cars hissing by, biding my time in the confidence that somewhere out there was the person with the open heart who would pull over and answer my prayer yet again.

So, it came as a surprise on this Saturday morning that after 20 minutes, then 30, then 40, that I found no connection. The river of cars, sparkling in the morning sun, rolled on quietly, taking no notice of my plea. That cruel voice was working in my thoughts, harping on the feeling that each car that passed by was a rejection. I waited there in the cold, my sanguine hope peering out into the passing traffic.

As the time stretched on, I began to grumble inside myself, "What's their problem? Why doesn't someone just pick me up? What's the big deal?!" Honestly, I was so used to it working with ease, that when it didn't, I was a bit offended.

It sounds crazy in retrospect, but I found myself getting angry. It was so obvious to me that there was only good to come out of it. I knew I wasn't dangerous. It could just be so simple. "How can they all be so cold hearted?" I lamely accused. I got more and more wound up.

How long I let those thoughts occupy me I don't remember. At some point a ray of reason pierced the dark knot of frustration. "Alex, you know that this whole process of hitchhiking is based on Love. How can you expect this to work when you're casting anger out into the street for all of them to drive through?" The rebuke landed. It was so true.

I was getting entirely in my own way. All these resentful jabs at the unknowing drivers. So counterproductive! So opposite of everything I know and love.

Humbly I walked over to the guardrail. With great clarity I felt, "I have to give up on getting a ride until I can get my thoughts in the right place." I laid my sign down against my bag and sat on the rail. I closed my eyes and turned away from the desire to be in a car moving towards my goal. I wanted so much to turn back to the thing I loved, the Love that binds us together. I reached out with that desire.

I thought of all those drivers passing by. All those good people. I thought of God, loving each one of us. Then, like a beautiful blanket, I felt in a new way I never had before, *"We are a family."* In a way that could never be undone by any darkness, by any cruel act, by any misunderstanding. God has created a family of beings, and we are it. I drank it in. I'd forgotten about the cars and the rides and the distance to Albany. I'm part of an enormous, love-soaked family. We are all under the care of this beautiful blanket of God's generous, universal love.

The frustration and anger I'd felt were gone. Replaced by this feeling of family. I opened my eyes and looked gratefully out over the flow of cars. They were zooming in from the highway, piling slowly up in lines at the toll booths.

As I sat there, my Albany sign leaning invisibly against the guardrail, my thumbs hidden in the pockets of my coat, a station wagon pulled over just beyond where I was sitting.

"I wonder why they're pulling over," I thought. Then, as it came more into focus, I saw in the back window, a sticker. "Skidmore College," it said.

In the split-second speed of thought it all began to coalesce. Could it be? I inwardly shook my head as it dawned on me what the generous spirit of Love was doing. I stood up with my things and walked over to the car.

"Heading west?" I asked.

"Yeah," she answered, "Going to Skidmore college in Saratoga Springs, New York."

I got in the car and we drove off into the day. Amazingly, it was a single woman, a college student. I boggled. In this world, where instead of being praised for your kindness and compassion, people are roundly rebuked for picking up hitchhikers, this young woman, alone, was not afraid. We chatted happily for the few hours of the drive. Inwardly I praised my God and basked in Love. A couple hours later she dropped me off in downtown Saratoga Springs, where I happily waited for my friends to arrive.

FIRST MURAL

When I was about to graduate from college, I felt a great weight on my shoulders—Ok, I love art, but how do I actually *do* this? How do I get people to see my work? And how will I pay my rent? I thought of myself, pitifully pounding the pavement, getting rejected by gallery after gallery. And frankly, who goes into art galleries anyway?? I wanted my work to be seen by people.

The greatest burden was the fear that I had no way to share my gift. My pictures, my images, my art, were the most precious things to me. They come to me in true inspiration, the deepest living thing. My relationship to them is as real, if not more, than my relationships with people. I owe these pictures my life for all the riches of love and meaning they have given me. So, what if I can't find a way to share them with others? What if the world hates them? Or worse, what if no one cares?

I knew my work was good. I knew it was powerful and honest. I lacked no confidence there. But it's a long leap from feeling good about your own paintings to touching someone else's heart. And another long leap from there to being able to make a life out of it. The picture the world lays out for artists is pretty bleak. A thousand actresses trying out for one sparkling part. Countless painters, ambitious and egotistical, amassing in cliquey art scenes to viciously compete for an ounce of limelight. Countless others cast aside like so much garbage. Where is there a place for the deep channels of true poetry? This fear sat in me for months.

In the last weeks of summer before finishing my final semester of college I decided to hitchhike up to Quebec City, Canada for an adventure. I had a week or so before I needed to be back in Northampton. I headed out from my pal John's place near Bath, Maine, and made my way to I-95. I got a handful of rides and by the end of the day I found myself 60 miles north, near Waterford, Maine. The sun was starting to get low, and the air was feeling chilly, more like the coming fall than the fact that it was still decidedly August. I took a walk to find a place to camp.

In my effort to not be seen and kicked out, I didn't find anywhere great. I set up my tent on a rocky piece of ground down by the railroad tracks, with a view of the rolling Kennebec River. Feeling glad to be done with the day's uncertainty, I took out my food and my sketchbook and got ready to have a relaxing evening.

When the light was gone and I could no longer read or draw I slipped into my little blue tent, with every intention of going to sleep. Instead, an uncomfortable, scared feeling settled over me like a mist. Sounds outside the tent were filled with foreboding. A worried voice in my head, "Someone's going to find me. They're gonna call the police." Every sound made my heart jump. I heard a car, then voices. My fear took those voices and turned them into the meanest hoodlums they could be. They would stumble upon me in their drunkenness, pull me out of my tent, beat me up. I lay there expecting it all.

The voices faded. The car revved and was gone. I lay in my tent thinking about my life. "What am I doing out here?" I wondered stupidly. "Why am I lying in this tent on the side of some railroad track, scared out of my wits?" I could find no reason. I thought of the upcoming semester. It seemed like a world away. I needed to put together some kind of final project to graduate. I hadn't thought about it, and didn't know what I would do.

I thought about other friends of mine. One had painted a mural a few years back. "That was cool," I thought. "How did she do that?" I thought about my studio, my pictures, the feeling of being in the thick of working. Then, like the most obvious thing in the world, I thought, "I'll paint a mural." Oh, ok. And just like that, I knew that the next day I would not be hitching into the north woods on the way to Quebec City. Instead, I would turn myself around and head straight to Northampton and start looking for a wall to paint a mural on.

Twenty years later it's hard to remember how each step was a wilderness. When it landed in me that I would paint a mural, that didn't mean I knew how to do it. In fact, I had no clue. All the things that seem so basic to me now were, at that point, invisible. There was no map. There was no one to ask. How do you find a wall? How do you find out who owns it? How do you bear the dizzying white-out feeling of almost total ignorance?

It did occur to me, as I thought of putting my art on the side of a building, that if this could happen, then nothing can stop my work from being seen. It was a way to cut out the middle man and go straight to the people with my best ideas. It was too new to even begin to understand, but I felt a glimmer that it could work.

It's really something to actually take the first step of something you don't know how to do. A couple days later, back in Northampton I walked out the door of my apartment. This little city had been my home for two years. Immediately my eyes fell on its streets and buildings in a way they never had before. Instead of running for the bus, or meeting a friend, I looked hard. How do the walls fit together? Where do people walk? Can people see this wall from the sidewalk?

Over the next couple of weeks I found a number of possible wall spaces and asked around at the stores, offices, and restaurants inside. I was excited, exposed, totally open. I felt too ignorant to know if I was doing anything right or wrong. I got phone numbers, called them, left messages.

I got a call back. He was interested to see a sketch of what I would paint. We met at his building. The wall was on one of Northampton's main streets. Hundreds of cars going by each day. And the answer was yes.

****

Soon it was the day to begin. I stood before the enormous red brick wall, considering. Up to this point the largest thing I had ever painted was 6 feet tall—a panel, which at the time had been overwhelming. I had never worked outside the privacy of my studio. The paints were there in their cans, the brushes piled up next to them. This wall was 16 feet tall and 10 feet wide. It towered over me. And hundreds of cars passed by constantly.

My design was an image that had been coming to me powerfully for some time. The main idea, a stylized tree, takes up the full space. The leaves, like a mandala, create a kind of spiraling pattern. The tree is both fruiting and flowering. It is the tree of life, a symbol of spirituality, eternity, God's creation. Below the leaves, at the bottom of the painting, a small city, Northampton, sits, dwarfed by the tree. The tree of life towers over our little town.

I went to put the first brush stroke on the wall—and stopped. Instantly, and with no warning whatsoever, I was filled with a fear the likes of which I had never encountered. I was overcome, paralyzed. I couldn't continue. Couldn't even put the brush on the wall. It was as if a physical force would not allow me to proceed.

I searched myself. *What is this?!* My thoughts were flooded with fear and fear only. "What if I fail? What if I start and can't do it? What if I make an enormous mess of this painting, right here in public while all these people watch?!" There was nowhere to hide. Nothing to protect me from the judging eyes of the world.

In my panic and paralysis I stepped back from the wall to regroup. I stood there in the parking lot with my brush in my hand and closed my eyes. I knew that the force behind the picture itself, the force that told me in my heart about the tree of life that towers over my little town, had also brought me to this moment. It had turned me around as I thought I was hitchhiking up to Canada. It had given me the idea of painting on a wall and set me to work finding this one. I took all the longing and desire I felt, and reached out to God in the privacy of my own heart.

My inner experience went something like this:

"What can I do?? What am I supposed to do?? I know I'm supposed to be here!" And then I listened, concentrating.

There came a new thought in the midst of the noise of fear. I remembered that I had been excited to make a beautiful picture—not so I would be seen as a good artist, but so there would be a beautiful thing there.

I began to think of the people in the neighborhood. The folks driving by. Folks coming home from work. Kids walking by after school.

Like a light in the darkness a new thought arrived, as natural as can be. "This is not about how they see you. This is about you giving a gift to them." The truth of it shone before me. It felt healthy, and clear, and *not afraid.*

I reflected. If it's not about me, then I have to be willing to think of them. If it's about giving a gift to them, then I have to believe that my work is good enough to be a gift. All at once I found myself shifting inside. Like tectonic plates, deep thoughts moved. It simply wasn't about me. It was about using my skills, my love, my desire to make something beautiful so that other people could see it and be blessed.

And just like that, after about five minutes, I opened my eyes and looked at the wall. The fear was gone, as if it had been washed away by rain. And what remained was a healthy, excited desire to do this thing I had never done before.

I spent the next 10 days working on this mural and my life changed forever. People rolled down the windows of their cars and cheered, hollering their support. Folks stopped to talk, asking about the mural, curious. For the first time in my life I felt the meaning of the word "community"—people connected. I became instantly addicted to creating in public. I could see the power of art happening before my very eyes. I invest my best ideas, my skill and desire as a creator, and people can literally see them and be moved. I could have a real power. A power to do something beautiful that would have a visible effect.

It's now 23 years later and I have continued painting murals every year since then. As of this writing, over 200 murals in 19 states and 4 countries. There have been several other times when fear rose up like a mountain just as I tried to do the thing I most wanted to do. But this was the first time. From it I saw clearly that if I'm doing the thing that is right—the thing I am supposed to be doing—I can be brave. I can learn. I can find the way to let go of whatever is keeping me from doing my work, and I and my community will be richer for it.

GOD GIVES ME SONGS

Knowing God is in feeling. We simply feel God. Though there is no outward evidence of it. Those God-feelings are simply more interesting, more convincing, and deeper than anything else we've encountered. A door opens in our understanding and we feel God's nature. It changes us.

My spiritual understanding and exploration of creativity were growing together. God visited me regularly with feelings of universal Love, a beauty that closed the mouth of my every complaint.

My girlfriend, call her Gretchen, had just left for a year abroad in Peru. I missed her and wondered what she was doing. I sat down to write a song. I thought of her, far away, beginning her new life. Then I thought of the Love I was learning. It was like an angel with wings 4000 miles long, joining us over continents and seas. I could feel it. That overarching Love.

I explored some chords on my guitar. They were fresh and new—chords I hadn't found before. I thought of that 4000-mile angel. The thought filled my chest and I felt enormously strong. I could feel Love linking all of us, looking down from above. Up in the sky, with that closed-eyed, loving angel, our towns and cities are so small, so cute. The people drive their cars like toys. Lights glitter on the dark hills and the angel loves us all. Eternity hangs over us with her great windy arms.

Then, as if that feeling were speaking to me, through me, there was a song coming out of my pen. I thought the thoughts and wrote them down. But they weren't my opinions, my concerns. It was speaking to me, comforting and correcting my concerns.

It said:

> Stop the presses, stop the fight
> Stop searching in terror night
> Stop wishing it would come out right
> My will is nothing, Love is all might
>
> Love is the answer, all along
> So please don't worry my dear, my love

It was as if there were two of me. One that was concerned, worried, excited, afraid, and another who simply knew. The one was speaking to the other. *My dear, my love.* The big, airy angel whispered to my skittering heart—stop. Stop even wishing. Stop pushing and hoping and fearing, because all the while, Love, God, is all there is.

It went on:

> When you're lonesome, it's still around
> And you can hear it, without a sound
> If you can listen, our love surrounds
> 'Cause we're all living in one little town
>
> Distance is nothing, Love follows you around
> So please don't worry, my dear, my love

I played the song to myself, singing the words. I could feel the truth of these gigantic, idealistic statements. When I'm lonesome, it is still around. And I *can* feel it without a sound. When I listen, I really know that Love, our dear, good God, Love, does surround us. The whole vast world, with its seas and mountains, nations and impossible distances, are, to that Love, one little tiny town. Distance is meaningless to Love because it's everywhere. I felt it all. I wasn't wishing. I knew it was so.

Then I wondered at the thing. This song was unlike any I'd ever written. I moved the pen to write the words. I thought the thoughts and felt the wonderful feelings. But I knew I had received the song. It was so much bigger than I could have made myself. It was deep—so instructive and so confident in ways that I wasn't. But there it was. And no one else wrote it.

With joy and awe, I accepted in my heart that God had written a song through me. It was a gift to me. Maybe to show me. I didn't know. But it felt like the best gift I had ever received.

****

My mom was kindly paying my phone bill. If you can believe it, the bill was $14 a month—a landline shared with my surly roommate, Walter.

Walter moved out. Over the months the bill had been adding up and Walter owed my mom something like $50. My ever-sunny, patient-as-the-hills mom had written him a letter politely requesting the payment. She received no response. Over a series of months, she continued to follow up with him, ever expecting the next letter to have the desired effect. But, a payment from Walter was not forthcoming.

Finally, one afternoon I happened to pick up the mail at my mom's house. In it was an envelope inscribed with Walter's choppy scrawl. I was glad and opened it, happy to have the drawn-out episode finally at an end.

Folded around a check was a hand-scratched letter. "Dear Anne," it began, and continued with a string of profanities and insults the likes of which I feel pretty sure my mom had never in her life encountered. It closed with a messy drawing of a hand giving the middle finger underscored by an angry "FUCK YOU."

It was impossible that these words were addressed to my sunshiny, entirely guileless mother. I thought of her. Addressed to her, these words made as much sense as ancient runes in the New York Stock Exchange.

The letter, the drawing, the anger, were so pitiful, so small, aimed at her. The virulence, and the intended shock and violence, were so poorly aimed, so powerless. Without thinking, I walked to the piano in the living room.

Taking my seat on the bench I laid my fingers on the keys. As if it had been waiting behind a curtain, fully composed in the 30 seconds since I read the letter, out came this song:

> You cannot steal anything that is real
> You cannot defame one who knows no shame
> All curses will fall, and die where they lay
> All anger is swallowed in its own decay
>
> Bend down, bend down and kiss the ground
> That your heart's hard toil may be lost in the soil
> Bend down, bend down, put your ear to the ground
> For God is within us, the earth and its towns

I could feel my relationship with Love defending me. It showed me, like a gentle teacher, that this curse, meant for us, could do nothing but die its own death. It would eat itself up. It had nothing to do with me or my mom.

Then it spoke words of humility. *Bend down.* Be filled with affection. Give up your struggles, your inclination to fight or be distressed. Instead, let them seep silently into the dark, forgiving soil. *Bend down.* Hear God's blessing. His intimacy, enormity, and over-arching affection.

I sat at the piano, adoring the words and their accompanying melody. I sang them over and over, letting them fill my throat, feeling their lessons. I drank in the images as I sang, feeling their protection. They were spiritual—leading me to further spirituality. They declared paths I hadn't known.

I'd had no intention to write a song. I'd never had these thoughts before.

No gift could be better. Nothing could be more intimately tempered *for me.* I felt my world expand and my understanding deepen. God knew me better than I knew myself.

I crumpled up the angry letter and put it in the trash, never mentioning it to my mom. I gave her the check and she was pleased that the affair had come to its conclusion.

FINDING A STRONGER FOUNDATION

Gretchen was away in South America. Before she left, we made plans that I would join her in Peru after I graduated.

It was fall in the Pioneer Valley. The hills and rutted corn fields trembled with the promise of the coming colors. The broad Connecticut River flowed confidently between Northampton and Hadley, reflecting the afternoon sky. I was deep in the labor of painting my first murals. Daily my thoughts were growing, pushing through creative challenges. I wrote Gretchen plenty of letters in my best (but not good) Spanish, telling her all about my expanding life, asking about hers. I released the floodgates of my thoughts, and let it all flow into letters that would fly 4000 miles to find her. In my mind's eye I guessed at what her mailbox looked like, the family she stayed with, the room she slept in. And the glory of opening my own mailbox to find one of these red, white, and blue "par avion" airmail envelopes peeking out at me.

By November she had been away a couple of months. The air was getting colder and the days shorter. I was telling her all about it in my letters, scrawling away in some study carrel on the 18th floor of the enormous UMass library. By contrast, Gretchen's letters were coming less and less frequently. I tried not to worry.

But I did worry. I needed to talk to her. Was something wrong? Was she mad at me? The longer I went without a letter, animals of fear and injustice prowled inside me, baring their ripping teeth. How could she not know I would worry?

I called the long, confusing Peruvian phone number and didn't reach her. Some days later I called again, waited through the inscrutable Spanish greeting on the machine, and left another message.

The letters that had been coming several times a week, had virtually ceased. I'd jumped off the cliff, certain of her presence with me, and she'd evaporated without a trace. Where was the one I'd been counting on? I was confused and hurt and badly needed to know what she was thinking.

One night the phone rang. It was Gretchen. Her voice was naked, parched. "I've been seeing someone," she said. My guts tumbled out of my body as if I was on a terrible roller coaster. Out of my mouth, inexplicably, came the words, "Bless us!"

All fall I'd been praying. My life was growing more and more spiritual every day. I could feel God's presence. I really saw and felt Love, deeply and regularly. I knew God was real—that Love was real and spiritual and everywhere. It was in everyone. It was in me and it was in Gretchen. She was better than this and I knew it. In that moment the words "Bless us!" blurted out of my mouth I knew she was spiritual and good, and I was spiritual and good, and God loved us. I knew it.

My mind raced. The moment burned. Then, my heart rose with clarity. "Well," I said, feeling as serious as I'd ever felt, "If you want to be with me you need to end it with him." She agreed.

As the days ground on, my rosy Love-feeling was shorn away. The spiritual feeling I'd marveled at was obliterated. More and more, and with terrible, abhorrent intimacy, I felt that the very thing that made me special, the most precious thing I held in my heart, had been trampled over, spat on, crushed and desecrated. I wondered how I could trust anyone again. I howled from my heart's red, raw throat. What is trust?!

I wept and wept. My eyes tired of crying. It was physically difficult to take the steps to get from here to there. The hurt. The hurt. The hurt.

In the 18 months of our relationship, Gretchen and I had been having sex. At first it was a surprise to me—up to this point my relationships had contained only lesser sexual expressions. I hadn't pushed for it. But it quickly became more and more normal—a fun, intimate part of our relationship. In the weeks after she told me she'd been with someone else, I devoured my own heart, killing myself moment by moment. I couldn't stop thinking about her, physically with some other guy. Each time the thought came, I felt my own preciousness ground down disgustingly, like a cigarette butt under a bootheel.

In outer darkness I flailed and beat at the air, reaching for an anchor, a north star. This was just a few months after I had started going to church. I knew almost nothing of the Bible. Now I poured myself into it, my life depending on it. Simply by searching the Bible, I admitted my need. The Bible was not my book. It was my parents' book. In going to the Bible my pride was crumbling. It was admitting that I wasn't able to figure it all out on my own. I could feel myself admitting that there was wisdom in the world. It was in things I had disdained. In the people I had rolled my eyes at. There are foundations already built.

One night I came upon Romans, chapter 12. (I didn't know the books of the Bible. I had no idea what "Romans" was referring to.) It was filled with instructions. I needed instructions, badly. I was amazed—I could feel them. I read it over and over.

> Let love be without dissimulation. Abhor that which is evil; cleave to that which is good.
> Be kindly affectioned one to another with brotherly love; in honour preferring one another;
> Not slothful in business; fervent in spirit; serving the Lord;
> Rejoicing in hope; patient in tribulation; continuing instant in prayer;
> Distributing to the necessity of saints; given to hospitality.
> Bless them which persecute you: bless, and curse not.
> Rejoice with them that do rejoice, and weep with them that weep.

Be of the same mind one toward another. Mind not high things, but condescend to men of low estate.

Be not wise in your own conceits.

Recompense to no man evil for evil. Provide things honest in the sight of all men.

If it be possible, as much as lieth in you, live peaceably with all men.

These instructions were full of hope. They gave me something to live for each day. I loved that it was right there in writing, "recompense no man evil for evil." Amazingly, it was comforting. Incredibly, it punctured the notion of evil. Somehow, it asserted that I didn't have to feel terrible because of evil. I could "bless and curse not." Looking at it in black and white it was less slippery. It was a relief. Yes, Love is real. The words were cheerleaders, deadly serious, chanting for me, reminding me. When you want to die, they will repeat to you words of health. They will repeat them again and again for as long as you want. All you have to do it open the book. They will be there. Somehow, in all the suffering, love remains.

Gretchen would return in several weeks. We kept in touch. What we were to each other was uncertain.

When she returned from Peru, I wanted badly to see her. I longed for it all to be ok. I dreamed that she would walk in the door, we'd embrace and all would be well. A deep, black chasm of hurt spoke otherwise. I paced the floor of my apartment, longing to stay calm.

When she arrived, she was with a couple of our close friends. It was meant to be a get-together. I'm not sure they knew about any of this. After just a few minutes I found I couldn't be in the room with her. I left the room and closed the door behind me. The suffering was too much. I crawled into my closet to be alone in the darkness. I couldn't stand the light. I couldn't stand to be seen.

In hell, I boggled at myself. Even I wondered, "Why is this such a big deal?" "Why am I incapable of being in a room with her?" I was not in control.

The Bible was becoming my foundation. I leaned into the feeling that I don't know it all and don't have to reinvent the wheel. I thought back to my years of Sunday School as a child. The 10 Commandments. The Beatitudes. I decided to look them up.

As far as instructions go, the 10 Commandments are like, the big ones, right? In some ways, they're so basic it's hard to think of them as really rules. Don't kill anyone. Ok. Don't steal. Ok. They're like the songs you've heard so many times you sing along without even noticing they're on.

But now I drank them in anew. These are the pillars of life. The rails on the bowling lane. For several years I'd imagined I lived in a world in which I could make it up as I went along. Like most of my peers in college, I'd thought I could handle it—that there were no consequences. Now I found myself getting used to living in a universe that *has* rules. Rules that give safety, order, desperately needed guidance.

Then, as I drank them in, I came to "Thou shalt not commit adultery." I'd never spent too much time on this one. It was too easy to blow off. No one, and I mean no one, I knew had any notion of sexual restraint. It was seen as ludicrous, embarrassing, not applicable. But as I put my actions, my life, in a biblical context, my vision changed. I didn't feel guilty for having sex with Gretchen. But I had seen the consequence. All I wanted was to do right. I wanted to be caring and care-full. I wanted to be going in the direction of God.

In a moment it all fell into place. "Thou shalt not commit adultery" is not there to keep us from enjoyment. It's there to keep us healthy and safe. It's pointing us to the higher enjoyment of living a healthy life in which relationships are cared for, secure, and nurturing. I hadn't realized how precious my heart is. I hadn't known it was made for a deeper love. I hadn't known! I hadn't known how capable of feeling it is. How much it needs to be cared for and protected. I simply hadn't known! So, I had put it out there in a place that simply wasn't able to keep it safe. Why had I imagined that this kind, but undisciplined relationship would be enough to maintain it unharmed? I hadn't known better.

And in that moment, I felt a new, deeply chastened love. We're all that precious. We all need our hearts kept safe and protected. I longed to see us all that way, letting our hearts connect with one another in good, patient, healthy time. We can allow ourselves to open up naturally, like flowers to the warmth of the sun, not forced open by impatience, lust, and cultural expectation. It can happen. We don't have to be foolish, rash, lazy, and careless with our hearts. We don't have to simply go with the flow and then be shocked when we're miserable. We, each of us, have precious, perfect hearts. We don't make up the rules for them. We can't pretend they don't want affection, intimacy, closeness, adoration. They do. And we equally can't pretend we're in the driver's seat. We must care for ourselves, care for those around us, and love in every way we can, even when it's as humble as the dust. It's not a step away from love, but rather, a step towards Love to be patient, caring, and care-full with our most precious selves.

Walls crumbled down inside me. With a feeling of intense independence, I realized I could agree with myself to utterly turn my back on the sexual expectations of society and my peers. Life was between me and God. The expectations of others had no power over me. I didn't have to have sex with anyone until it felt holy, safe, and humble before God. Whenever that was. I didn't need to know. I didn't need to hide, but I could be serious about keeping my precious heart safe and my life happy.

I felt an amazing exhilaration, alone with God, leaving behind one of the main attractions of youth, constantly on the minds of my peers. It was not for me. It was not the way God was leading me.

I relaxed in my new understanding, amazed at where life had brought me. I didn't have to be ashamed to be different from my peers. I nestled into a new safety, knowing that I was being moved by God's good hands. I am not in charge. I am a listener, a receiver, a responder. God is good and leads me away from danger, into new uncharted land.

STEVIE RAY VAUGHAN AND THE ART BARN

In the weeks after I'd learned that Gretchen had been unfaithful to me, I struggled to love her. I wasn't mad, I was just, destroyed. I didn't know if we were still seeing each other. I could barely think of it. Still, she'd been lost, lonely, far from home. She didn't mean to hurt me, and even if she had, anger wouldn't change anything. But, more powerful than my puny efforts to be good, it was as though the treasure of my being had been desecrated. Each day was hung with countless emotional burdens, bearing down within me like balls of iron. Each new moment I was stung by the thought of it, ceaselessly. I pulled myself through the hours, going to classes, trying to work as if everything were normal.

I'd been learning to pray. I longed toward God with all my heart. But I was a child on the front lines. The bullets and barbed wire were far too much, my muscles weak, my understanding flimsy.

After a painting class I took myself to my studio. The Art Barn was an ancient building at the far end of the UMass campus, where painting students had work spaces. It was, as the name indicates, an old barn, originally for use in the agricultural school, at some point transformed into de facto studios. White paint flaked from the aging wooden walls.

There were no keys to the Art Barn. The locked front doors shook on their hinges barely clinging to the frame. A secret in plain sight, a butter knife lay in the grass to right of the doors. We all used it to jimmy the lock.

I made my way in and stumbled hollowly to my space. Here I had worked countless hours. In solitude and among others I'd created, learning, seeing my inner thoughts become visible on paper and panels. These walls were beloved to me, infused with the innocent mystery of our discovered creativity. My supplies lay in piles on the floor. The walls showed innumerable marks, paint strokes and scribbles. They were jumbled with musings, phone numbers, notes from friends who had stopped by.

The rooms were empty and dark. Pale gray light slid in the windows like discouraged ghosts. I was glad to be alone.

But in solitude I could do nothing but ruminate. I could think of nothing but this rip in the fabric of goodness. There was no way I could paint, create, or do anything at all. All I wanted to do was escape, to be hidden, gone. The pain was too much. Like a physical wound, it ached and screamed. I paced through the dark rooms, helped incrementally by not sitting still. With stillness there was only the suffering. Walking, at least there was the motion, one step then the next.

Like a dog in a trap, I was frantic. There was nothing but the pain. I searched the walls, my thoughts, my imagination, for something to do to lessen the hurt. There was nothing. No veil between myself and my own violent debasement. There was nothing left but the cold cement floor. Nothing good or gen-

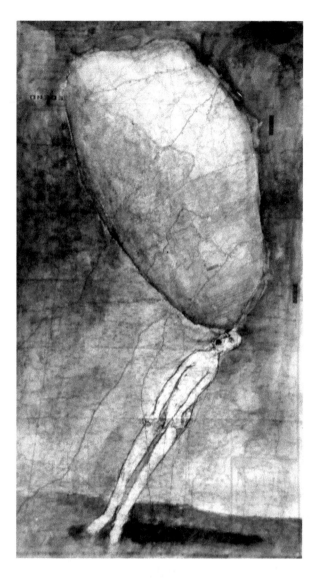

tle remained. Desperately I dreamed, I'll cry it out. I'll just weep and weep and weep and it will come out of me.

Clinically, as if I were going out back to put a horse out of its misery, I plodded to the stairs down to the basement. There it would be darker. I could bleed and strain and gush and no one would know. If someone slid that old butter knife into the lock I would hear it. I could pull myself together before they found me. The worn wooden stairs shuddered beneath my steps. The exposed stone walls of the basement were cold to the touch. They receded into darkness.

In the black shadows I threw myself on the floor and let all my worst thoughts crowd over me like insects. I relaxed my fists and surrendered my efforts to maintain myself. I prepared myself for a wave of sadness like a tsunami. It would wash through me, opening my eyes, opening the doors of my deep, unapproachable hurt. I would let it roar through the city of me, toppling buildings, destroying homes and hospitals. I would shake and suffer through the weeping, but when it was done, I would be cleansed. I lay there in the dark, squirming, longing, waiting for the deluge.

But it didn't come. I found myself simply lying on the cement floor in the lonely shadows. I tried again. I thought of the worst things. Cruelly, methodically, I called to mind my dear Gretchen, in the arms of her lover.

But I only lay there feeling worse than before, cold and unmoved as a stone. No tsunami came. No waves, no water at all. No relief. Only now, added to it all,

I felt ashamed. Helpless. Naked. I'd disrobed before this awfulness, and it only smirked and rolled its eyes. I felt the ice cold of the mindless floor inching in through my many layers. It wore its way through my coat, my sweater, my shirt, and ate into my shoulder.

I lay on the floor in the dark, dry-eyed, unchanged, and absolutely nonplused. I knew of nothing else to do. The pain remained like heartless weather.

After some minutes, squirming, squinting my eyes to produce tears, I gave up. Low as the dust itself, I struggled to my feet and made my way, stumbling to the stairs. I boggled at my desperation. No one would know I had lain on the dark floor of the Art Barn, impoverished, lame, and unable to help myself. No one would ever know I had squinted my eyes, trying to squeeze out tears like juice from a desiccated lemon. Life felt like that cold, hard cement floor on my shoulder. It did not give.

I brushed the dust from the arms of the winter jacket I'd been wearing. I wondered how I would make it to the bus to get home. What would I do when I got home? I could barely manage to walk across the room.

I made my way slowly back up the stairs to the door. I picked up my bag. Inside was my Sony cassette Walkman. Unthinkingly, I put the headphones in my ears and pressed play.

Like a shock of bright colors, music blasted into my brain. So loud, so bright, like the colors of a circus. The sounds were like streams of electric water, coursing into me, utterly irreverent, unknowing, and unmoved by my darkness. They laughed, skipped, and caroused like colorful birds. A second later I recognized it. Stevie Ray Vaughan sang rambunctiously, "Hey, hey, hey, hey mama, look at little sister, out in the backyard, playin' like this…" The guitars glowed and jangled like bright bouncing sunflowers, golden and orange. His voice was filled with delight, laughing and joyous.

All day I'd thought only gray and black thoughts. This music might as well have been from another galaxy, another creation. "Joy!" I thought, as if I'd seen a unicorn in the forest. "It…exists!" I could hardly fathom it. Joy exists. It's right here in this world. Stevie kept on singing in my ears as I waded through confusion and surprise.

I stood there in the open door of the Art Barn, taking in the song as if it were a waist high pile of gold doubloons reflecting the confident afternoon sunlight. Joy was here. It was recorded in tiny magnetic tapes purchased years before. Over the years I'd listened to this song so many times every note was burned in my memory, familiar as the voices of my friends. I'd biked through wondrous summer nights with these words singing joyously in my ears. He'd sung me his love songs year by year, unrelenting in his joy.

The song overmastered me. I had no defense against it. The element of surprise had won the day. With my eyes as wide as the moon I let in the facts—there is joy in this world. I can feel it. Warm tears rose in my eyes. They were grateful tears. Amazed and overcome tears. Stevie Ray, loving me through eternity, gone from this earth these seven years. He reached me. When my friends couldn't, when I couldn't reach myself. That man's joy blasted me out of my story.

I remembered my thought that I wouldn't be able to make it to the bus. But there was joy in the world. I thought to myself, "I'll take it step by step. I will take one step after another, and I will make it to the bus." The music continued to play.

As I made my way slowly across the campus, I was conscious of each step. Each one was a new decision to live. Each step could be a renewed willingness to make it. As I walked, I made up a rhyme, dead serious, a life-line to repeat to myself:

> Each step, a step of courage,
> Each step, a step of care,
> Each step, a step of forgiveness,
> Each step, we're already there.

Over the next weeks I chanted the words as I walked. They became second nature to me. Incrementally, they filled my time instead of the abrasive, cyclical rumination. Each step I could remember to be brave. Each step I could remember to care. With each step I could give in a little more and forgive the darkness, the suffering, the evil, and let myself see more joy.

INSTITUTE FOR VIOLENCE PREVENTION

Gretchen and I didn't stay together. So, with my Peru plans cast aside, and my final semester of college coming to a close, I needed to come up with a new idea. It was strong in my thoughts that I needed to go somewhere far away—have a new experience—start over. I cast about in my mind and quickly thought of my good pal Maggie who a couple of years before had moved to Athens, Georgia to study at the University of Georgia. I called her up and pretty soon we had it all hammered out. I had a couch to sleep on. I was going to be a muralist—all I needed were walls. Athens was as good as anywhere else.

When I arrived, I had enough savings to stay alive for a few months. Much more pressing though, was the ever-burning desire to do my work. I longed to be useful, to paint murals. Maggie and her friends came and went. They were hospitable and I was glad to have a roof over my head.

Every day I wondered what to do. The hours were long and empty. After a few days, under the constant pressure of my own mind, I plucked a tab off a flyer on a phone pole. It advertised a job working in a phone bank for a telemarketing company. I shrugged my shoulders. It would be a paycheck, and something to do.

A few days later, I had the job. On a warm autumn day, I walked myself down Prince Avenue to the address. I wondered what it would be like. Would I die of boredom? Would I hate it from the moment I started? Would there be a way I could make it fun?

As I walked, the addresses were getting closer and closer to the location of my new job. Then, there it was. I went to open the door, but before I touched the handle, I just kept on walking. I walked right on past and never went in. I felt a weight slip off my back.

The next day I was right back where I'd been before. Freaking out. I wasn't a telemarketer, but I also wasn't anything else. I couldn't watch another daytime episode of *Behind the Music*. I just couldn't.

In utter humility I opened the phone book (if you can imagine). I'd heard old-timey stories of people calling companies right out of the yellow pages. It had worked for them. I thought I'd give it a try.

But where do you start? I looked up "murals." But I hated the idea of working for a mural company that made commercial signs. I didn't call a single one. I looked up "art," but it was all galleries and things that weren't even in my world. I lost my focus and started bouncing around the yellow pages, looking at random things of interest. At the time I was deeply into American folk music. I'd been listening to old union songs of Woody Guthrie and Pete Seeger. For no other reason than that, I looked up labor unions.

Now listen—I was green. As naïve as a child. Everything I knew about labor unions was from these songs. Nothing more. Not a single thing more.

Under the bold text heading "Labor Unions," I saw a surprising listing: "Labor Mediation—The Institute for Violence Prevention." Amidst the hundreds of pages of listings, that title, "The Institute for Violence Prevention" was an oasis. It spoke a language I could feel. I'd always felt, in a wildly uneducated sort of way, a kinship with the concept of mediation. It had always come naturally to me to see the many sides of a conflict. And I did like the idea of preventing violence. Pretty solid concept.

I called the number.

"Uh, just calling to learn about The Institute for Violence Prevention, and maybe see if you're hiring…"

A couple of days later I was sitting across from the director, Louis Siegel, in a local coffee shop. By the end of the conversation I was an employee of the IVP.

I learned quickly that the IVP was Louis's brainchild, a small non-profit created to reach adjudicated and at-risk youth with the principles of mediation and alternative dispute resolution. One of the many services the IVP provided was a court-appointed community reintegration program for teens getting out of lock-up.

Though I had no experience with alternative dispute resolution, community reintegration, or at-risk teens, I was willing to try. In a way it felt natural. The main thing, at least as far as I could see at the moment, was to care. I did.

I didn't have a car so Louis and I often drove together to the many different

locations where the IVP had contracts. We got along well and usually enjoyed our sometimes-long car rides together. He was interested in me and my ambitions. I was happy to be asked about my art, my desire to paint murals, and my hopes of making beauty in public places.

One day, several months into my new job, Louis showed me he had been listening. He suggested, "You're going to make mural painting part of our curriculum." He invited me to design ways to engage our youth with community-focused mural projects. They could contribute to something positive in the community, we could give a gift to our neighborhood partners—it was a win-win.

I was moved to the core. What willingness! What an open, creative mind! My respect for him soared. I could feel his trust in me. How could I do any less than pour my heart and soul into the work? It became a model to me. *This* is how you work with others.

Being white and ignorant often made it hard. The basic love I felt made it work in the times when it did. It was often my job to make sure these young, mostly black, men did what they were supposed to do. I sometimes felt like the horse-riding chain-gang guard in a movie as the young men shot me eyes of hate while they carried out their court-ordered tasks. Other times we celebrated together at the completion of a mural or when one of them completed the program. Over the years I gained an affection and blessed familiarity with the places we went. The community centers in poor rural housing projects. Alternative schools. At one graduation celebration I drew over 20 ball-point pen portraits of our graduates. They lined up to watch their faces become recognizable as I drew.

I painted one mural with four 16-year-old boys who had just been released. They were like pent-up, stifled ghosts. So angry and lost. Imagination, fluency with ideas, seemed impossible. To enable them to participate, we painted what we saw, right there in the junkyard. We saw piled up paint cans—we painted piled-up paint cans. We saw a ladder leaning against a truck, we painted a ladder leaning against a truck. They could do that. Then, amazingly, a smiling sun. Then what I could only guess was a brown and blue moose in the far right, sporting antlers that looked like the mohawk of a 1977 New York City punk. I boggled at the mystery of these boys. Art could open doors. Art could allow them to say something. Make a joke. Try something new.

I often wondered if the work we were doing was helping. The lives of these kids were so hard. I knew I was often inscrutable to them. Yet, there I was,

spending my hours with them. Trying to brush aside the embarrassment I often felt, longing to be useful in the face of poverty and hardship. In one honest moment I realized there was no way I could know if what we were giving was helping. And in the next moment, I knew I had to have faith. I had to believe that Love, invested in the lives of others, was not for nothing. It had to trust it.

Anthony was the most difficult boy I worked with. Our program could be passed in six weeks if all the elements were completed on time. It was court-ordered, so it had to be completed. There was no getting out of it. Because of absences, fighting, and badly done work, Anthony took nine months. At one community service location, Anthony took my keys out of my bag and threw them into the dense Georgia woods. Week after week, with all my might I strained against my own frustration and anger with him. It was painful and hard to know if anything good was happening. When he graduated, we celebrated him like every other graduate and sent him on his way.

A couple of years later I was walking in my neighborhood one evening. A few blocks from my home, my eyes landed on a young man in loose shorts and a faded undershirt who stood smoking on his porch. I recognized the face, the stance. He offered up a subtle gesture of recognition. No one mentioned the past. He briefly told me about his job at the poultry factory, known familiarly by all the kids as "The Poultry." Many of them had parents, aunts, and uncles who worked there. Anthony the boy had become Anthony the man. He was clearly exhausted, smoking his cigarette after a long day at work. He asked about me. I said, yeah, I live around the corner. We wished each other well and gave the acceptable tough-guy "see-ya-round" gestures, and quietly moved on. I drank in that muted, peaceful conversation. After the dust had settled, we met as men, quietly, and, if I allow myself some dreaming, with a tired affection.

I worked with Louis and the IVP for four years, almost my whole time in Athens. This part-time job paid for my life during those years. The rest of the time I fought, struggled, labored, and began to work out how to be an artist.

In retrospect, it's humbling to see God's hand in leading me to this job. At the time, I considered myself a fine artist, simply paying the rent with a job that put me out in the community. I'd never thought of working with youth, and I'd certainly never thought of working with poor youth of color. I brought to it no appropriate education. Only the skills I happened to have and a desire to care for these young people whose lives were so unlike my own.

But, with the accuracy of a golden clock my time there prepared me for mysteries that were to come. These experiences cracked doors I didn't know I would be passing through. They gently tugged the strings of skills I hadn't known I had, or would have to learn in the future. They built the foundation for my life as a community artist—a dream I didn't have at the time.

THE GOLDEN TREE

A lot of our work at the Institute for Violence Prevention was done at an alternative school in Union Point, GA. All the kids there had been thrown out of their original schools for whatever reasons. We provided study help, and a "leadership" course, about good habits, community awareness, and responsibility. Needless to say, a lot of the time it felt as though we were swimming upstream. The kids wanted to be left alone. They would lay their heads down on the desk, pretending to sleep. After being asked a question, or to participate, several times, they might answer "huh?" as if it were the first time it had been asked. They also were jokesters, ever trying to pull a trick on a teacher. An enormous amount of time at the school, for us, the teachers, and administrators, was spent simply trying to keep kids on task. There seemed to be a new principal every year. At the same time, they were sweet kids, and every once in a while you could find yourself in a beautiful teaching moment, witnessing real learning.

After working there for a few years our bright idea was to give students the opportunity to paint a mural of their own design on a wall in the school.

I was really excited about it. It felt so different from the drudgery of the other "here's how to behave right" subject matter. But, when we told them about it, expecting lots of enthusiastic submissions, we got silence and exactly zero takers. It hit home that because our program was perceived as uncool (how could it not be?), that basically whatever we presented, it was going to be perceived as uncool. Even if it was painting a mural—the coolest thing ever.

Having my best idea fall flat I was stumped and a bit insulted. I took myself to an empty room and prayed. I quieted my thoughts, listening. I thought of God, loving these students, loving the administration, knowing them for real, in ways I didn't and couldn't. I tried to be comforted and not take the rejection personally. I thought of God, loving me. Then, in my quietness I had an idea

that surprised me: I would paint a mural on the wall of the school and the students WEREN'T ALLOWED TO HELP.

One cool thing about alternative schools (I've worked in several), especially this one, in rural, poor, black Georgia, is that because most people have given up on these kids. there aren't many rules that would keep you from trying something out. You don't need to get three signatures on a form before you can try a new idea. There's so little pretense. The kids aren't trying to be A students. They know they're headed on to lives of working at the local factory, McDonalds or Wendy's. The teachers aren't up for district teacher of the year. And the principals breathe a happy sigh at the end of any day where there isn't a fist-fight in the hall. There's a kind of humility in the silent, worn school. So, it was easy to change gears.

As I began my mural, I noticed more and more pairs of eyes peeping out of nearby classrooms, watching me. It was autumn and the warm Georgia days were filled with golden leaves. I painted a golden tree, using this opportunity to make something I could be proud of—and hopefully impress the kids. A day or two into it, after the image began to appear and they could see that it was good—not lame—some students came and asked if they could help. "Nope," I said. I felt the risk of my gambit—they might give up on me and painting forever.

"But," I continued, "you can make one of your own if you submit a design."

I think they were a bit stunned. It was clear they were used to teachers bending over backwards to accommodate their interest whenever it showed up. They continued to watch me paint, talking amongst themselves.

When I finished my mural a few days later, we had about 10 student submissions for other murals to be painted in the hall. More came after that. Over the next two years we made 14 murals in the school.

DUET FOR TRUMPET AND VIOLIN

A year after my dad died, I was living in a grungy apartment on Pulaski Street in Athens. It was April in Georgia and spring was going at a gallop. The blossoms on the dogwoods and pear trees came and went. They were replaced by small, confident leaves. The days were bright and warm. Later, a wide canopy of leaves arched over our street, dousing it in dark, lovely shade.

I'd moved to Athens just a few months before and was feeling new—excited and uncertain. I was trying hard to meet people, make friends, and feel at home. Maggie was my one connection. Ever the socialite, she had tons of friends and they included me in their parties and outings. It was a nice start.

I often thought of the events a year before—my dad's passing and the feeling that he, like Obi Wan Kenobi, had, in death, passed some spiritual riches along to me. First the dream—while I slept on the couch, he drove into the garage, walked up the basement stairs, and gave me a great fatherly hug in the very living room where I slept. Then, my walk in the reservation down the street and God's titanic message of spiritual reality, "Nothing has changed."

Those things lived in me like visible changes in the earth's landscape. Like beautiful stones revealed in an earthquake, they jutted out of the transfigured earth, changing the land indelibly. And still, the days went on quietly like all the other days, new life arriving like the spring leaves.

In this warm April I slept with my bed toward the open window. The balmy air came gently over me while I slept. Early one morning as the sun rose, I had another dream.

In the dream I awoke in my bed with the window open to the warm morning air. Dawn's birds cooed and whistled in the trees. I heard the sound of a car (a rental car—I knew it) rolling up the short driveway and coming to a stop. After a short pause there was a knock at the back door. I rose from bed, quickly dressed and opened it. There he stood, just like the last time I saw him, smiling, calm as a garden. Silently we walked to the car, a maroon sedan. He drove and I sat in the velour passenger seat.

I buzzed with excitement. He's here!

We silently drove out of town, on the highway, and then out to a rural road, flanked on both sides by robustly growing corn fields. The car came gently to a stop and we both got out. Joyfully, but without a word, he walked to the back of the car and popped the trunk. I followed. As if it were a plan we'd shared all along, he reached down into the dark trunk and pulled out his trumpet. (He had been a music minor in college and had just started playing the trumpet again in the last couple years of his life.) I followed his lead and reached down into the blackness. Natural as can be, I pulled out a violin (though I never played the violin) and lifted it to my chin. Then, as if we followed a well-practiced score, we played a duet for trumpet and violin that filled the sunny Georgia sky. I saw the notes, flowing up into the air over our heads, wrapping around one another, rising up and up into the steamy sun.

I awoke with my head by the window. I half thought I might find that maroon rental car parked on the cracked cement behind the house. I thought of that sunny song, rising up over the corn. His notes and mine, his trumpet and my violin. Like the first time he visited me in the days just after he passed away, it was more than a dream. It was Life-force. He visited me.

Who was this man, who came to visit me, not only as I slept on the couch in the home he bought and paid for, but who also followed me to this dumpy apartment he never knew? I knew him for 23 years as a thoughtful, portly authority, a classic dad. He'd lived a quiet certainty, expressing his love through sports, food on the table, and advice when asked. But who was he now, visiting me out of eternity? This was not a nerdy, suburban office manager. This was a *being*, something royal, something adventurous and majestic with a will to cross boundaries. I thought of him renting the car to come get me, excited to see his son who didn't know he was coming. I loved him, driving the rural roads of Georgia, perhaps consulting a map, side-stepping mortality. I longed to hear our song, the duet of those two strangely paired instruments. I couldn't hear it, but I could feel it. It was warm, joyful, the song of a father who will break the rules to show his son that he loves him. The song of a son who has been visited by his father, one year gone from planet Earth.

WRESTLING WITH ART

In my first decade out of college I didn't watch any television. I was too poor to watch movies or go out. I spent my time making art. I made my few hundred dollars a month from my part-time job at the IVP, and that was about the only interaction I had with the functioning world. The rest of the time I was walking, watching, writing songs in my bedroom, or making paintings- also in my bedroom.

What an enormous world of creativity I found, in the absence of many of the other things people occupy themselves with. I truly dreamed, and daily thought about, making perfect art. It was my daily goal to express Beauty—to actually do it. I didn't wonder if I was too young, or too inexperienced, or that it was too high a goal. It was my occupation—make the most real art. Write songs that describe the universe. That tell about God. That bare the heart.

My conviction that the universe, God, the heart, are there to be expressed, coupled with magnificent ignorance, opened the door to me. I knew I could do it, or I could at least try. I was dewy with ambition to take up the greatest subjects and succeed.

One afternoon I cut a length of paper from my huge roll. It was 3 feet across and 7 feet tall. I tacked it to the wall. I'd make a life-sized figure drawing.

I opened up my art-sense and out came lines. I watched them evolve and soon realized this was going be the figure of a youth, running naked in the woods. Two of my favorite, most expressive subjects, figures and nature. I continued to let the image appear. The young man was running away from us, his body thin and sinewy. He ran with abandon, his bare feet cutting a path between trees. I perfected the lines describing his body—the hips, the bend of the legs, getting the foreshortening of the calf just right. I explored and erased a million times, seeking the right curve for his shoulders and arms, swinging naturally in that forest air. I quit for the day after many hours of work.

The next day I picked up my charcoal pencils and eraser again. I looked at the boy, and asked what was next. He needed his forest. The trees began to appear. I put my weight into bringing out the depth of the space, creating light and shadow, giving him a real place to run. Leaves appeared on saplings. Branches reached across the canopy of the woods creating a thatch of grasping fingers. After hours of work in my bedroom studio the day's sunlight had come and gone. I turned lights on and continued drawing. More leaves. More branches. The twigs and fallen leaves on the forest floor.

The next day I began where I left off. The forest was further along than the figure. He was only lines, while the trees had deepened with shadows and texture. I felt into the curve of his muscles, thinking of the light falling on his limbs. His smooth body began to take form as I gently shaded the curves. After many hours he was *in* the forest. I worked and worked to give him real form, diving into the shadows with as much sensitivity as I could find. The shadow of his forearm on his side. The subtle profile of his cheekbone and jaw. Every effort to make it natural, against all the opportunities to make mistakes. So many mistakes made, then looking and looking to figure out what will fix each one. What will bring it to life, a natural feeling?

Another day bringing out the details, pouring effort into the realism, caring for each leaf, each part of the body. Bringing out contrast and gradation. Again and again, pulling in close to the paper, making a tiny change, and back across the room where I can see the whole picture. The floor is littered with shavings from my knife-sharpened pencils. The room smells of charcoal dust and the repetitive friction of the eraser. Deep into the night's hours I gazed at the work, wondering if I had run out of improvements to make. I pored over every section to see if they were all working together. It might be finished.

I sat down to admire my work, to revel in its completion. I expected to look over that large page, scratched and wrought upon with my tools, and to be drawn into that forest space, the feeling I had made. But, I didn't. As I took it in, I didn't feel anything. I looked more, and longer. Where was the world I had created? The drawing stared back at me, admitting nothing. My expectation stuttered. I've just spent 35 hours on this drawing. I've done every last thing I could think of to make it perfect! The figure was well rendered. The light and shadow felt real as it fell on his limbs. The trees opened up around him nicely. Surely this piece of art is finished, and done! A success!

But it wasn't. It didn't move me. I didn't feel anything. The figure was fine, but just… fine. The trees were good, but only, good. It didn't sing. It wasn't saying anything.

My will rebelled. I've spent my 35 hours of honest labor on this drawing—surely it is good! It's worth something! But I wasn't sure if it was. Was it worth something simply because I invested so much time? I compared this drawing against my high hopes for art: that it will reveal something about Soul. That it will sing of highest Beauty. That it will force me to feel and travel and love life.

With that comparison, it wasn't hard to know—this drawing wasn't doing those things. If what I was looking for was something to show that I was an able draughtsman, this might do it. If I was looking for art that would speak of the true, deep places, it wasn't.

I was stunned. I asked myself more questions. So, if this drawing isn't singing, is it worth *anything*? Is it the same as a blank piece of paper? If it has failed at the goal, is it as if it didn't exist at all?

I struggled to understand. But, like a beautiful, demanding beacon, a lighthouse in the darkness of doubt, my love of Beauty came forth. It rose up naturally in my thoughts, unbending. The love of good forces us to admit when we have not achieved the ideal. This is integrity. The simple question, "Have you achieved your goal?" My expectation resisted. "But, the hours!"

Deep inside, my heart was already so fully devoted to my dear Beauty, there was really no contest. Beauty gets what she wants. If She isn't satisfied, the work isn't finished.

Beauty left me no pretense. My tools were on the table, as if they had been unused. The hours of my labor had made no imprint.

I prayed, listening. "What can I do? What do you want from me? How can I proceed when my best efforts have been in vain?"

Then, a feeling. The only thing that matters is if it sings. The rest simply doesn't. The rendering, the accuracy, the shading, the time spent—none of it matters unless it is in direct service of the feeling, the soul. Then another feeling. Keep working.

I looked back at the drawing. Was there anything in it that made me feel?

Was there anything worth salvaging?

My eyes landed on a small bush in the lower left corner. The leaves, the curl of the branches *were* beautiful. I could feel it. All the rest could go.

I listened for more. And as I did, a new image began to take shape in my thoughts.

As if I were leaving home on a long journey, I took a deep breath and began to draw over my drawing. A new horizon asserted itself. I could hardly believe it. I had burned my boats. There would be no return. Only what lay ahead. The paints came out, covering the forest I'd spent so many hours perfecting. An orange sky wiped it away. I listened again. The land would be open. A small creek. And a boy, asleep at its stony side. These images, I felt them coming from far away, from deep inside. A different language than the facile beginnings of the first drawing. This land, this creek, this sleeping boy had a story to tell and this was just the tip of the iceberg.

I continued to work, amazed that I had destroyed the first drawing. It was a mess. Half of the old drawing persisted, making no sense in the context of this new painting—whatever it would become. I concentrated, to be rid of all from the first drawing that wasn't singing. I painted and painted, covering the charcoal trees with color, blotting out every line of the figure.

After 10 more hours of work I arrived at what turned out to be one of my favorite paintings I'd ever made. The sleeping boy rang with feeling on the white stones of the creek. Leaves of the one remaining bush from the first drawing hung over his head like a lamp. The dark sky over him was filled with stars and a nearby sapling bent over the boy like a concerned brother.

Step by step in the labor to bring out true ideals, I learn the path. It is false that you can do whatever you want. It is false that we are free. If we want to bring out true beauty, true justice, we are servants and life itself will make its demands known to us. They come like facts from the love we have found. They will not bend to laziness or fear. They demand obedience. But unlike obedience to a human master, obedience to Love and Beauty, invariably brings joy and success. It moves us deeper. We find that as we follow the lead of Love, we are doing what we most wanted, but didn't know. By this fealty to Beauty, we learn who we are and what we love. And when we live the courage, honesty, and persistence to be obedient, the way opens and our ideals are made real on planet Earth.

****

The other side of the coin:

In one of my first mural commissions ever I was asked by a church to illustrate Matthew 19:14—"Let the little children come to me, and do not hinder them, for the kingdom of heaven belongs to such as these."

I was excited about the commission but pretty scared about the subject matter. Over the years I'd had some desire to make some pictures of Christ, but they weren't going to look anything like the traditional picture of Jesus. In fact, when I thought of the true Christ (as far as I knew it), and how to express it in a picture, I wondered if I had the authority to do it justice. So far I hadn't tried.

I thought deep and hard about how to express the feeling, the spirit of the verse. One thing came quickly clear to me—I wouldn't be able to move ahead if the requirement was going to be to make Jesus in the traditional, blonde-haired, blue-eyed man sort of way. It was such a boring trope. If I did it, I felt it would be disrespectful to the two things I love most—God and art. At this early time in my career, commissions were few and far between, and I badly wanted it to work out, but that would be too much.

So, with my heart in my hand, and a lump in my throat I shared my thoughts with my contact at the church. I explained further that I wanted to express Christ's caring openness to the children in what I hoped would be a more spiritual, non-gendered sort of way. It seemed entirely possible that she would say "Thank you very much," and I'd never hear from them again.

Instead, I shook my head with joy and relief when I learned that they were open to my ideas. I was free to start.

I went ahead and made my mural, reaching out to feel the image as real as I could. I could barely begin to grasp the gravity of the subject matter. It symbolized whole worlds. It saved peoples' lives. How do you begin to paint the greatest expression of God's love? In full knowledge of the great meaning towering over my efforts, I just started, trying my best.

It unfolded. I felt pleased with my Jesus, that he was neither man nor woman, but authoritative, warm, and joyful. The children were innocent, sim-

ple, alive. I wrestled with the formal elements, striving for balance and beauty.

After several days and many hours I came to a place where I had done all the wrestling I could do. I couldn't think of anything else to do to improve the picture. Unlike the drawing in the story above, it was working in so many ways, but it just wasn't *perfect*. I'd wrestled and bent, made changes and changed them again. I'd shifted the colors slightly, changed positions of various elements in subtle ways—but the feeling persisted—it wasn't perfect.

I felt that I would cry. I'd been given this job to create beauty, not just by this church, but by God himself. I couldn't bear the thought of failing. Of actually giving up. But I'd done everything. I'd given every piece of feeling and understanding I had. It hadn't achieved the inner smile of wholeness that I often felt when I'd finished a picture. What was I if I couldn't bring my work to fullness?

I sat down, truly lost. At the moment, in this wrestling, I was the one with my shoulders on the mat. Was there one more adjustment I could make? I considered my situation. It was clear to me that I was the only one that could feel the distinction I was making. I knew without doubt that the members of the church would walk in the door at the next service and would love the mural. I knew it with certainty. They were going to love it. But was that enough? In the rest of my life as an artist the only standard I had was if it was good enough by my heart's inner eye. It was the standard I lived by. Why else make art at all?

This time, as I reached out in humility, I realized the bravest thing to do was to be grateful that it would be loved by the people it was for. I had done all I could do. There were no new ideas forthcoming. I thought of my dear Beauty. Beauty is not cruel. She is demanding but kind. She must be kind or She is not worth serving.

I longed to fix the mural. I longed to wrestle and win. After another hour of waiting, longing, hemming and hawing, in silent humility I admitted that I had done all I knew how to do and could do no more. I painfully pulled myself away from the mural and packed my things.

The church was delighted by the mural. They were so appreciative and threw a party to celebrate it. I was glad and celebrated with them.

I felt myself maturing. Striving for perfection is hard. Even though you may be used to feeling the beautiful flow, even succeeding at realizing beauty, you are only a learner. It was humbling to accept that on that occasion it was good enough that the congregation loved what I had done. I could feel myself being handled by the process. Once again, though my ideals are high, I am not the boss. I am a servant, walking the halls of Beauty. The walls are hard and do not yield. Again and again, I am the one who must yield. All the ideals remain in their purity and stature, while all that is weak or petty, fearful or false must yield and be swept aside.

LEARNING TO BE SIMPLE

I grew up loving artists who could draw. I mean, artists who could take a pencil and make a picture that looked *real*. In those formative years I pored over books of drawings by Albrecht Durer, MC Escher, and the poster artist Rick Griffin. With just marks they created worlds I could walk into and feel.

I pursued this skill. It was deeply satisfying to sit down with a blank paper and emerge, hours later, with a drawing of round, illuminated reality. Over some years of striving, I arrived at more and more ability to render things realistically, giving them form and weight. It became the language of my drawings.

My art turned more and more to an exploration of identity. I loved to draw figures and self-portraits. I passed joyful hours studying my figure in the mirror, striving to render the light, the curves, and the shadows correctly. The drawings expressed gravity and strength. The muscles, the joints, the gestures were real, serious.

I loved to throw myself into a huge drawing, knowing it would take 10 or 20 hours to complete. It was like walking through a garden, studying the plants, basking among the many fascinating wonders. As the hours opened, the

forms came to life before my eyes, and, as if by magic, the figures expressed things I felt but couldn't say. By holding my questions and convictions in my heart while I drew, they made their way into the pictures. The thoughts themselves, too big and unknown to put into words, naturally revealed themselves in these formative works. I gloried in the skill I was finding and the wonder of being with these big feelings.

I considered the work of my peers in the art department at UMass. The work they were making was diverse—abstract, expressionist, cartoons, minimalist. The language that spoke through me was this realism.

Leaving school, I continued. My explorations got more ambitious. I regularly went to the art store to buy my favorite charcoal pencils. And I regularly wore them down to unusable 2-inch nubs. I was drawing a lot.

One afternoon I was on the phone in my little Athens, Georgia bedroom. I was sitting on my red upholstered chair, holding the phone between my chin and shoulder. It was a warm day and I was wearing shorts. The conversation wound this way and that and minutes turned into an hour. Without noticing it, I had picked up a black ball-point pen and began doodling on my right thigh. It was something to do with my hand while I talked. Thoughtlessly, barely noticing, I drew and drew all over my thigh as if it were a pad on the counter or the margins of my school notebook. When the conversation ended I stood up and went about my day never thinking of the drawing again.

Sometime later I was on the phone again. Again, without much thought a black ball-point pen found its way into my hand and I drew all over my right thigh. All through the conversation out poured lines, patterns, and geometrical figures. And more, there were little beasts, a horizon, and simple trees and buildings made of patterns themselves. Again, when the conversation was over, I stood up and went on with life.

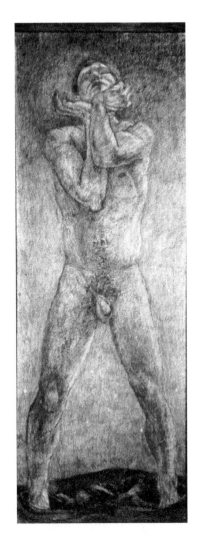

During this time, in my big serious drawings, I had begun to feel pangs that I was going over familiar ground. It had been a few years since college. What once had been sincere exploration was perhaps becoming just doing what I was good at. But I didn't know how to evolve. Or even that it was possible. The feeling continued and I chaffed against my desire. I felt strangely guilty, stuck and uncomfortable.

I don't know how many times it happened—doodling on my leg while I talked on the phone—before I noticed. But finally, I did. One such conversation ended and I regarded the figures I'd just scrawled on my leg. The lines were my own. I knew them perfectly. I knew the kinds of doodles I made. I always had. They were playful, simple and goofy. They were from a totally different place in me than the drawings I made when I sat down to create "art".

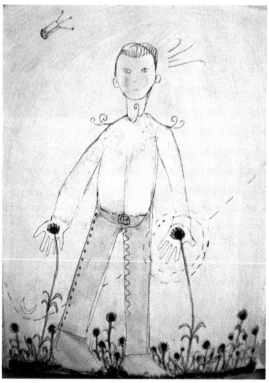

After a few more times, noticing and taking in the phone drawings, a message broke through. Like a merman crawling up out of the sea, the idea dawned. They weren't "just doodles". They were expressing something. *Something so simple.* They were as real as my serious pictures. When classified as "doodles", the communications were silent. I didn't notice them. But when I saw them plainly—as expressions—they proclaimed worlds. They were from over the horizon. They spoke their own language.

The drawings were from somewhere I didn't know how to get to. I couldn't just sit down and draw like that. I didn't know how. They were too simple. I literally wouldn't know where to begin.

In fact, my artist-self was entirely caught up in the notion that to be good, a drawing had to be realistic. I was invested in the idea that there had to be something difficult about it. There had to be this hard-earned technical skill to prove that it was good. Without knowing it, I thought, "Look! My drawings are good. I've developed this skill over these many years. It's something I can do and others can't. I can prove that I'm a good artist!" The idea of sitting down to make a drawing like these new ones—*and calling it art*—was too much. It was too slippery and hard to find. I couldn't get there.

Each time I made these leg-drawings, they survived only a short while. By the one-two punch of hot Georgia summer days and the showers that followed them, they were quickly gone.

The next time it happened I was ready. I found myself doodling while I talked on the phone. This time I watched. The conversation went on, but, sidelong, I took in the drawing that emerged. Gloriously, it continued unabated even though I'd become aware of myself. Somehow, the simple distraction of being on the phone was enough. The self-consciousness that didn't allow me to draw that way in real life, was somehow blocked by the fact that I was in the middle of this conversation. My hand continued to scrawl out lines, creating a little forest on my freckled leg. Beasties crawled to and fro between simple trees that looked like feathers.

This time, when I got off the phone I opened my sketchbook. Feeling insane, I copied the drawing from my leg into the sketchbook so I could study it. Like a student studying the Great Masters I copied the pictures made by my phone-talking self. It was like an artifact from a cave. There was only one and it needed to be preserved.

I began to regularly copy the phone drawings from my leg into my sketchbook. I became more familiar with their simple, innocent language. And after a little while I felt ready to try to draw this way without being on the phone. In stutter steps I used pieces here and there from the copied drawings. I saw the way phone-me had used a single line to denote the trunk of a tree and a burst of radiant lines to indicate the leaves. It was like learning a language, piecing together the lexicon of an unknown tongue using the Rosetta Stone of these leg-pictures.

After some time it was a language I could hesitatingly speak. I no longer had to refer to the copied pictures. Its ideas came more naturally. Concentrating, being brave, I reveled in the unbelievable freedom of being so *simple*. The figures that occupied this world weren't heavy and round like my old drawings. They didn't have muscles described in luminescent chiaroscuro. They were made of squares and circles and might have little wings jutting out of their shoulders. A castle might be made of simple arched lines with little plus signs as the windows. The sky was peopled with puffy clouds, some of which had upside-down lightning bolts poking out of them.

To the degree that there was room in my understanding for this simplicity, my smaller sense of art began to lose its hold. It was as if a burden slipped from my back. These pictures were so simple, they couldn't be used to prove my technical ability. It turned out that it's not about proving. The pictures delight my soul and that's the end of it.

Since then I've seen many times that our job is often to explore an idea until we've learned all we can from it and then, move on. Sometimes it's clear what to move on to. Sometimes it isn't. Often it's something outside our vision and beyond our experience—something we have to grow in order to see. We can't see it—until the moment we do.

LEARNING ABOUT THE VOICE

Growing up I didn't have many thoughts about nature. The closest I got to it was the flower garden in the backyard. And to me, flowers were for ruffly grandmas. I didn't care. I *did* like shooting bees and flies with my rubber band gun. That brought me close to the flowers in the yard. Outside of that it was sports after school, video games, and my neighborhood pals.

I didn't learn that I loved nature until I was in the midst of my first long distance bike tour at the age of 19. Even then, I barely knew it was "nature." My path took me endlessly over the hills of New York State. But the hills began to get into my blood. While I busted my ass pedaling, and thought my churning thoughts, the hills passed by calmly, in the golden wash of summer sunlight, in the curling air of a cool morning. The sky called out its confident blue song, and before you know it, I loved nature. Just like that I found that my life was married to it.

After that bike trip, in the next years I made three more—from Boston to Savannah, Georgia; Arcachon, France to Barcelona, Spain; and San Francisco to Eugene, Oregon. As those adventures unfolded, and I traversed the many hundreds of miles, I found that I couldn't really talk about my life without mentioning the way the air felt, the looming trees, the roll of the hills, the wind, the smell of the night. Soon, and without trying, when I went to describe my understanding of those trips, the ideas emerged using symbols from the natural world. All of those elements of nature taught lessons and corresponded symbolically to the many thoughts and mysteries of my insides.

Without ever meaning to, I came to love nature. It's endlessly filled with poetry. It's constantly speaking.

Athens is a southern college town, rowdy on game days, loud in parts, but mostly a quiet, suburban village. With just a little bit of effort, you can escape to the woods, to a creek, a quiet wilderness.

The years I lived there were a deep, dark struggle in many ways. I found myself in a deep depression. Without meaning to I questioned my every thought and action. Wanting to be good, I judged myself harshly, driving myself deeper into frantic worry. I was uncomfortable around people and didn't like socializing. Instead, I went for walks. Then I could breathe deep. Even if nothing else was going well, I could feel my legs moving, going somewhere. I would put on my jacket and set out into the neighborhood, no plans to be back until the walk was over. I sought out places I'd never been before, places I didn't know. I loved to get lost, to be gone from anything I'd known and just look. I opened my eyes and drank in the world. I followed my guts, the poetry that spoke to me, and went wherever it said. This meant down train tracks, over fences, into abandoned factories. It meant going curiously in the back door of buildings with a soft step and a readiness to run for my life. It meant the woods behind the housing development, the abandoned cemetery, down into the ravine and under the highway bridge. I walked through the projects and the suburbs, through the college and the farms.

I loved to walk. As the years went on, I had a feeling that this city was mine in a way no one could take away. I knew the secret places. I knew the foot-worn paths that led from the parking lot, out through the woods to the cul-de-sac. I knew where the white neighborhood ended and the black neighborhood began. I loved the trees, stitched through it all, bending in the wind.

The hidden places became my friends. My many escapes. One summer I spent my time in a sun-splotched glade at the side of the flat, brown Oconee River. In the distance, the cool, damp shade of a cement overpass. Its solitary underside was mine, where no one goes. From my rented room I made my way out the spring-loaded, paint-flaked screen door, into my dilapidated neighborhood. The grass was tall, pouring out of the cracked sidewalks. The trees were dark with their millions of leaves, making lakes of shade in the baking Georgia sun. I made my way down past the old Standard Oil sign, and turned left onto the rusty brown train tracks. I'd never seen a train on these particular tracks although gigantic trains trundled through town regularly with their enormous metal sides and deafening horns. These tracks, however, had emerald green grass growing up between the slats and a cavern of leaves, branches, and shadows arched overhead. I walked through the long forest tunnel and out into the sun. On the left, the backside of the water treatment plant, surrounded by strict wire fences, guarding weird, square pools. Just ahead on the right, a gravelly yard filled with piles of DPW equipment. I jumped off the tracks and scrambled down a grassy grade into the lot. There were piles of cement pipes, so big I could walk through them. Hundreds of smaller metal pipes, mounds of sand and salt, cement pavers and rebars. I made my way through the piles and back into the grass at the far corner. There the woods begin again and there's a narrow, foot-worn path leading into the trees. I

can hear the hiss and distant roar of the highway overpass. From here it has a quiet feeling. In the woods again and it's dark. The leaves are blowing and wiggling in the washing wind. Sunlight trickles in through the shimmering leaves. The path winds on and sidles up next to the broad, brown Oconee. A mile away this river is passing brightly under the main streets of the city, next to the University's celebrated halls. But here it is of no repute, passing silently between the wooded banks.

We're getting close to my spot. The deer come here to drink and rest. I can make out their trails, winding unceremoniously through the trees. The path goes right down to the thick brown water, and right there is a strong tree, broad

and old, growing out over the water. This is my place.

The tree juts diagonally out of the earthy riverbank. Quickly it flattens out, stretching almost horizontally over the water like a bridge. I crawl myself out onto its thick body and sit. No one can find me here. No one knows. The water moves in such a wonderful way. It's slow and fast all at once. It moves in one great piece, its surface rolling like a wave. The water might be deep. I don't really know. I'm too scared to find out.

I do go swimming here. Against the warnings of my friends. But I don't want to feel the bottom. I swim against its muscular current to stay in the same place. It's not a relaxing swim, but these days I'm never relaxed.

I sneak again to this river and this reaching, longing tree in the middle of a black summer night. The air is velvety and I am escaping my empty room and the long unrelenting minutes. I've made my way through the neighborhood, down the tracks, and across the DPW lot. I've felt with my hands for the trees in the blackness. The moon shines a dim, hopeful glow on the forest floor and on the gray surface of the moving water. I am away from all the eyes, except my own.

I crawl out on the round back of my friend, the tree, to feel the water roll by below my dangling feet. Yes, I'm afraid of falling in. I'd rather I didn't, but it's a fear I'll put up with to feel the feeling of sitting over the river. The millions of gallons flow under me like slow and certain herds of buffalo.

All around Athens I had my solitary, secret adventures. My open eyes. My opened heart. My panting for beauty and fascination. Longing for relief from worry and self-judgement.

I am an artist. I'm always listening, looking for beauty, for paintings to make. For ideas worth expressing, to make a statement to the universe around me. When I return from these walks I've collected treasures in the pail of my soul—the feeling of the puddles after a rain, the sound of the wind, whipping through the trees on an autumn night, the lonely pipes, piled up and unmoving in their sandy lot, so close to the river they could roll in and cool off. Each one of these treasures, and the thousands of others, are there, laid in my thought basket, perfect ideas. I drink them in when I walk, and I drink them in again while I work, loving them as I breathe them into my pictures.

I always kept a journal. I'd remember to myself where I walked, what I saw. Through it all I am wondering about my life, praying to my God, striving to move beyond fear, beyond my terror of my life. On my walks I breathe in these comforts—the black, naked trees on the far side of a rutted field, the unflinching pale purple sky on a winter morning, sparkling white headlights against a darkening sky. I lay them down in my journals like putting my baby to sleep.

Once I was reading through my journal and found something that surprised me. Again and again, through page after page, I found that I was writing about "The Voice." It was speaking all these things to me—the puddles, the fields, the sky, the deer, the river, the secret paths. In my years of walking and listening, escaping, and drinking in the poetry of the land, I made a friend of The Voice without even noticing it. In my journals over and over, there it was: The Voice. It had become so matter of fact that there *is* a Voice, that I wrote about it not noticing any more than if I wrote about a tree.

I put down the journal. There *is* a Voice! It has a capital V. The towering piles of riches that I found each time I set out my door to walk, they were spoken to me by The Voice. In this beautiful moment, of course, I knew, this Voice is my God. My God who I first heard of from others and imagined as a far-off lawgiver with no face—this very God is The Voice. This God is my best friend! He speaks to me in a language so deeply mine that it can't be spoken in words. It is so deeply mine that when He speaks, I learn about myself. My God reveals to me who I am as I walk and explore. I'd been writing and recording the dear, precious words of my God, not even knowing it was Him. He waited for me to understand.

There is a Voice! I remember to myself again and again. I'm celebrating. How can it be that there is a Voice, and it speaks, right to me? It just gives and gives and gives. The Voice blows me up like a balloon, lifting my heart right out of my worries, distracting me from my smallness and my vicious thoughts. The Voice gives me gift after gift, lifting me out of my judgement, and instead enriching me with ideas for paintings, drawings, songs. I am excited to make these things, to magnify and hail these living poems I've heard, and share them with some other heart who may be able to hear them.

Though my life outside of these walks felt like an electric fence, binding and cutting, The Voice pays no mind. It sings to me when I will listen. It sings at every moment of the day if I will let it. Its joy has no regard for my worries. For my fear. In line at the bank it says, "See the budding blossoms on the tree out the window! Aren't they like princesses in their maroon gowns?" Then when I've got my small cash in my hand, if I will forget my smallness even for a moment, it says "Aren't these dollar bills like ancient documents? What mystery! The eye on the pyramid is like your own eye that I have given you—it sees and sees and sees!"

And from that moment I took up a conscious understanding that I live in a life in which there is a Voice. I can listen to it at any time. The Voice has my best interests at heart. It has endless riches. It will say what it wants. It is honest. It is limitless. It does not respond to my will. I bend to its beauty and truth.

With all my heart, and not knowing how, I then strove to become a listener. God help me! I want to learn how to listen!

THE FIRST TIME I WROTE A BOOK

For years after leaving college the thing I perhaps feared most in life was empty days. But there's no map of how to be a muralist. Especially at the beginning, mural jobs were few and far between. The hours crawled, slow and cruel. Each moment they whispered, "You're doing nothing. You aren't contributing anything. You're worthless…" I frantically made paintings and drawings to prove them wrong.

I was waiting to start a mural at a bar in downtown Athens. It was going to be my second paid mural ever. They were doing construction on the building and my project was delayed and delayed. Each morning I woke up in the warm Georgia autumn and wondered what to do with yet another empty day.

Daily near tears, I read the *The Artist's Way* by Julia Cameron. It's a compassionate book that sensitively acknowledges the countless obstacles, outward and inward, that artists face, and provides practical responses. Her generous tone put me at ease and opened me up. Something in the book put a spark in my thoughts. It was simply, "When you are frozen with fear, just choose one of your ideas and start."

I felt a beam of hope. I could do that. I had lots of ideas.

During my years of bike touring and hitchhiking I had often thought, "People don't know that things like this are happening. Everyone tells me it's too dangerous to hitchhike. They say you can't depend on people to be kind. But every day these glories are happening." I had dreamed of writing a book, telling the stories of my spiritual, social travels.

In the humility of my need to fill my days, I realized, "I'll do it!"

I began to write:

As I sit down to write this book I am reaching into the sky, grasping to put my fingers around the moon. The idea is too big to get my hands around. Still, my hands are reaching. The winds of life are blowing and the creative juices are stirring. Something is afoot. The idea confronts me like a jungle cat—serious as death. Its demands are uncompromising. But at the same time, it is miraculously gentle, only asking me to meet those demands. Staring a huge adventure in the face feels like attempting the impossible. Whether it be writing a book or riding a bike a thousand miles, there is a feeling like proposing marriage. My thoughts focus, and the world trembles around me. A swarm of logistical problems and unanswered questions buzz and burp in my mind, screaming like a murder of angry crows. My mind fizzes and pops like exploding candy, seeing the seeming impossibility occupy the same space as the dream of success. There, way off in the distance lies my hope. And between that success and myself lie 50 miles of pits, barbed wire, and armed assassins. Still, the adventure begins. The idea has arrived, telling me with floods of inspiration that this is the path. The supersensible tug of intuition leads. And despite all the voices that would tell me the reasons I can't do it, I can. Or at least I can begin, and the road will open.

I walked from the dark old house where I'm staying, across the parking lot to the Golden Pantry to buy a thick notebook in which I would begin writing. As I stepped in the door of the mini-mart I felt the project teetering over me like a water tower. I got butterflies in my stomach and my hands began to buzz. Just like the first nervous miles of a bike trip. "This is silly. What the hell am I doing? Am I really doing this? Who do you think you are?" Like an out-of-body experience I'm noticing it all happening, as if watching myself from above. The voices are saying I can't do it, my heart is leaping so wildly I barely recognize it as my own, and there I am, walking into the Golden Pantry, buying a 100-page baby blue spiral notebook for $2.25. And I know full well that I can't buy this notebook unless I fully intend to write the book. Otherwise it will just sit there in my room mocking me, a symbol of this thing I could be doing.

I'll own up. Writing this book is as much a search, a floundering, scared, excited quest for goodness, worth, and adventure as any bike trip I have ever taken. I am a man who has no job other than the one God gave me. I am an artist. I am committed to spending my days, hours, and thoughts making beautiful things to feed the hearts of people. While this is a formidable and expansive job to take on, it doesn't have the 40-hour-a-week dependability that other jobs have. So, there is a lot of time waiting, planning, and wondering. I've been going crazy trying to keep busy, itching to work, to feel my life giving something. I sometimes feel the way I imagine men in the Great Depression felt— ready to work and nothing to do. Banging their aching heads against the wall of boredom and the struggle to feel worthwhile. I have a great creative fireball inside of me. I always want to be working on something, churning through the slop, picking out the gold.

This project is daunting. It towers over me like a mountain. It implies more work than any other project I have ever considered. Not only do I have to climb this mountain, I have to explore every corner of it, catalogue every beast and flower, and record every step I take. There are countless places to trip, fall, or worst of all, quit. What is a life that begins its dreams and then quits them, simply because the road was long? I must lift up the reasons I'm writing this book and hold them before my eyes continually. The responsibility for this project can't rest on my little shoulders. I would crumble under the weight. It can only rest on the continuous, unsolicited commitment that rises in me when I think of its beauty. These adventures have given me great fields of vision that have grown my life. They are my darlings. They are my precious gems.

"Alex, what in the world are you trying to do here?!" This question came to me forcefully, mockingly. I was *scared*. There were so many things to distract me. I was afraid I would fail. I was needled by the fear that the whole thing is crazy and I'm just lost and groping for something to latch onto. There was the daily fear of simply putting the pen to the paper. What if everything I write is stupid?

I worried that after a little while my zeal would peter out and my scrawled notes would sit, damp and silent on some shelf. The book would wheeze and sputter like a caught fish on the floor of a boat, pathetically suffocating. My heart broke at the idea. I coached myself sternly, "You don't simply raise a child until you begin to lose interest. You have to be committed to it." Dead serious, I asked myself, "Is there anything that can assure me that I will come back to this, day after day, month after month? If there isn't, maybe I shouldn't be writing this at all."

Answers began to come. If there's anything in my life I can see clearly, it's the overwhelming *goodness* of these trips. When experience is inspiring, it's worth sharing. On these trips I witnessed a red velvet carpet for the soul. There is richness beyond what the world will tell you. Something happened in those days and nights out in the world, riding and seeing. Whatever it was convinced me, way down deep in the invisible places in my heart, that life has the potential to be fantastic—not just good or passable, but wonder-full.

I got into the routine of picking up the notebook, getting on my bike and riding down to a little field I knew of. I made my place in the grass, leaning against the trunk of an oak tree. Most days I didn't know what I was going to write. I was scared as I pedaled myself the three-quarters of a mile. What if I can't think of anything? Are my ideas obvious and childish? But the idea sat in me like a king. It was right. It was good. It had arrived. Plus, what else was I going to do? Go back to not doing this? Where two weeks ago I was tortured by the endless hours, now I walked around in a flurry of new ideas. I knew I was on the trail of something big. I knew it was a door opening in my life. I didn't know what was going to happen, but there was something beautiful at stake.

More than once that I sat down by that tree, close to terror, and prayed. "God, I know you're moving me to do this. I don't know what to write about today. There is not a thought in my head. I know that you are doing this and you don't fink out on your projects." After I prayed, I would sit and think as simply as I could. Ideas came. They weren't passed from heaven in a cup of light and they weren't spoken in a deep and booming voice, but they came. They were ideas I'd had before. They were my ideas. But I'd never written them down to be in a book before. When they did come, I ran with it.

A distinct pattern developed. Daily, as I went out to the field to work, I felt resistance. I didn't want to go. It was scary and hard. But I knew that I really *did* want to go.

It's something to see and name the opposition that comes up in us as we are taking off on a new adventure. Thoughts saying it's not good, it's worthless, I can't do it. But the greater knowing is that we are *going* to do it. So, we do, and the opposition falls by the wayside. And that's exactly what happened. As soon as I would arrive at the field and begin working, the opposition would disappear. *Every single time.* Sitting in the grass, putting the pen to the paper, it was replaced by a creative excitement to move further into the idea. I could breathe deep and work.

Deciding within myself that I will spend the hours of my day writing, not seeking a paying job, without realizing it I was drawing a line in the sand. Others are spending their days working their jobs. Whether you like your job or not, it's one of the main ways we know we have a place in the world—we have a job. We're part of a system. As I wrote, sitting in the grass at the park, I would often think of the thousands of people in Athens, sitting at their desks, working in restaurants, schools, and offices. I often longed for the security of knowing I have a place in the world, a role. The fear of empty days might have driven me to find a job to fill those hours. But the voice inside gave different guidance. So, I went to write the book.

Just going to the park, doing my daily writing, I was *doing* it. I pushed back against the mocking voices. They kept tearing at me, comparing me to others. How could I possibly hope that my little work, sitting in the grass while everyone else is in jobs that matter, could be valuable? But I kept doing it. Over time, by tiny degrees, I felt the boulder shift. I opened my eyes in the midst of the work. I felt, in a small way, I'm allowed to do what feels right even if it's not the way others do it. Even if it's not the safe, known way.

****

Over a few months I watched the pages fill. I'd never written more than 20 pages of anything in my life. By the spring I had 90 pages, written in my tiny handwriting. The blue notebook was full, and the first two trips were recorded.

I'd always been a hand-writer. I'd never learned to type. If I could avoid computers, I did. I had no use for them. "I'm an artist!" my ego crooned. "I work with paints! I bring beauty to the earth!" In the unspoken recesses of my thoughts, like a dumb bully, I scorned typing. "What a bunch of nerds!" I never dreamed I'd need a computer. I never thought I'd type a word. I'd never turned a computer on. Now, the trembling path of my own creativity brought me to this impasse. If this book is going to exist, I'm going to have to get a computer. I'm going to have to learn how to type.

Pow! Look at this adventure. The project, this invisible idea, compels me with irresistible force, to change my life. It would be one thing if this were a marriage, to a person; then you expect to make adjustments—to compromise. But I'm alone. Even so, I can't have my own way. I am not allowed to remain unchanged. I have to alter my very lifestyle to accommodate the book. We are never alone. We are never not in relation. Life itself is pushing on us, forcing us to grow, to become better. It will not leave us alone.

So, knowing nothing, I bought myself a used computer for $150 from a Chinese exchange student at the University of Georgia. I soon realized I also needed a desk. The next day I came across a bunch of lumber in a dumpster down the road and lugged it back to my house. I sawed and schemed and after several hours I had a very homemade, very heavy desk. I heaved it up the stairs and soon had an attic office.

I was in it for real. On a bike trip it's easy to know you're in it—there you are, 500 miles from home. But in *this* trip, I'm at home the whole time. I know where I'm going to sleep. I know where my next meal is coming from. Physical necessity erased, the only thing keeping me in it is my desire. The love of this book demands that I do whatever it asks even when I don't want to. Only the desire to see the idea grow has the power to keep me moving into the unknown. Now I'm giving it my time *and* my money. What next?

For the next months I sat down at the computer daily, ready to type. "I don't care how slow it is. I don't care." I said it over and over like a mantra. It was a good thing I took that stance because it was excruciatingly slow. I had my 90 pages sitting there on the desk. Like a caravan of refugees marching thousands of miles with only a vague hope of a Promised Land my fingers ached around the keyboard. They yearned to hunt and peck. To fall back into it would be like returning to a bad relationship—the first embrace would feel like heaven. But the same old problems would return. With an iron will I forced myself to maintain the correct position. For hours I looked back and forth from the manuscript to the keyboard, forcing myself to keep my hands in the right place. Faintly, ever faintly, my fingers began to twitch intuitively towards the desired keys. The next day I made a rule that I couldn't look at the keyboard at all. I stared at the screen and watched the letters slowly—so slowly!—appear and turn into words. Again and again, I defied the powerful ache to look at the keys, catching myself a hundred times thoughtlessly dropping my eyes. The words drunkenly stumbled onto the blank screen, yawning and wondering where they were. As if asleep, my hands were doing it on their own. After only a few days I was running from friend to friend yipping and yelping about my success as a typist. "The words just appear! It's like magic!" I danced and leaped while the world looked on with pity.

I had to calm my head every day before sitting down to work. "I'm not writing a book; I'm learning to type." All I could do was be patient. That was my only tool. Like a schoolmaster, I still had to discipline myself not to look down at the keyboard. Every ten seconds my eyes would wander down and each time I had to patiently pick my head up and plant it firmly on the coolly shining monitor. The pages were like gridlocked traffic.

But I was making progress. For the last half-hour of work each day I let myself look at the keys while I wrote. Like a child let into the playground, I dove in and watched gleefully the speed with which I could make my fingers go. Just the sound, the clickety clack of the keys made me proud and stirred my willingness to come back and do more.

****

For the next months I transcribed all that I had written in the notebooks, editing on the fly. And then I did the obvious, yet unthinkable thing—I skipped the handwriting all together and worked directly on the computer. I launched into the second half of the book a transformed man.

For the next year I poured out my ideas. The book grew from 90 to 240 pages. After they were there on the page, I paced through them, organizing and correcting. I began to learn to write. Day after day I did what I'd promised myself I'd do—I loved the ideas. I considered the effect I hoped they would have on a reader. This love, felt each day, drew me further into the project. I wasn't in any in danger of quitting. I loved where it was going. I liked climbing this mountain. I liked its demanding path, the trees and flowers, recording my steps.

What had been a dream, an escape from the terror of empty days, was a real thing. It occupied my days and my thoughts. I'd set my hopes on it. I'd laid my own comfort on the altar for it. I'd changed my life for it. As I lived for it, I loved it. It was my baby, the thing I am giving myself to, working for, sacrificing for.

In the summer of 2000 I moved to a new house. I quit my job at the IVP and dedicated my days to writing. In my new surroundings I sat at the computer from about 10 a.m. until about 3 p.m. most days. Systematically I went through the book, working to fill in the gaps as if I were mending a dam as the river rose.

As I neared the end of one complete edit, I knew that I needed to immediately begin another one. I hadn't done it wrong, but different edits have different eyes. As I'd moved through the broad fields of the pages, I'd begun to feel that there was a great gaping wound in the book itself. All the stories were there, the reflections were solid, but the voice, despite my best efforts, was weak. During these two years of writing I'd felt glimmers of how strong the book might be. The initial fear evolved into robust, athletic labor. I knew it *could* be deeply inspiring. I watched myself understand more, gain skills, and feel more at home amongst these thousands of sentences. I could feel its voice, growing, longing to be more. Despite all that, it wasn't good enough. As I read through, the stories were a chain of deep and beautiful lakes, but between them, stitched into them, was shaky, childish talk. Right in the midst of my most beloved descriptions there were phrases that hung like dingy old socks. There could be no weakness when this work was done.

So, I resolved to do a massive overhaul with the specific goal to root out any phrase or idea that lacked authority. I would be merciless. Sometimes I dreaded what I would find. In two years of working, I'd become a better writer. "Ugh," I often thought as I found some lame turn of phrase, "I can't believe this stayed around this long!"

I worked with my simple desire. But as I labored, I found in myself a corrupt voice, making excuses, encouraging me to move on, winking at the problem. Sometimes I felt helpless, embarrassed, like the whole thing was written by a child. In those moment I was like the captain of a ship constructed of rotten wood. I could see in my writing the artist's worst enemy—begging, pleading sentences saying, "But it's good *enough*, right?" In the worst moments I feared I had written beyond my knowledge. There were always better ways to say things. It could always be simpler. Always another strip of fat to cut from the muscle. I learned that what most needed to be excised was the silent desire to get away with something. There was some little whisper in me that wanted to say it had finished the great and noble book, without investing *everything*.

It became vile to me. I couldn't abide the thought that such indolence could attend my precious work. The cloying hands of weakness were red all over its back. So, having seen it, I tramped through the book treating every weakness to the best dose of health I could muster. That meant finding places that had been written carelessly, and caring for each one. It meant banishing laziness. I came upon sentences that lay like novocained arms, like slovenly, self-satisfied kings. They never expected to be roused from their sleepy rule, safely hidden in bureaucracy. At this point, certain of these flaccid passages had rested in the armchair of my book for the full two years. They had slipped past the eyes of the previous edits. They were used to being let off.

But their time had come. When I wouldn't relent, the voice of laziness immediately insisted that the book would never get published and it wasn't worth trying. It complained that there was no way to improve the writing. "This is the best I can do!" it whined. But it wasn't. Until now this little temptation existed in the shadow of my strong voice, hoping to never be seen.

All the while, over me, hung my ideal—the Voice. The Voice I knew from my paintings, where my confidence was not a question. That Voice could be here, in my writing too. A Voice like the sky. A Voice with wide blue wings. A Voice like a showman in a black tuxedo dancing his enemies to shame. I could feel its impeccable expression, its unswerving accuracy. More than ever before I was daily aware not only of the tremendous tower of expression—but also the staggering, exacting dedication required to approach it.

Finally, I was at the end. I felt I had done right by the book. I'd cared for it like a nurse. It was on the mend. And now, after three months intimately rearranging its innards, I could barely see it. I knew every sentence. There were no surprises. I took a job in northern Michigan for the summer and resolved not to think of the book until the fall. Coming back after months away I expected to see it with new eyes. At that point maybe I could discern whether or not my baby was all grown up.

****

Upon my return from the summer, when I picked up the book, I didn't know what I would find. I hoped strength would outweigh the weakness I knew was still there. I perused the first paragraphs and was mortified to find it floundering as it had before. The weakness had not been eradicated. The chain of its speaking was deplorably mixed with the frail timidity of one writing his first book.

I'd come to my limit. I'd done every last thing I could think of to fill my book with health. I had edited it patiently for over 18 months. I had closed my eyes to still my defensiveness when I got criticisms from friends. I had opened my heart and my willingness to the widest aperture I could muster—and still, the book was not the muscular river I'd dreamed it would be.

Self-help slogans swarmed through my head. "Never give up!" they said. But I could only think it sarcastically. I imagined the thousands upon thousands of would-be authors working in their homes, full of hope. "Ugh," I thought, "We *are* a sorry bunch." It seemed impossible. If I didn't believe in my work, how could I expect someone else to? I looked back over the last three years of my life. They had been centered around the creation of this book. Its concepts and images composed a shining tower in my thoughts. I regarded the edifice I'd built. It wasn't that shining tower.

After reading some more I put the book down and didn't move. I lay on the couch knowing I was smack dab in the center of a moment of truth. I'm just a guy. All I can do is make my best decisions. I hope they will be intelligent, soulful, and kind. I have no more power than that. Like a father, I looked back over the hours of work, effort, inspiration, and prayer I'd invested. I had learned things I never imagined I would. I had an irreplaceable experience of dedication to my creative life. I'd honestly done my best. I left it all on the field. With a clear heart I said to myself, "I've done all I want to do for this book. There's no saving it. It isn't good enough." I could look myself plainly in the face and say, "Alex, you are not as good a writer as you want to be. You're just not there." And with kindness, I knew I had nothing to be ashamed of. Why would I expect to be John Steinbeck at the very beginning of my dealings with writing? Or even, at all? And with that I decided to put these years behind me, treasure the lessons, and move on. I lay on the couch, awed at my decision, amazed that my life had brought me to this strange place.

I lay silently with my heart, both sad and open. I'd just ended the longest relationship I'd ever had with a creative project. How deeply I had loved this book, how dearly held its message. And now I had to let go. The journey ended proudly, honorably, without a trace of laziness. With that, I looked forward into the open sky of the future, knowing that there must be something waiting for me.

FINDING THE FOUNTAIN / CHRISTMAS REVELATION

A couple of years into my time in Athens I continued to slog through the darkness of depression. I also continued to make art. It remained interesting. It was a path of escape from the fear.

The inspiration for my pictures had always been my feelings. If I saw a beautiful tree, I would paint the beauty I'd seen. If I'd been hurt or felt lost, those feelings would be the jumping off point for my expression.

One particular evening I had been out on my bike. I was riding around, feeling terrible, thinking about my life. In a burst of rebellion I thought, "I'm going to go home and make a picture! I'm going to pour this suffering into a vibrant, powerful work of art." It was what I had always done. I poured my emotions into art.

I got out a large paper and tacked it to the wall. I got out my charcoal and jumped into the drawing. I did what I was used to—I felt my feelings and let them flow out of me onto the paper. The feelings transformed themselves into images as I worked. I watched them come out of me, responding to the images as they arrived. I sculpted the pictures until they reflected my feeling.

But on this night I found the path blocked. I opened up, as I always did, to let the feeling out onto the page. But instead of the flow of feeling I expected, what came out was lifeless, without substance. I made marks on the paper, mimicking the process I knew. But the marks were dead. The feelings themselves were dead and couldn't provide a path to art. They had no soul. There was nothing good or alive about them. So, a work of art that grew out of them, died the very moment it was being born. There was nothing there.

I was stunned. This had never happened before. It felt as though the one tool I still had, my art, was breaking before my very eyes. I went back to the paper and tried some more. I pushed the charcoal around on the page, trying to lift the hopelessness I felt into something beautiful or true. I couldn't. I'd had one way, one remaining path that gave life value. It had been strong and passionate. It was dwindling to nothing in my hands. I was bereft.

In the days that followed I wandered, suffering through my wilderness. I longed to live, to make beautiful things as I had before.

Suffering is a crucible. It brings about unforeseen chemical changes. My losses pushed on me, hard. I'd lost my happiness, my confidence, my peace, and now, my art. But, though I didn't feel happy, or confident, or peaceful, in my depths something knew that they must come back or life is nothing. Something demanded that these losses must not be the end. There must be more. In the same way, in the root of myself, in the deep wilderness pool, a tiny voice began to be heard. It said, "Art can't go away. It can't be over. I still want to make beauty. I still want to sing." And though I didn't know how to proceed, the longing to sing a beautiful song emerged unchanged. It crept around in the wilderness, looking for a way to sing.

If my art wasn't about my feelings, what could it be about? Without them it was false, a lie—the opposite of beautiful. Without feeling there was no good art. There was no song. Feeling is what makes art live. If my emotions are dead and can't support beauty, what do I have? How can I make anything worth making? I had no answer.

The longing persisted. It was there, like an animal in the darkness, just longing to sing a beautiful song. It pushed painfully against the world of darkness that surrounded it. It was comforting and terrible all at once. This longing, like my prayers for healing, was pure and good. It remained unchanged despite the carnage in the rest of my thoughts. But it was so hopelessly small in the face of all the fear that occupied mile after mile of the city of my life. It was terrifying to think of resting my hopes on this longing, on these prayers, when they were so outmanned and outnumbered by fear.

The longing continued, searching, seeking, almost in spite of me. Its life was to sing a beautiful song. It knew only the desire to be beautiful. It could never be anything but that desire.

As the desire persisted, nosing around the darkness, seeking something to sing about, I felt a shift. The desire, my desire to express and make beauty, had learned, unequivocally, that these emotions couldn't support beauty. So, like one who has learned not to touch a hot stove, it naturally turned away from them. It no longer looked to them for help. Like a blind man, it was feeling around in the darkness—feeling, feeling, feeling. And then, it found something.

Imagine a darkness at the bottom of a cave. There are cold, wet stones strewn on the hard dirt floor. There is no light, and no hope of light. No one has ever mentioned light, or heard of

it. And the longing, a deer, is wandering around in the darkness, acting out its self-longing. It is leaning against the stones to learn if there is anything good to be found among them. It longs for light, color, softness, warmth. It can't ever cease seeking because it is longing. Then, it leans against an enormous, cold, boulder. Its deer body is small and weak by comparison with the stone, invisible in the blackness. But beyond explanation, the stone shifts an inch. The deer leans against it again, longing into it. The stone shifts again. In fact, it isn't hard to move this stone at all. The boulder shifts as if it were on an easy, smooth track. This stone was sitting on top of a spring, a fountain. Immediately its warm, refreshing, entirely foreign waters are gushing upwards, changing everything.

I imagined this darkness as the floor of my insides. The longing to make beauty turned away from the darkness it knew couldn't support it. It turned away, but it could not quit being itself—desire. Like a miracle, it found the source, the fountain. The fountain was gurgling with interesting ideas that had nothing to do with me or how things were going for me. They were just… beautiful. They were trees and travel, adventure, and declarations of the fountain itself. They were endless, and gushing into the dark cave.

In the next days I went to paint again. This time, I leaned towards the fountain—to understand, to accept what it was giving. In my mind's eye I saw a field of white flowers under a starry sky. Its peace and expanse could not have been more different than the angry, hurting image I had tried to make just days before. It was so new, so foreign to turn completely away from my emotions, and towards this other source. I was learning a new language, giving birth to a new thought. I struggled to be big enough to allow it in. As I did, I felt the angel, the longing, saying, "Yes, this is it."

I knew that good art was based on honesty. I had thought being honest meant telling about my emotions, my life. But this fountain didn't care about the small things of my life. It had totally different things to say, to tell me, to sing about.

Starving for joy I drank them in, despite the fact that the depression continued unabated. I found that this fountain of ideas was always pouring forth, no matter what I was feeling. Any time I could tear myself away from my preoccupation with my own feelings, I could drink it in, find fascination. There were field after field of ripe ideas, brilliant new flowers, fruits, streams and birds.

Without understanding where, or why these ideas were coming, I followed them. They were happy. They were colorful. They were deep and interesting. They were imaginative, fantastical, loving, sweet. It felt crazy to be engaging with such bright ideas when the rest of my world was so dark! I could hardly understand. It shattered my sense of where art comes from. Still, I could feel the fountain gurgling, flowing with beautiful water. It was in a place far deeper in me than I had known existed. I was learning that a person is deeper than I'd known.

In the next months I gave myself over to the fountain and its ideas. The depression and fear I felt continued unabated, but in the midst of it I found myself making some of the most joyful, sweet, colorful paintings I had ever made—or seen! And, if depression is a dragon, making this art and drinking in this beautiful water was a powerful wound inflicted upon it. Without knowing how, one of my arrows had finally pierced its scales.

I never looked back. The fountain became the source of all my pictures. My art was changed. Creatively reborn, I loved my paintings as I had before. Maybe even more. Amazingly, while these pictures didn't take my daily emotions into account even a little, they were deeply personal. While they didn't express anything about my personal life, exactly, they expressed things I loved more than anything.

I'd seen how powerless I was to create value when I based my art on personal emotions. Then this dauntless longing refused to die. It unearthed the fountain. I soon laughed at a thought that had once seemed so basic—that I am the creator of my art. No, I go to the fountain and receive. I am powerless as a creator. I can do nothing but go to the fountain and receive the gifts it bestows. I didn't make up the desire to express beauty. I found it in myself. I didn't make up my ideas. I found them on the path of longing and desire. I didn't make up my love of beauty, the song, or singing it. I found them all, and received them. I didn't choose to be myself. I received it as a gift.

All that year I'd been praying, hard. The unhappiness I felt pushed me to deep efforts to find comfort. The Bible was becoming my dear friend. Its stories and symbols shone in my thoughts. They made confident claims for the reality of the spirit—an eternal goodness untouched by the miseries of daily life. In my art I went faithfully to the fountain, deep down in the dark. In my prayers I was learning to do the same. As the months went on, I learned they were the same. The images coming from the fountain were the answers to prayers. They were God speaking to me, in the language that I could most easily feel. Art and prayer were not separate entities. They were the same, bound up inextricably in the desire to live, be good, and feel safe.

The images came and I explored them. They taught me the pictures I should make. They whispered their many meanings. I found myself dreaming of fireworks, exploding joyously over an old-growth forest. The picture came to mind and I swooned at the thought. I drew it in my book. Where were the fireworks coming from? Who shot them off? What were they celebrating? I could feel that there was no one in the forest. The beautiful eruptions of sparkling color spontaneously shot forth from the ancient trees. I made several paintings of the image, letting its message speak to me. I began to understand that these fireworks were God's spontaneous joy. The old-growth forest was to say, "You don't have to know where this joy comes from. It just is. Enjoy it. Look at the colors." This image, which I didn't make up, proclaimed the spontaneity of joy. There was a source of it, deep in the depths. Joy was pouring forth, like it or not, independent of what you think or feel. I did like it.

Summer turned to autumn. I dreamed a new image. A star fell to Earth and landed on the side of a hill. The star was not a flaming ball of gas, but five-pointed, as if it were cut out of paper or wood, fallen out of a folk painting. One of its luminous points stuck in the side of the hill from the fall. It glowed with all the brightness you can imagine. It felt like an amazing secret, fallen to Earth, way out in the country, miles from the closest town. Still, people in the towns saw the glow, pulsing from over the horizon. They wondered what it was. The bravest of them walked towards the mysterious light, crossing miles to discover it. I drew this scene many times, feeling for its meaning. I loved the star, hilariously poking into the hillside. I could feel its authority, its other-worldliness. Its light was so gentle, but inexplicably bright. As the people made their way, wonderingly, to the star, way out in the wilderness, they came with their hopes in their hands. I suspected that this star was wonder itself. Or maybe it was a symbol of this new voice I'd found.

December came and Christmas decorations sparkled sweetly around Athens. Colored lights shone humbly from trees and hedges. As Christmas drew nearer, I felt the familiar burn of its spiritual light. It pushed up against my daily sadness, shining on it in a friendly way. One evening I opened my Bible to read the Christmas story to myself. Its images sang. The angel speaks to humble Mary of a blessing to come. The angel tells humble Joseph that Mary has done nothing wrong and there are good things to come. The birth in the manger. The loving animals crowding around them in the hay. The guiding star.

And then I understood. My image is the Christmas story. The star is Christ, come to Earth! Only, it was spoken to me, directly in a language I could feel. I'd made several drawings and paintings of this glowing star, hidden on the hillside, not yet knowing that God was singing me the song of Christmas. And with that, I felt it. I understood like never before what Christmas is. It is the coming, in each heart, of the pure, unblocked, generous Christ—the message of God shining gently on our hidden hillsides, changing everything.

The star shone its light all through me. I understood, plain as can be—Christmas is no holiday. It is the very real influx of holy light, fearless of the dark. I thought of all the gifts that would be given between friends and family. It made so much sense. When you've received a gift, directly in your heart, from the Creator of the universe, all you want to do is give gifts to others. When you can see and feel the fireworks, exploding beautifully over the old-growth forest, all you want to do is explode and shine like they do.

YOU DON'T GET TO CHOOSE

In the depths of depression, though you don't know what to do, you do just keep on living. As I prayed, and explored, I made progress. Finding the fountain of ideas within me changed my art life forever. Receiving a revolutionary new understanding of Christmas brought amazing light, but neither of those events ended my daily battles through fear and complaint. I continued to struggle on.

I flew out from Georgia to Tucson, Arizona to help an old friend, a muralist, on an enormous project she had undertaken. I was sleeping on her couch, meeting her artist friends, going to their parties. The fear I wished I'd left behind in Athens was right there with me, dogging my every step. My social interactions were warped. I tried in every way to hide the all-consuming self-consciousness, but couldn't. For every one thought a regular person had, I had ten, each of them second-guessing the one that preceded it. I argued with myself instant by instant, questioning the basics. Who am I? What should I do? Why did I do that? Why didn't I do the other thing?

One evening I was faking my way through a party at one of the other artist's homes. Exhausted and freaking out, I ducked into the bathroom for a break from all the people. I looked in the mirror. I sat on the toilet. I picked up a book from the reading basket. It was a book of inspirational quotes.

Some people think inspirational quotes are lame. I don't. I love them. I learned that day how much I love them. I drank in ideas from Helen Keller, Winston Churchill, and the like. They were the opposite of people at a party. They didn't have eyes to see me. They didn't want anything from me. They simply said that life could be good. In fact, according to some of them, life could be amazing. Victories could be won. You could be proud of yourself. I read the entire book sitting on the toilet. And when I came to the end, I started again at the beginning.

I'd been tearing myself up over who I was supposed to be. I had a feeling I was supposed to be really good. I'd been good before! I had always wanted to be really, really good, in every way. But the pressure was more than I could bear. I didn't know how to know what was good or how to do it. My mind spun like a top.

That day, with those good inspirational quotes easing my thoughts, I felt a breath of fresh thought-air. In the privacy of that bathroom, I fought. "What AM I?" I asked, with hard, renewed energy. "What AM I?!" I demanded to the room, to God, to anything. It was the same question I'd been worrying and whining to myself for months. But this time it was like grinding stone on stone. I needed an answer. I refused to let it slip away. I ground the stone into the stone. The bathroom was empty—just me and the mirror, the counter, the sink. But then, in an instant, it wasn't.

"I have desires." The thought came, obvious but soft. "I want to paint murals. I want to make beauty." I looked at those things. They were true. I hadn't made them up. I found them in myself, realities. The fact that I liked those things was secondary. The first fact was that they were there, in me, like mountains in a landscape. I hadn't made them—I found them.

I continued the line of questioning. "Where did that come from?" I knew it was God. God gives me those things. But this time I understood, if God gave me those things then I *didn't*. Those things very truly did not come from me. I never decided to be an artist. I never decided to love beauty. There was no matter of choice about it at all. It was given to me by God himself. It was placed there, in me, by the hand of that Being.

I compared this with the common notion that "You can be anything you want!" It's thrown around cheerfully by hopeful parents, books, after-school specials, and posters in guidance counselors' offices. I'd witnessed myself, along with thousands of my peers, struggling to live up to it. "How do I know what I want?!" was our burdened, exhausted refrain. With an enormous, grateful gravity, I internalized in the most serious way—that statement is wrong. You can't be anything you want. You are bound to be what you *are*. You are something. And that something is good. What you are is given to you by God and no other. You *find* what you are by the untrammeled, unsolicited, positive desire that you feel. Whatever it is, that's what you are. You are what you love. And you don't get to choose.

You get to learn what you are, and be it. And, thank God, when you do learn what you are, you love it. You love it because God knows you better than you know yourself. In sincere self-inquiry you find out what you love. It's there like a treasure chest in the basement. It's often layered over with false desires, questionable motives, fear, and a thousand distractions foisted on it by the swarm of opinions swirling around us. We spend years doing what others say we should. We even wish we wanted to do things we don't want. But under all that mess, undisturbed, are our true desires—what we really, naturally, easily love. You may have never seen it before, but when you open it, it's the real gold. It's there.

We are not free to make easy, sexy lives for ourselves. When we do, we find that they aren't freedom but restriction. We aren't free to choose. We're free to learn what we are from the good, honest desires we find in ourselves. We're free to live those desires and let them lead us. We don't live without God. We can't pretend we weren't created by the Wise One. We found ourselves existing, mysterious and wondrous to ourselves. We are not self-ruling agents, free to choose shallow, self-aggrandizing lives. Or, if we seem to be, those elements get knocked out of us by suffering. We're not even free to remain locked up by fear. Our love ever chafes at the restriction, calling out from within. Instead, we find freedom, satisfaction, and peace when we let our true desires, *whatever they may be,* guide us.

This was a victory in my struggle. I threw off, to some degree, the notion that I was in charge of holding up my life. I internalized a little more that I was not on my own, battling to make a little beauty before I flamed out under the ceaseless pressure. Instead, God put me here. The struggling, longing events of my life are not a mockery of my hopes. Instead, God is expressing Himself in me and as me. I am here because God thought it was a good idea. The burden was not mine, but God's.

HITCHHIKING IN WYOMING

I'd fled the summer heat of Georgia, and the stinging fear of my everyday life in Athens. All I could think to do was flee. Fresh air, the open road, maybe they could offer some relief.

It was my third day out on a hitchhiking trip from Albuquerque, New Mexico to Missoula, Montana. The first lonely night had been spent in a cheap highway-side motel just short of the Colorado border. The second lonely night was spent camping in the shadow of a strip mall Applebee's just past the northernmost reaches of suburban Denver. I set up my tent on a cloddy plot of dirt behind the building. I was grasping at straws, beating at the air. I'd left Albuquerque, nervous and scared, bedeviled by my thoughts. No connections made any sense. Self-conscious to a fault. Nervous. A burning weight of fear in my stomach.

My sister was in Montana. Maybe a place to rest.

The third day, I-25 had brought me laboriously out of Colorado into flat, desolate Wyoming. I waited for what seemed like hours on a hill looking out over Cheyenne. Between hundreds of miles of flat earth to the south, and other hundreds ahead of me to the north I was insignificant and lost. And sick. I was weak and my head reeled. Sometimes I could barely stand on the side of the road, waiting. I'd sit down on the dirt until I felt strong enough to stand some more. Passing through a town, I tried to get a glass of water at a restaurant to cool my aching throat.

I got a ride and then finally, just as afternoon turned to evening, I got dropped off at a minor highway exit. There was nothing around for miles except an empty gas station and a silent highway rest stop. In every direction were the dry, rolling, brown hills I had been looking upon all day. As I always did, when I got out of the car, I walked over to the ramp to get back on the highway. I faithfully raised my thumb to the coming traffic and waited. Trouble was, there was no coming traffic. In fact, other than the car I had just gotten out of there was not a single car in sight.

I was used to waiting when I was hitching. But frankly, I was also used to being picked up. So, when I looked down the road, trying to peer over the horizon to see the next coming vehicle, I was impatient. I plopped my pack down beside me, and waited. 10 minutes, 20 minutes, 30 minutes. Not a single car.

There is a sign on any highway onramp that has on it a little picture of a bike, a horse, a tractor, and a person walking. Each one of these simple pictures has a red circle around it and a line crossing through it. I had learned years earlier that the law is this: if you are on the close side of that sign, you are A-ok hitching. If you're past it, you are breaking the law. I'd come to think of it as a rule of the road to stay within the letter of the law concerning this sign. Keeps me out of trouble, and, actually, most of the time it's at no loss of rides anyway.

But this was different. There were *no cars*. I was standing with my thumb out, as if asking the shrub across the street to pick me up. A little desperate, after having seen no sign of humanity since my last ride drove off, I haltingly decided to cross the line of the law and get up on the side of I-25, where at least I could hear the throbbing roar of cars passing by.

The speed limit in Wyoming is 75. If I had felt insignificant before, once I got onto the interstate, I was dust. Trucks, semis, and cars burned past me cruelly, throwing stinging clouds of debris into the air and casting aside the jetsam of the road—broken glass, shreds of tire rubber, metal. I raised my thumb hopefully, feeling as I did it that I had become a beggar. I knew it was a quixotic, meaningless gesture, pretending that someone would stop. Though I knew it was hopeless, my pleading, punch-drunk hope quaveringly persisted.

None of these cars were going to stop. They couldn't even see me until it was too late. The sheer speed made it impossible. Even if they wanted to, they'd be half a mile down the road before they made the decision to slow down. The poor orange sun crouched in the distant hills and car after car sped by, taking no notice of poor me, broken and lost in northern Wyoming.

There was nowhere to sleep. I had to keep going. But there was no way. Then, flashing blue lights. Slowing from 80 to 60 at seeing me, and then 60 to 0 a hundred yards past me a mean state cruiser pulled over to the shoulder. He stepped out and strode towards me, beckoning with his hand like an angry father.

I wasn't afraid. This had happened before. When hitchhiking you can't help but have some contact with police every now and then. So far, these interactions had been fine. Every situation is different, but at worst I would spend the night in the police station. And at this point that didn't seem too bad.

This is how it went:

"You can't be here."

"Yeah, I know. Sorry. There are no cars down there"

"Hitchhiking is illegal in the state of Wyoming."

"Oh, I didn't know that. I'm trying to get to Montana."

"You got 23 miles to go."

Then I played my secret card.

"I'll be out of your hair and breaking no laws if you give me a ride to the border." (I had used this idea with police a couple of times in the past and had found that it yielded surprisingly good results.)

He raised his eyebrows. "No. You can walk." He added, "If I see you out here again, I'm going to arrest you." He strode coldly back to his cruiser and sped away.

The sun had gone behind the hills and the sky was darkening. My hope was barren. No cars, no rides, and the threat of actual arrest if I tried my one means of escape.

I wandered abjectly back down the ramp to the silent road. Across the street was the empty gas station, vacant and sad like an Edward Hopper painting. I headed towards it with a grasping dream that there might be a person inside. I thought nothing more than if there was another person there might be hope. As I walked up the hill I noticed the rest area parking lot had gained a few cars while I had been up on the ramp. I could hang out in the parking lot casting my plight on the mercy of these rich souls whose lives were under their own control.

The first car I saw was an ancient orange Subaru station-wagon filled to the ceiling with someone's life. Boxes, papers, clothes, and tools were crammed messily into every possible space. Not an inch remained for another object. I considered. This person was going far. You don't pack your car like that if you're just going to the store. Instantly my hopes kindled. I waited like a lion waits for a gazelle. I tried out lines I might use to start a conversation. Everything I tried felt headlong and clingy, but I didn't care. After a few minutes a man ambled out of the restroom towards me.

He was disheveled, a little nervous looking. I approached him plainly. "I'm trying to get to Missoula, Montana. I've been hitching all day and the police just said I can't be up on the road. Can you give me a ride to the next intersection?" I tried to get it all out quickly, so at the very least he couldn't say no before he had heard the whole story.

"I haven't got any money," he said dolefully.

"Uh, I have a little," I said, quickly becoming the nervous one. Now he was listening.

Soon we had it hammered out. I would buy a tank of gas and pay him $15 and he would drive me 400 miles, all the way to Missoula. I learned he was on his way to distant Seattle and would be going straight through Missoula anyhow. My clenched fists almost relaxed. My terrified mind nearly rested.

As the last light left the sky, we sped off into the black north, leaving that cursed ramp behind. I asked him, "Why do you have so much stuff with you?"

Agitated, he answered, "You would be too if they were after you like they're after me. I had to leave the rest of it in my garage back in Iowa."

"The rest of what?"

"The whole photon phaser system! When you come up with technology like I have, the government wants to get their hands on it and take it right away from you. They want the blueprints. They want everything! But they won't ever find me."

"You have a photon phaser at your house in Iowa?"

"Have one? I invented it! You think all that Star Trek stuff is real? Well, it isn't until someone makes it real. I made it and I have it. Or at least, I had it until they started threatening me."

I began to weigh my options. 1) Make a break for it at the next rest stop, sleep in the bushes till morning and try again in the free state of Montana. 2) Bide my time, never sleep, and ride all the way to Missoula. I was bigger than he was. I honestly didn't feel too afraid about anything really bad happening. If push came to shove I felt I could either subdue him or get away. Driven by my desperation I opted for choice #2. I couldn't give up this ride.

He was a man, not a psycho. He told me of his wife who had died a year previously. He spoke with great, gushing sadness. And then an unhinged freedom. His voice quavered between tears and rage. I tried to say comforting words. He wasn't making sense. He was crying and telling me how many days and hours it had been since her death. He would begin slowly, but soon his deep, gnarled emotions took over and he was ranting and wailing. This went on for some time and I sat there with my hands in my lap, trying to find words.

In the passenger seat of that ancient Subaru I got as serious inside myself as I could. His suffering writhed in him, pouring out of his mouth. In this close space was a real life, more desperate, more tormented than my own. I wondered if he might explode. He might let go this very night and send his fists flailing in my direction. But I longed to comfort him. His internal control seemed gone. As I sat there, searching, it dawned on me that he would continue saying crazy things, worse and worse, unless something stopped him. I knew that something had to be me. He needed me, for the moment, to be his control. For his sake and mine.

"But you can't just tell a stranger to stop talking!" My fear talked back. "Let alone this crazy, unpredictable stranger who invented the photon phaser!" I sat in the seat of his car, buzzing, nervous, thinking as deeply as I could. I prayed. "My good God, what can I do?" I thought of wildness, pain, violence brought about by suffering. Would it actually be helpful to speak with authority to him? To tell him it was enough? I felt in myself the truth that people who are out of control are often longing for some kind of discipline—some reason or force that will provide guidance. I felt it. His pain had him by its cruel claws and was whipping him around like a flag in the wind. Finally, feeling that this was the kind thing to do, I resolved to be that voice to him. A voice of certainty and assurance.

As things were coming to a fever pitch my courage rose up. I interrupted, firmly, loudly, "It's time for us to talk about something else!" He instantly became quiet. And from his mouth, a nervous apology. But, a while later the raving returned, slowly growing in his tremulous voice. Again, I stopped him, "This is enough!" And again later, with certainty, "You must stop." Each time he stopped, the erratic, violent tone draining out of his voice.

At one point, in the deep of the driving night the conversation dropped off. Blessedly, there was no adversarial or tense feeling after the interactions we'd just had. I can only have faith that he felt my love for him, that he knew I did it out of love, not annoyance or anger.

The radio was on an oldies station. The songs were so nostalgic, beamed in from a distant world. Somehow, beautifully, we began singing along. One of us would join in with the song and the other would chime in. Oldies songs, it seemed, were our point of shared knowledge. So we sang 50's tunes, together, for an hour, lighting up the inside of that Subaru. Rockin' Robin, tweet, tweedly dee. It was brotherhood. A pure moment of brothers, flying through the star-filled Montana night. A moment too slippery and alive for the beasts of grief and terror. In that moment their talons released and were gone. I don't know how it happened but it did.

We drove until midnight when we pulled over to sleep. He stayed in the car and I, saying car seats hurt my back, took my sleeping bag and walked a hundred yards and hopped a fence to sleep in the grass. I knew in all the blackness of the Montana night he wouldn't be able to find me. But by this point I felt almost entirely sure that he had no bad intentions for me. We'd sung La Bamba in harmony, for goodness sake.

In the morning we resumed driving and by 2 in the afternoon he dropped me unceremoniously at a gas station in Missoula. Then he was gone. I do wonder what became of him—his packed-to-the-ceiling Subaru, and his flight from the powers that be.

I was suffering, lonely, sick and exhausted. He was suffering, hounded and squirming. But even then, Love was there. In the moments between our fears, we entertained love for one another. We were comforted. Even in my own pain, I found I loved him. I longed for his relief. And in that desire, my prayers to be a comfort were answered. That night was not filled with howling, ruinous tears. There were also harmonies, brotherhood, the self-existent inner light.

MY FRIENDS BULLY ME IN A GOOD WAY

A couple years into my life in Athens I flew back to Boston to be at a friend's wedding.

In my daily life I was pouring myself into making art. The work was coming fast and free. The images were there and ideas developing. In so many other ways my life was stunted and stuttering, but making art wasn't one of them. It was athletic and convincing, flowing from a deep source. I was in love with my pictures and they were feeding me.

Knowing I'd be seeing tons of old friends at the wedding, I brought a book of photos of my pictures to show them. Like a proud father, I wanted them all to see what I'd been doing.

As I'd hoped, they took a great interest. We sat around a table talking catching up. They passed the book around, looking at the pictures, asking questions about each painting. I was delighted to answer.

The year was 2000. The internet was beginning to have a healthy hum about it. I, however, was disinterested. I am always the last one (sometimes by several years) to have whatever is the latest technological advancement. I had no interest. I was too busy with the tools my hands liked—brushes, pencils, wood, hammers. I was perfectly happy taking my walks on the train tracks, seeking out mysterious places, finding the spots where the deer sleep in the tall grass.

These friends, though none were artists themselves, had always supported my art. I knew they admired my skill and felt impressed with my images. I drank in their interest, their validating, sincere questions. Looking at the murals I had finished recently Mike said, "Hey, you need to make a website to show your work!" I laughed, sure he was joking. Then Heather chimed in, "Really Alex, this stuff is good! You have to get it up on the web!"

It was frustrating. I was obviously not going to do that. I had no idea how, no interest, blah blah blah. Plus, this was taking precious time away from the conversation about the pictures, which I was really enjoying. I wanted them to get back to talking about the *art*.

When I make art, it's between me and the Voice. I listen and react. I make my decisions. I follow the leadings of intuition and Beauty in an entirely private way. I don't ask for help. It would dilute the process. I'm in charge and it must be this way. I feel the power of expressing, and living my love brings these pictures into being. Pure, deep, demanding life-honesty draws images up from the depths and onto canvases, papers, walls. It's a relationship, tender and exacting, between me and Beauty, and no one else.

I tried to ease the conversation back to the pictures. "Hey check out this one!" But the idea was in the room and the more they looked at the pictures, the more they all agreed. I needed a website. I thought, "Fine. Let them give me advice. Fine. I'll just wait it out." I smiled and nodded. "Ok, great. I'll look into that." But they wouldn't let me off the hook. It was like an intervention.

The thought of making a website was, to me, similar to making a working rocket that would take me to the moon. Sure, it would be cool, but way too hard. It's a joke, right? There were too many other things to do that I did like, that I was good at, and that needed my attention. Why would I even try to do something that would be so hard? That I would most likely fail at? And that would likely come to nothing in the end anyway? The idea came from so far outside my experience that I couldn't imagine actually doing it. Just to think about it hurt my head.

Finally, out of exasperation I blurted out, "I have no idea how to make a website!" To be honest, I was such a Luddite that I really barely knew what the internet was or what websites do. I didn't even have the words to have the conversation. But, some of them did. They began to explain. It won't be that hard. "I don't know who to talk to!" You can find someone to help you. *Your art is good!* You have to do this.

I started to understand that they were loving me. They really saw value in my work. My work that I loved more than anything. They were loving it. Loving it in a way I hadn't. They saw the step I needed to take, and in my ignorance and fear, I didn't.

I started to really ask what they meant. How it worked. By the end of the night I had a clear sense that I did need to make a website. If I truly did love my work, this was something that had to happen. Who goes to a wedding and gets homework?

In any case, they had convinced me. Over the next months I stumbled around, exploring. Two other friends who knew a little about such things did help me. The thing came to life.

The first version of stonebalancer.com went live in 2001. It has been a showcase for my work ever since.

The reason to tell this story is that what I initially thought was my friends bullying me, was the voice of care and vision, breaking into my life, yet again. Thankfully, they disregarded my bleating complaints. They knew better than I did. Again and again the pattern is that we want to stay small. Even when my dream to create Beauty was as big as it could be, I was blind to the steps to take to achieve it. But blessedly, if there is a grain of willingness, the voice of growth comes. Very often we meet it with resistance. It annoys us. It enrages us.

But if we will just shut up and listen. If we will get over the discomfort. If we will concede to love our idea more than we cling to our smallness, then we take the steps that move us forward.

I'm sure I would have made myself a website at some point as the internet became more and more an unavoidable part of life. But how many years would

I have waited? How many jobs would I have missed because my work couldn't be seen? I overcame resistance by bending to my love for my art, my life. My good friends had blessed me with their care. They'd seen an obvious truth and told me, lovingly ganging up on me.

VIRTUES ARE OUR TOOLS

Everyone has qualities they feel comfortable with. The ones that feel like home. Some folks are attracted to creativity, others to discipline. Some have a natural understanding of togetherness. Others like independence. Some like to run marathons and others prefer to gaze quietly at the ocean. These people often disagree about which is more important—creativity or discipline, unity or independence. But the virtues themselves don't conflict with one another. Despite the fact that they seem to be at opposite ends of a spectrum, they work harmoniously together. God's tools are not at odds with one another. Creativity is strengthened by discipline. Independence is enriched by community. Honesty is made more loving by tact.

We each find ourselves with varying abilities with the countless qualities and virtues. A person who is full of creativity but eschews discipline often comes to see themselves as a particular type of person. Another, with plenty of discipline, who doesn't get creativity, comes to perceive themselves as another type. We put ourselves in boxes, closing doors on our natural ability to grow and learn. When we attempt to learn a new skill, or grow in one we aren't good at, we often find ourselves opposed by loud inner voices. They threaten us and tell us it's useless. They mock and deride our honest intentions. They pose as our own thoughts. We don't like that feeling, and to avoid it, we often simply quit. Soon we come to think of our current cache of qualities as our identity instead of simply, *what we have so far.*

The death-blow comes when we begin to identify ourselves, not even by what we have, but by what we feel we don't have. "I don't have any discipline." "I'm not a creative person." "I don't have the patience for that." Growth becomes impossible. And if we can't grow, life becomes nothing more than a trap, painful and boring.

Our lives would be better if we made more of the virtues our own. The truth is, the qualities we need are present as soon as you can think of them. But we don't like the hard work of letting in a new quality. It makes us mad. We get impatient. We succumb to the inner voice that says we can't do it. But when we press on, knowing that these virtues are right there for us, as close as our own hand, we progress.

Qualities are thoughts. They are only a thought away. As such, they are there, all around us, just waiting for us to take them up, embody them, and witness the loveliness that comes from their use. I may be better at some than others, but so what? These qualities are true riches! Assimilating any one of them makes us stronger, more capable. But in order to bask in the affluence of these riches we have to be willing take them up and use them.

It's freeing to accept that these qualities don't come from our personality. Rather, we can think of them as tools, existing outside of ourselves. People say

EXPERIMENT

things like, "I'm not a patient person." And they stick to it—cling to it like an anchor. It's similar to a child entering first grade saying, "I am not a person who reads." We expect a first grader to quickly overcome that sense of him or herself. And we should expect the same of ourselves. When we think of qualities as tools they are no longer out of our reach. They are no longer bound to the notion of a limited personality. We simply need to learn how to use them. We can study, practice, and get better. If we insist that "I'm not a patient person" we will continue to be impatient until we begin to learn how to use the tool called patience. We will never *own* patience, but it is ours to use whenever we like.

Often necessity pushes us to see the value of a quality we don't feel we possess. When we realize we need something, we begin to see its value and desire it. For example, if an undisciplined athlete wants to get better at her sport, she will come to see value in discipline. At some point she must make discipline her own. She must come to see it as a tool whose use will generously help her achieve her goal. When she does, a treasure that was previously invisible to her becomes visible. The only thing that can keep us from using and enjoying the power of this quality, or tool, is not using it. If we believe our identity won't allow it. Then we're identifying ourselves by what we don't have. We become brittle and stuck.

How valuable then to consider the qualities and virtues that would solve our problems. We can think of those qualities and let them seep into our thoughts and practices. Then we must find ways to embody and practice them. Sometimes we begin humbly. We make small inroads. The resistance may be strong. Old thoughts yell and scream, "I am not a patient person!" and feelings of frustration bubble up angrily. But with a steadfast, forgiving dedication to growth, each and every one of these resistances wears away. Through patient devotion to resolving pressing realities of our lives, we have small victories. New qualities, the riches of life, seep into our experience. Small victories become larger ones. As we continue, we see that by the practice of new virtues we are traveling in places we've never been. We are living new aspects of life and bringing out new skills and abilities in ourselves. Soon we're making our decisions based not on what we lack, avoiding what we fear or detest, but on what we truly want and know is right. Amazed, we begin to see that our identity is not static. We were not born with a brittle personality that has some virtues and lacks others. The tools simply exist around us and we are elastic, using whatever and whichever we need.

What a relief it is to let go of the notion that virtues come from us, from our personalities. Not one of us made up patience. Or discipline, or creativity. If we feel responsible for "manufacturing" these qualities we will fall short. It will ever be a burden. We aren't capable of owning them or producing them ourselves. They simply exist, like gifts. We learn to use them by loving them and making them our own.

The undisciplined artist sees more freedom when he learns to live within some helpful boundaries. The tight, rule-oriented manager sees more meaning and joy when she values the feelings of others.

It's a stereotype as cruel as any to say that people are one or the other, expressive or disciplined, idealistic or realistic, spiritual or practical. In fact, the necessity of a happy, full life is that we make ourselves at home with *all of them*. There are boundaries to be crossed and walls to be brought down. The outcome is the unveiling of a world peopled

with broad, magnificent beings, successful and effective.

When I began my career as an artist I felt comfortable with intuition, feeling, adventure, and lots of other expressive qualities. But I was not great at paperwork, business, and numbers. When it came time to do my taxes each year I would get pretty bent out of shape. I was really at a loss. I didn't know how to do it. I didn't know anyone who knew how to do it. The page after page of tiny text seemed impenetrable. What could I do? I will admit to you I did actually cry real adult man tears.

I had a strong desire to succeed in my art career and also not go to jail. So, I disciplined myself to learn how to do those dreaded taxes. But as important as doing them, I also wanted to not hate them. It was miserable to hate these numbers. To feel left out from the ability to do it. So, as I submitted to the discipline of learning how taxes work I also tried to see value in it. I thought about why it's useful and appreciated that my little portion was going to be paying for schools, roads, and other public services. Admitting to myself that this was a reality that was never ever going to go away, I bowed my head, put aside my distress, and sat myself down with those papers. I read each page and tried to follow the instructions. The first couple years I probably did a bad job, but the job got done. I got better.

I'm never going to quit being an artist and become a CPA. But I do know from that experience that I'm not left out of the world of numbers. I'm not "that kind of person." And by the same token I know that even if someone doesn't get art, if they're willing to spend some time with it, not fighting it, they can begin to get it. We can all feel better, and less threatened than we do.

In fact, learning to do taxes was just the very beginning. In subsequent years life required me to learn a whole host of skills I never knew I had. The jobs that started coming to me were art teaching jobs, with kids. I'd never thought of myself as a person who liked kids. In fact, I'd never thought about kids at all. But that's where the path led. I learned that I love kids, especially younger ones. I learned that I could teach, despite having no training for it. Growing out of those teaching jobs, I was inspired to start a mural painting program for teens (that story is coming up in about 50 pages). I needed to learn fundraising, organization, community outreach, management, payroll, and interacting with other youth groups. Each one came through experience, seeing the need, and accepting that I could do it. After that I was asked to serve as a chaplain at the local jail. It was a crash course in expressing authority, discipline, and deep compassion, all in a very foreign, very structured environment. Then my prayers led me to change my career and begin making music full time. This project required that I learn how to perform with confidence and authority. I also had to find the right collaborating partners, get over my stage fright, and learn how to organize concert tours over several states. In each case I saw what I felt I lacked—patience, knowhow, authority, organization—but I had an increasing awareness that the qualities themselves are there for me. I could practice using them even when I felt I didn't have them. Over the months and years, each one of those skills and qualities became mine. My identity expanded before my very eyes.

The artist who focuses, disciplines, and masters her expression, utilizing a broader spectrum of the qualities available to her, becomes a superhero. Her art grows off the canvas and extends into relationships, strategies, and finances. She has the tools that allow her art to serve and contribute to society. The business manager who depends on creativity and imagination as a support to the rules, numbers, and necessities of the bottom line becomes a superhero. He is a surprise to the world, bringing to his field new ideas, resources, and a richer understanding of success. These people are stars, inspiring and uplifting all who behold the good they are doing. They are using tools from what seem to be opposite ends of the rack. They are living broadly, amplifying their own abilities. This experience is available in one way or another to each one of us.

IS YOUR LIFE A MESS?

Has it ever been?

I hope so.

I'm talking about break-ups, mistakes, upheavals, problems, bad decisions, dramas and difficulties.

Oh, the terror we feel at having people see our messiness! The stiff, brittle, seductive passion to appear flawless. The bitter, reptilian craving to appear perfect. How we mess up our lives as we strive for appearances and neglect to fix our failings. How we dig in our heels to prove our ease, while our fear grows like ill-gotten gains.

Fear draws our attention away from the natural, life-sustaining things it should be on—learning, growing, and living deeply. With iron claws it fastens our attention on appearances. How others see us. How we see ourselves. We present half-truths to cover our shortcomings. We're willing to pass over blatant wrongs if it will only allow us to put off facing them for another day. As fear bullies us, we're unwilling to try new things, to learn, or admit a mistake. We become paralyzed, terrified that we'll be found out. It's unsustainable.

But we do make mistakes. Sometimes lots of them. Sometimes really horrible ones. We aren't perfect. In fact, the only thing that makes speaking about perfection useful at all, is that God *is* perfect and we are His creations. We observe in our lives a seemingly endless distance between ourselves and perfection. But let that never keep us from striving towards perfection. In fact, the only way to become better, is to reveal, step by courageous step, the perfection of God within.

Messes are great for that. Often messes are so uncomfortable they force us to (finally) be honest with ourselves in ways we might never be otherwise. That blank, unsparing honesty is great for revealing God's goodness in us. The mess we experience is the mistake revealing itself, and our opportunity to correct it. Messes are nothing to fear. We serve ourselves so much better when we are less interested in appearances, and instead, long to learn from our mistake and fix it.

As uncomfortable as it is to be in the middle of a mess, when we keep our eye on God, it's our best opportunity to grow. When things are falling apart, we are safe as we strive to know God. God will not fall apart. Our relationship with Him will not be shaken. Our outward situation, our understanding of ourselves, will likely change, but who we are as God's creation will remain constant. The fear and pain of these situations can cause us to turn with open hearts to God for guidance and understanding. This is the way. Our focus changes. Because we see that they can and will fall apart, we learn to place our hopes less on temporary things and more on the eternal. We begin to see how unchanging, how safe and strong God is. It becomes more natural to place our tender hopes on Him, letting the outward appearances of our lives be dictated by our dedication to Love.

The danger is when we're so afraid of being or appearing messy, that we'd rather not learn about the mistake. We put off honesty, delay integrity, and pay for it later. When we fear a mess, we hope to find safety in the current situation, which includes the problem. We long to keep things how they are. But we're never safe in a life based on appearances. It's impossible. Sooner or later, that deferred honesty, the delayed integrity erupts in the life and creates a much larger mess than it would have been if it been addressed in the first place.

The kind of honesty that saves us holds the bar high. It's not easy. In fact, the only way to not fear these eruptions is to be willing to change. The safest place is to cultivate a single-minded interest in learning at the expense of all else. We must be unsparing in our desire to learn what life is and how to live it well. Then as we pass through changes, and mistakes are revealed, we'll be grateful for the opportunity to gain new understanding. We'll embrace the new and better path that is revealed. We'll feel more of God's consistency and goodness as the real constants in our lives. We'll find that safety comes from being and doing good, living the virtues. We become less and less interested in appearances, less preoccupied with defending ourselves. More interested in doing good.

Certainly, messes for their own sake are useless. And once we've learned a particular lesson, there's no reason to have to learn it again. But, if my life is to be one of continued learning, then I'm sure to continue making mistakes as the things I'm learning are more advanced. In short, a life well-lived will be full of mistakes. But it will also be much more full of good decisions, victories, and joy. It will be based on all the insights gained through resolving problems and cleaning up messes. The outward messes become less scary. We come to expect a mess now and then. We worry about it less. We know from experience that, whether fast or slow, it will be resolved.

Is a mess-less human life the spiritual ideal? Absolutely not. Outwardly, at times Jesus Christ had a messy life. He was consistently in conflict with others. He was in trouble with the law and had pretty pronounced conflicts with members of his family and community. What about other heroes? Any one worth his or her salt had messes. Probably some big ones. Jesus said "I am not come to call the righteous, but sinners to repentance." Jesus calls us to follow him, and in doing so, our messes will be revealed, and cleaned up. No one can be magically mess-less.

Living life's ideals—love, spirituality, forgiveness, purity, courage, etc., cleanses our lives of the things that cause messes—selfishness, dishonesty, fear. But the process of living those ideals is very often not a smooth road. And that's just fine.

****

I was working hard. My art was moving along in new ways. I was growing spiritually hand over fist. However, often after a long day's work, or in empty hours, I felt lonely. I longed for a romantic relationship.

I had learned enough over the years to approach my relationships with love, generosity, and unselfishness. I'd had a few. They had each been infused with real affection and learning, but none had worked out. Still, I was at home in romantic relationships. I felt good at it.

Around this time I began to notice a woman around my neighborhood. She was sweet, smart, and drop-dead gorgeous. With her long black hair and playful demeanor, she was the very picture of my longing. We would run into each other at the store, on walks. I began to think about her more and more. We had things in common. Like me, she was a guitar player. She'd played basketball in school and knew her way around the court. I learned she was a serious Christian. Erin was her name.

She was several years younger than me. As I considered moving forward with her it didn't feel entirely natural. It wasn't a really even match. Still, she was great, and beautiful, and my longing told me to go for it.

Soon we were dating and *it was horrible*. There were a hundred miscommunications a day and my feelings were constantly hurt. I love to talk about feelings. She hated it. I felt easy about moving into a relationship. She was stiff and chilly. You may think I'm foolish (I was) but my inclination when there's a misunderstanding is to talk it out. This is often the exactly right course—*except when the real solution is to not be in the conversation in the first place.* My longing pushed me to continue to try to work it out. She was so beautiful! She was excited about me! I was dazzled by the sparkling excitement of hope. Pushing and forcing. Never admitting that it simply wasn't the right place to be.

So, I spent months trying to get her to understand me. Trying to understand her. Trying to force this relationship to satisfy me. As time went on, all that became clear was that it was terrible. At each turn my tender hope for connection went unsatisfied. For every one good moment, there were 10 miserable ones. Finally, with a defeated heart, I decided to end it. When the time came, it felt like I was bound with a thousand cutting ropes, keeping me from saying the words. With great pain, straining against the pounding attraction I felt for her, I let her know that it wasn't going to work out.

This was sad, but not new. I'd had break-ups before.

But there were deep things going on I didn't know about or understand. A month or so later, she showed up, heart in her hand, saying, "I think it can work." She showed a spark of softness in a way she hadn't before. She was as sincere as she could be. A drunken slave to this lonely longing, my own heart

140

softened, and I agreed. For perhaps a week the ruse endured. And just like that, it was as if I hadn't done any of the agonizing work to extricate myself from this roadblocked relationship. I was right back where I had been, in the very wrong place.

We tried to work it out for a few more months, but it wasn't different. Despite our mutual sincerity and dedicated prayers, the road was closed, littered with pains and hurts. And again I told her, this time several notches more exhausted, it's not gonna work.

I returned to single life again. My longing was unchanged. It simply stayed, affecting everything I did.

And here is where I really became confused. Despite the fact that I had struggled and taken enormous pains to extricate myself from this obviously wrong relationship, I found myself continuing to think about her. I pined for her. We had countless friends in common and it was impossible to avoid seeing her around town and at social gatherings. After another month or two, we were somehow, monstrously, back in touch, spending time together. We agreed to "be friends," and continued to spend time together as if we were dating. I was as firmly in the trap as ever. As if by evil magic, I was embroiled in the very relationship I knew I should flee.

In all my life up to that point, I had always felt a pretty true sense of self control. When I discerned something was wrong, either in my behavior or in my situation, I changed it. I wasn't afraid of adjustments. I didn't resist new information. I was always seeking ways to be better than I had been the day before. So this was new. I'd heard people speak about being incapable of controlling themselves. They couldn't control their eating, or spending, or … going out with the wrong guys. I could never understand it. I always wondered, "Why don't they just make a change?"

It all came clear. I was one of them. I literally did not have the power to do what I knew was right. This relationship was so wrong I had already quit it twice! But I would hem and haw. I could imagine a scenario in which, if we could just change this and this, it might work. I often thought of simply pleading with her to tell me she wouldn't see me anymore. I didn't have the will to do it.

I will tell you, from day one of this relationship, I was praying. I was as true to God as I knew how to be. I prayed for myself. I prayed for her. I strained with all my might to be good. I had no desire to do wrong. No interest in getting away with something. Still, there I was.

My feelings were a warzone. I loved things about her. I hated the way she treated me. I was constantly hurt, and forever trying to do right. I hated the way I felt with her, but I couldn't let go of the fleeting hope of her affection. I strained with everything in me to be good to her, and I burned inside with lust and anger.

In my prayers I wailed, "How have You led me here? To this?!" I couldn't grasp how my sincere prayers could land me in such a painful situation. It was a mess.

One day, about two years into it, I reasoned with myself. "I've done everything I can think of to end this. I've broken it off, twice. I've tried and tried to stay away. What remains to do? How can I save myself?" If there was no answer, I was lost. I listened honestly.

A new insight appeared. "If I've done every outward thing I can think of and it hasn't stuck, *the problem must be inward.* If the solution can't be found in outward actions, my decisions, it must be a change inside myself." I was stunned. The implication was utterly disarming.

I'd been striving with every ounce of my moral muscle to do right...and failing. If the answer was not to be found in adjustments of my outward behavior, it must then be an adjustment in my thoughts that would bring about the resolution. I knew from experience that through prayer and willingness I could be changed from the inside out. I also knew that it was beyond my control.

From that time forward, with great amazement, I gave up on trying to fix the problem myself. To appearances it was utterly intractable. It was embarrassing, and I could see my guilt all over the place. Yet, I had to let it be and trust my prayers. I had to relax the fierce impulse to fix it with my own hands, and instead, trust.

As I moved forward in this way, I found blooming within me a patient, exhausted compassion for myself. I understood, deep in my heart that I was at God's mercy. For months I had felt a constant, agonizing guilt. With each passing week I was aghast and ashamed as my flaws were exposed in greater relief. But now, instead of a pressing, frantic fear, I sighed and thought of God. I couldn't do it. But I knew God could.

I prayed almost constantly. Powerless, in the teeth of the trap, there was nothing to do but pray. Prayer, which for most of my life was something I took time out of my life to do, became the rule. I prayed as I walked from here to there. I prayed as I drove. While I was at work I prayed. When I got home at night I prayed. One morning when I awoke, I realized I had been praying while I was asleep.

I pored over the Bible. I came across a verse in Psalm 100 that spoke freedom to my heart. "It is God who has made us, and not we ourselves." God had made me. Not me. Not my faults and failures. Not even my best intentions and successes. God created me. If God created me then this sin was not my home. I lived in this verse from that moment on. I said it to myself all through the day. I could feel the idea slowly severing the ropes that bound me, neutralizing my fear. It is God who has made us and not we ourselves.

My involvement with Erin continued for more than a year after that. I began to understand that the relationship was having a similar effect on her. It was painful, and revealing her own shortcomings to her. I came to see that she was as honest and full of integrity as I was. She was often embarrassed to have me see her do the things she did, the ways she failed. Her heart was on the line too. She was filled with longing to be loved. She was trying so hard to make it work. We both, in the intimate context of the relationship, were learning flint-hard lessons. We each prayed, asking God for guidance out of our own short-comings, afflicting us with each step. In a way, though we were often painfully at odds, we came to witness each other's redemption. I could feel that she was, in a way, my partner in healing. And I was hers. I began to feel a sincere appreciation of her many virtues. Her patience with my headlong lustfulness. Her love of God and willingness to learn. Her unsparing honesty. Though our personal connection was broken from the beginning, in the background a kind of spiritual sun dawned. We served a spiritual purpose in one another's lives.

As the months pressed on, we saw each other less and less. Gradually our lives ceased to overlap. There was no outward decision, just a natural evolution. Finally, nearly four years from our first date, I learned that she was seeing some-one else. Shockingly, like a serpent striking from its hole, I was overcome with an utterly illogical, yet violent pain of loss. Soon it wore off. With the certainty of separation that news declared, I knew the shackles were broken. I was free.

Like Jesus in the temple, the staggering pain of this snarl served to whip corruption right out of me. Ignorantly, I'd believed I was good enough to con-trol my own life. That notion was humiliated. I was forced to see it and admit it. And admitting it, I was comforted. God was in control. God would continue to lead me to my right life.

In years after this mess I was changed. The lessons I'd learned in that hard time made it impossible for me to be self-centered in the ways I had been then. During that time, my feelings had been hurt so often, and so constantly, I'd learned to stop looking to Erin for comfort or tenderness or companionship. Instead, I'd learned to look to God for those things. God became to me a closer companion than He'd ever been. With great clarity the lesson came: *You can't expect someone to be able to do something just because you want them to be able to. If you look for gold in a silver mine, you'll be disappointed. It's just not there.* And with that misplaced desire gone, I could no longer suffer from it. The longing that had ached in me uncontrollably was greatly diminished.

As time went on, I understood through and through that while we weren't a good match, Erin was pure goodness. She steadfastly lived countless virtues. She'd forgiven me again and again. The gospel of Christ was alive in her life and the world was blessed by it. I admired her!

I never want to go back to the way I felt during that time. However, now that it's done, I rejoice in its effect on me. I saw the inner workings of my own moral regeneration. In the depth of confusion and suffering, out of my pure need, I began to see the turning gears of the machine—how it works. I beheld, for the first time, redemption. I witnessed God turn my weakness into strength. Having come through the ordeal, I see the treasures it revealed. I'm cleaned up from dirtiness I didn't even know I had. I'd thought I was free. But God would not allow me to remain in my half-freedom. He revealed to me the bonds I was under. Then, through patient experience and prayer, He led me to see them fall.

Let's be honest with ourselves. The Bible tells us over and over that the effect of God is to overturn all that is wrong. Christ says, "I am not come to bring peace to the earth, but a sword." We have nothing to fear from God, Love, though God's action in our lives is often to overturn our wrong assumptions and mistakes. It is always for our own good, and brings healing and peace much faster than any other approach. That sword comes to destroy those things in our lives that would hurt us. We encounter messes when we cling to those very things. Every day is an opportunity to admit our mistakes and correct them. We must humbly accept the chastening that life brings to us, and work our way through it, becoming better. This is the way we most quickly pass through them, learn the lessons of life and love, and never return to those messes. Then, we are ever onward to new and greater labors and loves.

Is your life a mess? Breathe deep and be transformed.

LOOSEN UP, KID

From the time I was a junior in high school I knew that I was an artist. Over the next years the feeling was clearer and clearer. Images, ideas, stories, were enough to live for. By the time I graduated from college with a degree in painting I knew it was far more than a job—it was a calling, stitched deep down in me.

I was well aware of the notion of how hard it is to make a living as an artist, but that didn't bother me. I didn't care too much about having nice things. But I cared *a lot* about being able to do my work. I learned to live frugally—*very* frugally—and it was fine.

I created a lifestyle for myself. My single room in a dumpy house cost $150 a month. Week in and week out I ate pasta and vegetables and peanut butter and jelly. I didn't mind wearing thrift store clothes, buying day-old bread, or living in an apartment that smelled slightly of gas. It was working. I had plenty of time to make my paintings and write my songs. I went for walks in the morning. I worked at the IVP 20 hours a week.

But, as time went on, I felt a slowly rising terror about money. The slightest divergence from my strict frugality sent me into a panic. I spent only what I needed to avoid dying. But what about when a friend wants to go to a movie? Or a restaurant? How quickly the dagger of fear was in me, and I squirmed in my skin to not part with that $10. Simple things so normal to some, were to me, virtually unthinkable.

I clung to my plan. I unknowingly defended it to myself. How spiritual it was to be so spartan! How unworldly to need so little! How dedicated to my art I must be! And the terror grew.

I was rigid and petrified. Any unforeseen expense shook me to the foundations. When, after a few years, I began to have a sanguine wish for some diversity in my weekly groceries, I found no mercy in myself. It wasn't there. I wouldn't allow it. But, like it or not, I was changing, (gasp!) even expanding. My strictness, grown out of idealism and inexperience, was a chaffing, tightening belt.

I dreaded going to the grocery store. I dreamed of buying things as simple as cold-cuts and tomatoes, but I couldn't do it. It was beyond my ability. Everything would fall apart, my fear screamed, if I allowed exceptions. I walked the aisles of the store, tears brimming in my eyes.

And then, shame and confusion. How is it that I'm a man who cries in the grocery store? Why am I standing motionless in the produce aisle, debating with myself over purchasing celery? I had no idea how to make money. Or how to relax or loosen up. When someone suggested we do something that cost money, I stammered something about needing to go home.

In desperation, and with no tools in my figurative belt, I began to blindly push back. I made a list of comforting foods. One of them was bologna. I remembered having bologna sandwiches as a kid and feeling safe. I promised myself I would buy some at the store even though I never had, and it wasn't on the list of allowed items. Who knew buying bologna could be such a struggle? Though I trembled with fear as I bought it, when I ate those sandwiches it felt like a victory.

For some months, not knowing how else to proceed, I just pushed against my fear. I just pushed, trying to do some of the things I was terrified of doing. Every once in a while I tried to buy something new at the grocery store. I would psych myself up in the parking lot. It felt awful. So scary and lonely, driving into the parking lot of the Harris Teeter grocery store. And I knew it was crazy. No one knew. I never mentioned this part of my life to anyone. The very air seemed to mock, "Why are you scared to buy bologna?"

Time passed. I continued laboriously to push against this oppressive, imprisoning penury. I lived with it. I couldn't see out of it.

All the while my art was flourishing. I was making work that I loved. The images were coming constantly, like a gushing faucet. Thank God. Because everything else was hard. I continued under the pall of depression and fear.

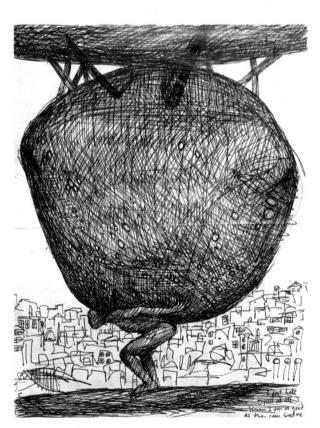

In the midst of all of this, I moved from Athens, back to cold, businesslike Boston, Massachusetts. With a thousand other factors at play, it was the right thing to do. I felt it in my bones. My rent tripled.

I got a job on the grounds crew of a nursing facility. Just to do something, I volunteered for some months at the Washington Irving Middle School, where a friend worked. It got me out of the house and left me less time to worry.

One day I was feeling the terrible clash of my dwarfed, strangled idea of money and my panting need for my art career to work. I wondered, like pressing my head against a wall, "*How* do you do it? How do you actually do it?!" Something had to give.

Then, a thought interrupted my fretting, "People pay you when they're grateful for what you do."

I considered it. It wasn't the kind of answer I was looking for. I wanted a bulleted list of instructions. It didn't make the path easy. But, I thought, not that excited, "That's probably right." Well, then, how do I make my art useful to someone? How do I get my pictures out of my sketchbook and into the world so someone can be grateful for it?

I thought of my pictures. They were beautiful. They were my soul. Songs of wonder, being alive. Hope, nature, adventure, beauty. Was there a place in the world for what I had to offer? When I thought of the world—the actual *world* out there—the notion seemed laughable. When I thought of my art, and the harsh, terrible, disgusting world, I knew I would die if they touched one another. And then my desperate fear, exposing itself in the crucible cried out, "How could I, who am nobody, ever hope to make any money with my art?" I know my art is good, but nobody else will! It was naked, helpless.

I saw, blankly, that there was nothing for it. Without the slightest excitement, and utterly crushed, I bent. I *will* try to find a way to make my art useful. I will take my heart into the absolute unknown. I will bare my naked navel to the world. I will ask it if it wants me.

With my heart in my hand I resolved to begin calling restaurants all over Boston to ask if they had need of a muralist. I began the next morning at the top of the yellow pages section, "Restaurants." As if I were pounding nails into my very own palms, my fear screamed, "This is useless! You'll never get a job this way! You're wasting your time!" It was difficult to even move. Each call was an enormous, painful weight. I left my name and number. I took numbers to call back later. I got names and addresses. I would do ten and take a break as if I'd run a marathon. I cried. I dried my tears and got back to the list. More pushing. It seemed more and more facets of my life required pushing against fear.

One day the phrase, "You have to spend money to make money." popped into my head. I leaned into it and it meant something more than the words. I listened, exhausted of my fear. I felt, with a dewy relief, *I have to spend myself.* I have to be grateful. I have to throw off this terror of spending, and give something. If this life of mine is supported by God, if my art comes, as I truly believe it does, from a holy source, then I just have to have some faith. I felt I had to act, right now, as though I had something to give. I decided to be more generous, to actively spend the money I had—gifts for friends, donations, whatever door opened and felt natural. This was my way of defying fear and materialism, stepping into my faith in God's supply.

On the way home one day I passed a dairy advertising homemade ice cream. I thought "I need to buy some for (my friend) Jude!" I pulled in and bought it, paying the $8 a gallon, way more than double the grocery store price I was used to. It felt good to be giving a gift. I could hardly believe I did it.

As this idea was growing in me, I got a call. It was a newly opening laundromat in the neighborhood of the Washington Irving Middle School. They had contacted the school in the hopes of finding a muralist for their giant outdoor wall. (Why did they think contacting the local middle school was the right way to find a muralist? Your guess is as good as mine.) But, amazingly, someone at the school remembered me (I'd only volunteered there a couple days a week for a few months) and passed on my info.

Soon, I was painting a huge mural, for the unbelievable (to me) sum of $2000. It was my first mural job in Boston. Then the business next door hired me to do their space. I was off and running. I noticed, when the murals were finished, that the folks who had hired me were honestly *grateful* for what I had done. The murals I created for them were filled with ideas, individual thoughts, decisions, ways of dealing with their subject matter. They were done in *my* hand, using *my* ideas.

Over the next months and years I watched as my financial and artistic life changed. As I was generous, I found I had more opportunities to be generous. As I gave, I felt love, and new freedom. The rigidness and terror began to drain away. I was participating more in my life, with my friends, and my world. I began to thaw and found myself looking more outwardly.

I continued to think of payment as gratitude. If I was going to be receiving money I was going to have to be actively doing things that others were grateful for. With this awareness came new ideas about how to make my art useful to others. I began to see that I had skills not only as an artist, but as a community builder. My art could not only be beautiful, but could also bring people together, provide jobs for young people, and provide a public symbol of life and health. I applied myself to this goal, honestly working to see my art bless others. As I did this, more contracts and projects came my way. More than once I received calls from people I had never met offering me jobs.

At some point I realized that all the fear I had felt about spending money was gone. I also became more aware of the value my work had in the community. It was wonderful to acknowledge that it was actually useful to others.

As I look back on this time and the decisions that I made, I feel aware that there is amazing protection in doing what you love. From the very beginning, my reason for making art was to

glorify God, to truly live and reveal beauty. The desire was so pure that it was impossible to be afraid, at least about that part. I was not interested in money, just beauty, just expressing the real thing, and sharing it with others. As I created, as I painted, the strength of those motives was at work. It made the work strong. It's what made my work good, worthy, and ultimately, valuable.

As an artist I'm always having to live by intuition. And this has been a great training. The spiritual truths lead and it's my job to listen and trust. Every step is a step of faith, trusting the value of the work and of the spiritual qualities leading it. Each step teaches new lessons and enlarges my understanding of what it is to be useful to others.

FAILURE

Imagine putting all your eggs in one basket—not out of laziness or wishful thinking, but because you know it's the right basket. Imagine seeing clearly the good work that life has set before you and setting out into the wide landscape of that work. For years you labor for the dream, moved by its beauty and goodness. It lives in you, a love that you did not create. You are driven by your love of the work and the good it will do. All along, the world is saying, kindly, condescendingly, that there is little or no hope that you will succeed, that you are too small, that the work isn't worth doing. Still, you push on, bound to this effort by deep conviction.

The time comes to see if that work will function. Can it prove its worth? Can it live beyond the walls of your own thinking and effort?

Can you imagine putting all your heart and soul into something, knowing it's right, and then watching it fail before your very eyes? All the heroes of the world have done that very thing.

We look on them now and remember only their success, but in their beginnings, in forgotten days of obscurity, they were all failures. What of their years spent in unrecognized toil? The dread and fear that they were crazy? "If I'm right," they say, "Why does everyone disagree with me? Why am I the only one pursuing this idea?" Yet the inner voice is clear. The vision is too beautiful, too important, to abandon. Don't you think that all our heroes spent untold hours agonizing over tactics, wondering how to care for this child they were bringing into the world? How to communicate their inspiration to others? The people who have most deeply expressed love, who have shown us creativity, honor, intelligence, and purity have not always *felt* inspired. They had no assurance that their work would be accepted—that it wouldn't just fall to the floor, useless. What was to make them believe they could succeed where so many others fall by the wayside? They have fought within themselves for assurance. They have rested, not on the certainty of success, but on the *rightness* of the idea. They have set their hopes on the necessity that the work be done, on their love of life, and on their desire to see it borne into the world. They have risked it all.

We are so afraid of failure! But failure is not failure. When you are doing what is right by your integrity, learning from your mistakes, bravely moving onward, you cannot fail. You can only learn, get bigger, humbler, and better. This is life. What did you think it would be? Not to rest but to explore. Digging deep ensures that we will encounter challenges. And there is nothing for it but to dig deeper, let our desire to do the work, be purified and transformed. Then, bit by bit, we find that the doing has made us wiser. We have learned some of the real rules—the ones that support the true work. We feel them and live by them though it causes us to stand out. We become less afraid of failing because we *have* failed and seen that it was not the end. We begin to flow more smoothly, and are less easily terrified.

Before the laundromat mural, (and often after) I was lost, burdened by fear, and lacking any outward evidence that I could do it. There was no map. No vision of how to reach people with my pictures. But that was in stark contrast with the depth and beauty I saw, and that I was able to express. In a way, that deepened the tragedy if I couldn't succeed. I felt trapped, a ready servant for Beauty, but utterly lost, lacking courage, swirling in doubt.

As I mowed the lawns, weeded the gardens, and swept the paths of the nursing facility where I worked, I was constantly aware of the pumping fountain of Beauty within me. I was daily heartbroken by the distance between my dreams and plodding reality. On my breaks I would run to the living room where there was a piano. It was usually empty and I would pour myself into deep chords, singing along, letting them fill the room.

One day as I sat at the piano, I picked up a book from a nearby shelf. It was about the painter, Monet. I had always loved Monet—his incredible depictions of light. Opening the book, the paintings were a relief to my nervous heart. He'd always been a hero to me. Such a towering success, a witness for Beauty! I knew from my studies that he had suffered plenty of rejection from the salons and galleries as he had developed his vision. He had pushed on and overcome.

I read a page I randomly landed on. It described an event from his history that I'd never heard. When he was about 30 (I was 28) he was impoverished. He'd given everything to make his paintings. They were rejected time and time again. There was no money coming in. There was no way to pay the bills. In desperation he tried to drown himself in the River Seine.

This lion. This master. This hero whose works are among the most famous in the world. This tower of Beauty whose paintings are on coffee mugs in every suburban home, *had tried to end his life* out of fear that he could not succeed!

It went on. His suicide attempt failed. And he soon resumed painting. He went on to be Monet.

I imagined him crawling onto the bank of the Seine, having failed even at killing himself. He must have climbed up onto the shore, utterly defeated. He must have sat there, considering what to do. Still alive, thinking thoughts in the wake of his admission of defeat.

Then, with what I can only imagine was the deepest, sighing humility, he went back to painting. He submitted to Love even though it had presented no hope of success. He gave in, and resumed his work.

I was *deeply* comforted. I thanked God he had failed. Oh Monet, thank God you lived! I longed to hug him and thank him, tell him how proud the world would be of him—how much of a gift he would give. That moment of resuming your work after life did not allow you to quit—I couldn't get it out of my mind. Alex, what if life won't allow you to quit? What will you do?

You press on.

Even in darkness. Even in the wilderness. Even when there is no path.

Let us work with all our hearts to succeed, but when failure appears, let us not fear it. Let us not think it reflects upon *who we are*. Let us get back on our feet and continue the work, altering it and reforming it to succeed where it failed before. Let it and us grow by experience. The work will change, and deepen. It will not be done in a moment.

Everyone who has really succeeded has come upon this. They have all failed. And then continued. They have been uncertain. They have been discouraged, beaten, utterly demoralized. And when they returned to the work, to the effort to serve, improve, and create, the assurance of its simple, obvious goodness worked in them, revitalizing and transforming.

HEROES

I've adored Mohandas Ghandi. He would not spare himself if Truth was the cost.

I've adored John Lennon. He sang his nakedness so we could admit we were naked too.

I've adored Nelson Mandela. He thought and waited and worked for a healing that was 85 years old by the time he saw it manifested.

I've adored Henri Matisse. He would not surrender from the face of Beauty.

In my need for a hero, these and countless others, were there for me. Their examples shone before me in my own darkness, proving that holiness can be achieved here on earth. They saved my life. They beckoned to me. They lifted a standard.

There are those who see the deep and do not shrink from its enormity. They step out into the waves while crowds of landlubbers stand behind and mock.

Let these heroes do their work. They are laboring with new life like a falconer tames his bird. We can't see them until they show us, yet when they lead those birds into our view, their long, magnificent wings beat a new panorama. These powerful beasts perch proudly on their forearms, making no move to escape. And soon we can't imagine zoology without them.

Harriet Tubman was a criminal for righteousness.

In retrospect, vindication is as plain as a stone in the hand.

Without heroes we are deep in our blindness. But, adoring them, we have guides in the wilderness.

Vincent Van Gogh jumped from the gallows of despair into a black and nameless place and came back with brilliant color. From the darkness he showed us play like sunlight.

They have put their heads into the gears of the machinery. They have lain down low to reach oily black pistons and rotors unseen to the rest of us. They have cut their hands on the unforgiving metal. They've gone places we didn't dare to try. They've found doors we couldn't find. They've repaired the slow and ugly in order to prove the graceful and free. They have taken each grueling step.

They are working for us. They are bending, craning, laboring overtime. After grinding failure they are trying again. We are the grass they seek to grow. We are the land they cultivate. We are the crops, the fields they pray over. We are the ones they are speaking to. Singing to. Weeping for. Let us hear them. Let us be led by the ones willing to do the work. Let us trust wisdom even though we didn't think of it first. Let us embrace our heroes and trust their labor. They sculpt the great thought.

Let us strive to do our own work. Let the love we have learned from our heroes cause us to labor for others. Let us lie down for Beauty. Let us accept that we are here to be heroes for one another. Let us push onward in our own line, thanking God that there are others following their light in other directions. Let us be brave in the wilderness and follow our guides.

These heroes have given everything. They've seen a vision of something better, and have done the work to bring it into the world—to show it to us so that we could see it too. They are in every discipline. They are everywhere. They are invisibly pouring everything they have into their work. They know that life is more than hours spent getting money to stay alive. They hear a song singing in their lives. There are ideas, people, beauty and service to live *for*.

Because this labor is so pure, so holy, so inherently spiritual, the pressures against it are intense. How will you eat? You're a fool! Your family will hate you! These heroes have held for dear life to that creativity, the love, which they knew was their life. But it's more than that. This clinging to purity, the life that is in service of Beauty and in service to hearts that long for Beauty, requires untold letting go of other things.

Life presents us, again and again with the choice, "Are you for Beauty or for personal safety?" "Do you want *all* of life, all eternity of it, with labor, learning, difficulty and glory? Or would you prefer 65 years, with approval?" "Would you rather be *effective* or popular?" Heroes are the ones who are making the larger choice.

These people have waged the wars of expression and dreams. All the bored world says, "Stop acting like a child. Get serious and live a normal life!" Yet that same world ceaselessly complains of its own hopelessness. The world says, "This is life. This is what you get. Make it through each week so you can rest on the weekends." But these heroes, these adults, have stood on Beauty with the weight of their lives saying, "This is more important." They have stood in that crucible that says, "Are you a rat in a race or are you better? Do you know more? Feel more?" And as it presents this question, all the devils of the world are snarling awful things about worthlessness, irresponsibility, idiocy, insanity. They mock, "Who do you think you are to imagine that you know more than others? Don't you think if it were right to express your ideas confidently, more people would be doing it? You can't do it. You will die penniless, ruined, friendless, and it will be your own fault." "Yes," they mourn, "Beauty is lovely, but, there's no place for it in this real, real world of ours." "Or," they bargain when they see the hero isn't budging, "with all your skills, you could really make it big if you just give up these embarrassing notions of beauty and service!"

But the heroes have said, in one way or another, "There is only one life and it *is* Beauty. I have seen the truth and it is holy. If there is no room for it in this world I will make room for it." They have said with their lives, "The invisible idea, beauty, grace, the Song, is enough to stand my life on."

They have clung to Beauty and let go of countless weaker notions. They must cast them off! This pile of garbage is large, and seeks to terrorize, and patronize: "Adults are beyond that. Do that when you're young, when you still can. You've tried, and now it's time to be realistic. You have to live like those around you. You will die if you do this!" Its voice is repetitive and tiresome.

These life-artists have clung to the love of their lives, and cut from it the beggars and lies, hacking and swinging with great life-knives. They have said yes to the first love, and been forced to say no to the thousand assumptions the world lives in, complains about, and clings to. A thousand things that would not help them on their way.

Meanwhile, Life is being lived in richer colors, with greater soul, and stunning generosity by all and any who say yes to their work instead of being afraid. These heroes have learned that labor is joy when it is the work of love. They have fought so hard that they have learned no bruise, no injury is enough to stop the Voice of the song that truly sings.

Our heroes did not give up and give in. No, they lived for Beauty, for giving a great gift to the world. They didn't settle in and let fear make them small. Rather they loosened up and threw more heartily into the openness, trusting their lives to Beauty.

FOLLOW BEAUTY

I was trapped. And my heart was breaking.

Daily I was pushing, pushing against what felt like walls of stone—fear, sadness, and pain that were encroaching on me in an almost physical way.

Over a few years in this struggle—an arduous, demanding journey that felt like a million miles in the wilderness—I could feel that if it really was a journey of a million miles, I had travelled a hundred thousand. Or maybe five hundred thousand. As I struggled, and prayed, and wept, and pushed, and failed, and failed, and succeeded and failed again, I could *feel* it. I was changing. I was putting miles behind me. And there were thousands upon thousands of miles to go.

In the midst of this, I have to live my daily life.

I had a painting show coming up. That meant that I needed paintings to show. I needed to get busy. But every day I felt as though I wanted to cry. And these weren't inspiring, cathartic tears. They were sad, hopeless, gray tears.

I went to the studio to work. I stood there, among my paints, canvases, and thoughts. I didn't want to make paintings about how awful I felt. I had been fighting and fighting to feel good. The progress I had made encouraged me that it was not all for nothing. I was striving to turn outward—away from the downward spiral of inner negativity, into helping others, and simple good things I could see in the world. I longed to the feel the healthy flow from the inner fountain I knew was there. I couldn't. Making paintings about the enormous well of lifeless tears inside me seemed absolutely wrong. And yet, to make paintings about something else (what would it even be??) felt dishonest and disgusting. Even if I tried to make happy paintings they would have no guts behind them. What would be the point? I felt utterly trapped. The way was locked.

A big part of my struggle against depression was prayer. In fact, I continued learning to pray. In my need I was learning to give up on things that didn't work, even if they were the things you were "supposed" to do. No point in prayers that don't work. So I'd been getting really willing to let God tell me what prayer is. A lot of what I had thought prayer is was falling away. I'd begun to understand that prayer can be nothing more complicated that reaching out and being open to what comes back.

In that trapped, awful moment, feeling the stone walls encroaching on me, threatening to make my life impossible, I did reach out. I just asked, with a real, deep longing in my heart, something like, "God, you made me an artist. How can I do this?" And I listened in my silent heart.

What came back was something I already knew. "Follow Beauty." I knew it was right, but what did that mean in this situation? I felt sort of let down like, "Ok, but HOW?"

I listened again for how to turn that directive into action for today. I concentrated. As I did, I realized that I knew, for a fact, that honesty and beauty are inseparable. There is no beauty without honesty. If something is worth doing, there's no faking any part of it.

If I was going to express something, it had to be a real thing, something I *felt*. I had to be honest. I knew this meant beginning with feeling—no matter how bad those feelings were. AND, I could feel that this was the more *courageous* option. It meant letting go of the notion that I was in charge, and being willing to explore and let things unfold.

I did begin making a painting about how I felt. It was about tears and loss and grief. It was ok. Not the best painting I ever made. BUT THEN, a magical thing happened. Things had been set in motion by simply beginning. In that same day I made another painting—this one fueled by my love of painting. That feeling had arrived *while* I worked on the first one. This painting wasn't about anything sad at all. It was a figure growing, exploring—and it was *honest*.

In the next two weeks I made 16 honest paintings, and only one of them (the first one) was about feeling terrible. The rest were new ideas that came as I worked. They were real, inspired, and came from exploring—a willingness to move forward at all costs. They were solid. I could feel proud of them, knowing that they were neither forced, false works, nor were they the navel-gazing complaints I had feared they might be.

I put together the show and didn't even include that first painting.

I can't create feelings. I can't manufacture interesting, life-filled feelings instead of bored or miserable or sad ones. But, from this experience, I learned that I am never trapped choosing between honesty and happiness. No matter how I feel, as I listen and am willing to live and progress, there *will* be a life-affirming feeling that arises in me. I didn't make it. It's not because I am a particular kind of person or have particular skills. It's there because Life is, and the moment I am willing to forget about my complaints, analysis, and terror, it's mine. No matter how intransigent, how cruel, the trap appears to be, it can dissolve.

I continued to labor for another year or so to be free from depression. This and many other moments like it were the waymarks on my journey.

I AM AN ARTIST

There's only one time when I thought of quitting.

The images, the paintings, the inspiration all came. Even while the rest of life was a moment-by-moment grind, the work was coming.

But, how do you bring your art to the world? How do you make a life out of it?

When I first began to try to make a life for myself in Boston I was fighting for every step. I was scared of everything, scraping for each inch of progress. The demands of looking for work tugged me in every direction, and each one was a mile outside my comfort zone. Cold calling—rejection. Knocking on doors—rejection. With each new effort I mustered my courage to begin a conversation, sell myself, show my work, and each time there was no interest. No opening. Every try required that I learn something new, try something I never did before. There was no map, no path to follow. Each new endeavor was a hope in the wilderness. The long hours of each day stretched out before me. I struggled to know how to fill them. I wrestled with my terror that I would die if I didn't create. Even though I had no buyers, I made paintings to fend off death. It proved that I was alive. That I had power. That I could do something useful in the world. I strove to find some kind of organization for my days, some kind of structure for my time. It seemed every day I had to get better at something I'm bad at or reveal some vulnerable thing in myself. The process of sharing my work publicly, the very thing I most wanted to do, was like a crucifixion.

The kind of art I was interested in making was about my sincere feelings and convictions. Finding them, exploring and creating them was joyful and life-affirming. After that, the demand was to somehow pour them out, into the world. My sanguine, longing hope was that these images that fed me the best things I'd ever found, might do the same for someone else.

But think of how people protect their feelings. Think of the lengths to which people go to keep their hearts safe. To hide their true feelings. To keep their sensitive parts safe from the judgement and scrutiny of callous eyes. Think of the defenses and armor that people use to avoid being rejected.

My dream to bring my beloved visions into public places where they could do their work required that I simply not have those defenses. The whole idea was to *not* hide my true feelings. It was to open up the most sensitive places. To reflect innocent, spiritual love into the world. So in addition to the labor of actually making beauty and finding work in the wide world, I also strained against the pains of the repetitive rejection of my most sensitive self.

These difficulties filled my days and nights. But working against them, standing like an ageless tower, was the certainty of Beauty. It was the impulse behind my desire. It was more than a personal desire. I would sacrifice for

Beauty. It was worth it. Beauty could save lives. It could bring life to broken-ness. I knew it could. It had. I had seen it. So, I found myself in the gears of battle.

It was harder than I'd imagined. Week after week the complete uncertainty. I longed for something in the real, visible world to tell me that my work would come to something. It didn't. I longed to see proof that my efforts, my suffering, weren't in vain. That proof was not forthcoming. I got so used to wondering, every day, if I would be devoured by the mean teeth of this monster of fear.

One night I was at the end. All the uncertainty, all the agitation and fear came to a boil. I couldn't stand it anymore. I needed to do something. In my desperation I thought, "Maybe I'll just…quit." With that thought came a wave of relief that I could just stop all my hopeless, endless *trying*. I could do some-thing normal. I could just get another job. There were all kinds of other things to do.

After the wave of relief came disgust and more fear. How could I just give up on Beauty? My dear Beauty? The one who had become my best and bosom friend in the dearest possible sense? She had sung to me, songs greater than my own small life. She had grown me, expanded me, never left my side. How could I leave her?

There was no answer. And the vice tightened.

With no comfort in sight I had to get out of the house. It was February in Boston, 10 PM on a black, crackling cold night. I pulled on my sweatshirts and coats and stomped out into the night. I didn't care about the cold. The air was good and the clear sky spoke of something better. I couldn't think. I just walked. I wanted to get lost. To just walk and walk and not think another thought.

After some time, naturally, I found myself thinking about my situation. But walking had done its good work. My legs were churning, my gloved-hands were stuffed in my coat pockets. I found myself praying. Just thinking and lis-tening for God's guidance. Just reaching out, deep and sincere. "I'm trying my best here. I need to know what to do. I need an answer tonight."

I tramped the sidewalks far into the frozen night. Away and away from my home. My thoughts began to shift. I looked into the good sky. The cold moon. The clickety-clacking twigs in the leafless trees. As my feet tramped the pave-ment, a thought unfolded in me. A good, solid thought, emerging, arriving like clouds in an empty sky. I realized, and not without a warm, heartening swell, that I AM an artist. It is done. It is stitched in me like cold in winter. It is a fact that God has planted and not my choice. There is no debating it or struggling with it. It was God's decision and it is not mine.

My muscles relaxed. I breathed deep. My life deepened. I am not a bug, skittering on the surface. I am in the thick, and getting deeper. I could feel the deep, black mountain of my identity, my work, my being, rising up on the horizon before me. It held enormous promise, freedom to be something. I drank it in. Contained in that mountain, bound to the promise were countless demands. They are so much more than I could conceive. And yet, they are mine to face and fulfill.

Though the answer to my prayer brought with it no new tactics for any of the problems I would face the next day, it settled the issue. It relieved my heart. There was no going back. I would do the work. It was a fact.

When I did get back to work the next day, and in the next months, I found this certainty *did* affect my efforts. Like ancient armies whose generals burned their ships so they couldn't go home without victory, I went on with a certainty that there was no going back. I often returned to the conviction that arrived that night. I AM an artist. I came to understand that whatever challenges come to me as I strive to see my work done in the world, these are my labors. I am not capable of avoiding them. I do not have the choice.

What a relief. I AM something.

WHO'S THE BOSS?

Amid my stumbling efforts to get on my feet in Boston I took some work with a friend of my mom's. They were doing work on their house out in the suburbs. My job was to dig ditches all around the house for new pipes to go in. As I spent my hours digging, I came to be friendly with these folks. They were glad to have their ditches dug and happy to support my staggering efforts at life.

At some point during this time my mom told me about a new dog our friends had adopted. It was a huge German Shepherd, she said, and mean. They called her "Moxie." The dog was so aggressive, she told me, that it needed to be chained up at all times. They kept her in a prong collar to keep her from lunging. I wondered, why would you get such a dog? Every time the dog came up in conversation, it was about how aggressive she was. How everyone needs to be careful and give her a wide berth.

In Athens I'd gotten beat down so hard I didn't know which was up. The suffering had gone on so long I just simply longed for things to be ok. I longed for kindness, gentleness, peace. I dug deep into the Bible, reaching out for dear life, finding strength and comfort where I could. I reached out to God day in and day out, longing and panting for relief. I was slowly, arduously learning to listen for God's voice.

One evening my mom and I were going over to our friends' house for dinner. She reminded me again about the new dog. Another warning. Though this would be the first time I'd met her, I didn't feel too concerned. I was never much of a dog person. I thought I'd just let her be.

Getting out of the car I saw Moxie. She was lying there on the wide porch, panting, chained to the rail. We walked up to the house, and as we did I watched the dog. She was quiet, big, looking to me just like a normal, if huge, dog. The mean-looking prong collar was around her neck. I didn't like to think of her lying there all day, trapped in that grim thing.

Then, quickly, as we approached, I had a feeling and I knew it was true. It said, "The dog needs to know who the boss is." Without thinking I walked right over to her and scooped her up in my arms. She melted, never struggling for a moment. I stood there holding her, her big body in my arms, her legs dangling down below. Then I put her down and petted her roughly, showing her I was the boss and that she was safe. I scratched her back and head. I handled her, showing her that I wasn't afraid, and that I knew I was safe with her. She was full of joy, rubbing up against me, and wagging her tail. We were best pals.

I don't know anything about dogs. But I did know that the feeling I'd had was right. She needed to know that she was safe. That there was a structure, and she fit in it. She needed to feel that she didn't make people scared and that her relationships could be comfortable and not marked with fear. To be sure, none of these thoughts were consciously with me before our small interaction. It just came in a moment. Simply, "She needs to know who the boss is." It came with a feeling of love and certainty which is the hallmark of God's direction.

FACING THE DARKNESS

In my college years I had done well. I had felt strong and alive, capable and happy. And I knew that I had done well. With great joy and learning I had seen my prayers answered. My paintings were powerful, reaching people. My friendships were deep and full of love. I felt, "I'm great at living!" When I graduated and moved on, I had a powerful expectation that life was going to continue to be great. I mean, really great. Perfect even. Having felt so much deep life, poetry, love, and spiritual depth, I knew it could be. But then, life is long.

I felt my life stretching out ahead of me into new seasons and unknown years. I began to feel a towering pressure to fill those years with continued success. Even to be "perfect," day after day, month after month. To live up to past successes. But not just scoring the winning goal, or making a good painting. Also, *feeling* inspired, being loving, feeling in the flow. In previous years I had *felt* the love of God. I knew it was real, and that perfection was something to shoot for. I had seen it and felt it. But I missed an important piece—I thought it was my job to be perfect myself. Like an untested and immature child king, without knowing it I made demands that no one could live up to. My eyes were on myself with an exacting, endless judgment. It was a terrifying burden.

The fear began to interrupt my life. I couldn't live as I had been. It was tearing me down from the inside out. And I was doing it myself—my own cruel thoughts.

After a while I called a friend from church to pray with me. She was older, tougher, and way more experienced. With certainty she reassured me that I was God's creation, good, innocent, and deserving healing. She was rock solid with me that that there was no bad or guilty self connected to me as God's reflection. I listened. I was constantly under attack in my thoughts.

Months went by and I thought of nothing except to be healed of this darkness. Every step I took, every thought that I entertained, I judged myself. Was it good enough? Was I doing the right thing? Maybe I could have thought something better? I was afraid of messing up, and afraid of being afraid. I couldn't see a way out. Yet I knew, in a way that wasn't really touched by how bad I felt, that there is nothing that can't be healed by God. God is just…God. But, getting to that goodness, I felt, was up to me. At times I felt so weighed down by what I thought was my responsibility to be "perfect" that it was only the promise of healing that allowed me to see any worth in life.

It had always been natural to me to share my problems with my friends. It was normal to tell them what was happening, ask for help, see what they thought. I told them about my fear. I described my feeling that I had to be perfect. That I was self-conscious all the time and felt constantly afraid. They listened and tried to be helpful. It wasn't helpful. I would leave these conversations feeling worse. They didn't know what I meant. They wondered why on earth I was concerned with being perfect. They shied away and were embarrassed for me as I spoke about God and spiritual things. They couldn't relate. And they didn't have any good ideas about how to fix it. That had never happened before.

It was like one of my best tools for problem solving, my friends, had evaporated in my hands. This problem, unlike any I'd had before, was completely beyond their reach. It wasn't going to get fixed by talking about it.

On the heels of this realization I came across this passage in the Bible:

"…when ye fast, be not, as the hypocrites, of a sad countenance: for they disfigure their faces, that they may appear unto men to fast. Verily I say unto you, they have their reward. But thou, when thou fastest, anoint thine head, and wash thy face; That thou appear not unto men to fast, but unto thy Father which is in secret: and thy Father, which seeth in secret, shall reward thee openly." (Matthew 6:16-18)

It's comforting to recognize your own life reflected in verses of the Bible. In this case, I knew that this terrible time was my "fast." Up till now, as I had been seeking a resolution to the problem by mulling it over, talking and talking and talking about it with my friends, I had been "of a sad countenance" with a "disfigured face." But, I considered, the best thing I knew was to be honest with people about how you feel! That had always been so clear. Such an easy thing to know and do. How strange it was to feel the Bible, the deep, solid Bible, giving a different instruction. As I felt it out in myself I realized that this wasn't about being honest or dishonest with my friends. It just didn't involve them. This was between me and my own life. Between me and God.

Taking in the next line of the Bible thought, I saw that I was to anoint my head and wash my face. I could feel that that meant I was to face each day brightly, openly, hopefully, despite whatever I was feeling.

This too was a new concept. Until this time I had felt that my job was to be honest about my feelings. The best way I had come across to live a life was to live both joy and sadness to the full, plumbing their depths. And this sentiment was supported by the thoughtful, artsy culture of my bohemian friends and lifestyle. But as I considered this horror I was in, I began to understand that there was no poetry in its depths. There was no richness to be discovered in its belly. It was just death. God was showing me that it was only there to be destroyed from out of me.

I knew that pretending doesn't work. Pretending doesn't heal. You can't just put a smile on your face and act like there's no problem. But that's not what this was. It was different. This was a new step towards not giving the darkness a place to live in me. It was an instruction to actively not allow the darkness to live on my face or in the way I interact with others, even though it continues to rage in my thoughts and feelings. This was a first step in reclaiming some of the land of me.

It was a powerful step in trusting God instead of people. I intuitively knew that for this approach to work, I had to embrace it completely. Give up on telling people how bad I felt. Stop wishing for a hug to take it all away. Stop looking for temporary solutions that aren't up to the job. Instead, this was a real step towards committing *to being changed inwardly*. This was cutting the ropes that tied me to the expectations of my friends, or the world, and instead putting my faith in God, and in the Word of God. I could feel the great, deep, stones shifting in me again.

This startling idea made its way through my system. How strange to leave behind the kind but vague humanism that we all learned in college. The answer to everything had been, "You need to talk to someone about this." "Share your feelings. Be honest with your feelings!" That was all fine, but it wasn't good enough. It simply wasn't up to the task.

I prayed almost constantly. I hoped. I felt afraid of God. He's too far away! He's too good! I'm so bad! But I knew He could make me good!

It was a mess. I imagined God, coming to my rescue, magically planting some new vision in me, taking away this fear. I imagined myself earning His attention by my efforts to be good. I was ever striving, ever pleading in my inner-most self. I repeated Bible passages and spiritual ideas to myself like mantras, hoping they would somehow parry attacks of the beasts that climbed all over me.

The attacks continued unchanged. My days were sour, tearful, trembling. With my memories of God's goodness longing in my chest I bent over backward to be patient. God will save me!

But the weeks and months went on. A scream, a tsunami, of frustration was rising in me. It grew, and ate like acid into my

patience. It grew more, scraping and scratching at the wall, but my memories of the vast goodness of God didn't budge. I would explode.

Every day was expanding my understanding of what suffering can be. I wondered to myself how life could be something so different than I had known before. I'd had no idea that my little life, once so hopeful, could reveal such depths of hurt and fear. I sometimes thought about suicide—not that I would kill myself, but just what suicide was. This is when I knew I was in the crucible. I knew, with certainty, from previous experiences with God, that killing myself wouldn't do me any good. I knew that I would just wake up somewhere else with my same problems, probably feeling worse than I was now. It was never the slightest temptation to think of ending my life. I knew I was incapable of it. God had not given me the power to escape living my life. So, I didn't try.

I read in the Bible about God's mercy. I looked for it in my life and didn't find it. I found no mercy. I thought of kinder, gentler times I had known. Sometimes there had been pain, but it always receded. That seemed like mercy. Now, everywhere I looked, in every corner, there were accusations and wounds, endless fears, but no mercy. When they spoke about God's mercy what did they mean?!

Then, one afternoon, the fear continuing as it had for months, my patience broke. Like a fresh breeze through an open window came a new idea—"There is no magic." Like a sword the thought severed my sanguine hopes that I'd be saved by a hand from the clouds. In that instant I knew, there would be no hand from heaven. No magic wand to take away my pain.

As if a veil had been torn away I saw in a plain, unpretty light, that I had been hoping on magic. I'd been hoping that the cruelty of cruelty itself would relent and just be nice. That evil would stop being evil and give me a break. But in a moment, I understood, it won't. Cruelty is going to keep on being cruel until the very moment you refuse it entrance to your mind. This darkness is not going to give you a break. It won't give you a day off. And the only way it's ever going to be gone is when you understand how and why it's gone. Magic won't do it. I'd been hoping on something to save me, to let me off the hook. But it wasn't going to happen. God doesn't do His work on a whim. Instead, we must live every step of a very real, wondrous transformation.

My soft, sanguine, hopes of being saved by a magic God evaporated. And as they did, I could feel, as if it had been uncovered, a deep living pool of desire to fight for my life. I hadn't felt it before. I'd been too entranced, expecting someone or something else to save me. But knowing it wasn't coming, I breathed in a fresh, windy, rock bottom desire to live. And this, THIS, was the mercy of God—to sweep away the scales that had obscured my understanding. This was a revelation from beyond myself, changing the landscape in a way I never could myself. Instead of magic, there must be learning. And from that learning, action.

In the absence of the illusion of magic, I now found myself face to face with my oppressor. This oppressor I knew to be implacable, and beyond reason. In fact, I had come to understand that it had nothing in mind but my destruction. It wanted me dead. This was strangely freeing. If your enemy has no place in him for reason, then there is nothing left to do but fight or die.

I began to notice my thoughts much more. As I stopped trying to be comforted by others, or saved by a fairy king, I was alone with them. They were on fire with complaint. Like a well filled with demons, my thoughts erupted with whining, fussing, kicking and screaming. "I want my way!" My inner world was alive with open wounds, voices of dissatisfaction, temper, irritability. All day, every day.

But how different—instead of seeking to be comforted, seeking to end the pain. A shocking, startling fact dawned in me. I stood before it, disarmed. I saw, with amazement - if you want to get better, if you want to draw closer to God,…here it is…*there is no complaining*. It was the healthiest slap in the face I ever felt. As if God himself were my parent (Is He really???) this holy chastisement landed directly in my heart and dried up those wounds. There is simply no complaining on this path. If you want to walk this path you cannot bring your complaints.

It was hard to swallow, yet I knew in my most honest self that it was a fact. Oh, this hard, healthy discipline! How disarming is God's path! How demanding and how comforting! This is God's mercy—He comes, not to serve you, but to transform you from the inside out so that you can better shine with His own light.

Over the next months and years my lesson would be then, *how* to rid myself of these complaints. It was an exacting process, step by arduous step. It required noticing the thought, and then, despite the fact that it felt like my own feeling, recognizing it as a burdensome, poisonous, shackle that I could let go of. And then, actually letting go of it. It was day-after-day labor, moment by moment, working for the sake of my life. It was hard to believe in. But then, in glorious reality, it started working. Beginning in days, moving into weeks and months I could feel the difference.

The thing is, as you let go of thoughts that have seemed normal forever and ever, you start to have space in your mind. New thoughts, better ones, take their place. And those old thoughts, the ones you thought were you, actually weren't. In their absence you become a different, better person.

In this work I was like a non-athlete training for a marathon. At first it was only pain, tears, disappointment. It was only a desperate, distant hope that moved me to try. A need to not suffer anymore. But as I got into it, and I began to see how it works, I found that behind the exhaustion there was always another step I could take, another mile I could run. Even the exhaustion was a lie.

At this time there was an almost constant voice in my thoughts whispering "You are worthless! No one cares about what you do! You'll never be able to make anything of your work! Look how pathetic you are!" It was hard to believe in my efforts to be rid of it. Each long minute, each interminable day.

As I continued praying with my friend, it became clear to me that there simply is no giving up. I felt horrible all the time, but it was clear that I had only two options—give up and remain endlessly lost, crushed, or rebel against the horror, committing myself to seeing past fear to spiritual truth. The choice was obvious. In those months I became much better acquainted with the holy texts I was studying. I realized with some amazement that my answers were in there.

My friend and I had prayed together for a few years. As the time passed, and despite the fact that I did not feel out of the woods, I had to admit that there was progress taking place. It was a kind of humility I was not used to. What a crucible it is that requires you to admit to progress even while the suffering grinds on. Right in the midst. With great amazement I began to witness that I was being healed.

Through it all, my friend was praying with me. She was tireless, ready for my call at any time. She was ever prepared with encouragement, and often an unbending reminder that God is in control. Many times I called her from social engagements or at work, at my wits end, utterly beaten. I would slink off to the bathroom, ashamed of myself, hiding my terror from those around me. I felt

certain they could see right through me, exposing the bubbling cauldron of shame and horror inside me.

I'd hear the same information again, admonitions to keep working, keep praying. A reminder of who I am as God sees me. I'd get off the phone, trying to haul myself back to a place where I could function. Listening, listening in my heart for the meaning of the words she was saying to me.

All the time I was working to separate myself from the terrible thoughts that were occupying my mind. Here's what I mean: I knew that God is real. I had a very clear feeling that I was somehow in God's care, and that this could be brought to bear on my life. But, as if someone had just unlocked the dark demon-filled basement in the house of my mind, these cruel fears constantly obscured my feeling of it. My labor was to see myself, inch by precious inch, as being related to God, good, and at the same time, to cease to claim these fears as my own, despite the very aggressive feeling that they were the very thing that defined me.

I boggled at the feeling of being so far from where I wanted to be, but having come so far from where I was. How dirt-bottom humbling, and yet, how white-light joyful to feel that I am traveling, truly traveling in this invisible land of spirit that had been, to me, only a rumor. I could see myself on the path, walking, ever walking.

A new feeling arose in me—a sinewy, closed-fisted defiance of one who has suffered much and endured. I thought, "This thing can't kill me," and I knew it was true. It had been pouring it on thick for three years. It was using its best weapons, and I was slipping out between its disgusting fingers. Though the suffering continued, it existed side by side with a feeling that even the suffering was a sign that I would win. It might make me hurt, but I would outlast it. It couldn't kill me.

Many times as the months went by my friend exhorted me to "have faith in the process." It often took strength beyond what I thought I had, but I did try. I sometimes found I was comforted by that thought. It helped me let go of the abrasive, acidic impatience that often hounded me. If I could keep the long view in mind, I could look forward to emerging from this experience a better man. I could rest in the deep breath of not having to finish it all today. I often wondered, "Who will I be when I am free from all this?"

I became an ardent student of the Bible. I found that it was an ever-deepening pool. First, a source of guidance, rules, a way to bring order to my life. Next, a thick library of spiritual and moral meat to chew on. I worked and worked. Read and read. I found a kind of home in the labor of reading and praying. There were answers in the stories and metaphors, friends in the characters. The sheer volume of ideas and material allowed me to feel very comfortable using things I could relate to and not worrying about things I didn't understand or that seemed beyond understanding.

There were ideas I read, and moved on from, because frankly they seemed wrong. One of them was this, from Jesus' parable of the talents: "Whoever has will be given more, and they will have an abundance. Whoever does not have, even what they have will be taken from them." (Matthew 13:12)

In the parable there are three guys who each have some money, lent to them by a richer man. Two of them invest it and return the money with interest earned. The last one hides his money and ultimately returns it to the lender unchanged. The first two are praised and given honors. The last one is chastised and his money is given to the one who made the most! It seemed the opposite of fair, kind, good—all the things I thought and hoped the Bible would be.

I prayed and prayed, observing my life, using my growing spiritual understanding and familiarity with the Bible. One day I was reading and came across that passage. What felt like the main thrust of the parable I understood easily: Use your skills, be active in your work, don't take your talents for granted. But on this day, the part that had been locked to me, fell open like a ripe fruit.

When I considered the passage that had seemed so callous, so downright unfair, I realized that it described my experience with my thoughts *exactly*. When I was spiritually active, when I was working hard and gaining new understanding, I could feel progress. There was hope. There was promise. And my spiritual riches grew. I was on the path. By contrast, when I was overcome with complaint, hopelessness and inactivity, I felt as though all was lost. I was destitute, bereft.

It dawned on me, Jesus is not saying what "should" happen. He was describing what does happen. He was telling me, as you labor for, and gain, goodness and strength, you make it possible for yourself to gain more. When you give in to fear and despair, you make it so much harder for yourself. You will feel the despair and fear you give into. I had always imagined that when Jesus speaks he is declaring the ultimate goodness of how things *should* be. But no, he was pointing out the dangers, the pitfalls, the tortures, and showing me the way out. He comes, not with a magic wand, but with a map. He was saying, with enormous generosity, look, this fear and despair is dangerous to you—and the way to avoid it is to give it no quarter.

It's not a soft lesson. But it was incredibly useful. I began to see that the Bible's riches were beyond the capacity of well-worn humanistic bromides. They were capable, robust, and incisive. They could unveil and eviscerate invisible corruption and truly clear out darkness. The ways of the carnal mind are not merciful. And Jesus freely gives us the way to leave them behind and be done with them. My respect for the Bible grew immensely. A new understanding of that scripture came because the unfolding private difficulties of my life had revealed its logic. My inexpressible private wilderness was right there in the Bible, reflected back to me with useful, steely insight. And it came from a line that I had previously judged as inscrutable and even cruel. With wide eyes I began to wonder, what other incredible insights have been invisible to me?

One morning as I was getting ready to go to work, I came upon the prayer that eventually led me to freedom. It had become normal to me to spend 30 or 40 minutes each morning praying and reading the scriptures to set the tone for my day. At its best it was inspiring, exploratory, and a deep inquiry into my relation with God. But, at its worst, it was a kind of terrified struggle to build up some defense against the darkness. On this particular day I had not had time to read and pray like I was used to. I'd slept through my alarm and was frantically running out the door to get to work on time. As I ran down the stairs, I stopped—terrified that I had not done my day's prayers. A wild fear stole over me that without this ritual, my whole life would come crumbling down. The wolves would pass through the defenses and tear me apart. I stood on the stairs—in the crucible yet again. Were these prayers truly holding my life together? Was it my effort? Was I buying God's love with the time I spend praying to Him? The clock was ticking and I was late! Utterly without pretense I simply prayed, "God, protect me today—I need to live my life," and ran out the door.

In the next weeks I began to treasure the meaning of that prayer. It was a shift to really trusting God, instead of my own paltry abilities, with my life.

In that moment of prayer, feeling my own inability to defend myself, I felt that yes, it's God who holds my life together—not me. The iron lung of false responsibility had caused me to fear every moment. This prayer cracked that leaden shell and small shafts of light began to sprinkle in. I began to try living life "to the hilt," as my prayer friend often said. Instead of trying to do things "right," I began to concentrate on living with *inspiration*. Doing things beautifully. It was like learning to fly. The false supports were coming out from under me, and I was held up little by little by the warm hands of inspiration. There was a lot of humble trusting. Simply, "Does God love me or not? Yes, He does."

One late night, after hanging out with a friend, I walked out to my car. I was very used to pushing my way through social engagements, having fun when I could and putting on a brave face when I couldn't. Walking out the door, the cold night air on my face, I relaxed in the relief of solitude. As usual, my dark thoughts, the memory of my broken situation, returned like leaden weights to their stubborn position in the wings of my mind. But this time there was a finality to it. It was as if every feeling of progress I'd felt was a dream. I'd been fooling myself. I hadn't made any progress at all. By the time I went to open the door of the car, the burden was unbearable. Every feeling of progress or light that I hoped on daily was nowhere to be found. The darkness was complete. I felt, *I can't even take one more step.* I didn't. I stood there on the sidewalk in the cold, empty night, and thought of my old friend inside the house. I wondered if he might look out the window and see me standing inexplicably, too long, in his front yard.

The minutes stretched. I couldn't find the will to move or continue in any way. If I could have ceased to exist, I would have. I couldn't understand how to continue existing.

Then, only because something needed to happen, I tried to resist the weight. Standing on the sidewalk I resisted the weight of the absence of hope. Every voice of death screamed my worthlessness with its lock-like logic. How certain they were that my resisting was useless. I didn't have any defense against what they said. I couldn't argue with them. They seemed right. But I didn't want to die. I didn't want to be nothing. So I tried to resist them, despite how right they were. I lifted and lifted, resisting the certainty of being swallowed in darkness. With whatever strength I had, and whatever that even means, I pushed. Like an athlete who has done every pushup he can do, and then must do more, I pushed. Locked in absolute, naked effort, I resisted.

If my friend had looked out his front window he would have seen me standing on the sidewalk in front of his home. Nothing more. No hints. Which, in this case, is what it looks like when a man uses every muscle of life to resist death.

Everything becomes the resisting. There is nothing else, only the pushing against the towering iron deadweight. I pushed and pushed. And at some point, anti-climactic as you please, the weight receded into the night. I felt only that I could, in fact, take the next step, get into the car, and drive home. Nothing else was different. I drove home and continued my daily struggle.

In the next months the depression began to lift. With each trusting step I began to see that the great responsibility to be perfect was not really mine. Life began to flow more naturally.

The final step was a very specific instruction. In prayer, deep into the fourth year of this struggle, I felt an idea in my heart. It was this: "Say yes to anything you are invited to." I sat with it. I noticed that it didn't allow for any choosing on my part. If I get invited, I must go. It made me nervous. But it was deep and comforting to recognize this as an answer to my prayers. I embraced it. It would be a rule to me.

Shortly after that, a friend invited me to a training for youth workers. Now, though I'd worked with teens in the past, I was not a youth worker. I didn't have any interest in it and had no plans to pursue anything like that. All the voices of "no" began their complaints, ganging up like always. But "yes" was my rule. I went.

On that day I met Anna, who in a few months became my girlfriend. The relationship was sweet, kind, and new. It was the first one I'd had since this fear began. As our time together went on, I could see how much I had changed. I was so much calmer. I just wanted to be good to her. I found joy in doing things for her and being patient with her. I was less interested in trying to get my own way. I found I had opportunities to comfort her and help her be less afraid. I felt strangely strong. Rather than needing comfort, I could give it.

After these years of fighting darkness in a cracked and empty land, there were moments of color returning to my world. These moments had character and nature. They were defined by what they are, not by what they aren't. They were characterized by going towards something instead of avoiding something.

Finally, I could feel some momentum. Little by little there were times where I was honestly glad to be alive. Those moments began to string themselves together. New people came into my life, new jobs, and opportunities. I found that at each step of the way I had a choice between self-pity and knowing myself as God's good creation. I got better and better at making the right choice.

Soon I was feeling like a normal person again. But it didn't end there. I began to see that I had opportunities to help others who were feeling bad. There were chances to be generous—to defy fears about my own situation by giving to others. I began to treasure and assert that I was not a patient, but a healer. I found new strength, and renewed, passionate desire to live. After having stood up to a monster of that size, walked through and come out the other side, I knew that darkness could be overcome. It will scream and threaten and do every cruel thing it can muster, but it need not win.

I gained oceans of spiritual treasure in those hard years, one of the most beautiful convictions being that God not only has good for me, He has wonderfulness. Having come through this mighty challenge I am a soldier girded with spiritual weapons. There is not a vestige of depression left in me and I know I will never be depressed again. I have gained a control over myself that I never guessed was possible. I can honestly say that God has made me "a new creature: old things are passed away; behold, all things are become new." (II Corinthians 5:17)

In retrospect, as I consider this path and the changes that took place in me, I observe that it was God causing me to learn to fight for my spiritual freedom. I was forced to learn—in the words of Jesus, to deny myself. Where I had thought that my personal feelings, thoughts, and fears were creators of my experience, I was shown, through hard practice, that, in truth, God is the only creator. Where previously I had had no use for the Bible concept of the "carnal mind," now I saw it, and recognized it as my enemy. It would lie, bully, and destroy until I oppose it, and by allowing God, good, to be all to me, cast it out of my experience. Then, in its absence, I found peace, usefulness, and rebirth.

Through it all, and with deep and humble thanks, I have gained a new joy with God and myself. I now know that perfection, God's work, is done, and it is my joy to live in and explore His creation. The depression, which for four years seemed like an impenetrable prison wall, was reduced to nothing. It was gone and has never returned.

BUILDING MY LIFE ON FAITH, AT A COST

After living in a beautiful apartment for a couple of years, the landlady wanted to remodel and my housemates and I had to move out. We had a few months.

After a long search, looking at rooms all over Boston, I found a gorgeous, perfect, beautiful situation in a big apartment over in Jamaica Plain. I'd be living with a couple of women, Kris and Liz, both of whom were great. All three of us were in our late twenties or early thirties. We'd enjoyed warm conversation when I interviewed for the room. Amazingly, my rent was going down by almost a third of what I'd been paying. I couldn't believe how perfect it was.

I felt a powerful sense of rebirth as I moved my things across the Charles River and into my new apartment. I was excited to explore the neighborhood and get to know my two new housemates.

I'd always felt very comfortable living with women. I've always had plenty of platonic women friends. It was a big part of my social life, and one I appreciated deeply for its emotional depth and ease of conversation. For a couple of years in Athens I shared a house with Maggie. Then, back in Boston, I lived with Arwen and Jude, both of whom became good friends. In both cases I liked the feel in the house, the kinds of conversations we would have, the warm, caring community. I expected this next situation to be similar.

It was! From the time I arrived, it was a great fit. Both of them, especially Kris, were quick with conversation and to include me in things. We shared meals or watched a movie every now and then. It was shaping up to be a really smooth transition.

However, as the first weeks turned into the first months, it turned out that Kris and I spent more and more time together. My relationship with Anna, the woman I met at the youth training, had ended after a year. Kris was interesting, capable, confident and attractive. Oops. By the end of the second month, I realized I was having feelings for her. And for the amount of time she was happily spending with me, I guessed she had feelings for me too.

Now, in times past, I may have thought, "This is great! New room, new girlfriend, all in the same place!" But I didn't. I learned from my battle with depression that I wanted to do everything differently. The chastisements had been sore and severe. During much of my depression years I'd been blundering through relationships, attempts at romance, and floundering intimacy. Toward the end I'd met Anna. We'd had a warm, well-intentioned romance and that companionship had been an enormous blessing, but it came naturally to an end. Through it all, and holding close to my freedom from sexual pressure, I'd stumbled my way through romantic encounters and matters of the heart. Now, blessedly, I was out of the woods and I *did not* want to go back. With my most serious face I was intent on doing it right. I was growing in my spirituality, trust in God, and appreciation of the Bible. I wanted to be moral, unselfish, and upright.

The question was, what does that mean? And, how do you do it?

I had plenty of examples from my own life, and in those of my peers, of how to do it wrong. It seemed the norm among my friends and in my larger social circle, was dramatic ups and downs, fear, breakups, and an assumption that unbridled sexuality was freedom. I had examples from my parents' generation, or from hard-line church folks, of picture-perfect marriage outcomes, as if out of a bridal catalogue. On that side of things, it seemed as though there was no room for sexuality of any kind before the wedding. I couldn't see how that was going to work for me.

I had also seen and felt things in intimate moments that I knew were just right. From my first experiences I had seen that it could be tender, kind, and truly intimate—a really sweet sharing. It had been very natural, from the beginning, to bring my whole honest self, my best intentions, my character. I'd also learned that I could expect to find in that intimacy the good, honest self of the person I was with. It could be something very real, very substantial.

I was surprised to find myself in this situation with Kris. I hadn't foreseen it at all. And yet, there we were.

I had a precious, newfound appreciation of restraint, patience, and a more Bible-based sense of morality. Almost in spite of myself I realized I was feeling that it wouldn't serve us best to pursue a relationship while living in the same apartment. But, I balked. It all got real serious when that thought was brought to its logical ends. It meant that I needed to give up on my feelings for her (which, I have to admit, were strong—or more honestly, my feelings of wanting a girlfriend were strong) and simply move on, while keeping the apartment. This seemed unlikely at best, and perhaps impossible. On the other hand, it meant moving out of this (perfect, inexpensive, well-located, and beautiful) apartment, to pursue the entirely uncertain hope of a romance with Kris. On top of that, it was only an educated guess that she even had the same feelings for me. I imagined a conversation in which I confessed that I was going to move out of the apartment in the hopes that we might pursue a relationship, in which she revealed that she had no feelings of the kind and what I did was my own business. Yikes. Was I willing to give up this holy grail of an apartment for a glimmering, unlikely hope?

Days went on and the issue grew and grew inside of me. I could feel that Kris, if she were like others of my peers, might think my willingness to move out of the apartment for an old-fashioned appreciation of morality was totally insane. In fact, by revealing it, I might be ending the possible romance anyway. My inner workings were going to be exposed. My spiritual growth (I hoped that's what it was) was causing me to make choices—go one way, leave the other behind. You can't have both. By the end of the week I simply couldn't go on without addressing it. I needed to make a decision.

But I was afraid. I wasn't only going to lose the apartment—I was going to lose it for a reason all my peers would think was actually crazy. None of them would relate. On a quiet Saturday morning, with a pit in my belly, I took myself out for a walk around the block to pray. I was resolved to make a decision before I came back in the house. I was going to decide that morning.

My heart pounded in my chest and the pit in my stomach churned. I reached out to God. I listened with all my heart and all my desire to do right and trust the guidance I received. I walked slowly, giving myself time.

By the time I was back, standing on the sidewalk in front of the house, the only guidance I had felt was that I trusted God more than myself. More than the norms of the society around me. It was God who had pulled me out of desperation and blackest fear. It had to be God upon which I built my life. And with that, the decision was made.

Later that day, and with much trepidation, I initiated a conversation with Kris. I told her that I had feelings for her. Her eyes warmed and she intimated that she had the same for me. I revealed that if she was interested in trying out a dating relationship, I would move out. Kris had recently been through a divorce. I was touched to see that she too had a very serious eye on handling these things with maturity. She wasn't horrified or embarrassed for me as I'd feared.

So, two months after I moved in, I began looking again for a room to rent in Boston. Over a couple of months I looked at 37 apartments. Not one of them was nearly as good as the one I was leaving. And all but the dirtiest rat holes were more expensive. I kept the faith.

By the time autumn was rolling warmly around I moved into my new place. The room was smaller and it was almost 50% more expensive. And, I'd be living with three sports-watching, beer drinking fellas. My too-cool artist self rolled his eyes a little. It was a leap from what I was used to. Moving forward had certainly felt like choosing the lesser of 37 evils.

Through it all I could feel something new emerging. While I navigated the specifics of where I would live, maybe dating Kris, and the tumbling uncertainty of all the outward elements, I had broken with the path of seeking out my own will. When I trusted God to lead me through this mess, I took a step out of basing my understanding of my life on its outward appearance. Instead, I placed it on my expectation from God. My new room was smaller and more expensive, the guys I lived with seemed gruff and unlike my usual sensitive art friends, and who even knew what would happen with Kris—but I'd placed my feet on a path led by prayer. That was more important than any of the outward elements. It was better to be on the path, willing to let go of whatever I needed to, in order to follow the guidance I received in prayer.

After all that, if you can believe it, Kris and I dated for about four months. With concerted effort on both sides to make it work, it came to an amicable end. And then, the justification gone, I was just living in this new house with the fellas. Outwardly, the whole thing had been for nothing. I didn't end up with the great apartment or a girlfriend. I pored over what had happened. At every moment I'd done my best and followed the guidance I'd received. The relationship hadn't worked. The new living situation was not my first choice. But, and this is everything, my spiritual connection to God was. I looked back on those months and felt proud. Wide eyed and a bit punch-drunk I considered what had happened. I didn't end up with any of the things I had thought I wanted. But I hadn't allowed myself to be bullied into giving up on God, my integrity, or my willingness to follow the inner voice. I hadn't been cowed into silence for fear of my inner workings being exposed. They *were* exposed. And I was stronger for it. I had been as brave as I knew how to be. What I emerged with was better than an apartment or even a girlfriend. I had established myself further in the thing I wanted most—I was willing to follow God at all costs.

I was elated.

My confidence grew. I saw, yet again, that prayer was my bosom friend. I saw myself protected by my prayer. Also, pushed to my limits and lifted out of them, into greater trust. And there, in the midst of a situation that seemed ok, but not great, I rejoiced that I didn't care. The thing I cared about was listening to God. Nothing else came close.

BEAUTIFUL, YOU'RE BEAUTIFUL

Despite having routed the specter of depression a few years earlier, one night I found myself feeling sad. I was lonely in the long, unremitting hours. I'd made plans to go to a party for the night, but now felt like crying, no reason to go—just another stupid night. I was wanting to be held, comforted, loved, close and warm. I wasn't lonely for company, but to be understood. Goodness gracious! In these hard years I have been learning that I am an amazing being—deep, with pools and wells of feeling and perception. Then who is it that can begin to see them? Name one person with whom I have been able to share it to its depth? I'm being honest—there's not one! I have lived a full and beautiful social life, yet there is no one on earth or elsewhere with whom I've shared the tenth part of my being. You may say I am talking selfish. Who am I to want such a thing? Or to wax so romantic. But you know, I open my eyes and I want to be loved. I want to be adored and embraced. I want to be assured that I am precious and special. I want to be smiled upon. I want it deeply and it's not going away.

Another thing—I'm tired of people being mean. We come to expect it and think it is normal. We see it all the time. But my heart of hearts screams against it forever and ever. My little boy wants pure kindness and nothing else. I'm tired of thinking of cruelty and callousness as normal. I'm tired of impatience and rudeness. My little boy, standing in the blackness, his toes in some dewy flowers in the grass, in a moony spotlight, he wants kindness and jokes. He doesn't deserve this crap. Really, he's heart broken.

So that little boy, standing in the grass, cooled by the night, standing in a place undefined, just surrounded by darkness and showered in a glow of light—that little boy turned to his father. I turned to my father, the father I can't see, but know is there. I turned to Him and thought, "My father loves me. He loves me in exactly the way that I most want to be loved. He loves me deeply and would never let me misunderstand His love." Then I tried to imagine that. I love my imagination. Because it can think of all these amazing things. I tried to imagine a love that could touch me in all the places that I am deepest, most amazing, most untouched.

And I realized that my father loved me the most in those places. Then I thought, oh my God, God is really my *father*.

In that place where all is calm and a breeze is blowing kindly through the leaves, in that place where the little boy is standing in a black summer night, in that place where each of his toes is safe in the cool grass, in that place, my father loves me forever.

Call me in 10 years. Does your father still love you in a perfect, warm way that leaves you safe from every danger? Yes. Call me in 50 years. Still? Are you happy and unthreatened? Yes. Call me when the world is falling apart. You can be sure I will be crying to my father, calling to that Love that is beyond the veil, in every place and condition.

In order to love anyone else, I need to feel loved myself. I really do. I need to know that my father loves me.

I realized as this was all going on that I *have* a father! I have a father that I can cry to at any moment. I saw in my mind's eye an image that made me exclaim. "My father has put me in a place apart!" I saw that He has taken me out of all the hurt, out of all the loneliness and longing to be understood. He has taken me out of all that incompleteness and unrequited longing because He knows me and is with me in all the ways I most want to be befriended. In all the ways I most want to have fun and share. In all those ways He has made me and is with me.

Then I shed my skin like a snake. I shook my old feathers and rose up and walked. I took my lonely, longing self, my self near to tears, my self over-whelmed at the thought of every decision and change, and I went to God, my father and said, "You are my father! You are my love! You are my everything and you love me just like I need to be loved. You don't ask me to pretend I don't want to be loved! You don't tell me it's selfish! You made me that way. You made me to want to be loved because that is exactly what you want to do! You want to love me and I accept! I accept your love Daddy!" And I said it to him ten times over, again and again, thinking of him loving me, hugging me, never letting me go.

And I could feel the loneliness falling from me like scales. I rode my bike out into the night and the words from an old song sang in my ears—"Beautiful, you're beautiful! As beautiful as the sun! Wonderful, you're wonderful! Wonderful as they come!" And then, newness. A push to live and to go. That I am strong and filled with freedom, a song, a wind.

I rode across town to the party. I sang quietly, with little tears rolling down my cheeks as I went.

I wiped my tears and rang the bell at the house. I knew I wouldn't know many people at this party and the ones I did know were only acquaintances. Minutes after I arrived one of the folks at the party said, "We were talking about you before you got here. Someone said you are a Christian Scientist and we had all kinds of questions for you." (It turns out few, if any, of them were religious, so to them I was a bit of an anomaly.) For the next two hours they asked me about my beliefs and understanding of the universe. They were honestly inter-ested, asking relentlessly. I answered plainly, loving God for this. Every single person at the party came into the room. They arranged chairs in a circle. They asked every question. I thought, felt, and told them every answer, opening the great wooden doors of my inner palace. When they asked, I showed them what was there. Deep into the questions they asked some things I didn't know how to answer. God said, "You're safe when you tell the truth!" I said I didn't know how to answer that one, and we moved on.

Though the questions were probing, I didn't feel afraid or attacked. Though the people were mostly strangers to me, it felt intimate, honest, and sincere. Though it was a total surprise, and sprung on me quickly, I felt comfortable, even joyful.

At the end of the night the acquaintance I'd known best at the party, a woman, said to me, "I know you better than any other person in that room tonight."

Preserve my soul for I am holy.
86:2

I'LL DO ANYTHING FOR BEAUTY

My years in Athens and then in Boston sifted me like flour. I'd learned to let go of weaknesses I hadn't even known I'd clung to. I clung for dear life to what I loved—God, and Beauty.

After my move to Boston, and with my growing, strong-enough-to-base-a-life-on faith, I poured my heart into creating. When I finished a picture, and it sang, I knew I'd done something worthwhile. Pictures and poems were more real than other things. They were enough to live for.

When I did get a mural job, every now and then, it was like walking in heaven. The great, glorious walls, rough brick and cement, larger than me, pushed me to my limit. I wrestled them, ran my brushes over them, revealing wonder where there had been nothing. I felt power coursing through me. Its amazing, life-asserting alchemy took emptiness and filled it with spiritual beauty, the love of my life. My best thoughts, my dears, my beloved babies, were now on walls, seen by hundreds, even thousands of people. Those pure ideas were free to do their work, influence lives, touch hearts, as they had my own.

More and more I had access to a world of pictures, poetry, feeling, mystery, stories, wonder. It was rich and better than anything anyone had shown me. In my listening, imagining, and working I received beautiful ideas. They changed me, lifted me, educated and embraced me. Except for the pictures I painted and the songs and poems I wrote, this world was invisible. Yet, I became completely confident of it. It never failed. It was richer than kings. It flowed, swollen like a river after rain.

Back in the world of rent and groceries I daily wondered how to live and progress.

But I'd fallen in love with Beauty. It was over and done. I was her slave. I longed to be at her service. And as this idea grew, a conviction grew with it. I will do this work. I will do anything to do this work. I will find walls. I will do it for low pay. I will do it for free. I will embarrass myself. I will go from door to door. Nothing matters but to make this beauty that I feel.

I didn't care if I was poor. In fact, I assumed I would be. That was fine. But I needed to be beauty-rich.

My sketchbooks filled with images. Page after page, ballpoint pens, acrylic paints, collaged maps and watercolors. The books filled up and I moved on to another. The books revealed the invisible world. I was amazed at how easy it was to imagine a magical place and then, simply create it. I sometimes imagined what I could do if it weren't so hard to get someone to let me paint on their wall. How many murals could I make in a year? The only limitation was time. I had endless ideas and endless energy. I longed for those walls.

I began to feel a mythological image of myself. In it, I am standing on an ever-growing pile of gold and jewels, endless riches. I am longing, laboring with all my strength and hope, to simply give the riches away. I reach down into the pile and fling them into the world around me. Gold doubloons, ruby rings, jewel-encrusted crowns. I can't keep up with the pile of gold and gems as it grows beneath me. And they are received so slowly, tragically. The desire to share burns and burns. The pile of treasure is constantly growing.

One spring afternoon in 2002 I was in Boston's Roslindale Square. A new bakery had just moved into a corner space. On one side was a brick wall, 75 feet long, 10 feet high, no windows. A virtually unbroken canvas.

I began to knock on doors. Who owns the building? Who can I talk to? Oh, there's a local commerce board I should speak to. What's their number? Who's the contact?

Some weeks later I rode my bike to a meeting with the building owner, the chamber of commerce rep, and the owners of the new bakery. I had my sketch in my hand. It was a detailed drawing of a sprawling, twisting tree, and a bounding team of kids climbing, running and playing around in it. A wooded landscape rounded out the scene, with distant mountains, a creek, and a stony grotto. It was my freedom dream—a vision of totally uninhibited living, innocence, and joy.

It would be a powerful statement. It would be art, a real idea, no commercial concerns. It would be humble—a vision of beautiful life, comprehensible to any and all. It would be a chance for me to use all my skills, to set myself free to create. I'd proposed that each of the three entities chip in $500, but the main thing was to get to do it. I didn't know what would happen.

My heart pounded as I waited for the others to arrive. The clean, professional feel of the conference room was foreign to me. I sat up straight, trying to feel like I belonged there. Would they laugh at my idea? Would they like it? I could only wait.

The bakery owners, Kim and Chris, arrived with Tom, the rep from the Chamber of Commerce. Tom announced that we were still waiting on Ashy, the director of a childcare agency housed in the building. She was in another meeting, running late.

We got started. I showed them my drawing. I knew it was good. It was so good, in fact, I naively hoped they would see it and rejoice. Each of them looked at the drawing, taking their time, asking questions here and there.

Ashy burst in the door -a small middle-eastern woman in a charcoal gray pantsuit. She was distressed. "Uuugh!" She moaned, "I've just had 10 million dollars cut from my budget!" I balked. Instantly I was smaller than an ant. Who am I meeting with? How am I even in the same room with this person? I thought of the pathetic $1,500 I was trying to raise. Immediately I feared this woman, smarting from her $10 million loss, would have no heart for art. My drawing could be as beautiful as a Raphael, but if she had no eyes to see it I was lost. I longed to sneak out and avoid embarrassing myself further.

Still, she sat down and asked what she'd missed. Tom filled her in, passed her the drawing, and launched into his hopes for the project. From the perspective of the Chamber of Commerce, this mural was going to be on a bakery, and should be related to the business. He began to walk us through images of the bread-making process—harvesting fields of wheat, making dough, the finished loaves. My heart sank. Inwardly I rolled my eyes. This was precisely the kind of thing that makes so many murals so bad. For the sake of "making sense" or relating to the community in super-literal ways, we throw art out the window. We give up on imagination and creativity altogether.

He confidently made his points, obviously familiar with the process. It was a win-win for everyone, he let us know. He listed the reasons: It'll draw attention to the bakery! It'll show that Roslindale supports the arts! Alex will get to ply his trade.

Kim, Chris, and Ashy all nodded their agreement. It made all the sense in the world. And I could feel my mural slipping away, like a chunk breaking off an iceberg. There was nothing I could do. Away it drifted, receding into the frozen water with an epic, tragic splash.

Broken-hearted, I considered my options. Would it be worth doing this mural if they were still going to put in their $500? (At this point in my career, making *any* money on art was a bonus, nothing to be snuffed at.) I tried to imagine myself painting Tom's idea. I was bored already. Was it better to wash my hands of the whole thing and try again somewhere else?

Inwardly I mourned. I had thought this was going to be something really beautiful. Hopelessly, I imagined sitting out the rest of the meeting, smiling and nodding, just waiting to be done. I looked around the room. Ashy was there in her fancy business suit, nursing her $10 million privation. Tom wore a trim black suit, his briefcase filled with supporting evidence. In my vast ignorance, I imagined him bopping from meeting to meeting, watering down ideas everywhere he went, making the world safe for commerce. Kim and Chris were, like me, in jeans and T-shirts, theirs puffed here and there with white flour.

But, something in me pushed back. "Tell them why your idea is better." Inwardly I snapped to attention. *I can't do that! She just lost 10 million dollars! I'm lucky if I see*

10 thousand dollars in a year. I'm nobody! This was so stupid. Why did I even think they would go for this? But it piped up again. "Tell them why your idea is better." It was better. It was filled with life. People would love it. It didn't need to make sense with the bakery. It didn't matter that a big beautiful tree had nothing to do with Roslindale Square. It simply didn't matter because people love beauty, and they know it when they see it.

I didn't know if they would laugh in my face. Honestly, I didn't know if Tom would slam his fists down on the table and rip me to shreds. I didn't know.

The only thing I had in my possession to say was that this design was better. It would draw people to it. It would make the neighborhood richer because it was itself rich. I could only tell them that it was good to make images of innocence and joy in public because innocence and joy make life good. I could only point out that the beauty of nature speaks to people, and perhaps precisely

because we are in a city, distant from trees like this, we should remind ourselves of them. I could only reveal my feelings, the simple, basic things that were enough to make me serve them with my whole heart.

I opened my mouth. When I did, the trepidation receded. It was all or nothing. I heard myself explaining my ideas, basic and human. I let it flow from my feeling. "Beauty makes life worth living," I explained. "It calls to people." With each claim I made I felt myself becoming more and more naked. Nothing covered my ideas or my dearly held hopes. I disrobed further, remembering to them the virtues of play, freedom, and exploration.

For a moment the room was quiet. Then, Chris mused, "I remember playing in the backyard as a kid. Digging in the dirt with a stick. That was the best feeling in the world." He went on, "Those Saturday afternoons when the adults have left you alone and you can just do what you want..." He smiled, remembering.

He spoke with a different tone than he had before. His business owner voice gave way to his regular guy voice. I could see him as a little boy, playing.

It was as though a drowned brother, dragged dead up on the riverbank, had moved slightly. I could see Chris considering the ideas I'd presented, feeling them with his own feeling, testing them. Then, with a smile he offered, "I'm with Alex. I think we should do the tree." He looked at Kim, his wife, to see her response.

Then, Ashy, whose face had softened while Chris spoke, observed, "These children in your drawing are like our children—the ones we care for at the facility. Maybe parents will see this picture and think of us, caring for their children." She smiled to me, showing me she understood. Instantly I understood *her*. In her real being she wasn't numbers and pantsuits. She was a lover of children, laboring for their safety and well-being.

Kim jumped on the bandwagon, and then, easy as you please, Tom agreed. "I guess we can see where we're going with this!" he admitted. We agreed on the three donations of $500, everyone shook hands, and the meeting was over.

I was in a cloud. I was floating, free, untethered, wondrous, disbelieving. I unlocked my bike and pedaled over to a nearby park and rode among the trees. They'd *believed* me. I'd convinced them. I said what I loved, and it touched them—first Chris, then Ashy, and then the rest. I had died and been reborn right there in the meeting. Invisible to them, I'd dived off the cliff. I'd disrobed my intimate ideas not knowing if my nakedness would be mocked or rebuked. But, incredibly, beautifully, it had reached them in the very place where they were naked—their feelings of being alive.

****

That September I painted the mural. I gave myself to it, life and limb. In the glorious Boston autumn I worked. In the warm, dry air, the sun, kissing and burning me, I passed endless hours in joyous labor.

This mural changed my life. I did my very best. Day after day I poured all my longing into this picture, making the shadows of the leaves, the reflections on the water, the deep, cool caves between the rocks. All my pent-up hope and desire—the pile of gold and treasure—gushed out onto the wall.

That would have been enough. But there was more.

****

I love to listen to music while I work. It was my joy to take myself to the wall, my bag filled with cassettes to play in my old Sony Walkman. I'd been doing it for years. It was my way. The music blocked out the sounds of the world, allowing me to float deeper and deeper into the world of the picture. Hours would pass, the work appearing on the wall, and I would hardly notice the time, lost in the tree, the leaves, the limbs.

A few times in the first days of the mural, people came up to ask me questions about the picture. After some awkward moments they tapped me on the shoulder, or, waving in my periphery, attracted my attention. I pulled the earbuds out, and, as if drawn out from a deep dream, tried to hear their questions.

The questions were usually simple. "What's your mural of?" Or, "How did you get permission to do this?"

After each conversation I found myself feeling humble affection for these folks, brave enough to step out of anonymity and ask their question. Thinking of them, I began to notice the people walking by more than I had. The neighborhood was diverse. Older Greeks and Italians, young mothers and children, recent immigrants from West Africa. There

were always people walking by while I worked. Every stroke of my brush, every color choice, and every mistake are made without a veil. They can see everything I do.

A few more questions came and I followed the same process. The bellowing music ripped away, the conversation starting while I try to remember where I am, listening to a new stranger present her query.

Over the years I had often noticed that lots of people feel intimidated by art. Or at least, they don't feel included in it. They feel that they don't understand it. And, they fear, if they don't understand it, they must be dumb. But I knew that wasn't true. Art is *for* people. If it makes people feel dumb it's probably the art's fault. Yes, sometimes art is hard and ahead of its time, but it can be explained. It can be unfolded, patiently and affectionately. I wanted *my* art to be for people. It was profane that art should make people feel small. Its whole purpose is to make people feel their meaning, connected and strong. I wanted to be a guide, helping people see their own connection to art, beauty, color, pictures and stories.

One morning I was pulling out my paints, ladder, and brushes, getting ready for the day's work. As if an angel had passed over, I had a feeling of warm generosity as I realized that today I would not wear my Walkman. My ears would be open to the wide world. I would be ready for questions as they came. I would step into my role as spokesman for the mural. I would be a ready voice, helping to bridge the misunderstandings.

As the mural proceeded, I didn't wear the Walkman anymore. Almost instantly my understanding of my power as a muralist virtually doubled. I am not just a painter of beautiful, spiritual, life-transforming images. I am a man in the street, open to every conversation. I am a face of love to everyone who walks by. The same love and passionate desire that I pour into the pictures, I can pour into my conversations with the people.

I felt my ownership of this art, my art mission, falling away. I knew I served Beauty. But now, I also served humble humanity. It's not about how I feel on any given day. It's about the questions coming to me in the mouths of strangers on the street. It's about *them*. It's about the hearts that will see these pictures and wonder. It's about allowing every facet of the project to express the innocence, joy, and freedom that the picture proclaimed.

I felt like the sun. Instead of shining my energy on the wall, my light shone in every direction. I felt as if a shade had been taken off of me, allowing me to do twice as much as I ever had. The people are a waiting audience. I was standing on my pile of riches, and this was a new way to share them. Answer their questions. Guide their concerns. Do it with a friendly voice, a forgiving tone, and never a moment of judgment. Be so grateful for their questions, their desire to understand, their humanity in conversation.

Naturally, as I opened that door, the questions and conversations flooded in. There were regulars who stopped by every day, saying hellos, noticing the progress from the previous day. Countless townies shared their opinions and made the obligatory "You missed a spot!" joke. My affection for them flowed easily.

Then, because I still longed for music, I brought my old boom box from home on the back of my bike. Deciding to ask forgiveness rather than permission I began playing my beloved tunes, loud enough that I could hear them at the far end of the mural. Loud enough even, that it might feel like a street party. I tried to play music that might make people dance, or just feel good when they walked by.

When the mural was finished I had lived my public prayer. I couldn't make a better painting than I had. It looked back at me and made me proud. I'd had countless conversations and taken on a whole new understanding of what it is to be a public artist. My power grew.

I stand on a pile of riches, longing to give it away.

THROWING OFF THE PALL

My years of battle with depression had shown me I could win. So in the following years, when a dark mood, or poisonous feeling settled on me, I knew I didn't have to be its slave. When they came, and from time to time they did, I knew I could push back. They still felt real. They felt like my own feelings. But I knew from dire experience that they weren't.

One day between jobs, with practical difficulties looming large and desolate, things were feeling very hard. In fact, despite all my growing, it felt as though fear was crushing down. It was surrounding me, climbing all over me. I noticed a thought pass through my mind: *All I want to do is go to bed. And maybe never wake up.*

But this time, I recognized it.

Like a watchdog, I became alert. "I know I don't REALLY want to go to bed and never wake up." Then a new feeling, "I don't ever want to feel like *this*, ever again." I reminded myself of what I knew from experience—this feeling is only a voice. It wants to overwhelm me with its pounding. It wants me to forget who I am. The only way I know of to really banish feeling terrible is to feel closer to God.

So, despite the *feeling* that it was hopeless, that it would never work, that I should just give up forever—I began praying. Just thinking of what God is. Thinking of eternity, of Love, of Love's love for me and everyone. It was instantly so different from the feeling I had been feeling. So different from emptiness and despair. And it didn't take into account at all any of the things I had been feeling bad about. It was in spite of them all.

That's the thing about prayer. It works, right in the midst of that terrible feeling. It doesn't matter that the dark, oppressive armies of fear are clomp-clomping in with their heavy boots. It doesn't matter that the sky is lowering and exhaustion moans that it can't take another step. Prayer is not asking about fear or exhaustion. Prayer is not asking them how they feel. Prayer is in blue sky. Prayer is stepping through the veil of threats to God, where there is no threat. Prayer is remembering that Love is right where every threat screams, and being more interested in Love.

I began to remember feelings I've had in the past that made me love God. Feelings that have convinced me that there is a God and that I want to dedicate my life to understanding and knowing that God. I was happy to remember them.

Fear screams, debates, reminds, scolds. It argues for hopelessness like an agile, implacable lawyer. It seeks to find a foothold in your mind and expand its colony. It will remind you of all its well-researched reasons for being afraid. It will pound and grind you with threats of suffering. It will attack your virtue and argue you into a prison cell. But prayer is turning away from fear. It implies, "I don't care about your threats. I'm listening to God who knows better than you do."

I held to those good-feeling thoughts of God. I let them grow in me as I felt them. I made a point of remembering that I'm not making these thoughts up. Rather, I recognized them as realities I've seen and felt. Almost like remembering a place I used to go. I held to those thoughts and let them be real to me. I let my desire to feel Love lead me.

And it began to shift. With a feeling of true fresh air, I could see and feel that the horrible feeling was losing its grip. The window had opened a crack and I breathed in a mouthful of actual hope. As I thought of Love, and felt it become a little more real to me, I also felt the darkness tune out a bit. Where two minutes earlier I had been entirely ensnared in its grasp, now I was partly free.

I'm familiar with this. It's like it's an arm-wrestling match.

So, I kept thinking of those strong, eternal, loving thoughts of God. I didn't try to do anything, or make any outcome. I just thought of Love, of eternity, of the times I have felt the big Yes. It was warm and healthy to take control of my thinking—to fill it with reverent and adoring thoughts of great goodness, instead of heavy, self-destructive ones. To draw up close to memories of true feelings of God's being, rather than all the reasons it isn't working.

Moment by listening moment, the windows opened further. A fresh breeze wafted in, beginning to fill the room, pushing out the rank, stale air. The fear couldn't maintain its grip when my thoughts were closed to it, and open to whatever goodness God would provide.

By the time I went to sleep I was cleaned out, humble, and hopeful. I was deeply comforted, not only that the fear had been driven out, but also to see that it was something I could initiate. Right in the midst of darkness, I could begin to refuse the darkness. I could follow the mental path of allowing better thoughts, believing them, giving in to them and accepting them, based on trust in the unseen Goodness.

I love times like this because, not only did it make me feel better that night, it will be yet another token of hope. I'll be that much more confident that the next time those cruel threats come. I can turn away from fear, loss, terror, and feel a little more of the sweet, humble saving light of Love.

NAVIGATING THE WILDERNESS

In the midst of the wilderness of life, it's often hard to see how it makes sense. A thousand things go wrong, our feelings get hurt, and we're tired of trying. All those things and more try to make us give up on the pure thing—doing right. If we let them, the endless arguments of the world will convince us that it's better to give up on simple goodness. We'll catch the contagion that says that life is too hard for doing right. It complains, "I'm too weak! No one else is doing it, so what's the point?" There are plenty of things trying to snuff it out in us.

****

After a couple years in Boston I'd had a few successes. I could take myself to the few murals I'd created around the city. My brushstrokes were on walls. It proved to me that it could be done.

Still, every day I awoke in my little apartment, silent—no leads. And every day I thought and prayed, longing to know how and what to do. I made my paintings in my sketchbook, pushing back against the persistent fear that it didn't matter. I did my work to the best of my ability, ever longing to progress.

Here's a very long story made short.

Somehow, I don't know how, I heard of a certain Father Waldron, a priest at a Catholic church way over in Dorchester, a place I'd never been. Whoever it was that passed his name on to me thought he might be amenable to creating a mural project in his neighborhood. I could barely imagine how it would work. I called him. He agreed to meet with me.

Some weeks later, in January 2003, I biked through the snow and slush, past the limit of my knowledge of the city of Boston, to his church. When I got there he didn't have any idea of how to start a mural project (why did I think he would?), but he did tell me about an organization he knew of down the street. His church had multiple services in many languages. One of them was a congregation of Cape Verdeans. This organization helped Cape Verdean immigrants.

I didn't know anything about Cape Verdeans, or immigration from a distant country, but he said he thought they might be interested in talking to me about murals. They were! The Cape Verdean Community Task Force was looking for a way to create positive associations with the Cape Verdean community, who, they felt, received disproportionately negative attention in local news. That summer, working with 25 Cape Verdean teens, I designed and oversaw the creation of a 152-foot mural about the experience of Cape Verdeans immigrating to Boston. (I learned from them that there are more Cape Verdeans living in Massachusetts and Rhode Island than there are in the nation of Cape Verde!)

I was overjoyed to have the job. I learned a thousand things. I had a new familiar feeling in a neighborhood that had been completely unknown to me. It was the largest mural I'd ever created. (It still is!)

Still, the calendar is long, and the days are endless. That three-week mural, as expansive as it was, ended. Would there be another one? How? In the back of my mind I was always searching, scanning the horizon.

Later that summer I received a phone call. It was the principal of Community Academy, an alternative school down the street from where we had painted the Cape Verde mural. He was looking for an art teacher and he'd seen my website written on the mural.

Soon I was in *way over my head,* teaching art classes a few hours a week. I'd worked with youth at the IVP, but classroom teaching is a whole different thing. And these kids were *rough.* Sometimes they simply walked out of the room and never came back. Other times they just laughed. In many classes the kids simply refused to do what I had prepared. Incredibly, in one such class, the school principal walked in and offered $50 to the student who did the best assignment. My mind boggled at how much we would be paying them by the Thanksgiving break. A jovial semi-pro football player hung around in the office and wandered the halls. His job was to break up the furious, violent fistfights that regularly flared up in the classrooms.

For me, being in that school was like being skinned alive. I didn't have the skills. I cared what people thought of me. I had no authority or control. At every step there was some mockery to reignite my shock and embarrassment.

All I had was my sanguine love of art, and a trembling desire to do a good job. As with most parts of my life at that point, I simply plowed ahead, enduring the pain, trying to keep my head above water. At ground level I was simply grateful to be working, less terrified than I had been the year before.

Then, a month or so into the second semester, the principal called me into his office. It had been hard to understand this guy all year. In a surprise move, he unceremoniously told me they could no longer pay my salary. Then, shockingly, he invited me to continue teaching without pay. He also offhandedly mentioned that if I wanted to, I could try to find a grant to pay my salary for the rest of the year. I couldn't have been more insulted and furious if he had reached back and slapped me across the face. I was so angry I could hardly see straight. It was clear to me that he wanted me out of the school. I didn't know why. (Maybe because I was a random, un-trained teacher he contacted through a website he found on a wall?)

Necessity got the better of me and I swallowed my rage. It was strangely unacceptable to me to give up. I couldn't do it. But I had no idea how to find grants, or really, what that even meant. Through what felt like the punches of a prize fighter, I found a library that had a listing of grants available for arts education. It was so unfamiliar I was dizzy. I thought I would pass out under the weight. The voice inside me screamed, "You're a fool! You're an idiot! You're can't write a grant! You don't even want to!" Somehow, under the anvil of that fear I found what I hoped was the right paper to fill out. I wrote out the situation as well as I could and sent it off to the address in the listing. It felt dead, totally without life and reason. It was clear that a fool like me would never succeed at writing a grant. What did I know about paperwork? Grants went to other people.

During the four years I had been praying about depression I came to see with different eyes. With great effort I weaned myself from judging my life by how I felt or by my circumstances. I learned to look to God, and the invisible certainty of His love, to tell me about myself. After all that practice I was no longer able to complain about uncomfortable or scary things. I simply worked. I didn't like suffering, but I knew—in fact, by this time, I felt in my bones— that there was no use in feeling sorry for myself. So, there was nothing left but to remember the invisible love of God, and keep working.

Imagine my surprise when a short time later I received a check in the mail, paying my small salary for the rest of the year. I was surprised, but the principal was shocked. It was clear he thought he'd seen the last of me.

I finished out the year at Community Academy. As the months went on, the kids who wanted to learn about art stayed in my class. The others left. So by the end, there were only a handful of us left and we were having an ok time.

In those last few months of the school year I tried, with all my deer-in-headlights might, to be part of the teachers' community. I became friendly with the math teacher. Mr. Carlos Pinzon. He was a hulking man with a friendly disposition and sunny Panamanian accent. Outside the school he was starting a Tae Kwon Do dojo for kids. One day he said to me in passing, "You're the art teacher right? Can you draw a dragon?" I said I could. I was happy to draw a dragon for him to use as the logo for his dojo.

During this time, outside of the teaching job, I'd been working on presenting myself as a freelance artist. Through much prayer and striving I'd coached myself to ask for what felt like the astronomical sum of $40 an hour. It was more than I was used to making—by a lot. It seemed like I might as well be asking for $500 an hour. But I wanted so badly to grow! It seemed preposterous to me that anyone would pay $40/hour for anything, let alone for my hopeful, dewy-eyed pictures. I was so afraid others would think it was as ridiculous as I did I could hardly get the number out of my mouth.

Towards the end of the school year Carlos let me know that his wife, an administrator at the Dimock Center, a local social services organization, was looking for an art teacher for their upcoming summer program. A week later I was sitting in her office interviewing for the job. I was disappointed when I learned that it was only four hours a week, June to August. I was so tired of these rinky dink jobs! A few hours here and a few hours there, trying to scrape together enough money each month to live on. It was barely enough to pay the rent, and only a slight distraction from the gnawing fear that my art career was going nowhere. I hardly cared if I got the job or not.

So, when she asked me for my hourly rate I blithely said $40/hour as if it were the most normal thing in the world to me. I didn't care if I priced myself out. I assumed I would. A week later, and much to my surprise, I got the job, if I could accept $30/hour. $30 was still far more than I was used to and I accepted.

I worked the summer and the people were nice. When the summer ended, they were planning for the coming school year. They asked if I would stay on. But for the school year the job was four hours a day, five days a week! I couldn't believe it.

The job brought a kind of security I had never known since leaving home. $30 an hour, 20 hours a week?! It was a kind of luxury I'd never dreamed of. The job was from 2-6 in the afternoons. It was a 5-minute bike ride from my home. I could work on mural stuff in the mornings. And it was all in the same place! I couldn't believe my good fortune.

It was another teaching job, and I still knew virtually nothing about teaching. But these kids were little. Like, 6-12 years old. I soon found that I loved them! Until this point, all the teaching jobs I'd had had been with teens, and mostly teens who were in deep trouble. All the kids I'd ever worked with were either getting out of jail or had just been thrown out of school. The kids at this program were little, often friendly(!), and I could connect with them. They liked to play. They were a wonderful breath of fresh air.

From my previous jobs working with teens, I'd come to think that I didn't like youth work. I had poured myself into it because I wanted to do my job well and had no other tool than to try to love these kids. And teaching jobs were the jobs that were coming. But every step had been a struggle. In my new position, I found that with a few small adjustments inside myself, I was right at home. We got along great, and never once did we think of offering them $50 to do what they were supposed to do.

I worked at this job for four years and it became a kind of home for me. At one point I said to myself, "Some of my best friends are nine years old!" and it was absolutely true. I was able to catch my breath financially while continuing to work on mural projects. I learned that I loved working with kids. I was good at it and didn't need to fear them.

Our mundane personal lives are often wilderness. We are lost and off-balance. We wonder which path to take. I thank God for the spiritual North Star that shines on, declaring with its light, "Only keep doing right! Only keep up your effort and your hope! Because God is real, there is good and you can do it and be it!" As I made my way, slowly but adoringly towards that North Star, my mundane personal life was lifted up. I made progress in my work. I made incrementally more money. I grew in confidence. With attention on what could be, instead of on the suffering of the moment, my hope held its ground. I found new wildernesses that it was my job to explore and grow through. The star never waned or moved. It has ever been a living, pulsing certainty that Love is real and can be lived. There may be loss and fear and suffering, but Love can be lived in the midst of it. It may look like a beautiful mural, but just as easily it may look like stumbling to the library against all odds to ignorantly write a grant to finish the year's teaching. Or it may be the courage to resist the devil's voice and ask for a higher wage. It also may be the bike ride through snow and slush to another wilderness meeting with a stranger, in a place beyond the small known world. God's love feeds every push of rebellion against limitation and fear. It leads out of the wilderness and turns it into a garden.

CREATING ABC

During the last couple months of the school year at Community Academy I had some students who could really draw. One boy in particular. Alberto, like all the other students in the school, had exhausted every academic option in Boston Public Schools. He'd been expelled again and again and had landed here, at the end of the line. But man, he could draw. He was 19 years old, about to age out of school. He knew he was good at art. "Do you want to learn more?" I asked. "Yeah," he replied, sort of shrugging. He told me about his difficult family situation, that there was no money coming in. No one he knew cared about art or had any interest in supporting it in him. My heart strained at the idea of someone being so talented, but finding no way, no reason, to pursue it.

Summer was coming up and I didn't have anything planned. I needed work, not just for money, but also just to do something—to pursue my own life. Between the desire to fill my own days and my small awareness of the needs of these teens, a few ideas began to coalesce. Alberto, and one other of my students, Caitlin, were *artists*. But they had no idea how to do it. They could barely get their homework done let alone work independently to develop their art skills. I saw their eyes glaze over in virtually all their other classes, but when it came to drawing, they lit up. They were capable. I even saw some of the beginnings of real enthusiasm. I witnessed their skill, but they hardly did. There were no voices in their lives telling them art was valuable.

I thought, simply, "I could show them how to paint a mural." I asked Alberto and Caitlin if they would be interested in spending the summer learning how to paint murals. Yes, they said, and both indicated that they had to have paying jobs over the summer and wouldn't be able to do it otherwise.

The gears were turning. Could I pay them? How? Where would we paint? And with those questions, a thousand more. I was interested. Maybe I could do it. My learning muscles liked the feeling of flexing. It was much better than the prospect of the endless months of summer, churning to find mural jobs, driving myself crazy. After only a little hesitation I said yes inside myself. I was going to do it.

I have a degree in fine art. I'm well educated in painting pictures, thinking about art, and expressing ideas. I was not *at all* educated in organizational management, teaching, fundraising, community organization, finance, or youth work. So, I jumped in with both feet.

The summer was coming fast. I decided the program would hire five teens based on artistic ability and financial need. It would be six weeks long. I would pay them $7 an hour. By the end of June we would need three walls to paint on, and enough money to pay for the whole thing. If there was anything left at the end, I might get paid too. It would be called ABC—Art Builds Community. I made a list of all the things I needed and set myself to finding them.

I needed students. I wrote to all the high schools in Boston and let them know I would be interviewing teens for the program. I needed walls. I kept my eyes open as I drove, biked, and walked through my life in the neighborhoods of Boston. Whenever I saw one that seemed like it could use a mural, I talked to folks in the building, called the owners, and made my pitch. I needed money. I laid out my plan and sent it off to everyone I knew asking for donations—people at church, my ultimate frisbee team, old friends, the art community, people I knew around the neighborhood. I let them in on my vision of providing real-life art training and paid experience to young artists growing into their understanding of their skills. I shared my desire that the project would give opportunities to young people who struggled to find them elsewhere. I told them about my students and their skill despite their academic inabilities. Most of all I laid out my heart—that I wanted to impart my hard-earned skill to young artists who might find themselves in this work, and the glory of putting beauty into public spaces. I walked up and down Centre Street, the main thoroughfare in my neighborhood, and spoke to the owners of every business that would see me. I had lots of opportunities to hone my ability to express my vision.

Up to that point in my experience, the greatest opposition to creating something new came in the inner voices that demeaned and mocked, doing their best to stop the project before it started. But I'd been resisting those voices for years now. I was used to it. In fact, it was basically part of my daily routine. Pushing through them, the creation happens. Beauty is revealed.

My special terror this time around was that I would be able to assemble some of the necessary parts, but not all. I would find students and money, but no walls to paint on. I would find money and walls, but no students. Or I would find students and walls, but no money. If any of those things happened it would all come to a terrible, embarrassing halt. This concern hung over me like a storm cloud. Pushing through it, I worked.

Except for painting the murals, virtually every element of creating the project required skills that were new to me. On almost every side I worked to overcome my ignorance. I strove to understand how to think about money, organization, and leadership. As always I plowed ahead, pouring in hope and effort. And, one day, deep into the work, an idea bloomed in me with a warm light. It said, "Do every aspect of this as if it were your art." Gratefully, I drank it in. I didn't fight it, though I was amazed that I didn't. I agreed. I will seek out walls as if those conversations were my paintings. I will seek funding and write grants with the same sincerity and expectation of beauty with which I paint in my sketchbook. I will allow that this whole process can be done by the combination of intuition and reason with which I run my artistic life. And at the very bottom, I will let myself feel at home in this work because I will do it by bringing love to every aspect of it. I will disregard my fear of business by bringing love to it. Love can be at every meeting, inform every decision, support every conversation.

The hundreds of emails and brochures I sent, the research into mural locations, the outreach for possible students—throwing all that energy into the world—set the project in motion. It was out there. People were reading about it, seeing it, considering my proposals. Donations began to trickle in. People handed me checks for $20. $50. Sometimes $100! Perhaps more amazingly, I began to receive phone calls from the parents of high school students asking about the project. Strangers, calling me to find out how their child could apply. I boggled that this idea, which began out of embarrassingly humble circumstances, was now attracting attention.

At the same time, I began to get yesses from building owners. Walls to paint on! First one, then a second, then the third. The stones were falling into place! Each one landed with a powerful boom, building the structure of the project, gushing with relief. I could see the parts coming into view.

As I thought beyond necessities and logistics, one thing was clear—this project was about art and artists, not money. Yes, I was paying them. It was a good and necessary element. But we were there to make art and to develop the vision, skills, and passion of artists. To that end, a new understanding revealed itself. I was the boss. I needed to embrace it and live into it. I was the one with the passion. I had the skills and the discipline. I felt a fiery desire that this would not be a time for screwing around. It would be focused, serious, and demanding. I'd seen so many teachers and programs get pushed around by the youth they were supposed to serve. But my love of beauty, the glory that's possible in painting a mural, wouldn't let me be pushed around. If we could find the students, the walls, and the money, we would make real beauty.

As the time drew nearer I interviewed prospective students. I didn't have an office so we met at a local ice cream shop to have our conversations. Meeting with these young artists was like seeing wildlife in the forest. They came out of the wilderness of the city to meet with me. Who knew what they would say? I'd been clear in the program information that this opportunity was only for teens who already considered themselves artists. I asked them about their art, how they saw it, and what they were interested in. I asked to see sketchbooks, journals, and drawings that grew out of their own interests and artistic visions.

Growing up an artist, with the mind and inclinations of an artist, business felt foreign. Beyond a few negotiations for mural projects I had virtually no insight into business norms and procedures. With this ignorance firmly in place, my sense was that it was made only of numbers, margins, and mindless, soulless bodies in gray suits. I just had no idea. So, when businesses began to give dollars towards my idealistic youth art project, I was surprised. In fact, it opened a new reality of the world to me. I pounded the pavement, asking to the see the manager or the owner of various businesses. Some were small, locally owned stores, others were larger companies, magazines, insurance companies. I was meeting my neighbors. They'd been invisible to me, hidden behind a cloud of ignorance. I found that some simply gave because they thought it was a good idea and they loved the community. Others gave, and generously, in return for the promise of a "thank you" to their company, written into the mural. I'd not known I could have a conversation with a business. In fact, I'd truly not understood that businesses were made of people. People who love kids, who have concerns, who want to contribute.

The budget was coming into view. We were going to make it. And equally amazingly, I now knew the owners of businesses all through my neighborhood. I could hardly walk down the street without running into someone I'd spoken to recently. I kept thinking to myself, "You can just talk to people! You can just ask. You can put it out there and see what people think." How easy it had been for the "no" voice to just run on repeat: "They won't give you any money. They're just businesses. They don't care about anything but the bottom line." It was just a lie—a lie I couldn't refute because I didn't know the truth. But exploration and an open heart cause the scales to fall from our eyes. And in their place, I found that I lived in a community that contained good, interested people. People you could talk to and reason with. People who, some of them, would say yes.

And then, all the parts were in place. Out of about 20 applicants from around the city, I chose five. The first was Caitlin, from Community Academy. I had been planning on having her in the program all along. When it was time to commit, her Community Academy counterpart, Alberto, was nowhere to be found. I drank in the cosmic lesson that, while he was the original reason I had the idea in the first place, he didn't need to be in the program for it to be a right,

good, useful idea. The other students I chose were Anthony, Lucy, Nancy, and Johnathan. The funds were there, enough, at least, that I wouldn't *lose* money on the program. And we had three beautiful, public locations to paint over the next six weeks. All that remained was to do it.

The night before our first day, I lay in bed trembling. *I* was going to be in charge. Everything rested on me, my skills, my ability, my decision making. I was about as exposed as I'd ever been.

Within the first week there were important decisions to make. The first-day jitters came and went and soon we were humming along. The kids were getting along pretty well. It was glorious to see them naturally relating to one another, becoming friends, joking around. Our first mural was a colorful forest scene with a city in the distance. A few days in we were beginning to color in the trees. We had painstakingly drawn them out from a sketch I'd created. Because I had chosen them based on their artistic skill and desire, I spoke to them as artists. I depended on them being able to follow me into the world of feeling, imagination, beauty. So, describing the way to paint our forest I said, "You have to imagine yourself in the forest. Think back to the last time you were there. Feel what it feels like to be there. Drink in that feeling and let it tell you what colors to use." I wanted them to base their work on feeling more than technique.

But in response to this instruction, Anthony asked, "What if you've never been to a forest?" I assumed he was joking. "What do you mean?" I boggled. He wasn't joking. He explained to me that in his whole life living in the city of Boston he'd never been to a forest. He didn't have any way of thinking back or imagining what it felt like. In a moment I understood that there was no way he could do what I'd asked him to do. Our mural was a forest. How could he know how to paint it?

The next day we all piled into my little Mazda 323 hatchback and drove the 20 minutes to the Blue Hills Reservation. We spent the morning hiking over hills and rocks among the trees. They brought their notebooks and I asked questions to draw their attention to the things they would need as we moved ahead with the paint-

ing. "What do you notice about the shadows? What does the sky look like through the branches of the trees? How does the sunlight feel, filtering through the leaves?" Though Anthony was the one who revealed that he had never been to a forest, it was clear that for many of

them nature was a distant, unexplored concept. The whole thing revealed to me that what seems most basic to one, may be entirely outside the experience of another. A trip to the forest had to be part of the process of creating this mural. We were improvising at every step.

Over the years I had seen the work of several youth or community mural projects. When I compared it to the murals I loved, I didn't like them. I mean, I admired their work with youth, but the truth was, I didn't think the art was good. From the first inklings of ABC, I'd committed to striving for both a robust experience for the participants *and* for actual beauty. It was a model I didn't see elsewhere. In the programs I saw it was one or the other. I needed both.

As the first mural went on, a dire conflict arose in me. As I directed the students, delegated jobs, and did my best to keep the work moving forward, *all I wanted was to be doing the painting myself.* I stood on the curb, across the street behind kids, watching them work. With their every stroke of the brush I felt painful pangs as if I were being beaten with a stick. Their brush strokes were so clumsy! Their choices so elementary! The wall—our precious wall - was getting covered with their clumsy, elementary efforts. I reeled. I could see the whole mural in my mind's eye, finished, the way I would do it. Why couldn't I just do it myself? And then another pang—this time guilt and regret—why would I think that?! Why am I *such* a jerk? Of course they're clumsy! Of course their approach is elementary! This is their first time painting a mural! Why would I think such mean, unreasonable things? And yet, the selfish, controlling impulse surged in me like waves of the sea. If only they would just go home and let me paint the mural myself!

I was a mess. While the team worked, I stood behind them, silently tied up in knots. Inwardly I was being drawn and quartered, pulled in opposite, irreconcilable directions. I'd poured in hundreds of hours of labor, battled fear and stepped out of my comfort zone in countless ways to make this project happen. I'd laid myself out there like never before and received donations from people all over Boston and beyond. I was beholden to them, to the students, and to my own efforts. And yet, despite it all, and despite my own desires, my passion to make beauty fought against it. I wanted to do the painting my way!

Somewhere in one of those long mornings it became too painful. "What do I do?!" I cried out inside myself. And quickly, under the force of that honest question, I knew the answer. I reasoned—I must do one of two things: Either I send the students home, return all the donations, and paint the mural myself, or I accept that right now I am not a painter—I am a teacher. Of course, the answer was obvious. It was painful and difficult, but it was obvious.

The course of the events that had led to the creation of the project had assumed it. Here, I am a teacher, not a painter. My prayers and listening had brought ideas and inspirations of how to proceed. I had embraced it from the

beginning and labored for it. And all that labor and prayer had made it a reality. The final piece, I found, was to accept it myself—to submit absolutely to the necessities of the way as it unfolded. So I began. Like scaling a mountain, there was nothing complicated about it—just one step after another. But it was arduous and exacting. At each step over those days and weeks I reminded myself of my role. I said it over and over to myself, "Alex, right now you are a teacher, not a painter." I knew it was the truth and I worked to let it be true to me. In the next moment, I'd be engulfed in a burning longing to send the kids home and make the mural myself. Their beginner's hands, the simple colors and inexperienced work struck at my heart. An opportunity to make true beauty on a public wall was slipping through my fingers!

As soon as I could gain perspective again I would remind myself, "Alex, right now you are a teacher, not a painter!" And each time, as soon as I could accept it, just a little, it calmed the burning and reminded me that I was part of something bigger than myself. It began to dawn on me that while this mural would not turn out the way it would if I were painting it alone, I was still laboring towards a work of beauty. It was beauty larger than a picture on a wall. This time it was a beauty that included other human lives. Once again, it was God's hand growing me, growing us all, making our lives bigger and more beautiful.

Though it was painful, I loved to find the guidance of God, directing me through simple reason. I could see, almost as plainly as a road before me, the things I needed to do, and the ways I needed to think. How firm was the hand that revealed to me that right now I must be a teacher and not a painter. How firm was that hand that directed me to loosen my grip on my most beloved object—an opportunity to make a mural as beautiful as it could be. And in letting go, I could witness a larger beauty and an expansion of my own ability to participate in beauty. How firm that wonderful hand that enabled me to let go of an idea of myself too small for what was to come—even when that idea of myself was the most beloved thing I knew.

While I strove painstakingly inside myself, the outward labor continued. The first mural filled in like leaves in spring. The teaching happened. I didn't jump in and do it all myself. (Thank goodness) Instead, with great discipline, I waited and watched for moments to impart useful information, encouragement, and recognition of things well done. I took them when they came and held my tongue a thousand times. And then, the first mural was finished. In addition to signing our names, we each signed the mural with a bird of our own creating set among the trees.

We stood back from our creation and felt proud. The students had done well. In just a couple weeks they had grown, learned new skills, and used them. The mural was strong. Because its underlying organization was mine, it felt structured like one of my pictures. But within that, I could see many details and choices that expressed the hands and hearts of the team. Anthony had painted the whole sky, learning to blend colors as the sunset darkened into night. Caitlin had brought in a picture of her cat and adoringly painted him perched on a boulder. One had only to look at the boulders to see where we had studied shading to create a three-dimensional feeling. Or the tree trunks to see the lesson on contrast causing elements to jump into the foreground. Or the mountains and fields to see where they had learned that more neutral colors recede in the distance. And while the students were learning those things, I was learning to see the students gently, helpfully, and embrace my new role. The whole thing felt full of life, reflecting the team and each of our individual efforts.

We moved on to the second wall. I continued my mantra firmly: "Alex, right now, you are a teacher not a painter." By degrees I came to know it and feel it. The pangs were less frequent. Feelings of joy at the students' humble successes came more often. Like a heavy-laden freight

train, the team gained momentum. The program found its rhythm and the work continued.

One morning Anthony brought in his sketchbook to show me. Touched, I pored through it, taking in his images. With each page I drank in what it offered—a view into the life of this young, creative man. Standing there with his book in my hand, he watched me reacting, taking it in. I could relate to his book. In many ways it was similar to one that I kept when I was his age. It was his book of drawings, yes, but more, it was his book of exploring, pondering, all his young efforts to figure out the puzzle of existence. How I loved him as I caught glimpses that while his life was so unlike mine, he was a thinker, creative, a dreamer, an idealist, like me.

Page after page, among the drawings there were musings and lines of poetry. Little phrases of insight and self-expression wove in and out of the pen-drawn images. Next to one such drawing, scrawled in his dark, messy hand was a line that stopped me. It read, "When you learn to see without your eyes you'll see something more potent, more true, you'll see you." The words were his, but it was a sentiment that I would assert. I took it as a simple statement of his felt spiritual vision. From the wilderness of the city, this young man had emerged into my experience. And this young man, independent and honest, was having his experiences of reality. He'd felt that there is vision beyond the senses that reveals deeper, stronger truths. It was just what my life had told me, and the thing that I fought for every day.

I'd been looking for ways to bring the students more deeply into the creation process. I wanted them to feel their own investment in the images, more than just applying the paint on the wall. In a moment I knew we would use this line in our next mural. I wanted the community to consider this young man's assertion, his discovery. If he'd felt it, others had too. Our work could support this important idea in the lives of the thousands of people who would see the mural. I asked Anthony. He was surprised but willing. His words would be on the wall.

Beginning with Anthony's words, as a group we imagined visual ideas that would illustrate this statement of mental freedom and spiritual vision. We arrived at an image of a woman, lying on her back on the skyline of a city. She is at peace, perhaps asleep in this very public, larger than life situation. While she dreams, a forceful flock of birds flows out of her head, soaring into the sky above her. When the image was finished I printed the line across the bottom like a caption. I treasured the chance to put these idealistic words into a public space, so much more often dominated by commercial concerns. I hoped Anthony felt proud.

When this mural was finished, we had done a new thing. Where the first had been an exploration of techniques, this one expressed an idea. It sang with an airy idealism. It was an image you might find in one of my sketchbooks, but it was a different beast having been made by six sets of hands. The symbolism and imagery were mostly mine, but the teens had made it their own. Lucy painted every one of the birds with a colorful curling pattern. Caitlin gave the woman a pair of bright green slippers. The buildings had a wobbly character that I would never have arrived at myself. Some years later I rejoiced when this mural was voted "Best in Jamaica Plain" by readers of the local newspaper.

Finally, for the third mural, we worked with youth from the Cape Verdean Community Task Force, the ABC kids serving as team leaders. A broad arc of skills and roles from week one to week six. Over that time I did my fumbling best to provide enough structure to keep everyone knowing what to do, while making ample room for the kids to go with their own ideas when they had good ones. Every moment of it was a navigation and I slept very well each night.

By the end of the summer I was a different artist than I had been. Never had I been so aware of the community. They weren't just recipients of the art. They were supporters of the work. They were part of the conversation. I knew their names and they knew mine. I could no longer think of the community as a faceless public who I hoped would benefit from my murals. In the last weeks

When you learn to see without your eyes you will see something more potent, more true—you'll see you.

of the program I had largely mastered the desire to do the painting myself. The pangs had fallen away, replaced by a healthy appreciation that, for now, the program itself was my work of art. I rejoiced with each successful payroll cycle. The students' victories grew in my vision while the longing to be the painter decreased. And in the final mural I watched with gratitude as the ABC students used newfound confidence as they took on leadership roles among less experienced teens.

I continued as director of ABC for the next couple of years. ABC continued as a program under other capable leadership until 2009—a five-year run. It was my first taste of many things that were to come: fundraising, community collaborations, and facilitating groups rather than working on my own. It was my first great leap into the whole array of non-art skills and tasks that are a necessary part of being a working artist.

THERE ARE NO BODIES BETWEEN US

I was about as far away from my home as I had ever been. My mom and I were visiting her brother in Brazil. He'd recently married a Brazilian woman and moved to Goiania, a huge city I'd never heard of. We would ring in 2005 with his (our?) new extended family. Having never been there, and speaking little to no Portuguese, I was in a mode of mental athleticism. On the flight to Sao Paolo I prayed about the trip and my approach to it. I received a beautiful conviction that I could turn entirely away from fear and feel confident about my God-given ability to learn, grow, and excel. A really clear assertion. Basically, God said, "Don't spend another second worrying about it." For the duration of my time in Brazil, I felt a joyful motivation, and affluent ability to communicate and connect (in a ton of ways, many of which were not even about spoken language).

Towards the end of our trip our hosts took us to a water park. This was not my first choice of how to spend my day and, once there, I began to pray about the purpose of our time there. I humbly went to God, knowing that His grace was there, and despite the fact that I didn't particularly feel like spending a whole day (one of my few in Brazil) doing something I could very easily do at home, I knew that God's purpose of good was there. Soon I began to notice all the wonderful relationships that were happening around me. Parents were caring for children. Friends and family were laughing and playing together. I gently realized that it was a beautiful scene of humanity.

Another thing I noticed was that the swimsuits people were wearing were unbelievably small. I mean, these bikinis were all strings, almost no cloth at all, and they were everywhere. Needless to say, there were body parts going every which way.

I was about 30 years old at the time and I was deeply engaged in the healthy work of trying to do right by God. In years past I'd had my heart torn up and broken in my romantic and sexual relationships. At the age of 23 I'd breathed a sigh of relief as I let go of the societal pressure to have sex, but that was only a first step. What remained was the very real longing for connection and relation, not to mention my own desires. Each relationship required navigating these intimate details—communication and experimentation. I continued to have my interactions, trying to balance it all while feeling loneliness, nervousness, and a bright, ebullient hope of meeting someone wonderful. Over those seven years I had a handful of relationships, each marked by sincere affection and goodwill, but hobbled by various emotional weaknesses and sensitivities. And through it all, naturally, I labored to navigate sexual encounters in way that would care for each of us. I was so tired of being led by the nose, this way and that, by the tingling temptation of sexuality. These days I was earnestly trying to do it right, to keep myself, and everyone else involved, safe. This meant that

I was trying to see myself, the women I was dating, and everyone, as spiritual creations, loved by God. I was trying with a sincere heart to be less selfish, more generous, more spiritual and moral. Though my thoughts were often scattered, my heart was fixed—I wanted to see and feel the safety and love of God in my relationships.

At this water park I was surrounded by bikini models. And, it seemed to me, when these ladies weren't at the water park, they must have been spending plenty of time at the gym. It was distracting to say the least. I felt like the park was even intended to be a showcase for bodies, almost opposite from my intention to see spiritually. Among many of the people, the showcasing was unmistakably sexualized. I felt confronted by the intention to be seen sexually. It was far too easy to be drawn into gazing, dreaming, imagining. Instantly my feelings would not be my own. They would be headlong, beyond my control, stumbling in the very direction I longed not to go. I realized, with an empowering clarity, that if I was going to have any kind of a peaceful day I was going to have to work hard to let God fill my thoughts.

With a feeling of relief I made prayer the activity of the day. Though it looked like I was swimming, going down the waterslides, playing cards and chatting, I was praying. Everything else was peripheral. Prayer was central. I thought about God being the source of our identities, each and every one of us. I thought of God, loving these women and men, loving me, making us for useful, healthy purposes. I felt love for us. As I did, a single statement crystallized in my thought. "There are no bodies between us." I knew that God made each one of us, pure, innocent, and spiritual—not material—not a spiritual being with a material body. I thought of true Beauty, the holy perfectness that comes from being God's creation. I knew that no one is really beautiful or attractive based on their measurements. That whole notion was the way to misery and distraction, spinning our wheels, getting nowhere. We, the children of God, are created to connect with one another, to relate and express the danger-less joy of God. But no physical body is needed or included in the holy mandate that we have wonderful, connected relationships. "There are no bodies between us" became my mantra for the day. It played through my thoughts, leaping into action each time lust made its aggressive move to haul me away.

The day continued brightly, hopefully, as I worked. I could feel an increased clarity and cleanness in my vision. I was peaceful, yet mentally active, standing on the rock.

Towards the end of the day, many of our party were relaxing around a picnic table under a huge shade tree. Warm sun filtered through its dusty leaves. I noticed a couple of bees crawl into a soda can sitting on the table in front of me. I thought little of it and continued in the game I was playing with the others. About 20 minutes later I happened to take a look in the can and saw them both floating in the half-finished soda. Their thin wings were stuck to their bodies. They didn't move.

I was glad to accept another chance to pray. Having spent these many hours in active, agile prayer, the death of these bees was too unlike God to accept. I silently subtracted myself from the game and began to concentrate on the bees. I thought of an account I had recently read in which Mary Baker Eddy, a Christian healer and founder of Christian Science, was called to heal a young boy. She told the mother of the boy to leave them alone in the room and not to return for one hour. This spoke to me. It said that she, a towering healer and spiritual hero to me, gave herself time to work. I felt comforted that I too could give myself time.

I closed my eyes and began to know for the bees just what I had been knowing for the humans all day—their being is spiritual, derived, not from biology, but from God. As I prayed, I began to realize that these two bees are as important to creation as anyone or anything else. God included them in reality on purpose. That meant to me that they are eternal, perfect, shining ideas of Holiness. They could not possibly be subtracted from creation. They could not ever lose their life.

I made a deal with myself. I agreed that if I opened my eyes and saw that the bees had not moved, I would not be discouraged. I would not take it as any evidence that could contradict the truth of my heartfelt prayer.

I opened my eyes and looked at the bees. (I had poured them out on to a napkin.) They lay there motionless. I kept my deal with myself and simply went back to work, adoring the bees as created by Love. Eyes closed I returned to the ideas I'd been loving. The bees were as important as me, as the nation of France, as the Himalayas, as anything you can think of. God had included them in creation because He thought it was a good idea. I found that I really loved these bees. I knew that God adored them, and it felt natural that I would too. I began to feel enormously proud of the bees. The feeling swelled in me as if they were my very own son or daughter scoring a goal in the soccer game. I rejoiced in their little, adorable selves.

When my prayers felt complete, I opened my eyes again and found that one of the two bees was standing up on his legs, cleaning himself. The other was still stickily wrapped in his own wings, but moving slightly. I felt very clearly that it was not bodies that had changed. It was thought. Love and Life had been recognized as ever-present and I could feel its lively presence surrounding the two bees. Filled with joy, I returned to my prayers, knowing that nothing could stop these two wonders from having life. I felt so proud of them, so overjoyed at their intimate connection to God.

When I looked at them again they were both up and cleaning themselves. Soon they flew away.

I was deeply humbled, and felt very loved, to be privy to the spectacle of Love. I saw how dedicating my day to prayer had paid off for all three of us.

THE GREEN STREET SCULPTURES

I acclimated to my new home, living with my three male, non-artist house-mates. I hadn't watched sports since I was a kid, but in this new scenario, it was a way to connect with them and be a part of the gang. (And it was a good time to do it—this was around 2004. The Red Sox were about to win their first World Series in 86 years, and the New England Patriots were just beginning their Brady/Belichick dynasty) I found I had the language to connect with these guys, even though they weren't the type I was used to hanging out with. Just required a bit of adjusting.

One spring evening, arriving home from work, I found one of my room-mates, Matt, in the backyard playing catch with one of the neighborhood kids. They had their baseball gloves on—throwing the ball back and forth in the asphalt backyard. Tall, white, shy Matt in a gentle back and forth with rail-thin, brown-skinned, spark-eyed Jose. The boy was wearing his uniform in prepara-tion for a Little League game later in the evening. It was a beautiful moment. I began to understand that there was more going on in my apartment and in my neighborhood than I knew.

Our neighborhood was dumpy. The buildings were old, owned by absentee landlords. Graffiti sprawled messily over the building's vinyl siding. The back yard was an undulating rectangle of cracked black asphalt. Tree roots made their way under it, pushing it around like black hills. Wire fences hemmed it on two sides. As May pushed into June, the jungle that Boston would be if there were no asphalt at all, gorged mightily through the cracks, splitting them further.

Until I saw them playing catch back there, I'd never thought of spending any time in that yard. It was just the route to take the trash out to the dumpster. It was an ugly space.

As the weather got warmer, we left our back door open most evenings and weekends. More and more, kids from the neighborhood climbed the iron stairs of the fire escape, knocking on our door to see if we wanted to play. We would often hang around in the yard, under the newly sprouting leaves, play-ing with the kids—throwing balls, answering questions, and listening to their schemes. They were between 5 and 13, and lived in the buildings surrounding the cracked lot behind our building. They spoke English and Spanish.

Watching them, I remembered my own childhood. They tore around the neighborhood, over fences and down alleys, engaged in invisible after-school adventures. They jumped around in the dumpster in the alley, scouting for building materials. One of them, Raivel, had found an old bike in the dump-ster. He'd pulled it out, spray-painted it gold, and rode around the neighbor-hood as if he were the king. They knew the neighborhood inside out, slipping through kid-sized holes in fences.

Soon we were all pals. A few of the more confident ones began to simply knock and then join us in the house. We would play video games or watch the Red Sox. We had tentative, stumbling conversations.

One sunny weekday morning I stood on the landing of the fire escape looking out over the decaying back yard. The warm spring air made me want to be outside. Gazing over the surface of the asphalt, I noticed several really big cracks cutting across it. In a flash I had a thought totally unlike myself. I would rip up the asphalt where I could, and plant a garden in the earth underneath.

I had never in my life thought about creating a garden. I'd never had any interest. Honestly, the many times friends of mine had professed their own love of gardening, I found my eyes glazing over. I'd never understood. Well, now I did. Something about that cracked asphalt was like an invitation.

I bought myself a shovel and $50 worth of impatiens, the cheapest flowers I could find at Home Depot. For the next weeks I spent many hours with that shovel, prying up the asphalt where it would come. I threw the chunks in the nearby dumpster. Jamming the end of the shovel into the biggest crack, I pulled back, and great slabs of the asphalt broke off like bark from a dead tree. Repeating this I made my way around the yard, pulling and prying where I could. After some time I had broken up all the places that would come. Three large, organic shapes revealed themselves in the asphalt. Their borders were shaped entirely by the way the cracks had cracked. I just broke it up until I couldn't anymore.

Next, I pulled out hundreds of stones from the earth these holes revealed. They piled up impressively at the side. Finally, I planted my impatiens.

During this time, on trash days, I too would walk around the neighborhood, looking for things to build with. I'd been getting excited about found-object sculpture—I needed to find some objects. There were always piles of old furniture and other surprising things among the bags of garbage. After some weeks

of doing this, I had a growing pile of items in a corner of the back yard. I'd amassed all kinds of wood, broken chairs, tennis rackets, a ripped kite, and various pieces of metal and piping. The pile trembled in anticipation of what it was to become.

One day as we were playing with the backyard kids, Jose, the leader, asked me about the pile. Pretty soon I was showing them how you could make something out of junk. I brought out my saws and my paints and brushes. The group of kids grew as I explained it. I showed how you could make an animal out of the arms of a chair and some discarded wood. They were amazed.

Later that week they came back en masse and like the most natural thing in the world, we made a sculpture together. I helped them cut the boards, nail them together, and decorate it. In an afternoon we made what we called the Green Street Phoenix. They felt proud of the sculpture, and I felt proud that it had happened. It was so alive, so surprising, this collaboration with neighborhood kids. To me it felt like something that would happen to someone else—someone much cooler than myself. I thought, we have to show this off.

I constructed a little stand for it. We walked ourselves across the street to a fence around a vacant lot. Within minutes, the Green Street Phoenix was fastened with wire to one of the uprights. We took pictures and celebrated.

After that they were around all the time. There was plenty of ball playing too, but now there was an equal amount of art-making. They knocked on the back door asking for paints and brushes, smocks, and something to paint on. Pretty soon we had a mini after-school program happening on the iron rungs of the fire escape.

I was grateful for this evening respite from my very solitary workdays. At the time, I was cobbling together a living teaching art at a few different schools and every once in a while, a mural commission. I spent the majority of my time at my desk in my room, trying to get mural work, or laboring over my own pictures. I spent a lot of time alone.

After a long winter, fighting it out along these lines, pushing against resistance and breathing in great gulps of freedom and joy when they came, I needed something new. I was lonely. Making art was too solitary. I had to get out.

I thought of the kids. The Green Street Phoenix. It had just...happened. By some magical force we'd been brought together, and the outcome was a simple, but somehow glorious and embracing, collaboration. We *played* together. I needed more of whatever that was. How could I bring more of it into my life? How could I be less lonely, but still spend my time making art?

I listened. And, quickly, an idea. I had this pile of junk in the backyard. I had tools and space, and the weather was getting fine. I decided I would make up a flyer and put it all over the neighborhood. It said this:

Neighborhood Art Making Party!
48 Green Street—come around back
This Saturday at 2 PM
to make a sculpture together
No experience necessary

The next Saturday I spent the morning getting things ready. The tools, the paints, the space. 2 o'clock rolled around and no one came. I started to feel embarrassed. Who invites strangers over to make art? Have I embarrassed myself yet again? I imagined people walking past my flyer rolling their eyes. They had better things to do.

But by 3 o'clock, a few people had showed up! They walked tentatively down the alley, peering around the corner of the house. "Is this the...art party?" Then, over the next hour, more. By 4 o'clock there was really a gang in the back yard. There were MassArt students from my building. Others were total strangers. Everyone was ambling around, looking at the pile of junk, waiting for instructions. Then, I was on.

I introduced myself and showed them around. I walked them through the pile of wonderful items, the tools, paints, and supplies. I introduced some basic sculpture ideas and asked folks what they wanted to make. Quickly, I understood that my job was going to be to invite peoples' creativity, and at the same time be the final decision-maker, the one who makes it go forward.

The ideas came, first tentative and gentle, then faster and more assertive. We decided we would make a dragon. I cut out some big wooden pieces to guide the overall shape. Everyone else was looking around among the items to see what spoke to them. Within minutes this group of eight strangers was working industriously, fastening things to the body, decorating scales, working individually and in small groups.

Over several hours, from the afternoon and into the evening, we worked. And over the hours everyone became friends. I mean, you could feel the love, right there in our junky back yard. Birdo, a long-haired maintenance man with

the Boston Housing Authority, worked on the dragon's body with Ko, a MassArt student. Katherine, another artist, cut slats for the jagged teeth. Everyone kept an eye on Carolina, Birdo's 4-year-old-daughter. I watched these strangers share ideas, try them out, change them, and feel proud of what they'd done.

Some of the first folks left after a few hours. New people came. It was a real live party. It evolved that our dragon was named d'Artagnon, after one of the Three Musketeers. Everything was flowing. For a moment I stood back and watched the whole thing unfolding. Like a proud father I went up to the fire escape, taking pictures of the process. This love, this togetherness, was the art. I hadn't known it would be. It was as lovely and alive as any painting.

Like I said, outside of ABC my art-making life was almost entirely a solitary activity. I was used to being in charge, diving in after my highest hope of beauty, and laboring until it was achieved. But this was totally different. There were people in this group who had never made a work of art in their lives. They were just here for a fun Saturday. I'd invited them. I was responsible to them. On the other hand, some of the folks who had come were talented artists in their own right. I'd invited them too! There were opinions and ideas of all kinds, swirling around, including my own. I was responsible to this group and to my surging, pushing desire that we create something truly beautiful.

Every moment of it felt like walking a tightrope. The way to make beauty was changing right before my eyes, in real time. I had my own strong, almost

relentless inner voice with its very clear ideas about what was going to look good and what wasn't. But I was responsible to this sweet group of people

who had arrived out of the ether, responded to my flyer, and brought their own opinions and hopes. Yet, I was the guide. Inwardly I worked to be agile, decisive, forgiving, liberal, allowing, all things at once, and each one at the right time. It was exhausting and wonderful. The dragon must be beautiful, fun, and powerful. But at the very same time, the hours we spend making it must be equally beautiful, equally fun. The space has to be free and open for these new friends to explore, laugh, and let their hair down. The time spent has to be as soulful as the sculpture.

Some five or six hours later, as the sun was almost fully down on this mid-summer Saturday, d'Artagnon the dragon was finished. Sawdust and wood scraps littered the asphalt yard. Brushes protruded out of open paint cans. We had forgotten about the hours. The guys had their shirts off. Everyone's hands were dirty and knees scuffed from kneeling to work. We felt proud.

D'Artagnon was seven feet long from end to end, swirling and curving, decorated with strips of ripped maroon velvet and daubs of paint. His horns were arms of a wooden chair. A broken bike chain drew his eye. The dragon's scales were formed of lath board from inside the walls of a nearby home, currently under construction. His beard was an abandoned scrub brush. Four of us laboriously carried him across the street to the fence where the Green Street Phoenix had flown proudly for a few months.

This dragon was big. I didn't know who owned this empty lot, but as we carried him over, I began to realize this is different. He is not a humble little bird made by kids. People are going to notice this. People might have opinions. But everyone was so proud of d'Artagnon. We'd agreed we had to put him on the fence. We drilled small holes through the dragon's plywood body to run wire through and then around the fence uprights. As we wound the high gauge wire, attaching our roiling beast to the fence, I could feel him overshadowing the Phoenix. It was a big, snarling dragon.

When he was fast on the fence, sturdy and immoveable, and after we admired our work, the party kept right on. After six hours of creative labor, the new friends were ready to relax. Soon there were burgers on the barbeque and phase two was fully in motion.

Toward the end of the evening one of the guests

217

asked, as if it were a foregone conclusion, "So, when are we doing this again?" Then they were looking at me.

"How about two weeks from today?" I asked. And just like that, it was agreed.

Amazingly, and only by what I understood more and more to be the glory of God, we met every two weeks for the rest of the summer. We made five large sculptures together, each of which was attached further and further down the fence. By the end of August the entire fence was covered with this menagerie of characters and creations. From left to right it was d'Artagnon the dragon, a flying 8-year-old girl, a tree whose limbs were the traced arms of its creators, a pirate ship, and a flying horse. It was impossible to miss. It was a statement.

No meeting of the sculpture making gang was ever comprised of the same people. Each time it was a different social recipe and a different creative outcome. The ideas and the cooperation arrived, right on time. Over the five sculpture parties, 25 different people participated. Children under 10, lots of art students, and neighborhood parents lent their hands and inspirations.

At times, when the collaborations were not moving along easily, or when the participants had more questions than I had patience, I wished they would all leave. I would take myself aside and breathe, reminding myself to be patient, and to serve. Because that's what this was. I was learning to look out into the community. My eyes were being opened. Art could truly serve. It could be so loving, so human. But if it was going to do that, it needed someone to be the guide—to take responsibility.

The friends of a nearby park reached out to me. Would we be interested in a commission? We made another small dragon for the park and with the $300 payment, financed our end-of-the-summer blowout party. I invited everyone who had been involved. We reveled in what we had created.

Through it all the garden was growing. By the middle of the summer the plants overgrew the meandering sides of the plots I'd created. The flowers appeared to grow naturally out of the asphalt. The garden became a real thing before my eyes. I was bursting with love for it. I could feel that backyard space transforming.

I began a new project of arranging the stones I'd extracted from the earth into patterns in empty areas. Every corner of this yard could be cared for. There was room for baseball, room for art, and room for flowers. Actually, I began to notice that the more the space was cared for, the more other people were beginning to set up chairs and spend time there. There was room for simply hanging out. The backyard became a heaven. The flowers boomed. The pile of junk got used and turned into five sculptures, imbued with the spirit of that neighborhood. I found an old papasan chair and hung it like a hammock from the great tree in the shady back corner of the yard.

Some years later, an acquaintance was giving me directions from here to there. I'd since moved away from Green Street. She walked me through the steps from one location to the other. She went on, "Ok, so you're going up Green Street and, you know those sculptures on the fence right there? That's where you make a left."

In that moment, and in many others like it, I felt what we had done. People saw them. They knew they were there. Those sculptures became part of peoples' lives. Hundreds of people, living in those neighborhoods, driving through, had seen them. Children grew up walking past them, knowing that there could be dragons, pirate ships, and flying horses in the neighborhood you live in. They were famous around the neighborhood. People who had no idea where they came from were proud of them.

Then, eight years later, in the fall of 2013, while I was on a music tour, they were taken down overnight and never seen again. A friend emailed to let me know. My public artist's heart swelled and sighed. It's all part of it, I thought. Whoever owns that lot could have taken them down the moment we put them up. They didn't. The grass in that empty lot was mowed several times a season. It wasn't abandoned. Someone was aware of it. For whatever reason, they gave us eight years of joy to celebrate color, community, and turning garbage into beauty.

THE 4th GAME

Once, thinking of painting with total creative freedom, I noticed it felt like I was flying. I soared, doing what I'm meant to do. In those moments my engagement with my life was as full as it has ever been. Living was complete. The Voice pouring out of me, adoring God, loving the open hearts who would see it, sharing beauty, and being its vehicle. Firing on all cylinders.

I considered that sensation of flying—total freedom, no opposition. I looked through my life. When else do I feel that way? When else are all my muscles, all my efforts, working together, flowing like a lusty river, unencumbered and joyful? When else does my 100% effort, pushed to its limits, feel not like labor, but like play?

I feel that way singing a song I love. I feel that way hitchhiking or adventuring, pushing into the unknown, depending on intuition. And, I feel that way playing sports.

Running on the field of play, I forget my body, and long only to succeed. Like making a painting or writing a song, the field of play is a vehicle for the expression of perfection. It's a means to free the desire to participate in perfect beauty, absolute exertion.

The sport I've played most in my life is ultimate frisbee (or just "ultimate"). On the field the door is open to pour in every drop of desire and passion. All of life's longing to do well gushes out over the grass, moving us to run, dive, and push against limitation. I find myself running, locked in competition with another whose skills are equal with mine, letting go of that thing that would hold back. We're racing down the field, chasing the disc. We're both giving everything we have. Our desire is unleashed. In a moment, the hopes of our lives are expressed in our churning legs, our eyes on the disc. And finally, we see, in our thought-free athletic intuition, that we may catch it if we will leave our feet, throwing ourselves into the air, abandoning every thought but to catch that object before it hits the ground. With every other hope forgotten, the desire to catch the disc blazes like a star in the center of our being. We are flying together, through the air, our bodies parallel with the lay of the earth below us. The disc arrives from its arc above, our arms outstretched, fingers open to receive it. One of us, in that moment of perfection, has achieved the better position, and grasps the disc between his longing fingers. The crowd, our teams and friends, erupt into elated cheers as we crash to the ground. Our life desire cascades through us, flowing out onto the grass, filling the moment, filling our hearts.

At the end of each ultimate season there is a two-day tournament. We play four games on day one, and another four on day two. Playing one game with a full heart and pure desire is a beautiful gem of effort, but to play eight games over two days is an invitation to glory, requiring the athlete to love the game more than he loves physical comfort.

On one particular tournament weekend my team was shorthanded. It meant each player had to play more points and take fewer breaks than usual. But we were doing well. We made it through the first day and began the second.

In the first game everyone is warming up, our bodies remembering the feeling of running. In game two we're in our prime. We have re-entered the place of joyful striving. We are working as a machine. In game three we're exhausted. We have today's two games, and yesterday's four games behind us. But we're getting closer to the championship game. We want to win. This is what we're playing for. We pour ourselves in. If we lose, we'll go home. But we won. Which means there will be a game four. It begins in 10 minutes.

I looked at my dear, shorthanded team. We were walking with our bags from one field to the other, where we would begin the final game. It's three in the afternoon in mid-August. It is 78 degrees outside. Everyone is drenched in sweat. My teammates' faces wear a look of wonder and exhaustion. Their hair is matted to their faces. Scrapes of dirt on knees and uniforms have turned to mud. We all want to win the tournament, but we have nothing left to give. We've been taxed too far. We don't have enough players. The desire to give up is beginning to creep in. Maybe it's too much.

I'm exhausted too. I won't allow myself to think of sitting down, or worse yet, lying down on the grass. My legs don't want to run anymore. It takes concentration simply to walk across these fields. But in less than 10 minutes we'll throw ourselves over the cliff again. We'll be running. We'll have to run.

I watched us walking. My team is women and men. They are my friends. In a way, throwing this disc is like a conversation. When we complete a pass it's a connection. When we work our way down the field, connecting again and again, it's a kind of communication. There's an intimacy about it. Just like a conversation, when we connect, we understand each other. Affection grows. Communication happens and a kind of real love rises up naturally between us.

So, I'm watching them walk their exhausted selves over to the sideline where we will begin again. I'm praying. I'm praying because I know that all good things come from God. I love to bring God into my running, striving, longing efforts. I'm comforted to think of God's endless strength, agility, and endurance. I envision God as the fountain of all those things. His strength is flowing and flowing and flowing. I think of that fountain pouring through me, creating me, moving my legs and my desire. I'm feeling comforted. As I watch my friends feeling the burden of exhaustion, I feel for them. I love them.

A surprising thought arrives in me, with a feeling of joy. I'll give them a gift. I'll make a law for myself that when this game starts, the fourth game of the day, I will not come out of the game. I will not skip a point. I will stay in every point of the game and make it possible for the others to have more time to rest. As it dawns on me that I can do this, I feel great pleasure. I'll do it silently. I feel a genuine care for them. I'm grateful to think of them drinking in a few extra moments of relief.

The starting seven of both teams hauled themselves out onto the field. I made sure to be one of them. The first throw went up and the game began.

Something was different. I knew in my heart it was *a law* that I could not come out of the game. This law existed as a fact of nature. Like the weather, it was not something to disagree with or argue about. It was a simple fact. And with it was a feeling of Love. It was a law of love that I would do this.

Then, knowing it was a fact, I gave up all hope of having a rest for myself. I ceased to hope or desire that I might come out of the game. And in that moment, as if a door had been closed, the exhaustion I'd been feeling began to swiftly fade away. As I ran, embracing the fact that I would never leave the game, a new energy filled my limbs. As I let go of the hope of rest, as if by magic, the need for it drained away.

The first point ended and the second began. Then the third and fourth. With each opportunity to leave the field I joyfully declined. I loved to think of the one person, whoever it was, on the sideline, getting to rest for a few more minutes. I felt stronger and stronger. As the game progressed, I was a new man. I loved to run. My limbs moved freely, loose and limber.

I never did come out. I played every single point, that fountain of God's strength flowing through me, washing away the dread of exhaustion. It was fueled by the joy of giving comfort to my teammates. By the game's end I was in full victory. I don't remember who won or lost the game, but I stepped off the field like a king with his crown. The royalty of God's inspiration filled my heart and empowered my body. God's gift to me was a desire to be generous, and a thought of how to do it. Then, the great desire to give a gift, as strong as the desire to catch the disc, lifted the burden and opened the way.

ALL I HAVE TO DO IS TELL THE TRUTH

A friend called and asked if I'd go with her to a storytelling event she was interested in. I was game, and off we went. Alas for us, we got lost on the way and didn't arrive at the small gathering until it was almost over.

As we walked in, the last storyteller was just beginning his story. We quietly made our way to the back row, the top of the inclined classroom seats. The storyteller was an old black man with white hair. He seemed to own the stage. We were still getting our coats off, no idea what to expect. As I settled in, not fully listening yet, I took in images from the story he was telling—a voice, a mountain, a horn. He spoke about having a voice as strong as this towering black mountain. He told us about the horn, confidently bleating its notes into the sky. I forgot everything and gave in to him. He spoke of himself, seeking, longing to have that voice. He followed its call. It led him up into the mountain and up its craggy paths. His horn crooned it's song into the infinite sky. *He was telling my story.* And then he was done, everyone clapped and they were closing down the event.

I was on fire. That story! The voice. He knew about the Voice! His story had opened up the sky inside me. It lit my desire and spoke to the very place I was most alive and most alone. My voice, my precious voice! This old man knew all about it. He's done what I long to do. He knows about that mountain. He's climbed it and made it his own. He knows about the horn, and playing it into the sky without fear!

People were putting on their coats, getting ready to leave. Desperately, I hollered out, "You're not done, right?" I needed more. I needed more stories like this.

"No, we're done," he replied. Others in the group looked back at me, blankly. It couldn't be over. I needed there to be more.

"Just tell another one!" I cajoled, my need overshadowing my understanding that the event was obviously over.

He paused and I thought he might reconsider. "No," he repeated, "We're done…but you can tell if you want to…"

I'd never in my life been a performer. My actor friends in high school often asked me why I didn't try out for plays. The answer was that it held absolutely zero interest for me. A better question was why *would I?* Like most people, I hated public speaking. I was lost, totally self-conscious. In my longing to share my music, I sometimes forced myself to open mics, sweating through the songs, miserable the whole time. I usually messed them up, and felt embarrassed afterwards. With great pride I showed my paintings to anyone. I happily played my recordings for my friends. But I'd never emerged from a performance experience with anything better than discomfort, wishing I'd never done it.

With his invitation ringing in my ears, I took stock of myself. Everyone in the room was looking at me.

"No, thanks," I said, "We just came to listen."

"Ok," he replied, "But you can, if you want…" He looked at me, waiting.

Then, as if I had a trap door inside me, I felt the floor fall out of my soul. Whatever that means. The answer was yes. I was going to tell a story in front of these people. The most normal thing in the world, to *not* stand up in front of a bunch of strangers and tell a non-existent story, was gone. Just gone. I felt myself standing up. I began walking down the steps to the front of the room. The stage was getting closer. I began to realize I was going to need to have something to say when I got there. *I need something to say!* I kept walking towards the front.

The world moved in slow motion as I arrived at the stage. The room, my mind, buzzed. I turned and looked up into their faces. Closing my eyes, I looked into myself. Then my mouth opened and I began to describe what I saw.

I spoke of seeing pictures in my mind as a boy. The beauty that surrounds me. The beauty that buffets me on all sides. I kept my eyes closed, watching what I could see inside me. The words arrived in my mouth, describing what I saw, like a movie playing in my chest. I told them about the Voice coming to me, leading me, loving me, saving my life. Then, the story of my first mural. The gripping fear, reaching out in silent listening, and receiving a message that opened the way like a key in a lock.

And with that, the movie inside me went dark. Quietly I opened my eyes. I remembered that I was standing in front of a room full of people. Everyone clapped. Ten minutes had elapsed.

As I walked back up the steps I was amazed—reeling. "I did it. I just told the truth *in front of people*." I'd never known the feeling. Never even come close. But this was it. I'd told the truth.

It felt completely different than any other time I'd made any kind of presentation in front of others. I'd felt comfortable, even at peace. It hadn't felt like I was putting on a show. I didn't hope they would like it. I didn't even wonder if they would like it. I just told the truth. No uncertainty. I knew it was good. I knew it was interesting. I knew I'd done well.

I became a regular at the story swap. Each week I told a new story. Listening to my Voice, I easily discerned that what I had to offer was stories from my own life. I could tell them, watching that inner movie. It would show me what to say, what details to include. It would provide the beauty, the feeling, the poetic moments. Having told the truth, I knew there was no going back. This was the real thing.

Storytelling became comfortable. I enjoyed speaking to live audiences more and more. I loved the process of taking what was on the inside and sharing it. I loved the feeling of bringing out the humanity in the room by sharing my intimate details. We all have fears, longings, loves. They so often go unspoken and unshared. But look, when you reveal your humanity, people are moved! They feel love because they relate. They're comforted, or inspired, or moved to laughter because they have their own unspoken details. As I looked over my experiences, there were countless stories. All I had to do was tell the true details of my experiences, my desires, the intimate moments of my life's adventure. Life itself is fascinating, moving, incredible—all I have to do is tell the truth!

****

After several months of attending weekly, the folks at the storytelling group asked me to the "feature" for an upcoming event. That meant that instead of telling for 10 minutes I would tell for 45 minutes. I swallowed hard but said yes.

It had only been a few months since I started telling stories. I didn't have a teacher or a coach. I was learning by doing, week after week. The truth is, I was just at the very beginning of knowing myself as a storyteller.

There were all kinds of different ways to do it. Some told folk tales. Others shared funny vignettes of their life at the office. Others told about their experiences in love and friendship. They were all over the map. Everyone did what they felt.

The stories I wanted to tell were about my learning, my breakthroughs and adventures. It felt so natural to lean into those poignant moments, the intimate, emotional details. I could feel as I shared that as I took off the veil, my vulnerability made the stories compelling. I knew from my explorations of art and music that the more I honestly, unflinchingly tell my own story, the more others can feel it. We all have our private inner lives. Amazingly, as I was vulnerable, the better the stories were, and the safer I was.

I found my sweet spot. I would think through the moments of my life that stood out to me—dramatic moments, transformational times. I would close my eyes and be right back in those places. I could see, hear, feel the details in my mind. Not just the feelings, but the furniture in the room, the smell in the air, the creaking floorboards. And I would simply open my mouth and tell the story as it played like a movie in my thoughts. All the poetic details presented themselves like ornaments on a Christmas tree.

It felt so good to get up in front of the group and let them in on my life, my secrets and precious observations. After that first time, walking down the stairs, not knowing what I would say, I began to comprehend how it worked. That night I had leapt into the inky unknown. I opened the door and let go, somehow trusting that there would be something interesting to say. I saw that if I jumped off, didn't hold anything back, and simply revealed my true being, the story would be real. And when it was real, people would feel it. The room would vibrate and people would be moved.

I could see it almost like entering a room through a door. On one side was regular life, and on the other side was this dark, spacious place of memory and expression. If I hesitated, or stayed in the doorway I'd be ruined. But if I walked all the way in and just revealed what I saw, everything flowed. That place was filled with good stories, a million things to say. I found, to my wonder and amazement, that I could freely walk through the door.

But when they asked me to be the feature I knew I had to come up with something different. 45 minutes? It was an almost unthinkable amount of time to fill.

I'd arrived at a number of stories I would tell. They'd be connected by songs. There was the one about how the high school baseball coach had balled us out after a loss and made us run until we couldn't run anymore. I'd tuned him out and sang Queen songs to myself to keep my spirits up. There was the one about singing old time shape-note songs as I waited at the side of the road while hitchhiking. And there was the one where I fell asleep on a frozen creek in the woods on a bracing January evening. When I woke up there was a song in my mouth about falling asleep in those woods on that frozen creek.

The material was all there, but I needed to be able to remember all the details, the transitions, the important moments. So, in the week before my performance, I sat down to make myself an outline. I wrote out all the parts. More and more important details came to mind. The pages were filling up. I wouldn't be able to read it. The text was too small. There was too much. I felt farther and farther away from the good feeling of being in that room, through the door, telling the truth.

I forced my way onward. I tried to memorize it all, like I was studying for an exam. For several hours that night I paced and quizzed myself, trying to get it all into my thoughts. Trying not to worry about the 45 minutes. It was feeling longer and longer. The stories were turning to sawdust in my hands. I couldn't remember it all!

Feeling miserable, I stopped myself. It's not supposed to be like this. I looked inside myself, quietly, seriously. I'm an artist. This is what I *do*. I'm not going to be bullied by my own art! This art is freedom, not fear.

In a moment, a certainty dropped like ripe fruit from a hanging bough. With a deep draught of faith, I realized I am not a storyteller who uses an outline. I speak from my thoughts. I go through the door and rely on the magic. It's what I'm built to do.

I threw away the outline I'd made. I took out a new sheet of paper and in big black letters wrote the names of the three stories. That was it.

****

On the night of the performance I took my single paper with the three story titles onto the stage and laid it on the floor at my feet. Then I walked through the door, into that dark and windy place where the stories revealed themselves. Natural as can be, the first story was there, like a tree in an orchard. I told the story, picked its fruit, and passed it on to the audience. I was in it. I could smell the grass of the baseball field. I could hear the clomping footsteps of my team as we hoofed endlessly around its perimeter. I sang "My Melancholy Blues" by Queen, as I had sung it to myself that day. It's notes, which I had sung to myself countless times over the years, came coursing out of my mouth, vibrating my throat. I held nothing back. It poured forth splashing all through the room, meaning everything it meant to me. When the song ended I looked down at the paper at my feet and saw the title of the second story. Sure enough, it too was right there, through the door, real as can be. I opened my mouth and out it came.

It was happening. Like a surfer on a wave, it was no power of my own that filled that room with energy. The audience waited on each word, each song. The power was real and we were all riding it together.

I moved on to the third story, walking around its tree, passing the fruit along. I sang the songs, holding nothing back, knowing they were seeing my naked being. They could hear my breathing. My pauses between notes. There was no veil between us.

When the third story was over I walked out through the door, and back into regular life. The audience was applauding, long and joyous. I soon learned that my stories had gone over time significantly—about 55 minutes total.

SELF DENIAL

How can you feel connected with God when you just don't feel connected?

The answer is simple, though not easy. It is, as Jesus makes clear, to "take up your cross, and deny yourself." Simple, but not easy.

For the sake of our own happiness, denying ourselves should become normal. It should be our first reaction.

To me, "self" has come to mean not my identity, but rather, any voice or inclination I encounter in my head or heart that makes me think of myself as a separate being, without God. It's a sense that for better or for worse, I'm on my own. I'm making my decisions, I'm responsible for the outcome of my life, and how I feel defines who I am. It's this sense of life that makes us do and feel all the bad things we do and feel—fear, hatred, greed, loathing, shyness, lust … the list goes on and on. By contrast, when we feel and understand that we are eternally connected to God, the source of all goodness, health, and harmony, we are simply not inclined to fear, hate, lie, or any other bad behavior. When you're safe with God, there's no need for those things.

To deny yourself doesn't mean to keep yourself from doing things you love, or from having good things. It just means denying the inclination to think of your being as a separate thing—a self - apart from the Whole, the Source.

To many people, Jesus' counsel to "deny" ourselves basically means being mean to ourselves. There's a feeling that God wants us to punish ourselves for the ways we've messed up. Like, if we beat ourselves up enough, or stop ourselves from having fun, that will somehow show God that we're really actually good and worthy of His love. It's a notion that you can somehow buy God's love by being miserable and giving up all the good things in life. That is definitely not what Jesus means. No, Jesus is telling us to deny in our hearts the inclination to believe that we are vulnerable, separate things, wandering around a loveless, random, dangerous universe. This denial enables us to see, feel, and experience what Jesus' whole ministry was trying to show us—the present reality of God's love.

That feeling of separation and the blighted vision that grows out of it hide from us the peaceful, abundant, spiritual feeling of God's creation. Jesus said, "The kingdom of heaven is within you." It is. It's there, all along.

The main difficulty lies in the fact that we've spent our lives believing the voice of this "self." It fills our thoughts from the time we're young with fears and anger. To the degree that we see our life through the lens of self, we perceive it as filled with uncertainty, slights, and threats. Something could go wrong at any moment, and when it does, it's proof that the voice of self is right. It makes its case again and again: "Life is dangerous and hopeless, and everyone is against you." The only time it doesn't have the floor is when we entertain

thoughts and feelings that can't harmonize with it—unselfish love, joy, enthusiasm, willingness, virtue. We're often so entranced by the clinging, clamoring narratives of self that we can't imagine denying them. To question them feels insane, arbitrary, irresponsible.

But when we feel love, we find that there is a reason to disbelieve the claims of separation and lovelessness. We begin to witness a crack in the lie. As we pray, listening to God, we find an awareness of goodness growing in us. We're less likely to define ourselves by our passing feelings, or think of others as our enemies. Little by little, as the Bible says it, "The great dragon was cast out, that old serpent, called the Devil, and Satan, which deceiveth the whole world." (Revelation 12:9) Because God is real, if we're believing the threatening, God-forgetting voice of the self, we are being deceived.

The problem is believing that moment by moment how we feel tells us who we are. For example, if I *feel* separate from God, then I *am* separate from

God. We get so used to thinking that our feelings are us, that we find it impossible to defy them. We believe they rule us and that they are inextricable from our being. We're offended at the notion of denying them. It's a basic problem and to reverse it, we have to go to the root of it. Our passing, human emotions are not us.

We are created by God. Our real identities are pure, strong, and defined by love. We get the best glimpses of our real selves when we feel and act on love. In those moments, we sense our wholeness.

Denying our "selves," means being willing to let go of the negative overlay of thoughts and suggestions whose source is not in God. They obscure our vision and lead us to believe all kinds of wrong things about ourselves and the nature of life. At first blush it seems uncomfortable, and probably very hard, but to practice self-denial yields a gloriously consistent sense of happiness, security, and meaning. We'll be changed. We find ourselves free of bonds and limitations we thought were built into our very identity. But the identities of God's children aren't good and bad. They're just good. Denying self is taking the blockage off of the naturally flowing spring of good ideas, happiness, and inspiration that flows from God, right out of the middle of each one of us.

I find this story touching:

"A donkey fell to the bottom of a deep pit a man was digging for a well. When the man saw that this had happened he was very sorry and sad because he saw no way to get the donkey out. The hole was too deep and the donkey too heavy. He could think of nothing to do but fill in the hole and start over. The unfortunate donkey would die.

But, as the man began to throw shovel-full after shovel-full of dirt down the well he soon had a smile on his face. He watched as the dirt fell down the hole and landed on the donkey's back. Each time this happened, the donkey shook the dirt off his back and it fell to the ground beneath him. With each and every shovel-full of dirt that was hurled down the hole, the donkey shook it off, and little by little the hole began to fill in under him. After much labor by the man, and much patient dirt-shaking by the donkey, the hole became so shallow that the donkey climbed up and out of it."

So it is with us. The world, our feelings, our swirling thoughts of fear, spite, and dislike, are the dirt thrown down on us. We feel as though we were at the bottom of a dark pit, and our fate has been decided for us. Any unwholesome thought we accept into our being begins to weigh us down. We feel totally justified in entertaining them. The self cries, "All you have to do is look around to see how unwholesome and broken the world is!" But we can't deny ourselves, we can't be free, if we look to the world for evidence. We have to look to God.

But we feel that these things are us. Hence the word "self." Yet they are the very thoughts that cause us to suffer and diminish. Jesus' counsel to "deny yourself" is an instruction to see evil (done to you or by you) as useless and vain, not worthy of entertaining. We are called on to shake off fear, criticism, impatience, anger of every sort, and every other poisonous burden. Each time we shake off the dirt, again and again, and instead reach out to God, goodness, *unselfishness*, we are transformed, and we are naturally lifted out of the hole.

There's no part of this that's about being mean to yourself. There's no part that's about punishment. In fact, Jesus is giving us, clear as can be, the way to be happy. He's pointing out to us the very thing that makes us miserable, and revealing to us how to be done with it forever. It is entirely an invitation to be free.

There's also no part of this that we can do without depending on God. It's not about being personally tough. We can't deny ourselves, *by ourselves!* That really would be miserable. And it could never work. The whole point is to replace the feeling of being a separate, independent entity with the reality that we are entirely dependent upon God, the unseen source of every good idea and act. We're willing to do it, more and more, as we find out how incapable, stupid, and prone to suffering the "self" really is. It's not good at living.

As we deny ourselves, the whole cosmology in which self is the center of the universe, which seems so normal to us, is washed away. We make room in our thoughts for God's idea of who we are. We begin to see that God is the center of the universe. We feel into our truer, God-created selves. We learn that we aren't what we thought we were. We're less easily hurt. Less inclined to lash out. We have more buoyancy and resilience. We feel more at home in our skin. We're less easily convinced that we could be separate from God, good. The more of the old "self" we deny, the more we witness that our being is simply God expressing Himself—innocent, fearless, successful, and real.

RED SHOES

As I mentioned, I came back to church in my last year of college after about 12 years away. That was the beginning of a long, rich, and demanding journey. I attended church regularly during my years in Athens. And when I moved back to Boston I quickly found a church and attended services twice a week, with almost perfect regularity. By the time I was 30 my dedication to the teachings of Christian Science was deeply established. I loved the Bible and depended upon it for guidance. I drank deeply from the insights I found in the Christian Science textbook, *Science and Health*, by Mary Baker Eddy. I passionately wrestled with their deep assertions, and trusted in them daily, knowing they had saved my life.

Though I knew in my bones it was right to go back to church, it wasn't easy. The church I attended in Boston was an enormous stone edifice, and the services exuded a kind of formality that I didn't relate to. I felt *very* different from the other members of the congregation, and very uncomfortable. I'm an artist. I had long hair. My clothes were from thrift stores, bright and messy. I didn't have any money. They all seemed to have it together. I guessed they were business people, or something. They wore suits and nice dresses. I felt a rift of difference between us.

At the time I wore a worn-out holey pair of sneakers that I had painted red. They were my favorite shoes. I felt comfortable in them. When I looked around in church, every other person looked so different from me, I self-consciously wondered if that was how you had to look to be close to God. Yet, I loved God. I was truly conflicted. I stuck out like a long-haired, hand-painted sore thumb.

That's just the surface though. Looking more deeply, I was so focused on myself, so ignorant of the other folks in the church, all I could see was our differences. In fact, I hardly thought of them having their own individualities. Rather, they were, through my darkened lens, a homogeneous group—the church, I guessed, who agreed on all things and acted as one body. They were in the club and I wasn't. Honestly, I had no idea what church is for. In my great inexperience I thought it was a monolith of rules to which I needed to conform.

In every other part of my life I idealized *not* conforming! I followed my feeling, my own path. I practiced hard at listening for intuition, what was best, and it had revealed all the goodness I knew - my paintings, my friendships, my very approach to life. But now, my sincere path had brought me right to church. I was, all at once, filled with hope in God's guidance and trembling with fears that I wouldn't be good enough, I'd be exposed as a fraud, and I'd lose my individuality by submitting to this institution.

Still, reverence was foremost in my heart. I took myself to church twice a week, Wednesday nights and Sunday mornings. I leaned into the sermons, listening, drinking in the scriptures, the prayerful feeling, and the sharing. I pushed through the nerves I felt in the hallways, walking past eyes I suspected were judging me.

One Sunday, after the service, as folks milled around chatting, the head usher ambled over to me in the crowd. As if it were the most normal thing in the world he asked if I would be willing to be an usher for the Sunday morning church services.

I was stunned. The tone in his voice had even sounded like he felt that I'd be doing them a favor! How could that be? I considered all the male ushers I had seen. They wore suits and ties; they looked and acted entirely different from me. I was sure they'd all grown up in the church and never had an impure thought. They were the way an usher should be. Right? Me, I was afraid and off-balance—a total mess.

However, right next to that fear, my love of God was serious. I would give my life to grow spiritually. In fact, I was committed to doing that very thing. I knew I was a mess, but I was doing everything I could do grow closer with God. I had an unwritten rule: "If you're given an opportunity, take it." So, I told the head usher that I would be there the next week to usher.

That next Sunday morning with a gnawing nerve in my stomach I set aside my normal clothes, and put on a suit and tie. Instead of my favorite red sneakers, I put on the shiny brown shoes that normally sat untouched in my closet. I didn't feel like myself, but I was ready to play the role. That's what church is, right? Playing a role? Arriving at the usher's meeting I was sure my playing dress-up would be exposed. I felt embarrassed and stiff, but I was there to do my best. I pushed through. I was sure they were laughing at me. "Who's the kid? Why's he here? What is it, picture day at school?"

I was enormously uncomfortable; it was so far outside of my familiar life. After the meeting was over we were meant to go to our positions to prepare to greet people for the service. Before I could, the same head usher came over to me. I expected he would give me some further instructions for the job. I nervously tried to remember all the details. Instead, he asked with a smile, "Where are your red shoes?"

I couldn't believe my ears. My mouth opened a little. My eyes brimmed with tears.

My red shoes? He, this perfectly coiffed, short-haired executive type, had seen them? And, then, had thought I'd wear them to this? I could barely grasp it. He'd seen something about me and thought it was good.

I began to realize that he hadn't asked me to be an usher expecting me to change who I was. He had asked me to usher because of who I was. He had seen me, appreciated something about me, and asked me to contribute to the group. He hadn't cared that I looked different. In fact, he'd been so aware of me, in the way I presented myself, that he noticed when I traded out my red shoes. Immediately there was a steaming fissure in my illusion of church as a stern, unforgiving monolith. It began to crack as I realized that church was made of individuals, trying their best to live the ideals of God.

My fears about not belonging in church began to crumble away. The next Sunday I came to the ushers meeting dressed in my regular clothes. I served on that usher committee for a long time, feeling more and more comfortable and useful with each service.

Over the years, I've had many opportunities to serve and learn in church. I'm filled with awe when I think of that head usher, humbly listening for God's guidance and being told to ask me to help. (Later he told me this is what happened.) I'm so grateful that he listened, and then acted on the intuition when it came. It initiated what was certainly a profound change in my life. When I think of the blessings that have come to me and others because of that simple act, I am deeply humbled.

Some time later a woman, a long-time employee of the church, took me aside after another Sunday morning service. She knew I was an artist. She could see the way I was, the way I acted. She said, "Alex, this church *needs you*. You have things we need. We need you to be the way you are, in this church."

Amazed and humbled again, I drank it in. She loved the church. She wanted it to succeed, to be healthy. And she saw something in me that she felt would help strengthen it. This was an invitation to believe that I could give my gifts, different as they are, despite appearances, right here at church.

I've come to see that church is simply not made for conformity. Rather it exists to thrive on diversity. Church needs each of us exactly as we are—revealing our skills, insights, and hearts. Church changes us, and gives us opportunities to serve and grow. It gives us opportunities to check and overcome pride and selfishness too. Church is alive when we honestly, lovingly, and soulfully share who we are.

I WILL BE A FOOL

This morning I lay in bed, gray and unmoving, frozen with fear. I'm a fool. I've thrown in my lot for Beauty. There's only a trickle of money coming in. My paintings are not hanging in galleries or museums. I'm past the time of life where people excuse capriciousness. I'm nearly ten years into these efforts to make a life out of art.

I prayed myself a warm bath and melted the fear. Like many mornings. I'm learning how to do it. Then, as I lay in the warm bed, feeling new ability to move in the freedom of effective prayer, feeling God's ownership of all things, including me, I felt the insistent push of life itself. It chirped, "Out!" and without thinking, I leapt out of bed.

I'm learning the robustness of defiance. I am learning it—and its necessity for the health of my soul. I'm learning how a hanging web of drab expectations lies in wait to smother all that is surprising and truly happy. And without robust defiance, without its readiness, my agile stance, prepared to do battle, to leap, to lunge, dive, and roll—without all that, my voice, my breast companion of all these years, will be turned aside. My beauty, my holy mission, will bend and fail under the heavy, redundant wet blankets of routine and fear.

So this morning, shoved playfully from bed by one of God's trillion hands, I put on my many winter layers. I walk out into the gray, misting, messy, ice-melting morning. This walk is not for exercise. It is the day's first step into defiance. This is not for fun. It is a walk of crying with my whole heart for hope and vision. I need to be with the graceful lace of ice on the sidewalks. I need to sway with the burnt lavender trees. I need to breathe in their branches made smoky in the mist across the white hills of the golf course. This is a walk to loosen up my voice, sleeping in the depths of a warm bed. It is to loosen up the frozen voice, to swing my arms, to sing again with my life.

To let this walk do its work means taking myself through these city blocks to the woods. Then maybe it means getting down on my knees among the trees. Maybe lie face down on the wet leaves, drinking in the tenderness of last night's rain from a curled leaf. It means arriving at a brook, frozen hard, and, after sliding on it with my shoes, lying on its smoothness with my shoulder, feeling its cold through my many layers. It means drinking in the fire of beauty that lives in every moment of every single day, on every stoop, in the dark of every door, in the trees, on the rooftop, in the sky. All this beauty goes unseen for lack of defiance.

I am an adult. I see my peers rising up in their organizations, leading meetings. They are buying houses, having children. Maybe I'm a fool. My adult responsibility is to defend and battle for the dignity of expression. I see beauty. I live beauty. I throw off this sleep!

And I'll be brave enough to return home, where bills wait on my desk. I'll open the door and walk upstairs to my studio where work will remain undone if I am not brave. In the death of that empty room I will bring the breath of this walk. I'll bring my defiance to the empty hours, and fill them with color and stories.

Every morning I wake into a world in such deep need of beauty, of expression—of love-filled wildness. But on the radio, wave after wave of daily frustrations, bad news, boredom. It weighs us down. It turns us aside. We forget beauty.

I will fight for it. I will use my weapons. I will be the radio for God's immaculate transmissions—I'll escape the bound and burdened haze of adultness with this great, sweet defiance. I will be a fool!

GOD TOLD ME TO DO SOME CRAZY STUFF

I was looking forward to the beginning of the summer season with my ultimate frisbee team. I began in college, on the university team. Now, 10 years later, I play in a competitive coed summer league. As the first game approached, I felt the jumping, happy desire to see my teammates again after a year away. I searched around my thoughts for something to do to show everyone my bouncy joy to be back running, joking, competing like we always do.

Like waiting for the perfect birthday gift idea, I let this desire pace about in my thoughts and watched it, to see what it would come up with. One morning soon after, I woke up laughing. I'd had a dream in which I ran onto the playing field in a gorilla suit. It cracked me up! I was filled with delight.

I asked an actor friend, if he had, or knew anything about where I could get a gorilla suit. "No," he said, "but I have a bear suit." A bear running across the field made me laugh as much as a gorilla. Soon it was in my hands and the adventure was underway.

I love the way thoughts develop, open, and lead us. It is in our thoughts that our lives unfold. In our thoughts we learn who we are and what we will do. Truly, thoughts are the meat of life. We are used to respecting educated, intelligent thoughts. But are thoughts about animal suits as real and respectable as thoughts about political strategy or parenting tactics? I'm used to thinking of God as the source of good thoughts—peace, forgiveness, love, order, etc. But what about jokes, unbridled joy, creativity, hilarity? If hilarity, joy, and expressiveness are good, then they are certainly from God and teach us about His nature. Rather than letting my preconceived idea of God cause me to judge the thoughts that come to me as crazy, should I not earnestly seek to "try the spirits whether they are of God?" (1 John 4:1) And will I not "know them by their fruit"?

It dawned on me that for the joke to work I had to arrive at the field dressed in the suit. All humor would be lost if I showed up and put it on after everyone had seen me. I ride my bike to and from these games—7 ½ miles from my home in Boston to the field in Cambridge. I could change in the public bathroom when I got there, or something, but a new idea skittered up to me with a great, wriggling joke in its hand.

There is a kind of ridiculous, wild thought, which, when it comes, throws old conceptions of reality out the window. Your old sense of normalcy has fallen off the sill, and is plummeting to the earth below, and you, without that old encumbrance, are giggling, bouncing, laughing and light. This was the idea—to ride all 7 ½ miles in the suit, through the streets, the medical district, past Boston University and Harvard, in and among thousands of rush hour cars, and arrive, heroic, like in the original dream. I stood in my room, unable to keep from dancing—no cool dance with rhythm and sway, just the dance of a child, overcome with Christmas morning joy. Laughs like bird chirps sprang and bounded from my mouth.

The day came and the ride began. I put on the bear suit in my room. A big brown, furry thing with bear gloves and bear feet, and a furry brown head with little eye holes. I trembled my way downstairs and got on my bike. There are some moments in our lives when each of us is alone. Everything is new, or different, and we have no frame of reference for how to act or what to think. Inside the furry costume, my heart pounding, my breath condensing on the inside of the mask, I tried to control the fits of laughter that burst from me. I had told no one. Pedaling up the street I scanned the world through the small eyeholes. I was alone. Nowhere did I see anyone else dressed like an animal. I set off on the familiar roads to Cambridge, my heart leaping in my chest.

An amazing thing happened. People were seeing me. Turning their heads. Pointing. Tapping their young children on the shoulders, lifting them up to see me. People were laughing, amazed. Something good was happening. My joy began to grow as I realized that this was not only giving joy to me, it was causing others to open their eyes, to be surprised, to see and be delighted! It continued for the entire 35-minute ride. Again and again, peoples' eyes widened, smiles illuminated their faces. They laughed in their cars and on the sidewalk. This was some real-life magic.

I rode in the street like any cyclist. Cars had to be aware of me, move around me. As they slowed and lined up at red lights, I slipped between them, passing close by the windows. As if it were any other bike ride of my life, I rode confidently, making my hand signals, left and right. My mind was filled with helium. I'd jumped off a cliff and was flying through the air, making no sense. I was a living, moving joke—a fool, a star, a bear riding a bike through rush hour traffic.

I arrived at the game, heart and mind blown open, burst with a firecracker, and leapt out onto the field just as I had dreamed. One of my teammates, threw me a frisbee of recognition. We played catch for a few minutes before I took off the mask and revealed myself. We all had a good laugh.

Ideas do what they want. They aren't done until they say they're done. In the following days I thought about the feeling I'd had while riding through Boston, dressed as a bear. It's rare and spectacular to feel as free I had. I began to feel like I had a glowing, golden treasure in a box…I could do it again.

I began to go for bear rides. Soon I was going for almost daily rides around various neighborhoods in Boston, usually in the morning rush hour. As I did, my understanding of the bear as a character began to gather form. I lost all sense of fear about it, and gained a feeling of pride. My smile widened inside the fuzzy brown mask.

People! They see me. They laugh. The kids jump and clap. "Oh ….!" holler the teenagers, amazed and cracking up as I ride past. Some simply stare, their jaws actually dropping. I began to feel that it was my place to wave. If I was going to do something so incomprehensible, so unusual, I could help folks be delighted by it by doing what I could to be warm, loving, and inclusive. I began to understand that this was truly not just for me. In fact, in a way, it was a gift, a work of art. It was fun for me, but the amount of people who were being caused to smile, laugh, and delightedly shake their heads, was convincing.

Over many rides my confidence blossomed and I reached out to my audience. I lifted my hand high into the sky and waved to kids in school uniforms, ladies in office attire, men with briefcases, construction workers. I blew kisses and pointed at people like they'd just passed me the ball for the winning slam dunk. And what do people do? Most of them wave back! They crack up just like I did! Or their eyes widen and they try to drink the thing in. They take pictures with their phones as I pass. They beckon to me to come over for a selfie. In the wake of this inexplicable, joyful bear people experience a moment of wonder.

I did bear rides for a couple of years. Over the countless rides I understood it better and better. I settled into this art, totally new to me, totally unlike any art I'd done before. This is a way to love people. I could feel that my safety was in giving over to total confidence. This bear is nothing but love. He makes no judgements. He speaks in a goofy voice. Every once in a while he might bellow "Hellooo!" to a group of teens at the bus stop. I thought of the bear not as me, but as him, the bear. He was a different guy.

Many months into it I felt it needed to change somehow. Just like in my other art, the idea has to develop. The exploring reveals new creative perspectives. Instead of just riding around I started going to crowded intersections, getting off the bike and doing a show. I would dance, do cartwheels, and jump around. I would go to a park and do the hula hoop and jump-rope. The audiences were invariably dumfounded and delighted.

God has told me to do some "crazy" things. "What?! God doesn't act like that! That is not something God would tell someone to do. God isn't like that." Actually, where else would a thought so joyful, so harmless, so utterly child-like and wonder-full come from? With total seriousness I asked myself these questions. I could come up with no other source. The outcome of this idea was exclusively good. It made me happy and it made others happy. It caused walls to be broken down and its harvest was joy. It caused no harm, and it blessed unconditionally. Is that not what God does? Admittedly, the fact remains that it was not a "normal" idea. It caused me to do something totally abnormal. Yet the outcome of that abnormal, "inadvisable," "foolish" act, was joy and blessing. God has told me to do some crazy things.

At some point I fully accepted that this idea had come to me from God. But then, this means something. I have to begin to rearrange my understanding of the universe, and of God Himself. It means that *God does this kind of thing*. I'd never heard from anyone in any religious community about God giving this kind of guidance. It just isn't the reputation that God has. Still, there it is. And God only gives thoughts that are like Himself. So now I know with certainty that in addition to being eternal, good, holy, and righteous, God is also hilarious, surprising, and simply not governed by human norms.

I began to have special interest in this statement in First Corinthians 4:10, "We are fools for Christ's sake." And how that "foolishness," that willingness to follow inspiration even if it leads to something very unusual, is life-giving, even holy.

Here's another one.

I owned a little white car that I called Carla. She was a 1993 Mazda 323. Not much to look at but she got me from here to there.

One day an image showed up in my mind. It was Carla, painted like a little brown bird. Not flashy. No eagle or condor. A humble little brown bird. A thrush maybe. She had sweet little brown feathers, painted lovingly all over. "Aw!" I thought. "How sweet that would be."

I enjoyed the thought. I would think of it and be made happy by the sweet image, kicking around in my thoughts. This went on for about a year. I began to notice, "This thought isn't going away." As a watcher of thoughts, I considered, "Is this a thought I should be taking seriously? Should I do this? Should I make my little bird-car a reality?" And after just a little bit of mulling it over, the idea descended from the clouds and landed on the table, solid. I thought "Yep! I'll do it!" It would be wonderful. There was nothing keeping this little word from being made flesh.

So, one day I took my supplies down to the driveway and began to draw the design on the hood of my little car. I would begin with pencil, draw the whole thing out, feather by feather, and then paint it in. But, just as I began, sharpened pencil in my hand, I was gripped with a shocking, vice-like fear: *"People are going to think I am actually crazy. I am going to lose all my friends. People will pity me, the crazy man, as I drive down the street. I will lose my identity and become known only as the actually crazy person who couldn't stay normal."* The fear, unannounced and entirely absent the moment before, was staggering, pummeling. It came down like a landslide the moment I went to do what my sweet little inspiration had told me to. I hadn't felt a stitch of fear until I began to put my thoughts into *action*.

For the time being it was more than I could do to continue the project. I stood in the driveway holding the pencil lamely in my fingers. I couldn't go forward. I didn't *want* to go forward! All sweetness and delight were gone, replaced by a truly evil avalanche of disdain and derision.

I prayed. I reached out to God. "What should I do? I'm not crazy, am I?"

As I listened, longing into the great space of eternity, a series of wonderful thoughts came gently over me. It went like this:

"Do you believe in expressing beauty?"

Yes, I do.

"Is there anything that could ever make you think that expressing beauty is wrong?"

Well, no, there isn't. Beauty is always good, never wrong."

I felt, "I'm willing to stand on that as an eternal truth. It is only good to express beauty." I felt it. And as I did, it dawned on me that I was standing for one of the very things I love most. I realized, "I'm not afraid to be seen as crazy because...I'm right!" No matter if I am the only person in the world who has a car painted like a bird (which I am not) it is still good, and it will never be made bad by human opinions. I will stand for it. I will stand for beauty and expressiveness. I will be the one. I realized that this gift of beauty was not to make a statement about who I am. Rather, it was to put a statement of beauty, of wildness and expression into the world. It was a gift, from God, for my neighborhood.

The fear was gone. I knew I was standing on solid, clean ground. The threats were nothing. I didn't care about them. I went ahead and made the painting. It came out just as I had hoped, humble and kind. The rich, brown feathers

wrapped around the hood and the doors like beautiful wings. Soon I was a man who drove around the neighborhood in a little brown bird.

What followed was far greater than anything I had imagined. Just like with the bear, children clapped and jumped. People laughed and pointed. Fist pumps and cheering. I received a note under my windshield wiper once that said, "You have the most beautiful car in the neighborhood." Imagine, my little 1993 Mazda 323—surrounded on the streets by fancy, new, expensive cars— the most beautiful car in the neighborhood!

It's worth noting how the voice of fear tries to come just when we would act, working to make a reality of our best ideas. It comes with its array of arguments, sounding like wisdom, sounding like common sense, sounding like threats and cruelty. This voice will try to make your creativity, your love, your insight, your inspiration seem worthless. It will try to block your forward motion, your growth, your ability to give your gift to the world. But it can't do it if you will resist it.

God speaks in ways that are so far outside the norms of human activity. God is wild and beautiful and expressive. He speaks right there in the center of the mainstream too, but He is not limited to the path well-trod. Not by a long shot. The magnitude of God's expression is like the power of the great Pacific Ocean compared to the human sense of normalcy—a little ripple on a puddle. But, despite its power, the enormity and vastness, saying yes to that beautiful voice cannot bring destruction—only health, joy, depth of life. God's thoughts, His ideas, broaden and enrich our conceptions of life. They grow us into fitness to accept the next bigger, even more powerful and expansive idea.

So, once God has told you to put on a bear suit and blow kisses to the city of Boston, once He has told to you paint your car like a bird and shown you in your prayers, step by step how to overcome the fear that would arrest the project, how then can you proceed in your life without expecting more strange and wondrous directives from the Holy of Holies? The precedent has been set. God is the great Artist, Comedian, Joker, Healer in every unexpected way. God destroys observance of human norms that don't serve Him. God explodes your limited sense of who He is, and pours in riches.

KENYA MURALS

Over the years I met a number of people from Africa at church. They were from lots of different countries—I don't remember which ones. But I do remember one thing that seemed to run powerfully through all of them. They expressed a deep, bright humility. It was a kind of humility I hadn't seen before—a ready joy and gratitude to simply be there, accompanied by a willingness to help and assist in any situation. It made a deep impression on me.

I wanted to be like that. I didn't see models of it in my regular life. It was like American humility magnified 100x. I knew that humility was the way—maybe even the key to life. I longed for it. Over some months I solemnly considered these people and what they were showing me. It quietly dawned on me that I wanted to travel to Africa. I didn't care about safaris or wild animals. I just wanted to see where this humility came from.

I soon realized how silly it sounds to speak of "traveling to Africa." For goodness sake, there are 54 countries! You can't just "go to Africa." I did some research and decided I would travel to Kenya. From what I had learned, my very uneducated guess was that it would be among the more natural first places for an American to travel in Africa. They speak English. The government seemed relatively stable. My church has a presence there. That was about it.

Through internet exploring I made some connections. I connected with African Colours, an arts organization in Nairobi. When I told them I was thinking of coming, they invited me to lead some mural projects with their artists. I was overjoyed! They had procured funding to pay me and the other artists to create a number of murals around the city of Nairobi. It was a dream come true!

These plans had been in the works for a few months when I finally arrived in June, 2006. I was staying in an apartment in a shiny blue-tinted high rise in downtown Nairobi. The African Colours offices were on the second floor of the same building. It was the farthest I'd ever been from home and felt more foreign than I could understand.

I was delirious with excitement to work. With butterflies in my stomach I made my way into the office. Kenyan artists were hanging around in the waiting room, meeting with consultants. Framed paintings by lots of different Kenyan artists covered the walls. More paintings leaned against the walls in stacks.

The director of the organization, Andrew Njoroge, invited me into his office. He was friendly but nervous. He came out with it: The leader of the organization that was funding our murals, Transparency International Kenya (ostensibly an anti-corruption organization), had been indicted for embezzlement. Consequently, all the funds for our mural project evaporated. In about two minutes he made it entirely clear that there was no chance of those funds being returned. The whole project, the meat of my activity in Kenya, was gone. And, just like that, instead of my new collaborating partner, I sat across from an embarrassed, defensive, stranger.

I was 7000 miles from home and my reason for being there had gone up in a breath of steam. In place of the perfect plan, there was…nothing. I sat quietly for a while, my mind whirring. What should I do? Pretty quickly the naked reality of the situation revealed the next step. I'm not here to make money. I'm here to work—to meet people and see the world and learn about humility. Like stepping over a deep but narrow crevasse, I told Andrew I didn't care about the money. We should continue as if nothing had gone wrong. We could find walls to work on. I'd work for free if the other artists would.

It turned out they would. In fact, they were delighted to have a project to work on at all. None of them had ever painted a mural before. I would soon learn, from them and from simply walking around the city, that there was virtually no such thing as a mural in Nairobi. At that point public art was almost non-existent. (Since 2006 there has been a rise in public art in Nairobi.) The team was enormously excited to make public works of art in a place where it would really be a first.

Frankly, I was used to beginning with nothing. It was not foreign to me to think of setting out into the streets and simply looking for walls to paint. I knew that the shortest path from point A to point B is a straight line. If we wanted walls to paint, we needed to find them and talk to whoever owned them. Andrew was more used to running an arts organization through his computer and his art world connections and I think the idea sounded crazy to him. (Frankly, 7000 miles from home it felt crazy to me too. But what else was there to do?) So, we said we would think on it and meet again soon.

It was July Fourth. A long weekend and I was homesick. My days were not filled with amazing adventure and new friends. They were empty and desolate. It's scary enough to pound the pavement in Boston to look for mural walls, but…in Nairobi? Kenya? I'd put on a brave face, but I felt lost. I took a walk down to the cracked sidewalks of nearby Jomo Kenyatta park in downtown Nairobi. I felt as though I'd been catapulted into outer space. There was no reason for me to be here. As always, I hated empty days. I wondered what I was for.

I heard from a connection at a nearby church about a July Fourth celebration at the American embassy. I was so despondent I nearly didn't go. But I did, finally, peel myself up from the couch in my soulless apartment. A kind person from the church picked me up and we rode through the seemingly endless streets of the sprawling city. High walls and spiked fences surrounded many of the buildings. Images of poverty and abundance weighed heavy on me. They were so close to one another, separated by only a wall. Finally, we were at the embassy.

Inside, the grassy yard was made out like a regular American barbecue. Burgers, hot dogs—the whole thing. I was shy, sad, and couldn't think of what to do. I got myself a burger and stood on the grass, self-consciously munching.

Then, as if by magic, I was in a conversation. A cheerful, upright man told me he had recently moved to Kenya to serve as a leader in the Salvation Army. They were working at a large number of orphanages, or "children's homes" as he called them, around Nairobi. He had a bright, joyful smile and made me feel like I had a dad. I liked being near him. He told me about the great need there was to care for orphans in Kenya, and his hope that they'd be able to do it well. He pointed across the grass to his family who had come with him from their home in Indiana.

"And, what do you do?" he asked expectantly. I told him the whole story—the murals, the funding falling through, our need for walls to paint on. Cheerfully he offered, "Well, we've got a lot of walls at our children's' homes…"

It was glorious to find a yes. Something that *worked*. Something that wasn't "no" right off the bat. Everything had been saying no. So foreign. So lost. The anti-corruption organization being corrupt. The money gone. But with this connection I could feel life coming back into me. My shoulders relaxed a little bit. We had a lead! There was something to do.

By the end of the weekend we had worked it out. We would be welcomed at the Kabete Children's' Home the following week. On Monday I returned to the African Colours office and told them the great news. It was not, perhaps, the high-visibility location and art world attention the original spaces would have provided, but it was good. It was real. We'd be painting beautiful pictures for children in a place that could use it.

A couple of days before we were to begin I met John Kamicha, Jeff Wambugu, and Simon Muriithi, the artists with whom this mural was to be created. We met for a few hours, sharing our work with one another, talking and scribbling down ideas for the mural we were going to create.

I had been in Kenya for about three weeks at this point. I was constantly observing what felt to me like the amazing differences between Kenya and my home in the US. I was trying hard to pick up as much Swahili as I could, and struggling to be understood, even in English. Touchingly, when I got to meet and work with these artists, many of the cultural differences melted away. There's something special about artists, people who have made the great decision that creativity, beauty, truth, are worth working for, worth pursuing even in the face of societies and standards that don't agree. Having made this decision, I found, made us able to understand one another. We could talk about these things that we love in a way that we could all just *get it*.

The designs came together easily and simply. On the morning we were to begin, we were joined by another artist, Faith Nancy Cowie, and our team for the Kabete mural was complete. For the next several days the five of us worked, laughed, consulted, and got to know one another. As the work proceeded, I watched two beautiful phenomena unfold before my eyes. The mural, as always, came out differently - more alive, more individual, and more full of personality - than the sketches we had prepared. And the team grew together with creativity and real love. When we began we were strangers, linked only by our art and our affiliation with African Colours. But by the end of just the first day of work, I could feel each individual bringing their gifts to the table. We laid out our designs for a mural that would begin in the dormitory entrance and wind its way up a stairwell to the second floor.

By the end of the five days we worked on the mural at Kabete, it felt as if this team had been working together for years. We quickly trusted one another's creative intuitions, asked questions, and went with ideas as they arrived. They also answered my endless questions about Swahili. We all were joined in our love of the children. Each one of the artists, in our own ways, reached out to the children at the home, giving them opportunities to paint, coaching them, joking with them and photographing them, to their delight. As the work progressed, many of them tentatively, and with great awe, took the brushes from our hands and worked with us, filling in the shapes with color.

By the end of the week we learned some more good news. The progress at the Kabete Children's' Home had inspired Andrew Njoroge and he'd come up with something else. Connected as he was in the Nairobi art world, he'd had a conversation with some directors at the National Museum of Kenya. There was talk of our team painting a mural at the museum! We were all stunned and didn't know what to make of it. I wanted to hoot and holler and yell and whistle, but in the next moment I knew it could just as easily come to nothing. We tried to be calm and not get our hopes up. The deal needed to unfold. They

needed sketches and waves of approvals. It was going to take time if it happened at all.

Meanwhile, we had a team of artists chomping at the bit to work. The blessing at the Salvation Army orphanage had shown us all that it could work. The Kenyan artists were as delighted as I was and we were hungry for more. No matter the language or the culture, there is nothing like making a work of art in a place where it really can serve.

I began thinking about what we could do next. With the first mural behind us, and the museum project seeming distant and unlikely, I felt that unless we just pushed ahead, we'd spend the next week doing nothing. I suggested to the artists that we simply go out into the city, walk around, and see what sort of project we might scare up. I'd done it at home and seen it work. To me, sitting around doing nothing usually feels more painful than feeling like a fool proposing murals to strangers out in the wild world. The others felt the same. Kamicha, Faith Nancy and I took to the streets.

It can feel foolish, hopeless and stupid—unless you do it with great wide-open eyes and an expectation that something can come of it. But you have to face the absurdity. So we walked around watching and waiting for something to happen—an idea, a conversation, something. Having left the office, we'd left apathy behind. We were willing to be fools for art. We wanted to use our skills. Would life meet us halfway? Kamicha spied a long corrugated tin wall around a construction site and turned to me, "Should we ask if we can paint it?" "Of course!" I shrugged. He ambled through the rusty door and approached the owner. I heard their conversation in Swahili. After five minutes, as easy as that, we had that most precious thing—permission to paint the wall.

We spent the rest of the day finding and buying black and white spray paint, resolved to begin our new project early the next morning.

I've painted many murals in highly visible public places. I'm comfortable talking with strangers while I work—helping them understand what I'm doing, why I'm doing it, and what public art is all about. But I have never experienced anything like what happened that next morning.

In my time in Nairobi I didn't see any murals anywhere. Maybe they were out there, but I didn't see them. Either way, I could feel that if we painted a mural on this wall in a normal, everyday neighborhood, we would be doing something unusual. We would attract attention. Not to mention that I am a mzungu (a white person). These two things in tandem were bound to raise some eyebrows. But again, I'm used to that. In fact, I look forward to it. The showman in me loves to be the center of attention, being creative, blasting color into public places while people look on in wonder, delight, and confusion.

So, I was feeling great as Kamicha and I began our painting at 7 that the morning. People were walking to and fro behind us, but as soon as the first can of paint began to spray I could feel the eyes of the crowds turning to us.

A symbol I use a lot in my art is dragons. I've been using that image for years. My love of it comes from the Chinese use of dragons as a symbol of energy, life, prosperity, and vitality. To me it's a symbol of everything lively, imaginative, and fantastical. So, I make them lot. Kamicha and I had agreed that while we would be improvising most of this mural, we would base it on a theme of animals and beasts in a sort of cartoon style.

I began my waving, curling 20-foot-long dragon in bright white spray paint. It appeared in great arcing lines on the steel gray corrugated metal. Just as I had hoped, a crowd of 50 or so people were lining up behind us, talking about the work. They were pointing, and staring, not sure what was going on. Soon I broke the barrier of silence that was between us by bidding them all "Habari za asubuhi!" (Good morning!) in my best Swahili. This seemed to warm the relations a little and people began asking what we were doing. "Are you an artist?" "What is this?" "Where are you from?"

The dragon was coming out nicely. Kamicha was making this great lineup of three animals seated in chairs looking like Egyptian gods. I was feeling in

myself, "This is it! This is what life is all about!" I was watching a fabulous, flaming, expressive mural open its wings on this dirty old corrugated wall, doing the work of creation right before the amazed and startled eyes of a crowd of strangers. This to me is the height of life.

After about an hour my dragon was looking wonderful. He was shining. His eyes were bright. His body curved powerfully and the look of the spray paint on this old wall made it look tough as nails, dirty, and rough. To show his enormous size I drew a city skyline below him. I felt he was coursing through the air over it, flying with confidence and

skill. I continued bringing him to life—his scales, the stars in the sky around him.

By this time it was 9 a.m. and the crowd behind us had grown. Hundreds of people were passing by moment by moment. The crowd of onlookers continued to point and speculate. At one point, I walked across the street, away from the mural to get a look from a distance. One of the spectators pointed to the city I had drawn. "Is that Nairobi?" he asked. I hadn't really meant it to be, but because I wanted them to feel connected to the piece I said, "Yeah!" and walked back across the street.

From that point, as I worked, I felt a change in the crowd. I could feel them behind me, becoming cold. The tone of their conversations became dark and short. I looked back at them. They were just standing there, as before, talking. "Is this real?" I wondered, "Or am I making this up?" I couldn't tell.

The next time I walked across the street to get a look someone said to me, "This picture, it goes against our way of life here in Kenya." I didn't know what to say. The coldness enveloped me. I felt naked and afraid. How could my wonderful, curling dragon go against anyone's way of life? Another man said to me, "You are a good artist. Are you a Christian?" The two didn't seem to follow one another. "Yes," I said, "I am a Christian." A puzzled look was on his face. Soon I was surrounded by chilly, prying questions that I couldn't understand. I walked back over to Kamicha, working diligently on his trio of Egyptian-looking beasts.

"What's going on?!" I challenged. He didn't know what I was talking about. He hadn't noticed. I said, "I have to get out of here. I need to tell you what they've been saying." He was confused but agreed. We put away our paints and escaped to a nearby restaurant. A theory was coalescing in my mind and I told Kamicha, my new artist confidant, my best guess.

Images are innocent. But culture puts meanings to all these images which then give images great power. During my few weeks there I had begun to understand that Kenya is a deeply Christian nation. And the culture of that Christianity is in some ways very conservative. As I listened to the words of the crowd it dawned on me that the great majority of the folks behind me were seeing my dragon through a literal Biblical lens. This dragon, which to me was symbolizing life, prosperity, and strength, was, to them, the red dragon, the very *devil,* in the book of Revelation. While I have many ways of seeing a dragon, these folks, the residents of the neighborhood I was visiting, had no way of seeing a dragon except through this lens. Without meaning to, I had painted an image of Satan devouring the city of Nairobi.

I had a pit in my stomach as I feverishly strained to understand what to do. Should I erase it? Should I leave it? Should I take off and never return simply to save my own skin from this mob that probably want to stone me right here and now?

Art has the power to change and even create culture. It has the power to lead people to new ideas and new understanding. But, I knew, a poorly placed image also has the power to uselessly enrage and confuse people, further leading them away from a healthy enjoyment of art, creativity, and images. Another voice inside me insisted "This is my art! I have to stand by it!" Was I getting pushed around? Plenty of artists I love had fought for their right to express. They were heroes for it. Was I being a pushover? Should I stand for freedom of expression despite the obvious anger from the crowd?

After wrestling within myself I understood that the best thing to do was to change the dragon into something else. I felt more clearly than ever that my priority was to make art that would love people. Art that could be understood. A desire to understand humility had brought to me to this place, and that

desire rose up that morning. It unseated the complaint that I was the artist and had made the image. That somehow I had a right (or even responsibility) to stick with it because I had made it. Humility revealed to me that I wanted to do what Love would do. I wanted to fight on the side of Love, not necessarily on the side of my own self. I felt an enormous cheer at having come to the right conclusion.

We made our way back to the wall and resumed work. I stared at the dragon, trying to see through it to what it should become. Quickly it came into view. The two great curves of the dragon's back could be wings. The head could become a star, and the whole thing would become a bird, flying in the night sky.

I breathed a greater sigh of relief an hour later when no remnant of the dragon remained. The very air seemed to have changed. During this time Faith Nancy and Jeff Wambugu had arrived and had been working with Kamicha on the rest of the wall. For about 90 feet down the wall their images were arriving—scenes of trees and animals, fish, and huts. They had even invited some of the folks (there were still lots and lots of folks standing by, watching) to paint with us. A brave teenager and his friend took up cans of white paint and made some additions here and there. For the rest of the time as we painted, we talked to people, answering their questions and trying to entice them to paint with us.

With the dragon gone, the morning's terrors erased, a happy ease returned. I shook my head in stunned amazement at the day's events and the consolation of having done the right, the loving and beautiful, thing.

In the next days we learned that the mural at the National Museum had been ok'd. Our next step was to look at the wall and make a design for approval. The wall was 10 meters high and about the same width—a very different kind of wall than we had worked on before. The theme that was given us by the museum was "Kenyan cultural heritage." Between Kamicha, Jeff, and myself we came up with a design that powerfully used the size and shape of the space. Two large figures reach to the sky, their arms wrapped around a brilliant sun. Their bodies are filled with symbols of Kenyan culture, from the ancient to the contemporary—from cattle and masks to cell phones and matatus (ever-present taxi-like minivans used for public transport).

We sent the sketch off for approval and while we were waiting for the response, I set off for a trip to Mount Kenya that I had arranged months before. My flight back to the US was leaving on Sunday, in one week. Frankly, knowing how long it often takes to get ideas approved, I held little hope that this mural would happen. There were so many things to get done, not least of which was getting and financing a scaffold to enable us to get all the way up on this enormous wall.

When I arrived back in Nairobi on Thursday I was delighted to learn that the sketch had been authorized. And I was blown away by the work that had

been done in my absence. As seemed to be the pattern in our projects, there had been a pledge from a local company of a nice metal scaffold, but there had been hemming and hawing and the scaffold never arrived. Then, heroically, Kamicha, Jeff, and a new artist, Peter Walala, leaped into action, building a scaffold out of long wooden uprights and

plywood scavenged from a nearby garbage dump. They secured it to nearby trees with tightly tied cables. They spent three days building it.

Gazing at the jury-rigged scaffold, I joked to myself that we really could forget the mural altogether—this scaffold was art enough! It was three levels high, with makeshift ladders at the sides and twine wrapped from pole to pole, ostensibly to keep us from falling off.

Beginning in earnest on Friday morning, the new team, consisting of Peter, Kamicha, Jeff, and me, as well as three new artists, Willie Wamuti, Martin Muhoro, and Sam Kimemia, began the arduous task of scraping the wall in preparation for priming and painting. The building was ancient and crumbling. With each pass of the scrapers, great chunks of old paint flaked off and fell to the ground.

By the end of Friday the wall was almost completely scraped. And we had two days left to finish the mural before I flew back to the US. I got myself used to the idea that we would begin the mural, but it would only be finished days after I was gone. I didn't like the idea of starting a mural and leaving before it was finished, but it seemed like a hard reality.

Over the next two days, I had the pleasure of watching our two great figures come into existence. And at the same time, as the work was being done, I watched our team, now seven, make that beautiful artists' connection. The lines went up. The figures reached 30 feet into the sky, towering over us. Their gestures, cast upon the wall, became meaningful, symbolic, and important. The team worked with urgency, having already invested so much. The colors began to arrive, filling in the bodies, the sun, and the sky.

One thing about painting murals—the work is so big, so beyond our normal scale, that you can't see it correctly when you are right there working against the wall. The artist must, many times throughout the day, walk from the wall to a place 50 or 100 feet away, where the whole picture can be seen. The scaffold was so high

that to get down and back up again was something of a commitment. It was an interruption of the work and no one liked doing it. We got used to calling down to the folks who were already down on the ground, asking for guidance. "How much higher should this arm go?" one hollered down. The guys begin gesturing, hollering back, "1 foot! 18 inches!" The artists asked for the eyes of others, trusting their judgments, humbly making changes recommended from the ground. In this way the team came to act largely as one creative being. A beautiful trust blossomed among us.

The mural was being painted on some of the National Museum of Kenya offices. At one point one of the administrators poked her head out the door and regarded us working on the scaffold, ever climbing up and down. It was clear she was skeptical. She hollered over to us, "Do you have insurance for that thing?" The entire team burst into peals of laughter. Inwardly we were proud. No one answered the question. We could feel the distance between our process and her expectation. There was no money for insurance! There wasn't even money for a scaffold! Only creativity, willingness, and a great hunger to work. We all knew—the proof was before our very eyes—you can make something beautiful if you will disregard the reasons why you can't.

It was as the last glow of sun disappeared on Sunday evening that the final touches were put to the wall. The enormous figures rose out of the ground, holding a radiant sun over their heads. Many hands had indeed made light work. The entire mural had been painted in a matter of two long days. The blue sky over the sun, the highest point of the mural, had been painted by the outstretched arm of 6'5" Martin Muhoro. From the fourth rung of the homemade ladder we borrowed from a nearby construction crew, he just reached the top while two others held the ladder firm on the third level of the scaffold.

The clock ticked. 6 o'clock. 6:30. 7. My flight to Boston was to leave at 10. I was desperate to get a photograph of myself with the team before I left. Exhausted, and delighted to have finished the work in the time we had, we began the work of disassembling and pulling down the beloved scaffold, which obscured our finished work. After an hour of hammering and sawing, we pulled the construction from the wall and it fell with a great crack. Victorious, we sat on its fallen skeleton as Andrew's flash popped in our faces, capturing the last scenes of the work.

Back in Boston I could never be the same. How could I ever be afraid of plans falling through, when they already had? And 7000 miles from home to boot? My feet were planted that much more firmly in the path of improvisation and trust. Things can change, even fall apart, but I can no longer believe it's the end of the story. If there is willingness there is a path. I'm that much more confident in the desire to follow the shining idea and serve it with *humility*.

PREPARATIONS OF THE HEART

In the years when I hitchhiked people said to me all the time, "That was fine in the old days, but the world is too dangerous now." At least in my case, they were not right.

Hitchhiking was the ultimate improvisation. It's like surfing. The waves are there, but in order to ride it you have to give up on going under your own effort. And once I'm cast, then there is only the living of it. You get what you get. Yes, and…

People are connected. Why are some people inclined to pick up a total stranger? Why do they invite them into their personal space? *How* are we connected?

Stepping into a stranger's car is like a first kiss: Can it be? Are these lips actually touching mine? Instantly you're in someone's intimate space. The car smells like a life. The vinyl seat cover has a rip and the stuffing is coming out. A pine tree air freshener hangs from the rear-view mirror. There's a half-filled back-pack on the floor. The person has a voice, they ask a question, they're nervous, or not, but they're real.

God was introducing me to the notion of loving everyone. Daily I was thinking of the people I saw on the street as adorable and adored by God. I was more and more convinced each day.

In order to put out my thumb I had to let go of a few things:

1) The mainstream notion that hitchhiking is bad, shameful, stupid, irresponsible, and only for bad, undesirable people
2) The notion of total control of my situation
3) Independence

Over the years hitchhiking brought out in me a skill I hadn't known I had. I found that I could connect—*really connect*—with strangers. Whether it was a bearded fisherman, cursing out his wife in a rusty pickup, a soccer mom in a pristine SUV, a long-haired college student, or one of a thousand other types of people, I found I was connected to them, cared about them, and appreciated their willingness to open their door to me. More often than not, especially on longer rides, after some initial pleasantries, the driver would begin to tell me their story. Whatever was on their mind, out it would come. And almost invariably, especially if the story was angry or tragic, as I listened, the tone would warm and soften. They could feel me listening. I was interested. I didn't judge them. I could pay full attention to this beloved human, spilling their guts to a stranger.

Because we would likely never see each other ever again, the stakes were low. So it was easy to ask real questions and get real answers. Naturally, we felt close to one another.

I knew this was at least partly because of how I was. I wasn't threatening. I was friendly. They could feel my sincere interest and my love. I know it. These conversations were different than most of the conversations in my life. I began to see them as something I could try to guide.

My hopes for a hitchhiking trip expanded. It was not just to get from here to there anymore. It was to connect, and even, to help someone if I could. I began to have confidence that I could bring my love into the car with me, and if there was a need near the surface, I would have a good chance of bringing some comfort. It was a simple matter of exerting no will of my own, but simply responding with love and attention to whatever was brought up naturally. The confidence I felt brought a feeling of safety to the conversations, which invited more sharing.

A necessary piece of this equation was that I felt almost no self-consciousness in these situations. I knew that my presence there was good, strengthened by this new thought that my listening ear might be a comfort. This absence of self-consciousness was due, at least in part, to the fact that just to be there I'd jumped off the precipice of normal expectations. I'd had to let go of knowing what was going to happen. Many of us know the feeling of hesitation at a dance party. We arrive in a stiff, mundane frame of mind. Folks on the dance floor have loosened up, they're in the groove. It takes some time to let go of the self-consciousness of normal life before we can let go and use our bodies in the loose and expressive way that is dancing. These conversations were just like that except that once I put my thumb out, any hope of normalcy was out the window. It was going to happen. Just like good dancing, it was loose, expressive, and beyond the clutches of self-consciousness.

****

Years later, in 2007, my friend Spike asked me if I would take over for him doing weekly visits at a local jail through our church in Boston. He had been going for some years, leading men in Bible study, praying with them, loving them, caring for them. He was moving away and needed someone to take his place. The idea was so far outside of anything I had ever thought of I hardly knew what to say. Still, I'd been persistently practicing my principle: If an opportunity comes your way, say yes.

So, after mulling it over for a day or two, I did say yes.

The feeling at a jail or prison is unlike anywhere else. First, it's so serious. No one is there because they want to be. People have been forced there. People are making other people do things against their will. People are not free there.

When you enter (even as a volunteer) you are no longer living on your own terms. You are living on the institution's terms. It's harsh and hard, the rules and the surfaces. Just walking into the place you can feel the mental environment, like going to a foreign country where all the assumptions are different.

The first few times I went to the Nashua Street Jail, the feeling of foreignness was overwhelming. My heart pounded in my chest at the reality of seeing these men behind actual bars. It's staggering how movies can make prison seem cool, when the reality is only heartbreak—lives stunted and broken.

It was Christmas and Spike and I went to the jail together one time. We had brought specially sanctioned Christmas packages for men in a couple of the units. They contained things like soap, powdered soups, and deodorant. We were loaded down with them and walked from cell to cell, briefly wishing the men happy holidays and giving them the gifts. I noted how Spike spoke with great tenderness to the men. He shook their hands, lingering long enough to love each one individually. After a while I tried my hand at handing out the packages, stumbling to say something appropriate.

When we walked out into the lobby the enormous mechanical door clanged closed behind us and I felt like I could breathe deeply for the first time in hours. In the following weeks Spike moved away and the work was mine.

The first time I came back by myself my expectations were blank. I had a list in my pocket of names, units, and cell numbers of men who had requested a chaplain visit. I navigated my way to the unit of the first name on the list. Feeling like an imposter I knocked on the thick glass window of the officer's booth announcing myself as a religious volunteer. I was directed to a small, private room, empty but for two plastic chairs with fake-wood school desks attached. The guard motioned for me to wait while the man was summoned. Again the heavy door crashed behind me. Another door was across from me, leading into the unit where the detainees were. I could see men in baggy tan uniforms passing by the thin window in the door. I sat alone in the cinderblock room and waited. I put my pile of Bibles and magazines on the floor beside me.

After a few minutes an officer opened the door across from me and a young man in his tan uniform entered the room. He was slight and had curly brown hair. His face and manner were nervous. He sat down in the chair across from me. I wondered what we would say to one another.

I greeted him seriously and asked how I could help. He began to tell me about his situation. He had been high. He broke into a store. He needed money for his next fix…As I listened to his story I began to have a strange feeling that the conversation was all so familiar. The feeling in the room, the feeling between us. "What is it?" I wondered while he spoke. "Nothing about this is familiar." I thought about the scary, foreign place I was in. The young man continued to describe his fearful, stuttering life on the streets. But then, easy as can be, I realized, "This is just the same as hitchhiking." The truth of it dropped in like a perfect fitting car part. It made so much sense! Within minutes I felt foolish for feeling nervous about being there. These were just people—people with stories, heartbreaks, jokes, needs, desires, just like everyone else. In a heartbeat I realized this was easy. Just love him. Be on his side. Be human with him.

I had plenty to learn about the ins and outs of the jail, how to run a Bible study group, and a lot of other things. But after that morning I knew that this work wasn't going to be a stretch. It was right up my alley. I could bring my confidence of God's goodness. I could let myself love them, resting in our natural, God-created connection. I could ride the wave.

THE DEVIL WANTS YOU TO FORGET YOUR WORK

My work as a volunteer chaplain at the Nashua Street Jail was a far cry from the way I usually spent my days, painting murals and teaching kids. It was a place of rules that don't bend. In my world, there are rules, but they all bend. There's room for listening, taking in the specifics, working out an approach appropriate to each situation. At the jail there's nothing like that. There are the rules. Within those rules live 700 detainees and several hundred officers and administrators.

After just a few visits to the jail I knew this was my work. I walked from unit to unit on the echoing cement halls, visiting detainees who had requested a chaplain visit. The conversations were real. The men opened their hearts to me, asking about the most serious things. Can God forgive me? How can I pray about my fear? How do I forgive someone who's hurt me and my family? How do I get right with God? How can I forgive myself when I've hurt so many people?

I loved these men. It wasn't relevant to me what they had done or were accused of. They were there. I was there. The truth of God applied to them just like anyone else. I wanted to help if I could.

And, unlike much of the rest of life, I found I could help, *every single time I went*. They needed help and they knew it. They longed for it. When they asked questions they didn't get glassy eyed as I answered. They didn't chomp at the bit to tell me what they thought. They listened. They considered the ideas I shared. They drank in the Bible verses, and loving attention. Every time I left the building, after a two-hour visit and maybe six conversations, I knew I had been there for someone in their time of need. A human heart had been comforted or encouraged.

Every Tuesday morning I took myself over to the jail. My visits began at 9 and went until 11.

For all of my adult life I've been at least partially self-employed. That means that if I don't work, I don't get paid. If I don't paint, my work will never be seen. If I don't write songs, they'll never be heard, and no one will ever pay me to perform them. I *need* to be motivated.

And the good thing is, I am. It's much more comfortable to me to work than not. I don't like sleeping in. If I do, I can feel my mission, my ministry falling away, slipping into obscurity. Fortunately, I've never had too much trouble getting out of bed. When the alarm goes off, I jump up and get on with the morning. It's not my favorite, but it's no big deal. From the beginning, I've felt in my bones that my life is about working to make beautiful things. The best rest is in seeing the good you've done and the progress you've made—not time off. You may get paid, you may not, but only you can make sure the work gets done.

Over the years my practice of self-discipline has been honed in the crucible of self-employment. I don't worry that I'll slack off or make myself crazy pushing myself too hard. There's a healthy, hard-fought balance.

So, it was very, very strange when, at the buzzing of the alarm Tuesday morning at 7, I longed only to close my eyes and fall back into the warmth of sleep. I looked at the clock. 7:01. "I don't even want to go to the jail today." I thought. It felt so far away, so cold, so difficult and uncomfortable. Why would I even go? They wouldn't miss me just this once.

Thank God there is a thing in me that just doesn't change plans. I pulled myself up from the bed like a man who's been hit by a car. I forced myself to my feet, feeling six times the gravity of a normal morning. Everything was heavy, meaningless. Why didn't I just take it easy this morning?

But I didn't. I forced myself through the morning routine. Clothes, breakfast, prayers. I braced myself against the cold and walked to the subway. After a long wait in the January freeze, the train came, filled with listless urbanites. In the smash of bodies on the train I thought of the jail. What a depressing place. I thought of the stony face of the guard at the front desk. I dreaded the interaction I'd have with her. I thought of the steel doors and the way they crash when they close. The gray painted cinder blocks. The empty, sad feeling of the building.

I arrived at the jail, showed my badge and the steel doors banged closed behind me. Five minutes later I was in the visitation room with a detainee who asked me how to pray. I searched my heart and understanding for a good way to answer his question. We searched the scriptures and spoke about God's merciful openness. The warmth and love in the room were palpable. I loved his humility, his desire to grow and to know God. All the darkness and resistance I'd felt that morning was burned away like mist in the sun. It was no more. I wondered how I could have ever felt it. I spent the rest of my time there joyfully buoyed up by the spiritual desire and love I saw in these men. When I left the building two hours later I was filled with energy, delighted with life, and sure that I'd done the best possible thing with my morning.

So I was very, very surprised when, the next Tuesday morning when the alarm sounded, I wanted nothing less than to get out of bed. A heavy, gray burden cast itself over me. I couldn't think of anything good about going to the jail, and all I wanted to do was stay home.

I slogged through the heaviness, feeling uninspired and listless. The train made its way sadly through the dark tunnels and dropped me at North Station where commuters rushed coldly to their destinations. And when I arrived at the jail, the very same thing happened as the previous week. Almost immediately after the doors crashed behind me, the weight, the dark, listless, heaviness, simply disappeared. It was replaced by the warm, sunny feeling of loving these men. I listened to their questions, their hard stories, and a natural, basic love welled up in me like a fire in a furnace. There were lots of dark, hard things to hear and confront at the jail, but from the very beginning it was clear to me that my job was only to be on their side. It wasn't my job to worry or be terrified for them. It was to love. To be a listening ear and a solemn, certain voice, recognizing their value and belovedness to God, regardless of whatever had happened. I knew that God did love them. And we could make progress daily, seeing and feeling it more. Again, when I left the jail two hours later, I was filled with energy and love. Life was real and good.

When the next Tuesday rolled around it was the exact same thing. From the moment I awoke to the time I walked through the jail's unforgiving doors, it was as if the jail were a reverse magnet, repelling me with a constant force. And then, as if the feeling were controlled by the steel doors themselves, it was gone, replaced by the natural, life-rich feeling of love and deep spiritual connection. Week after week I saw hearts comforted and understanding deepened.

This process continued and I pushed through it. The resistance feeling was there in full force every Tuesday morning. By contrast, every other day of the week was as normal as could be. I ably began my mornings, working on other projects. I didn't feel a twinge of the resistance. It only happened on jail days.

This went on for about six months. Every Tuesday morning, like the Eye of Sauron pushing me away from my God-given task. And each morning I pushed through it, knowing it was my duty to be there. The pattern was conspicuous, almost laughable. As clear as can be it was the resistance of the devil, the adversary, the carnal mind. It doesn't matter what we call it, but I knew it from plenty of hard experience.

It had come countless times before as I embarked on the work that would help someone else or initiate my own spiritual growth. I recognized it from my bike trips, and various creative endeavors that would expand my abilities and power to bless. I had come to see that this mental influence arrives mercilessly, forcibly posing as my own thoughts and feelings. It floods my experience with fear, hatred, annoyance—resistance to doing what is right and God-planned. And, unless it's resisted, it wins. It will keep you, me, all of us, from following God's guidance, until we refuse to be influenced.

In this case, I felt enormously grateful for my natural inclination simply to do what I'm supposed to. I did feel gray and listless, but the thing in me that keeps promises was too strong. There was no way I wasn't going to the jail. I'd said I would. So I did. And thank God. It enabled me to put the heavy, burdensome feelings to the side and simply go about my business. It took six months but at length, the resistance gave up the ghost and never came back.

I was also grateful to see it for what it was—a lie working against my inclination to serve God. When I saw that it came only on Tuesdays, only in the hours before I went to the jail, the mask was lifted. These weren't my feelings, as much as it seemed that way. I could see through them to the truth that I did love to do this service. I loved the men at the jail. I loved to be with them and see them grow, losing fear and gaining confidence.

I continued in this role for seven years. I fell deeply in love with it. Soon I was going two and sometimes three times a week. I led Bible study groups in English and Spanish. There were countless conversations, the kind you dream of having, in which a life is truly transformed. It changed my life forever, deepening my love for the Bible and showing me that I was an able teacher in these important spiritual matters. I saw that it's never my job to create love. It's just there, for *everyone*, no matter what they've done. My confidence in the scriptures soared, my faith in God gaining in great strides.

JAIL IN THE MORNING, KICKBALL IN THE AFTERNOON

In my second year of chaplaincy at the Nashua Street Jail I really hit my rhythm. Every time I went, something wonderful happened. I felt useful in a way I almost never felt in the rest of my life. Every day I was there someone opened to me, and I was able to provide something useful. My tools, the Bible and *Science and Health*, were ever capable, and my understanding and ease with them was increasing by leaps and bounds. I was at the jail every Tuesday and Thursday morning, sometimes doing services in English and Spanish on Sunday afternoons.

On the weekdays I was in two different units on the sixth floor—the two murder units. In each one I had an active Bible study group of between three and ten men. Naturally, the conversations were serious. The personal tragedies were real—lives, families, and hearts broken. But, at the same time, they're just people. Sometimes the guys were playful with each other, making good-natured jokes, passing the time. Once in a while, one of the guys who was really being helped by the group would bring a friend. It was gratifying to see that the ideas we talked about were being discussed in the unit, shared, and lived.

And people *were* being helped. There is nothing more beautiful than a grown man, in his need and desire, asking about God's love, truly hoping. I helped them explore the gospels, psalms, and countless Bible stories, talking through the themes, applying them to their situations. I brought in study guides and assigned homework. The men were progressing, praying together, continuing the conversations outside the group.

It was in one of these murder unit Bible studies that I met Carlos. He was 20 years old with an athletic build and black buzz cut. He showed up one morning in the tan scrubs worn by every detainee in the unit. It was quickly clear he was on fire for the Bible. He was often first to offer up an answer to a question or pose a question of his own. He did his homework with care and consistency. He was a model student. I came to love him very much.

I learned that Carlos had found God in jail. He'd been arrested, charged with murder, and was looking at a possible 20 years in prison. Not surprisingly, in his need he turned to God. He found the promise of love and redemption in the Bible and it changed his life quickly. He often spoke of his efforts to live completely differently than the life that had led him to jail. From his demeanor he seemed to have truly felt the deep, real forgiveness of God. Carlos was cheerful, progressive, and hopeful.

After coming to the group for several months Carlos let me know that his trial was coming up. It was likely that we wouldn't see him anymore. One day after the group he stayed behind, waiting for all the other guys to clear out. "I wanted to ask you something," he began, and paused…"Do you think I could do what you do?"

My heart glowed. With all my force of conviction and support I assured him that yes, he could. Wherever he was going, there would be people in need, and with the confident, certain message of God's love, he could be a help to them. He had felt the power of God come right into the darkest place, and make it brighter. He knew it was real, that there were no walls to God. He knew that Love was real and he could take it with him. I shook his hand, wishing it were a gigantic fatherly bear hug, and looked him proudly in the eye. After a beat he smiled and walked out of the room. As the heavy glass door closed behind him I prayed that he would continue to see God's love working in him, opening the way of life, inspiration, and usefulness.

In the midst of my months with Carlos another new figure appeared. His name was Brian. He showed up like a ghost and sat silently during the whole 90-minute session. He looked as though he would rather shrink into nothing and cease to be. I tried to involve him in the conversation, asking him questions, but he quietly, shyly demurred. The next week he was back, and again, said nothing. At this point in the group we were making our way systematically through the gospel of Mark. At each meeting we would discuss one chapter that everyone had been reading during the week. We went through the text verse by verse, going over points of misunderstanding, connecting it to previous texts, and getting the feeling of the unfolding gospel. Brian sat in silence every week, enclosed in his little shell, looking like a deer in headlights. But he kept coming without fail.

After several months I knew something important was happening when Brian took me aside, away from the others. Nearly silently, trembling, he told me that in a drug-induced rage he had killed his wife. He had loved her and didn't have any desire to do something like that. They weren't even in a fight. But he had done it. "What can I do?" he asked.

My heart went out in a way it never had before. He was gentle as a lamb, mortified and destroyed. As if my words were my arms I tried to embrace him with what I knew about God. The words came, serious and rock bottom. There is nothing God can't forgive. You are precious. You have good in you. You are not worthless. You are not defined by mistakes, no matter how awful they are. After a few minutes the conversation was over and he walked slowly back into the unit with the other men.

The next week, Brian was there, silently listening as we talked through the next chapter of Mark. Over the next months it was plain to see that Brian was changing. He began to sit up straighter. Every so often he humbly contributed a thought to the conversation. I saw him smile once or twice. It was clear that he, like Carlos, was drinking in the message of God's love, turning away from the horror of the past, giving himself over to the promise of hope. After several months Brian was transferred to another unit, but I continued to visit him on a one-on-one basis. It was slow, humble going, but like a child, he applied himself with pure effort. Sometimes it was clear that he was learning to read while learning the spiritual ideas.

Then, he too was about to go to trial. He let me know that after a few more weeks he would be sentenced. In our last conversation, as he looked out into the likelihood of many years in prison, he told me that he planned to share what he was learning about God. He spoke with a warm, gentle manner. The horror that had dominated his demeanor when we first met, was replaced by humility. I saw him speak to younger men in his new unit with a gentle, fatherly care. It was easy to see that he was naturally kind—a good man. With all the seriousness of my burning hope for him I told him I knew he would help people when he got there. He smiled like a kid who got a good grade.

That day, after the sessions, I walked out of the jail, the thick metal doors clanging closed behind me. I walked out to my red bicycle, locked up outside the giant concrete facility, home to so many tragedies. I rode the five miles back to my home in leafy Jamaica Plain, on the other side of Boston. I ate my lunch and after a short rest, biked to work at the Dimock Center, where I was the art teacher in in an after-school program for 6 to 12-year-olds.

After picking the children up at the bus, helping them with their backpacks, homework and snacks, we tumbled outside for kickball. The kids hooted and ran, chasing and leaping around the fenced-in urban yard. I knew them all, each one. They were beautiful. Tiny, slight Melissa, a second grader, was the pitcher. Arrayed behind her, the infield and outfield, awaiting the thwang of the red playground ball. A sixth grader named Carlos was at the plate. He booted it with all his might.

How I loved each of them. In my years at Dimock I'd laughed and played with them all. I'd disciplined them and been patient with them. This time I looked out over the group and thought of all the dear people—some right here in the yard, and some five miles away in an unthinkable place. This world is so full of dear people, innocence, mistakes, effort, heartbreak, love—and finally, God.

I thought of God shining His beautiful light out of the faces, leaps, and laughter of these kids. They are the center of the universe to their parents. I thought of God shining His serious, eternal light in the hearts, minds, and courage of the men I knew at the jail. How I loved each of them! Beyond their glaring, terrible mistakes they were fighting for their lives in ways that many of us will never know. Together we were valuing their innocence despite all appearances. We were holding to the fact that God could redeem their lives, and bring that innocence back to the surface. I saw them living it day by day, walking away from fights where previously they would have jumped in with fists and fury. I saw them taking joy in sharing their modest belongings—a new deodorant, a pack of instant soup, with someone who needed it more. Their innocence was there, returning like the warm, white light of the sun emerging from behind a cloud.

THE POWER OF BEING WATCHED / DOOR OPENERS

"Nearly everybody is looking for something brave to do. I don't know why people shouldn't write poetry. That's brave." –*Robert Frost*.

I've loved this quote from Robert Frost for many years. I know the feeling of longing for something brave to do, something good, even glorious. But while Frost's comment is about writing poetry, there's a larger meaning about having faith that our acts matter. We don't all write poetry, but we do all have the power to influence the world for the better, even through our smallest actions and decisions.

Most of us would dearly like to be able to have an effect on the world. Many of us long to use our skills and our love to make the world a better place. We look for jobs in which we can do useful work, we volunteer, we care for those around us.

But we have another power that often goes unused.

I'm always watching the ways other people do things. If I see someone do something I don't know how to do, or wish I could do, I usually feel impressed and interested. Noticing that I observe others, it dawns on me that everyone does. We are all watching one another.

We're almost always surrounded by people. No one always knows exactly what to do or how to do it. Everyone is wondering how to live, how to be happier. And we're all observing the people around us to see what people do, what's normal, what's happening.

Silently, in our inner worlds we're taking in the actions, non-actions, and reactions of others. We are making our judgements, being surprised, annoyed, disappointed, delighted. Day in and day out, we are witnessing countless other people living their lives, making decisions large and small, deciding what their priorities are. We are comparing their decisions to our own, their skills to ours, and to some degree, seeing where we fit in the social landscape.

Often, thinking of others watching us makes us afraid. We feel self-conscious. We're afraid of being judged. It's only natural if we are judging others, having our own unkind opinions. We assume, and often rightly, that everyone else is doing the same. We believe the eyes of others are a source of constant critique.

So we protect ourselves. We wear masks. We dress ourselves up. We hide. We show off. We try to fade into the background. We find a thousand ways to avoid revealing who we are.

We hardly consider the power. There are people constantly watching us!

People long for fame, for the eyes of others to be on them. They long to be noticed and celebrated for the good they do. The fantasy is kept safely at bay by the unlikeliness of becoming famous. But, if we can be brave and kind, if we can let go of our self-consciousness, we can breathe in the good news—the eyes of others are on you *right now*. Every day people are seeing you, aware of what you are doing or not doing. If you do good, brave things, they will be noticed.

This *gives* each one of us power. If we will only see it as an opportunity. If we can find a way to value what we have and who we are. If we can let go enough to understand that our gifts can be valuable to others. If we can get over our fear that we won't be liked, that they'll roll their eyes or we'll be belittled, then we can give the gift of ourselves. We can show others the virtues we know and love. We can prove, in steps small and large, that actual, inspiring goodness is here, right in our midst.

The thing is to find the courage to live our best ideas. At any given moment, what you have to offer the world is the best ideas you've encountered—your loves, your enthusiasm, your delights. When we do this, we're useful. As we live our love, putting our best efforts into solving our own problems with virtue and courage, we are models for others. As we solve our own problems and fight our own battles, striving to be good, we're serving those around us by being an example.

It's not egotistical. It's the opposite. It's the ideas themselves that serve. They bear the weight. They do the inspiring. We simply love them enough to bring them into the world. We serve the virtues, doing what they require, and they give the gifts.

The things we love are qualities and virtues. It may be kindness, or humor. It may be courage or grace or self-control. Behind our love of things, experiences, and people, what we love are qualities and virtues. We love them because they are loveable, inherently.

The people who impress us are the ones who are living the virtues we love. Their lives have been touched by them. It may be a musician whose life has been changed by beauty or freedom. It may be a mom who's seen the power of organization and efficiency. They stand out to us because they're showing us how good these qualities are.

Our power is to express virtues. Our power is to fall in love with virtues and pursue them. Live them. Put them into action. Then, because people are always watching, it's powerful. As we work to practice the virtues we love best, we are not only doing the good work that those virtues cause us to do, we are also showing other people that virtue is possible, right here on earth.

I had a coworker at The Dimock Center who seemed to be almost entirely without self-consciousness. He loved to tell jokes. Many times I'd be sitting in a stiff meeting with people who weren't used to talking with one another and Frank would burst in and guilelessly make some ridiculous wisecrack. He would do this without taking notice of the stiff, self-conscious mood of the room. He seemed fearless. And because of his easy silliness, amazingly, everyone loosened up! Body language changed. We were laughing, charmed, more relaxed. Because Frank had been a fool for us, no one else was afraid. The ice was broken. Soon, folks who had been holding back, not engaging, were connecting and the meeting took on a new ease and humanity.

It happened time and time again. The mood in the room was chilly and quiet until Frank arrived. Then, after he shuffled in with his joyful energy, the feeling in the room would change, and folks would relate in a different, better way.

All along, the people in that meeting *wanted* to be connecting. They wanted to feel loose and free of self-consciousness. But, for whatever reason, there was hesitancy or fear to do it. Frank's demeanor opened the door for the rest of us to do what we wanted to do, but were afraid to initiate.

I began to see we have the power to open doors for one another. Frank didn't think of himself as a leader in that context, but he was. I don't think he was even conscious, exactly, of the service he was providing. Still, he allowed all of us to follow him through that door, and leave our stiffness behind.

We become leaders. When a child walks into a room, filled with joy and play, that child often leads all the adults in the room to feel more joyful. When, in a fearful situation, one person is calm, the others see it and are then "allowed" to be less fearful.

There is no time when this kind of service isn't possible. At the jail sometimes I spoke with men who were struggling with how to be feel useful while they were incarcerated. It was especially pressing when one of them was looking at an extended sentence. Each incarcerated heart bawls, "How can I be worth anything when I'm locked up?"

The question is answered beautifully as men in this position have taken to heart the fact that even in jail, they're surrounded by others watching, hoping. Just like Carlos and Brian from the previous story, even in prison there is an audience. Each of them, in their way, intimated to me that he knew his purpose was to help others, right there in prison. They would not allow their God-given power to contribute to be taken from them. In their need and humility they understood that they were surrounded by others who needed help. They could be the ones to provide it.

Don't compare it to name-in-lights fame. Don't belittle human life with the thought that your daily audience isn't big enough. There are real human eyes, with human hearts and feelings that will be affected by you. Do your brave, exploratory work. The virtue lived by one, seen by another, works its way into thoughts and feelings. It silently inspires. It moves in the one who witnessed it, causing new growth.

Because everyone is watching everyone else, every time we live the virtues that we love, we are revealing treasures to the people around us. The person who feels fear, and sees another person stand up to fear and overcome it, has been shown that it's possible to overcome fear. When we model kindness, we cause others to think of their own relationship to kindness and remember that it can be done.

This power succeeds when we know that it's not about us. It's about the virtues being expressed. Our self-concern slips off when we're so in love with kindness that we aren't shy to be kind, despite anyone else's opinions. We know that kindness is right, so we don't fear the consequences. Life becomes much more interesting. And we are that much more free to be what we love.

We all have this power, today. The world needs our models of courage, persistence, patience, and the whole colorful spectrum of virtues. In fact, it's what the world most desperately needs. All the while, the virtues are right there, in our hearts, ready to be used.

You may say, "I'm not courageous! I don't feel persistent! People are too annoying!" But, the thing is, everyone else has that voice working in them too. Everyone else is suffering under the influence of those same fears and doubts. Think of how much the world needs proof that courage exists. Consider how powerful it is to see someone actually *being* courageous. Love leaps up in our hearts when we see it. You have the power to give that gift to someone else. Maybe even a lot of people.

We all have the work of life ahead of us. That work is to do good, to be better and better, to love others and to love God. It's been a great help to me to see that as I fight my battles honestly, using the whole array of virtues to the best of my ability, I'm not only helping myself, I'm helping others as well. The world needs each of us to write the courageous poem of our lives—for ourselves and for the sake of those around us

AFTER HORROR, THE INNOCENT DESIRE TO BE GOOD

During my time as a chaplain I saw, beyond a doubt, that the qualities of God are alive and well, living and being lived in this place that would otherwise be very dark. Lots of people, when they go to jail, find themselves face to face with the mistakes they've made and the problems they have, and want very badly to get past them.

One day I was talking with a man, call him William, who had had a very sad life so far. He described being raped at the age of 13, drug abuse, friends lost to murder, and the list goes on. He was relating to me how, now that he was in jail where he couldn't get any drugs, all the feelings he'd been pushing away by using drugs, were coming out. He spoke sincerely, calmly, soberly.

His basic question to me was, "With all these terrible things that have happened to me, how can I be free from these intense feelings of sadness, loss, and grief?" It is easy to see, when you hear him talk, what an honest, kind man he is. So, I began to speak to him about knowing himself as God's creation, not the creation of a terrible human history. We spoke about knowing ourselves as spiritual creations who are defined, not by what we've done or had done to us humanly, but by God's love for us. I also mentioned that it's useful, when we feel miserable, to turn outward instead of inward—to seek to love and serve someone else, instead of getting stuck on ourselves.

He seemed a little confused about what I meant. He asked, "Do you mean like this?" He went on to tell me this story, without pride.

There's another man in this unit—call him Joe. Joe is older and had really let himself go—long, scraggly hair, not showering, finger and toenails long and curling. He was a mess and obviously unhappy. William, feeling sorry for him, asked Joe if he could help him, clean him up. Joe said no. End of conversation. But, rather than take no for an answer, William tried bargaining. In jail each detainee has their "canteen" which is extra food and supplies that one buys using their own, usually very limited, money. William asked Joe if he would let him clean him up, cut his fingernails and toenails, etc., at the cost of a certain number of food items in his canteen. At this Joe agreed.

When William told me this story, I looked over to the couch and saw Joe there, hair and nails cut, shaved, clean face, and a smile on it too. William asked, honestly wanting to know, "Is that what you mean by serving others?"

Tears nearly rolled from my eyes as I said, "Yes, William, that's just what I'm talking about." I quickly told him that *he* was also teaching *me*. That is riches of the heart. To desire so much to do an act of kindness to another that one buys the privilege of cleaning up a messy, smelly, surly brother.

In the following weeks as we did our Bible study, it was easy to feel the calm respect that existed between Joe and William. Joe's physical cleanliness (which had been maintained) was a testament to William's tenderness of heart —an enormous natural compassion. Also, where he had been surly, Joe now joined us, timidly asking questions and participating in our conversations.

We've all heard inspiring stories of people who have made it their life's work to help and serve others. Often we think of those people as "saints" or somehow better than us. Seeing this story play out (and many others like it) has shown me that it isn't that way. Tender acts of forgiveness, generosity, and mercy are happening anywhere someone is willing. They even happen in prison. I can't imagine someone with a darker human history than William's. Yet, he demonstrated, beyond doubting, that darkness and human history can't overcome the desire to love, and to feel the blessing of loving another.

BEAUTY REVEALED

One morning in the summer of 2008, I took myself out for a walk around Jamaica Pond, passing the time between jobs. It's a place I went regularly to breathe in the open air.

I looked out across the water, the morning sun shining back at me, reflecting. It reflected in a million different ways. I saw a huge, bright blotch of light, the whole sun looking up from the water like a submerged turtle. There were thousands of tiny stars, twinkling and dancing, coming and going. There were soft, gentle touches of light surrounding the larger reflections, some parts of the pond dark and some parts lit with a vibrant golden filigree like a sequin dress. I stared into this happy spectacle, but instead found myself staring through it, into the meaning of it. Past the spectacle into the meaning of the spectacle. In a moment it was all so simple, just sitting there right before my face. There for all to see. I thought, "The face of God is plunked down right before me—nothing between me and it." And I knew it was true. In those minutes I smiled, actually giggling, witnessing the simplicity and beauty of it.

Spiritual vision is almost like walking into another room. I could feel that I was seeing the same old thing I always see. The light on the water. It's part of a mundane weekday morning just like any other. It means nothing. It's silently there as the cars hiss by, as sales are made in the stores, as the seconds tick by on the clock. Who cares? It's just an empty day! And I could remember that it often feels that way. But I had new eyes. As I stood there on the path, my vision was soaked with meaning. I couldn't look away from meaning. The riches were served up on a shining golden platter.

What was the meaning of that spectacle? Light on water didn't have to be part of the world. And yet, it is. And, given interested and open eyes, it elicits delight in the human heart. Why? And why is this true of trees, the ocean, rocks, and countless other beauties? How is it that they feed us spiritually? The meaning is simply, yes, we are surrounded by a creation that, when listened to, when watched with ready eyes, *feeds* us. We live in a creation that readily, day after day, showers us with spiritual gifts.

As I gazed out on the water, I was delighted. Each star of light reflecting the morning sun became a word. Each swath of light a paragraph. The morning a clear, distinct, pointed essay. Then my eyes were opened to the same thing in other phenomena: A duck's head. His blurted quack. A grandmother hunched over a baby in a carriage. Each one speaking the indelible language of being. The just-almost-violet beginnings of buds on the trees across the pond. The whole of creation, I see. I see. I see.

Every aspect of goodness, written with the pen, and carved with the knife of God, is seared into being. It can never be undone. Duck's head, its face, is a word. This duck-head-word speaks of dearness, of longing, of experience, of "Yes, I AM." The duck is small. It has no voice to people. Yet, it is indelible. It has the stamp of eternity on its little, feathered face. This little face is not only adorable, not only happy, sweet, but speaks of defiance of death. "I am," it says. "I am, and I am nothing but what I am."

The next day I returned. Could I feel, see, that same thing again? The day seemed to hang with its own mundane nature—the opposite of wonder. Same old, same old. Then, for a moment I looked out and I saw that same light, far across the water, sparkling, dancing on the other side. It was spectacular. The lights, the tiny, tiny lights came and went like eyes in a dark cave. They blinked and sparked, opening and closing their hands, in and out like Morse code. Then the sun came further out from behind a cloud and like a breeze entering through an open window, the white morning light washed across the water, setting all the tiny sparks free and they scurried around the face of the pond like skittering bugs, like a white-hot crowd of a million pilgrims on the road to the holy land.

I stared and stared, looking into the simplicity of it. "This happens every morning," I thought. This happens a hundred times a day right here, with people walking past, noticing, maybe not noticing. There was no denying the perfection, each single sparkle on the water, perfect, never to be undone. Perfection exists.

Here is the crucial point: I could have walked right past and said, as the voice will say, "It's just light on water." Or, it may even admit the beauty of the light on the water, but it will still say, "It's just beautiful light on the water. What good is it?" Blindness says, "What does all this beauty do for me?" and leaves it at that, turning away from the riches. "Great," it cries. "There's beauty in the world, but how does that pay my bills? How does that fix my broken marriage?" But, if we would see beauty, and benefit from its riches, we must stop arguing for blindness. The difference comes in looking *into* the phenomenon. Like Moses investigating the burning bush. "What is it? What is it saying?" It's there and there is nothing to be done about it. It is fact. This light on water will never be undone. It is.

Looking *through* the thing into the simplicity of it, into the meaning of it, reveals the idea of it. Then I could see the nature of the thing. I could see that this is one of the infinite poems written by God, which He is reciting constantly. This is one of the infinite languages God is speaking, singing to us all the time. Saying very specific things. There are no words to put to the meaning of light on water. The meanings are only communicated through the things themselves. But they are there, meaning something. Don't seek the words, seek the meaning!

As I gazed into the light on the water, admitting that it wasn't useless or extra—that in fact it was communicating something irreplaceable—it was revealed to me. Its communications speak health, boldness, and worth. This beauty *does* pay the bills. It *does* fix the broken things. Because it is eternal. It is pure. It is what lasts.

I stood on the shore laughing. All around me was the unveiled creation of God's own self. The duck quacked and I cracked up. The light danced and I felt the opposite-less goodness of spiritual creation. The wordless words of God's poems sing in meaning that takes no time or intellect to understand. They are spoken in the shifting light and air of the day, the afternoon, the evening. In the light on the water, as in the feathered face of a duck, I AM THAT I AM. Regaining myself, I looked around and it was an entirely normal morning. People walking their dogs, cars driving silently on the road at the pond's distant shore. But here it all is, done for eternity.

I see the riches. Beauty is around me everywhere. For all time I can drink it in and reflect it back into the world. There is no end of God's goodness. Beauty is in no place, but at hand always. And beauty is not a painting on a wall, but the very voice of eternity. It is not useless, but changes the game, showing that all is Soul, all is beauty, all is indelible good.

Admitting beauty, looking into it with interest, we see it. Then, studying it, living with it, noticing, admiring, and becoming familiar with it, we adore it. It speaks to us. It changes our lives. The indelible nature of its language deepens our understanding of communication itself and of what there is to be said.

DOING MY BEST

As I think I've made clear, as I set out into adult life I was a lunatic for murals. I had them on my mind almost constantly. As ideas came, I worked them out in my sketchbooks like a private laboratory, exploring and testing. I was constantly smitten with the notion that these tender, private inspirations could be released and unveiled to be their beautiful selves in public. There was something amazing about taking those images, so direct from my inmost imagination, and showing them off for all to see. It was incredible. Dangerous but safe. It felt like alchemy, doing something impossible, yet plain as day. And each time I was able to do it, I felt like a superhero. I knew I was telling the truth, revealing something good, bringing something honest to places more used to carelessness and convenience.

So, as I walked or drove or rode my bike from place to place, I was always looking for walls. No matter what was happening, my eyes were open to it. I might be mid-conversation, but if we passed a big, unbroken wall at a well-traveled intersection, I would have to stop, note the address and take some mental pictures. As the years wore on, I had a mental map of countless walls around Boston. Some I had researched, made the calls, had the meetings. Others I couldn't find out who owned them, or had come to a dead end or a flat out "no." Others I hadn't gotten around to, or didn't know how to begin. Meanwhile the pictures in my sketchbook were great, and plentiful. As always, I felt like a little boy sitting on the pile of gold and treasure, begging to give it away.

Sometime in 2007 I passed a wall on Tremont Street in Roxbury. It was huge—75 feet across and 16 feet tall—had no windows or doors, and could be seen from the road by hundreds of cars every hour. It was perfect. I wondered how I could get it.

Doing this research is always an adventure. You just have no way of knowing what will happen. I always began with a hope that I'd be able to do some kind of amazing picture and also make some money. Most often the answer was simply "no" and I had to move on. But sometimes there was interest and the conversation would continue. Sometimes they had their own idea about what kind of a mural it should be and then I had to decide if it was enough like what I wanted to do to make it worth doing. Basically, from the beginning, every aspect of the conversation was a variable. After several years of conversations like this I thought of it like batting in baseball—if something good came out of it three times out of ten, I was doing pretty good.

I walked around the other side of the enormous brick building, looking for the entrance. The sign over the door said "Boston Housing Authority." I walked in and after some time I found myself sitting at the desk of a manager. "I'm a muralist. Your wall would be so great for a mural! Thousands of people would see it. A great contribution to the neighborhood!" Soon I was out in the parking lot again, with a big, bored "Not at this time" ringing in my ears. Oh well, nothing new about that.

But the next summer I found myself riding past the same wall on Tremont Street. It was too good. How could it *not* have a mural on it?? It was almost painful to me. I screwed up my courage, got together some photos of my work, and took myself back to the BHA office. I waited among a handful of folks in various lines to pay their rent or complain about maintenance issues. And then I was sitting in that same office. And in a few minutes had the same answer—"Not at this time." Ho hum.

I'd been learning about the spectrum of projects I might take. At one end of the spectrum were commissioned murals in which a building owner or organization would tell me the images they wanted and I would paint them. At the other end were projects in which I had a lot of creative freedom to use my best ideas and really create a poetic, imaginative work of art. Most of the projects I did were somewhere in the middle. I felt very blessed that the majority of the people I found myself working with were willing to trust me. Very often they didn't know exactly what they wanted and I could help them get there by using my own ideas. Most times I felt that it was my job to take the structure I was given and fill it as full as possible with beauty, expressiveness, and poetry. I loved to be able to work with these people and do a good job for them. It was heartening to find that often I could influence the conversation and show them

an idea that might be more visually interesting than the one they originally had. I learned a lot about having these conversations, discerning what their real interests were, and finding a way to satisfy their needs with images that were interesting to me.

All that said, I *longed* for total creative freedom. I fell over myself with desire to make murals that spoke, not even a little bit about commercial or organizational interests, but about pure beauty and imagination. I was like a raging fire of ideas and artistic passion, trying to pour my oceans of beauty into bathtubs.

Outside of the paying jobs, I worked for Beauty. I wrote poems and walked in the woods. My creative life was alive and deep. It was my best friend, my lover, for whom I would do anything. It was independent of a job or career. Only that I wanted these images to be my job and my career.

Then, that summer, I had the experience I described in the last story—I saw the voice of God speaking in the light sparkling on the surface of the Jamaica Pond. It turned me on in a new way to the holy voice that is speaking around us all the time in nature, light, shadows, just the way everything is. That summer I was surprised to find my inner compass taking me into the woods in the effort to make realistic, adoring pictures of nature. I wanted to see if I could invite that holy voice into my paintings. If I could love the trees, stones, and sky as much as I knew they loved me. It was like going out on purpose to meet God and reflect a small stanza of His immaculate mega-poem into my sketchbook.

This effort was deeply humbling. The beauty and detail of nature was so much more than I had even guessed. In my efforts to be faithful to what I saw, I came to understand that there is no copying nature. I will never be able to do it even 1%. But I also understood that that wasn't required. It was enough just to be its apprentice. I continued to go out, understanding my total inadequacy to create a truly realistic reflection of nature. Instead I felt grateful only to be with it, hear its voice, and reflect some of its infinite ideas into my pictures. In fact, I loved being shown how stupid it was to try to capture nature. Inwardly I cherished my utterly humble role with nature, the voice of God. It invited me, endlessly, to drink in the beauty, and try my very best, knowing I would never, ever, in a billion years, capture it. Yet, with good listening and honesty, coupled with my best efforts and the love I felt, I learned hand over fist. And I often emerged with pictures I loved.

My understanding of trees expanded. My ability to render light and shadow on stones was more mature. After many months of this study I was thinking in this language. More than ever I longed to create a mural into which I could pour everything I was learning. A public mural of the pure love-feeling, God's own voice speaking in the language of trees, stones, leaves, and sky.

So, the next summer, in 2009, when I passed by the Boston Housing Authority office I had to try again. And this time I didn't care about anything other than getting to paint on the wall. I didn't care about money. Just gimme the wall. I didn't care about time. I had the month of July completely free. I wanted to spend it making this mural. I would beg. I would plead. I agreed with myself that I would tell them plainly, "I do not want any money for this. I just want to make the mural." I also agreed that if that's how it panned out, I would require absolute creative freedom.

Then, I was sitting in that office again. A BHA administrator sat across the desk from me. I laid out my plan. I'd made two detailed sketches of the forest I wanted to make. She took it in. I could tell she was inspired. It would

be my magnum opus. The administrator called in the head maintenance official to look over my proposal. Still, they seemed unmoved. The looks on their faces were blank, impressed by the idea, but indicating zero openness to actually doing it. I spelled it out for them, "I don't need any money for this. Just let me do it."

The feeling in the room changed. "Oh." They seemed to say. "That may work." They were used to City of Boston contracts, construction companies, work orders, complaints, rent checks. They regarded me as if I were a sparrow or a thrush who had just flown in the window and said the very same thing. They didn't know quite how to respond. But over the next few weeks, we worked it out. They agreed. I would be free to paint my forest. And they would supply the paint. The wall was mine.

In the weeks leading up to the creation of the mural a thought landed in me. *This is my chance to see what I can do.* It had been a long time since I'd painted a mural without any influence from anyone. With wonder and a bit of awe I considered the concept of doing your best. What does it mean? What does it look like for someone to set aside everything else and do their actual, very, best? Where do you see that? I thought, I'm going to do it. I have the opportunity to see what my best is—where I am, what I'm actually capable of. I didn't know what it would be. I indulged myself. I will not quit until I have spent every piece of inspiration and understanding I have at my disposal. I will pour in everything I know, everything I've learned about the forest, the trees, and the voice of God speaking through them. I am a 34-year-old man, and I am about to see what my best is.

When July rolled around I leapt out of bed every morning. I spent my days doing what I was built to do. I flexed my muscles and painted. I reminded myself of the thousands of people who would see this mural over the next decades. I thought of their lives, their difficulties, their hearts and hopes. With those things in mind I poured in all the beauty I had.

I'd learned to enjoy the social aspect of working in public, but in my heart of hearts my love was painting by myself. I loved to move unrestricted, unharried and undistracted. So I was very surprised one morning when I diverted myself from that path. I'd just finished drawing the whole forest on the wall. The whole thing was laid out in lines like the world before God created it. That morning I was just beginning to fill in the first of the shapes.

As I worked I noticed a mother and her four children get out of a banged-up old station wagon. They'd just gotten home from grocery shopping. The mom directed each of the kids to carry the bags from the back of the car into their little apartment in the nearby public housing block. The kids did as they were told. I liked them. They were bright and loose, walking in their jangly kid way. When they were done with the groceries they were just there, hanging around in the sun, looking for the next thing.

I thought, "I bet those kids would love to put a brush on this wall." And then, almost against my own will, I walked over to where they were playing around near the car. I told them about the mural—what it was going to be. I asked if they wanted to see it. They did. I called to their mom— could they come look at the wall? She said ok. And then, just like that, I had four kids working with me. I couldn't believe myself. What had I done? And yet, it was a summer day. I was mixing paint for four awesome kids, and we were making a mural of a love forest. I had to admit, it was wonderful.

Pretty soon, with some cajoling, a few more kids came to help. And just like that it was established. Neighborhood folks could come paint if they wanted. Over the next few days, the news spread via the kids and others. I made myself ready. I understood now that this was part of doing my best. This was going to be a LOVE forest and part of that was to love the people in the neighborhood. People dropped in organically. The kids came back. They invited their friends. A professional house painter with a huge, tall ladder came and filled in some of the highest parts. A homeless man jumped in for a little while. I began to invite my friends. After a week or so we had filled in everything that could be reached without getting up on the really big

ladders. I'd not even suspected, but part of doing my best was to move when the inspiration struck, and let Love invite the people to help. It was just right.

And then I took over again. For the next three weeks I was up and down the ladder so many times I couldn't count. The leaves began to arrive, first flat and then with deep shadows and illuminating detail. I knew in my humble heart that compared to a real forest it was like a child's first scrawl, but I felt a rush of joy as it began to exude a feeling of rich, natural affluence. In big, confident letters, sitting right there in the forest, I wrote the words "LOVE" and "AMOR." It felt strong and real to write those words, 5-feet tall, public and unashamed in the wide, uncaring world. Each night I came home exhausted, riding my bike in the summer gloaming. My muscles told me how many times I had visited every square inch of that wall. The leaves 14-feet up in the right-

hand corner. The trunk of the great tree whose shadow I painted over and over again until it read as real light. There were endless details and each one needed to be there. I rejoiced with each incremental step I took to bring the forest to life. Each degree closer to the feeling of the real light in the leaves, the texture of the bark, the shadows on the great stones.

And then, I couldn't think of anything else to do to make it better. I stood before it and tried. There was nothing left. I stood back and gazed upon this mural that was, in every way, the best I could do.

I stared and stared. It was like looking at my child. I *was* as proud as a father. It was in the world and, at least for now, could not be undone. That evening it was very hard to leave. I would get on my bike to ride home, but just stay, straddling the bar, looking a little longer at what I had done. Finally I did tear myself away. For the rest of the summer, and in some ways, for many years after, I went through my life always living in relation to it, knowing it was there. I often remembered it, existing, just sitting there in the world, and felt proud. The deepest part of me, the best thing I know, *is* speaking. In that one place, on that one wall, the middle of my middle, and the all of my all, is doing its thing, free for anyone to see.

MY DREAMS COME TRUE

It had been a rough year. I'd been praying about a relationship that was going nowhere, and bringing up things in me I wanted to get rid of. In addition, I'd being painting murals for 10 years and I was getting restless. I began to feel that a change was coming. I didn't know what it would be or why, but I wanted to go deeper, do something better.

I gave myself to prayer. I listened and listened, in a constant pose of reaching out.

As the year went on I felt it more and more—a change is coming. I'd been loving my time as a volunteer chaplain at the Nashua Street Jail. I thought that might be it. I looked into going to divinity school to be a chaplain in the military. My interest was piqued, but I learned that in order to fulfill the army's age requirements I would need to drop everything right that second and start down that path. I couldn't do it.

The months wore on and my reaching out continued unabated.

Then, late in December, after nearly a year of praying this way, I received a very clear answer. A very clear vision, an idea. It was an instruction. "Every weekday, between 8 AM and noon, do nothing but be creative." I sat with it. I could feel what it meant. No email. No phone calls. No errands or other work stuff. Just being creative. Four hours every day. It was *so specific*.

It was crazy to think of four hours every day only to be creative. No plan. No job. No ideas. It also meant that I couldn't spend those hours as I often did, seeking paying work. "But," I asked myself, "What's the point of praying if you don't accept the answer when it comes?" I would begin the discipline in the new year.

The time came and I was nervous, but ready. I honestly wondered what would happen. I speculated that I would find myself making some new series of paintings. The first morning came. I knew I had to be wide open and willing. This wasn't about forcing myself to make things. It wasn't about getting down to business making paintings. This was God's direction. He's in charge. I don't know what He's up to and I don't want to get in the way. That morning, as I listened, I felt that I had to be kind to myself. I had to let myself feel good in these four hours. I had to abandon fears about productivity, speculation about what would happen, and especially *fear that I was making the whole thing up*.

To that end, I started off by taking myself out for a walk. To open my eyes, get the juices flowing—to say yes. It was a cold January morning. I did what I love to do, walking around my neighborhood, taking in the houses, the birds, the trees. This was a brand-new year, and I was beginning a crazy new God-given discipline. I felt myself standing on a precipice. Life has me in its hands.

As I walked, I sang to myself. Not a song, as such—just whatever came out.

What did come was notes, a bouncy bass line. It kept me company as I strolled among the familiar streets. But wait, that bass line is kinda cool. I listened to it. I sang it again and made adjustments.

By the time I got home, the bass line was rocking funkily. In the previous months I'd been recording some songs I'd been writing. I walked upstairs and laid down the new bass line.

I'd spent 2007 living in the Bible. I went to it daily, drinking it in, snuggling up to it. In my confusion, its deep, spiritual messages became my home and my hope. Its characters spoke to me, taught me, admonished me. I was constantly considering the scriptures. At the same time I was teaching them at the jail. The Bible became the language of my heart. I loved it like I never had. Its images were my images. Its stories were my stories.

After laying down the bass line, it needed some words. I began to write what I'd been feeling in my prayers. Simple images, basic feelings. I tried just to say what felt true, describing God in a way I could feel. As I wrote, I found various Bible images making their way into my words. All that week I worked on the song. Soon it had several guitar parts, a funky groove, vocal harmonies, and a bunch of verses. It was a song unlike any I'd written before.

In the past I had sometimes longed to write songs about God. I'd longed to bring my love of the Bible into my songs. But I couldn't. It was too big. I didn't feel the authority to do it. I couldn't see how I could make a Bible song without it sounding preachy and stupid. The idea of making bad art about my God made my stomach turn. I never tried.

That spring I maintained the discipline—four hours every morning only for being creative. In that time I didn't make a single painting, but I did write and record 25 songs. They put into words and melody my spiritual searching, and later, my rejoicing. Once it got going it was like a faucet. Idea after idea came tumbling out. My relationship troubles being what they were, many of the first songs were my relief and gratitude for God's forgiveness and mercy. There they were on the page, in my own language, in my own words. But as I continued writing, I felt God's creativity. The answer to my prayer was real and I was in the middle of it. The songs were more and more about feeling strong and knowing I was loved. By the end, the songs I was writing had a totally new feeling—joyful, powerful defiance of self-consciousness and fear.

The whole thing was deeply alive. I had prayed for months, waiting and longing, feeling only that a change was coming. Then the instructions. And then, this outpouring of new ideas. The chord progressions were new to me. The style of the songs, the vocal ideas were fresh and beyond what I was familiar with. Some songs came out and I thought to myself "I don't know how to write a song like that..." But there it was. I watched myself become a better songwriter. New ideas grew my understanding of songs and how they work. They grew my abil-

ity and confidence. With each new idea I could feel the circle of my thoughts expanding. Sometimes I wrote a song that was too hard for me to play. Too many changes and chords that were more complex than I was used to. I had to practice and practice just to be able to play my own song. One song required me to sing faster than I'd ever dreamed I could. In fact, after writing it, I was certain I would never be able to sing it. I simply couldn't do it. But pushing through that certainty, and with weeks of practice, I could. My guitar playing, singing, and delivery progressed by leaps and bounds.

At one point, when I began to realize that I was going to be writing songs that grew out of the Bible, I panicked. I'd always hated Christian Rock. Pretty much all of it I'd ever heard was the very opposite of what I loved. A lifeless, artless, rehearsal of words without feeling or insight. It was as if they injected a canned recitation of praise into some clean, thoughtless chords, and sent it straight to radio. And here I was, about to make…Christian Rock. It was a terrifying prospect. How do you make good music when there's no model of how to do it?

In all my life I loved music. My heroes are musicians, poets. It's impossible to express how much love, comfort, joy, and the simple, beating, pulsing feeling of life I had felt from music. None of my musical heroes were Christian. They mostly didn't sing about spiritual things. But the music was great. The words were moving, filled with real experience. At the same time, I loved God with all my heart. I'd learned that God has nothing to do with anything lifeless or lame. God was the very source of every good piece of music and art ever created. God is sopping wet with honesty, soul, guts, meaning and everything that good art expresses. Why on earth did the combination of those two amazing things end up so lame?

And now, I was about to make an album. I was going to make a Christian Rock album. My stomach curdled to think of my art being like the sing-songy, over-sincere glib-rockers that give Christian music such a bad name. I couldn't proceed if my music was going to be like that. I wondered if it was possible to avoid it. Knowing no other way, I resolved with a fierce passion that my music would be real art. I would forget every vestige of what I knew about Christian Rock. I would remember only the deep gushing reality of God Himself, and the pounding, soaring flame of music. I would never skimp on poetry or feeling. I would demand honesty. I would never act like this is easy.

At the heart of it was the pure longing to make beautiful art that spoke honestly and truly about my beloved God. That desire burned with a white-hot flame. I worked each day, facing my fears and concerns, pushing back against the seemingly ever-present threats that the whole thing is foolish and will do nothing for anyone. I coached myself. I reached out in my heart to fight for my love. And in that listening, just like the songs, I received hearty, healthy thoughts, the antidote to these threats. All through my ever-burgeoning song book I wrote notes to myself:

I am an explorer. Don't miss the opportunity to really explore.

Hold the standard high. WORK. Make these songs better than ok. Work them. You will not love them if you don't intend them to be *wonderful*. Make them magic.

The world has need of wholesome, healthy, Soul, unveiling-the-beauty music.

Don't let them go without submitting to Beauty. To shining, white-sun, blown-mind, gently-watered Beauty. Do your work, artist.

Listen. With all your longing, with all your heart. Listen for beauty, for soul, ideas directions. Say yes.

God is the only maker of beauty. I am the reflection of the infinite Mind—no ideas of my own—about the business of infinity.

An artist works. Doesn't accept the nothing of no idea, no movement. The artist works and tries and experiments and builds, discards, arrives, makes decisions, and sees something wonderful. Not giving up and not accepting less than wonder!

Serve by defining Soul. Not selfish to live for Beauty. Unselfish to contribute to the world's understanding of Soul.

Art that is harmless, impersonal, glorifying, cleansing, broadminded, fun, joyful, playful, calling upon innocence, grace, eyes and ears, souls of those who can see it and live with it.

God owns sound and Soul and rock 'n' roll.

Prove, through music, the existence of God—not in words—in feeling.

May rolled around and I was swimming in songs. A new era of creativity had been ushered into my life. Where I'd never been able to write about the most important thing to me—God—now the floodgates were open. I saw the potential for these songs to serve. It was their job. I allowed the four-hour discipline to fall by the wayside and my creative life resumed a more fluid structure. I continued writing and the songs kept coming.

After church one evening I was approached by a woman I didn't know, but had seen around. Apparently, she had ended up at my website and found some of the recordings of the new songs I had posted. She told me she'd been amazed by the purity of their voice. She intimated that they'd become a safe place for her. She listened to them and was comforted. Not knowing what an important thing she was saying to me, with longing in her eyes, she said, "Keep going." Surprised, humbled, delighted, I felt her comments deeply. There is a woman out there who has been supported by my music. She's a stranger. She wasn't just being polite. It was real.

During all this, I had my great job teaching art at the Dimock Center. The pay was great, the hours allowed me to work on my own art in the mornings, and it was a five-minute bike ride from my home. But under it all, I knew it was not my destiny to teach. I knew, like a tidal wave deep in the murky darkness of my soul, that I AM an artist. At some point I will move on. As one year became two, and two became four, I felt the question waiting in the wings.

That spring, as a beautiful deluge of life-changing songs poured into my life, I began to feel that it was time. When I thought of staying for a fifth year I could feel it growing stagnant. "But," I argued, "what will I do instead? Just having a bunch of songs doesn't mean there's anything to *do* with them!"

Over the weeks, as the songs were coming, I prayed. I understood more and more that this would be the last year at my job. But what would I do?! Then, as I continued to listen, I heard in my heart, "Quit the job. What you are about to do won't fit unless you give it all your time."

I bowed my head in awe and gratitude. It was hard to believe. Yet, lots of things had been hard to believe, but they came to pass. I thought of the beautiful swath of songs, vibrating in my book. I thought of the newness, growth and regeneration I felt in writing them. Just a few months ago they were nothing. They were absent. Now, they are reality.

"What you are about to do won't fit unless you give it all your time." I silently, seriously considered. God is really, actually giving me my life. I am listening, and He is providing. He is communicating with me, in feelings, intuitions, and understandings. I felt as though I was in the shadow of the towering mountain of destiny. Yes, I will listen. Yes, I will trust. Yes, I will obey.

I loved the songs. I loved them with all my heart. They were my gift from God. They were teaching me—about music, about myself, but most importantly, about Himself, God. They were my treasure. As I lived among them, playing them, figuring out how best to play and record them, I longed for them to do their own work. I wanted them to reach others, to serve.

All along, as I prayed to have the courage to believe in the songs, I'd felt a strong, healthy rebellion against all the voices that would belittle them. In the absence of a person to play the role, I listened to the inner cheerleader. In a strong river of thoughts, it urged over and over, "These songs can serve. You're building them to help and heal. You're creating them to meet people where they are, to love and comfort, and inspire the hearts of real people!" I longed for it to be true.

The school year ended in June and I shook hands with my friends and colleagues at the after-school program. I loved them. I'd miss working with those good folks, caring for the children, daily laughing with them, helping them, disciplining them. But the mountain of destiny was quietly looming on the horizon. Its demands were iron, beautiful. Its promise was the deepest thing I knew. This was life itself. I let go of the happy, family feeling, the comfort of daily routine, and the weekly paycheck, and set out into the open sky.

I poured myself into all my creative endeavors, listening and ready for whatever was next. Over the summer the idea came. These songs are going to be an album. And it won't be an album like the ones I've made before—recorded on my laptop at home, limited in countless ways by my own weaknesses as a musician and recording engineer. The vision came into view. For this album you will hire skilled musicians to play all the parts. You will hire an engineer to record it. I wondered if I was even supposed to sing. I felt no ownership or need to do anything. All I wanted was for the songs to be their best.

The vision was clear. And I had no idea how to make it happen. So, with fear and trembling, I began to explore. I met with people and asked questions. I wondered how much it would cost. I wondered what I would do with it. For nine months I explored. In the fall I had some sessions with an incredibly talented instrumentalist and engineer. On the day I received the first mixes of a few of the songs I was overjoyed. The songs were infinitely better than they could ever be if I was doing it all myself. They sounded so much better than my

ALEX COOK

Tree of Life

songs had ever sounded! Still, after a handful of sessions, it turned out we had different visions for the project. After half-completing four or five songs, we parted ways and my search resumed.

Finally, in early 2009 a friend introduced me to a talented sound engineer who agreed to do the whole project to completion. He lived in Southern California. So, with my heart and my songbook in my hands, I bought a plane ticket and spent a month in Encinitas, crashing on his couch, working 10-hour days recording.

I played the rhythm guitars and sang the lead vocals. Justin played bass and lead guitars. We hired musicians to play drums, horns, cello, and a female singer for background vocals. When the horn player, a music professor from a nearby university, gave us his fee of $800, I had to take a serious moment of prayer. I'd just quit my job. Making this album was already far more expensive than anything I'd ever done in my life. The songs would still rock without horns. No one would ever miss them. Maybe? I closed my eyes and listened. "Is it right to move ahead with the horns?" A question came in reply. "Have you held the bar high all this time, only to lower it now?" I hadn't. I would invest in the songs—in my life. With that, I was assured. I will rise to the moment. I will hold the standard high.

As we worked I realized the album would be called *Tree of Life*. It was my image. The subject of my first mural. It spoke to me of eternity, spiritual life, towering over our lives. A friend helped me design the cover using a painting I'd made.

After the sessions I flew home and waited for the mixes. When they arrived I was stunned. Were these my songs? They sounded like they belonged on the radio! They were incredible. I drove around in the car, windows down to the summer heat, blasting my songs. My songs! My words! My love of God! Bouncing, streaming, shining in glorious colors in the streets of Boston.

When the CDs arrived I was jubilant. It sounded better than I'd dared to hope. I felt a golden glow of joy inside of me. It was here, in my hand. My holy hopes, the spirit made flesh. All told, I'd spent $7000 to create it. It was by far the most money I'd ever spent on anything. I wondered what I would do with it.

I was ignorant. But things were moving around me. I didn't know how to market a CD. But, I hadn't known how to make a CD either. I just loved to hear my beautiful ideas becoming real. I only knew to listen to God, and follow the guidance.

I mentioned my new music to some friends in passing. One of them was an organizer for a church singles event in Michigan. She asked if I'd be the entertainment! I was delighted to be asked, and at the very same moment, terror rose in me like a fire.

Though I had learned to tell stories in front of an audience, I'd never yet had a musical performance that felt good. Not one! The weight of years and years of uncomfortable performances bore down on me. But storytelling had shown me that I *could* shine the bright light of honest art in a performance situation. I just had yet to do it musically. And things had been changing. These songs were different, and made me feel different. A shift was occurring and I was in the middle of it. I couldn't tell what was happening. I said I would do the gig.

What was happening is that I knew these songs weren't just for me. I knew that God had given them to me, to help others. As I honestly listened and let the songs flow out of me, I wasn't trying to express myself. I literally was trying to express God. Yet, because they were *my* artistic voice, I felt them with all my heart. I wasn't passing along someone else's message. The songs were God's gift to me, but at the same time, they were intimately mine. As the songs came, I was visited by regular inspirations urging me onward. They assured me that these songs really could help someone else. In a word, I didn't wonder if they were good. I knew they were. I wasn't looking for approval, I was looking to be a comfort, an inspiration, a healer.

So when I was asked to perform I was in a different place than I'd ever been before. It's true that for most of my life performing music had been a self-conscious burden. But now there was something like a fountain of confidence pouring out of the very middle of me. It wasn't about whether they liked me or not. It was about touching people.

Still, when the night of the show rolled around I was *nervous*. Trembling and sweating cold sweat. Seventy-five people waited in the theatre for their evening's entertainment. Before this I'd never performed for more than 20 or so eye-rolling, impatient open-mic attendees. All 75 of them were waiting for me. For a few minutes I prayed. I thanked God for bringing me to this place, for giving me these songs, this voice, this opportunity, these people to serve. I thanked Him with my pounding heart, knowing I was in the right place.

It was time to go on. I made my way up the stairs to the stage. As I did I felt a very strong, very clear message. It said, "You are the boss. You own this room." I stepped out onto the stage.

The 75 people were splayed out all over the place, chatting, not paying too much attention to what was going on onstage. If I started playing they'd be free to keep chatting, missing the music. The importance of the message, the art, would fall apart. On the heels of the message I'd just heard came another one. "Tell them all to come to the front." At the speed of thought I stuttered and balked at the idea of demanding all these people do anything, let alone come hear me. At the very same moment, I felt in my bones, "I *am* in charge. I *do* own this room." Everything hinged on having this authority. I opened my mouth, and said, not faking, "I need everyone to come down to the front so we can all be together." The authority was Love. Easy as you like, everyone listened, coming right down to the front of the theater.

That night I had them in the palm of my hand. The veil was lifted and I did bare my soul. I looked out on their faces and I knew they were feeling it. They were drinking in the fountain that was pouring out of me. I did own the room. Love's authority was in me. I loved them as I sang. The songs poured forth, filled with feeling and conviction. They showed their colors, their passion, and honesty. Finally, and after months of listening and labor, I was free to simply give away the riches I'd found. The soul-treasures gushed from me and that audience drank them in.

From that time forward I never again worried about performing. On stage that night I'd felt more comfortable, more at peace than I do when I'm *not* performing. Now, rather than feeling nervous, I longed to perform. It was my joy, my freedom, like flying. A towering burden of pain and fear rolled off my back like a cliff breaking off a mountain. It fell harmlessly into the sea and never bothered me again.

That summer, a musician friend, also a Christian, asked me to join him and his band in a performance they were giving at a church youth conference in Victoria, BC, Canada that fall. My interest was piqued, but it seemed awfully far away. And a bit crazy to fly across the country to play a concert, make $100, and fly back.

While I was recording in Encinitas, one Sunday morning I had taken myself down to the local Christian Science church to worship. Afterwards I chatted with the folks, and mentioned we were recording an album of Christian rock music. Folks were interested and asked questions. I thought nothing of it until later that summer when I received an email.

Unbelievably, incredibly, and utterly from out of nowhere, one of those church members asked if I would like to fly out and do an album release concert in their space. They would pay for my flight.

An invitation to perform in Victoria, BC. An invitation to perform in Encinitas, CA. An idea stirred in my mind. A tour.

I reached out to everyone I knew on the West Coast. I told them about the CD and the tour. And, slowly but surely people were getting back to me. There was some bubbling interest. I pushed myself to be brave but flexible as I negotiated my fee for each concert. I sent hundreds of emails to churches up and down the coast and by the end of the summer the tour was set. I'd play 10 shows by myself on the way up from San Diego to Victoria. Then, I'd join the band in Canada and we'd play another 15 shows driving all the way back down to San Diego. A friend (the same one who had met me in the lobby of the church a year before) donated her station wagon, "The Hairball" for the tour. It fit all four of us, three guitars, banjo, bass, amps, various percussion instruments, an accordion, and all of our belongings.

As the tour began, I recognized the feeling I love—flinging myself into the adventure. Both in the planning and in the improvised days of travel and performance, friends and strangers came out of the woodwork to put me up and give me rides from here to there. With each passing day there were new friends, new connections. I marveled and inwardly crowed with pride as I made my way to the bank after a show, a wad of cash in my pocket—money from strangers in exchange for my songs, my voice.

In Seattle I showed up for a small concert. The room was intimate. I asked the organizer how many people I should expect. 30 or 40 she said. I spent the hour before the show praying and warming up. When the time came for the performance I peeked out through the curtain from backstage. I was mortified. Struck to the quick. There weren't 40 or even 30 people there. There were six.

My pride reeled. I couldn't walk out into that empty room! Waves of shame washed up in my face. So embarrassing! How could I sing deep and honest when all I can think is how nobody came to the show? I was sure they were all embarrassed for me. In my disgrace I reached out to God for a lifeline. "How can I play this show?!" I pleaded. Another voice showed up. The voice of the tour, of the songs, and their mission. It asked, "In all your life, how many people usually come to you and say, 'Share your riches with us!'" I thought of myself sitting at home in my room, writing songs, making pictures, longing for a way to have an effect. I had to answer, "Usually none!" The voice of the tour answered, "This is six more than none!" And in that moment I loved those six people. I longed to make them glad they came. The room wasn't empty. It had six real people in it. They'd come to be inspired, enriched, loved. I could do that.

I walked out onto the stage and gave the performance. It was intimate and special. The folks sang along and everyone enjoyed themselves. After the show one of the six thanked me for the songs. She let me know which ones touched her the most deeply. Soon she was opening her heart to me, telling me of her recent divorce, and how these songs had spoken to her, comforted her, reached her. I listened, treasuring her. I thanked God for this mission, and for my prayer before the show. How pride would try to keep these heart-healing connections from happening. It would try to block us up, scare us into thinking of ourselves. But no. It's not about that. It's ever about service, about loving those in front of us, letting Love be there with us. I could never again worry about the size of an audience.

In Victoria I joined the others. We spent a week learning each other's songs and headed back down south. Before each concert we prayed that the message, God's love, would be heard and felt. We prayed for each other, for our audiences, for ourselves. We longed for our music to be holy.

Going back 15 years I had dreamed of being a traveling musician. I had longed with a desire so strong it hurt. For years I had tried to start bands, find musical partners to achieve the sound and feeling I heard in my heart. And for all those years my efforts failed. None of it went anywhere. There were precious few shows, no momentum, and the sound never came close to the glory I knew was possible.

And now, as if it fell from the sky, I found myself with wonderful friends, singing what we felt, moved by Love.

At the end of the tour, in December 2009, the world was reborn yet again. I'd seen with my very own eyes that a tour was possible. People would come to the shows. They were moved by the music. They sang along. They bought CDs. I had a whole new trajectory for my life.

Over the next several years, from 2009 to 2013, I toured extensively. During that time I played upwards of 220 concerts around the country. I wrote and recorded a new album every year. The faucet continued to pour– songs about God, new ideas, year after year. Each album was a new exploration, new learning, new growth. I made my living from performing and selling CDs.

As I toured, I found a new iteration of my old love of hitchhiking. Night after night I stayed with members of the churches I performed for. Week after week, new friends opened their homes to me, eager to show me around their town. The love I'd felt hitchhiking and on bike trips was right there, ready to go. How I loved lying down each night in a different place, feeling the adventure all around me, each day arriving with a thousand improvisations. My address book filled with locations where I had standing invitations.

Since I moved to Boston in 2001 I'd labored to grow my artistic reach. Longing, ever longing to see my art have a loving effect. Over the years that labor had enabled me to paint several murals around the greater Boston area. By 2013 though, after five years of touring, I had connections in states all over the country, and here and there I was getting requests to paint murals thousands of miles from my home.

I could feel momentum growing. I got more and more invitations to perform around the country. I began to keep a running document of the grateful messages I received from people who'd been at concerts or listened to the albums. When I began writing *Tree of Life*, I was alone with my hope and faith. No one was asking for it. There was no inkling that it would be a success, or find its way into peoples' lives. I defended myself constantly against a thousand fears. These emails were heart-healing vindications of my most precious hopes. I received messages like:

"I can't say enough how much your music is blessing my thought and life"

"I have been listening to this CD day and night. It's awesome and inspiring. Obviously you've plumbed the spiritual depths and come back with some nuggets of gold."

"I need to tell you that your music heals. Your song was huge in helping me to forgive someone."

"I wanted to thank you again for your songs. It's my favorite album of all time. I listen to it in my car, and I had a healing on a 50-mile bike ride yesterday just from thinking about the message. Thanks for your inspired music."

And one that went straight to my heart:

"If you ever doubt whether what you are doing is blessing people, I can vouch for the fact that it is."

Going back to my year of prayer in 2007, I had no idea what was going to happen. I didn't have the slightest hope or plan of becoming a traveling Christian musician. I never dreamed that it would support my life for those years or that I would get to travel all over the country performing music to comfort peoples' hearts. I had labored in vain for years to create a life of music. But a year of prayer and humble listening, brought on by suffering and confusion, revealed these dreams come true. It enabled me to do my work at a capacity far beyond my hopes.

JEALOUSY MEETS THE GOD OF DESTRUCTION

I sat in the velveteen darkness of Boston's Jordan Hall. The concert was students of the New England Conservatory performing Americana music. Each performer was an impressive talent, interpreting old American tunes, playing a broad spectrum of instruments.

About a year earlier I had begun performing my songs professionally. I had one tour under my belt. Each day of it had been a revelation, the steps appearing as I took them. Virtually every piece of that puzzle had been unknown to me. I was making it up as I went along.

I never studied music. After six months of guitar lessons as a teenager, I quit and never took them up again. But I couldn't stop writing songs. Year after year I wrote and wrote, learning the guitar simply by the demand to play the songs I had written. Twenty years later I could get around the guitar fine.

However, the previous year, when I recorded *Tree of Life* and hired professional musicians to accompany me, the process had opened my eyes to the enormous breadth of skill out there. By comparison, it had shown me how limited my technical skills were. Every day in the studio I was very aware that I was the least skilled musician in the room. Mostly I was delighted about that. It meant that my album was going to be much better than I could do on my own.

At the same time, it was sometimes very embarrassing. Many times one of the instrumentalists would ask, "So, you want me to play it like this… or like this?" I listened, and, after some uncomfortable moments, had to admit that I didn't hear the difference. I could feel the instrumentalists and the producer looking at each other like, "What's the matter with this guy?" I felt myself struggling to keep up. I prayed to remain confident in leading the project, *my* album. I became aware of just how talented and skilled some musicians are. It was a humbling experience.

The students in the concert at Jordan Hall were all much more developed instrumentalists than I had hope of ever being. And they were 15 years younger than me. I thought of myself at their age, the embarrassing recordings I was making at the time. These kids sounded like professionals.

An act ended and the audience cheered. In the decaying applause, four young women took the stage. They announced themselves as the Sail Away Ladies. They prepared their instruments—cello, banjo, fiddle, and mandolin. The audience went still and they opened their mouths. Suddenly the room was filled with beauty as if it were a stream, curving and flowing in the air above our heads. Their voices were colored ribbons, waving in a perfect breeze, individual, but locked in immaculate harmony as if they were from one mouth. My heart rose in my chest. I adored them. I felt that I would rise up into their stream and swim around within it, my every desire satisfied.

In the same moment, like a razor in my reverie, I was struck with a poison thought, "They're more beautiful than I'll ever be." I fell out of the sky over the audience and back into my seat. My joyful swimming ceased. The beautiful music continued, now equally cruel and heart-breaking. With each swell of adoration I felt, I was pulled downward, against my own adoration by a red, acidic jealousy. They were too gorgeous. I wanted what they had.

From a child I loved vocal harmonies. I'd swooned, feeling the very presence of God, when I first heard the Tallis Scholars, their voices rising and falling like the praise of angels. Any time human voices rise in harmony, I'm touched. It's the language I feel in. I always wanted to be that harmony. It sang directly to my soul. In my own modestly created songs, I tried with all my might to create harmonies that approach the sound I was hearing.

And here it was, achieved to perfection by these prodigies, as if they were simply walking down the street. I felt as if I'd been lit on fire. The beauty was all around me like the most delicious meal or a long-desired embrace. But I couldn't hear it through this jealousy. Instead of uplifting, it mocked. "This is what you will never have!"

I sat in my seat, amid this sea of listeners, suffering. Like a medieval criminal, I was being drawn and quartered, pulled apart by the song. The beauty lifting me like a pure North Star, envy like a leaden weight, pulling down to the depths. The Sail Away Ladies continued, perfect and calm. Their joy shone out over us like sunlight.

Shocked at the violence of my reaction, I inwardly stumbled to regain composure. "I have to do something!" I wrenched myself out of the hypnotizing feelings and turned my heart to God. Even as I did I felt a pang of shame: "Who freaks out at a concert?!" But the pain was too much and I reached out to Love in longing, "What can I do?!"

My thoughts continued. I was indignant. "How can my reaction to beauty, the love of my life, be evil?" It was clear to me that this jealousy was evil. Not some random human foible—this was evil. Beauty is the star of my life. It has been the guide, the muse, the wind of inspiration over these many years. I have fought and fought within and without myself to see it and be part of it. Beauty is *holy*. Beauty is my best friend, my love.

So, to find in me this response to beauty was repugnant. I was disgusted.

I continued to pray. I thought more of Beauty. She with her capital letter. She, the outcome of the living God. God is the source of beauty. There is no beauty that does not flow directly from the fountain of Him. These Sail Away Ladies were singing God's song. In them, I was seeing God. I opened my eyes and let my gaze fall on them. Their mouths were open like dark O's. Their faces, moved with the emotion of the song. They were feeling it.

This beauty, I admitted, comes from God. The admission grew in my thoughts. I could feel it beginning to crowd the jealousy and its dark complaint. I grew indignant again: "Beauty does not cause me pain!" It gained momentum and I yielded to the push. It became clearer and clearer as I listened, concentrating. "Beauty is the song of holiness itself and I am not at odds with it—ever. I am not in a petty fight with God. I serve beauty. I admit its holiness. It is always right. Where beauty shines, I am blessed. I am never, ever cursed by beauty. It's just not possible. I won't allow it."

The whine of jealousy retreated and ceased. It was nowhere to be found. Where it had been was only letting, allowing. I gratefully admitted, I love beauty. I'm never at odds with it. I was at peace. The Sail Away Ladies sang a few more songs, which I drank in humbly, joyfully.

After the show I took the subway home. I was lit up with the music I'd heard. I'd long desired to write songs in the old-time folk style they played. Their songs continued to play in my thoughts. I drank in what I'd felt in my prayers. I shook my head in gratitude and relief to be free of the pain of envy. As the train rumbled through the tunnels I poured out the inspiration I'd received at the concert. Line after line, stanza after stanza, the night's event became words on the page.

As I wrote, I could hardly keep up with the lessons as they grew clear in my thoughts. I felt grateful for the beauty that had called up that jealousy within me. It lifted its head and revealed itself. Then, that sincere prayer, allowing the goodness of God to fill the space, had destroyed it. It was no longer there.

I'd never thought of destruction as a good thing before. I'd never thought much about God as destroyer. I knew God only as Love, guide, goodness, etc. The part of the Bible's old testament that speaks in those terms, I'd always passed over, not taking much note. But now, how wondrous to have a God who was a destroyer of evil! I marveled at what He'd done. He could reach inside me, move things around, and destroy things that hurt me, if I would let go of them. My prayer had been to allow the nature of God into my thoughts, handle the element that stood against beauty, and be done with it. It had happened right then and there. My head spun.

The words I wrote built themselves into a ballad as the train rolled along. With that old American folk sound ringing in my ears, images came through that lens—a 19th century hymn, imagining the awe of beholding the coming of God's army. The fear one might feel, seeing its power and vastness. And the grace and relief realizing that army is capable only of blessing, ridding the world only of what hurts and haunts. It became, "I Can Hear the Marching."

Open up the doors and the windows of the house
For the army of the Lord is coming
His legions fill the hills and they do just as he wills
I can hear the awful glory of their drumming

Open up the doors and the windows of the house
For the angel of the Lord does now approach
He will let not one thing stand that was not made by
    God's own hand
All flesh feels the fire of His reproach

And I can hear the marching of the army of the Lord
He is coming, He is coming, feel no fright
Only render up your lives, trusting ever in His grace
Which will come like a thief in the night

Open up the doors and the windows of the house
For his sentinels are presently arriving
They fill the sky with light, burning everything in sight
While the creatures of his hand are gently thriving

Open up your windows for the Lord is at the door
He will enter this your house, which he owns
Open up your hands and reveal all that you have
Because nothing will be left of these old stones

And I can hear the marching of the army of the Lord
He is coming, He is coming, feel no fright
Only render up your lives, trusting ever in His grace
Which will come like a thief in the night

The Lord comes to destroy without mercy on the wrong
Like a hunter with his eye upon the quarry
And as we stand and gape, we learn to love is to escape
And always for our good and to his glory

And I can hear the marching of the army of the Lord
He is coming, He is coming, feel no fright
Only render up your lives, trusting ever in His grace
Which has come like a thief in the night

Come O Glory, to this, my house, burning from the
    south unto the north
You are my savior and by your fire, you cause me to
    come forth
I am saved by fire, I kiss the holy cross
God's glory is revealed, it fills the mountains and
    the fields
Light is all around me, my savior came and found me
And nothing but his love can I feel.

EVERY KNEE SHALL BOW

In 2010 I had the opportunity to travel to Lagos, Nigeria for a week to participate in a church event. I would perform music and lead a mural-painting event with the 300 people assembling from all over Nigeria.

Once at the event I learned that the content of the mural was to be an illustration of a portion of Matthew 11:28, "Come unto me, and I will give you rest." They requested that the design be an image of Jesus, his arms spread out to the world, calling people to him.

I was excited. It's a powerful challenge to create works of art that express the enormity and depth of Bible ideas. It requires me to be very serious about the image, considering how to bring out its feeling, not simply a familiar or easy reading. Also, any time it's a picture of Jesus, one who symbolizes so much to so many, there's great gravity involved.

I planned the image. I would need to draw the whole thing out before the conference participants began filling in my design.

There are countless paintings of Jesus that I love. Most of them are from Europe, from the first centuries of Christianity up through the modern era. Some of my personal favorites are from medieval Europe. They sing of eternity. Many of them are incredibly serious, truly endeavoring to express the gravity of God's message to mankind. No small feat for an artist. These works are stunningly deep and beautiful. Interestingly, because they were painted by white-skinned people, who were making images for other white-skinned people to relate to, in these paintings Jesus is represented as a white-skinned person. He usually has romantically long auburn hair. Sometimes it's even blonde.

As much as I love those paintings, when I consider creating a painting meant to represent Christ—God's message of salvation to mankind—I am not tempted to emulate that aspect of them. My interest is in trying (perhaps in vain) to represent the spiritual nature of Jesus. I have a much clearer sense of what's worth depicting about Jesus from his teachings and character than from considering his physical appearance. That said, if you're making a painting of the man Jesus, you still have to paint something recognizable as a human. It's an interesting and difficult problem. Over the years I've come up with a few different solutions to it, with varying degrees of success.

In this case, since the mural was in Nigeria, where the vast majority of people seeing it are very dark-skinned, I planned to make Jesus a dark-skinned black man. The notion of making this white-skinned Jesus, as a white artist in Nigeria, was laughable. It was embarrassing to think of. It didn't cross my mind.

While the hundreds of participants listened to lectures and discussed contemporary Christian issues in workshops, I began to draw the mural on the wall. I wanted Jesus to appear larger than human scale to enunciate his spiritual, universal nature. To that end, I made an enormous, sprawling city, like Lagos. Jesus rose out of it like a tower, his open arms, gigantic over the city, spread through the sky. I did not give him long hair, but instead, a short, close-cropped haircut like the one I saw on most of the men at the conference. Though I knew we would be painting over my initial drawing of the face, I tried to give him an expression a deep calm—a beautiful certainty and mastery.

While I drew, three male elders from the church came out to the courtyard where I was working. They were wearing brightly colored, patterned clothes. The drawing was looking good and I was excited for them to see it. I knew they would be excited too.

"What is this?" one of them asked.

I didn't know what he meant. Confused, I went through all the parts of the mural. Here's the city at the bottom…At the sides are two trees to frame the image. Jesus is in the middle, arms spread, just like we agreed. We'll put the text of the verse over the top at the left and right…"

"No, no," he continued. "That's not Jesus." The other men agreed. I still didn't understand.

"Jesus has long hair."

Aha! Now I understood. I began to explain my thinking. I told them about representing Jesus as a black man given the context.

"No, no, no. This isn't right. Jesus needs to be white. He must have long hair."

"But, don't you want people to be able to feel that Jesus is like them?" I asked, entirely off-balance.

He went on. "If we make Jesus a black man, no one will know it's Jesus! They will wonder if we are even a church. Our neighbors will think we are not a Christian church! Jesus must be white. He must have long hair."

The three men thanked me and went back inside.

I could hardly stand in my own skin. I hated what had just happened. I felt disgusting, and at the same time, trapped. On my own terms, I couldn't imagine making an image of that traditional white Jesus, even at home in the United States, let alone in Nigeria! It was tired—a caricature of itself. I couldn't think of any way to bring it to life. I didn't want to bring it to life. It was perfect in 17th century Germany, but in the 21st century I couldn't do it. I couldn't bear to imagine myself—my white self, coming to West Africa for a week—and what I leave as proof of my visit: an image of a white Jesus on the wall. I wanted no part of it.

But, at the same time, here is a hard fact: I am a guest here. The very same desire to be respectful, to not support the violence and racism that made that image feel so wrong here—that very desire mandated that I listen. Like a wrestler, I was pinned to the mat. My desires were powerless. They were not the issue. Their desires were what mattered. This was their home. Their church. What I wanted didn't matter. It was my job to hear their concerns and let the art reflect them. I was here to serve their church, not to impose my own ideas on them. I was trapped between layers of racism and colonialism, poverty and desire.

For a few moments I contemplated going to the conference organizers and simply letting them know that I couldn't do the mural. I could simply not do it at all. But, as I closed my eyes and listened, humbling my heart, I knew that I could do it. I asked God to let me do what is most loving. Let me do whatever is most loving. Most like God.

And then I knew I would do it. My pride was pinned to the mat. It had nothing to say or do. My love for these people, for this church required that I bend my will to theirs. I could proceed because I love God. God can go before me, loving them. I will follow and do what is required. My pride was humbled. My love of God, exalted. It was growing like silent grass between breaking, cracking cement.

I went back to the wall and changed the face of Jesus. I gave him long flowing hair as if he were a hippy from 1972.

The next day I led 50 Nigerian youths in painting the mural. Not one of them ever asked why Jesus was white or why he had long hair. They dutifully, seriously, and joyfully filled in all the elements of the mural over a couple of days. When it was finished, they took selfies in front of it. A parade of the young men took pictures of themselves standing below the larger-than-life Jesus figure, mimicking his open-armed pose. They were absolutely serious, feeling the weight of the idea, demonstrating their own desire to be part of it, open-armed and glorious like Jesus himself.

Invariably when I finish a mural I post pictures of it on social media. I'm always proud to share my work, my best ideas. But this one I would never share. I almost didn't even want to take pictures of it for fear that they would somehow make their way onto the internet. Horrified, I imagined the furious comments that would pile up if my community at home saw this mural I had made. It would stay in this small corner of Lagos, Nigeria. It could serve this church. They knew their community, their own hearts.

HOLY, HOLY, HOLY

In the autumn of 2013 I was booked to give a concert at a prison in Ocala, Florida. I was on a tour in support of a brand-new album, *Songs of Deliverance*. A year or two earlier the same church had brought me in to perform at the prison. It had been a small concert—just 25 guys or so. I'd performed in a little classroom off the rec room of the monochromatic facility. The men sat in their loose-fitting tan uniforms around a table like students in school.

Every time I'm in a prison I'm filled with a feeling of humility. I think of the hard lives of these men. Many of them have done terrible things. And yet, here they sit, trying to learn love. I looked out at their tattooed faces and bulging forearms. Countless tragedies brought them to this classroom, these uniforms, listening to me sing songs of God's love and forgiveness.

Over the years I had given a handful of concerts in prisons. It's serious business to consider how to let my songs really be helpful to them. I loved to invite them to ask questions about the words, the melodies, anything. I wanted it to feel totally conversational—a chance to just be open about God, our questions, fears and stories.

I sat in the passenger seat on the way to this concert. Spanish moss hung from tall trees. The jungle of central Florida was thick and dense at the sides of the road. Then, the trees opened up and the immaculately shorn lawn of the prison lay before us. Tall wire fences surround the tawny block-like structures. I asked what to expect for the concert. My host, Jeannie, replied that it would be similar to last time, same classroom, same number of guys. I'd prepared 14 songs—more than enough material to fill the hour-long slot.

Entering, I remembered the setup—metal detector, search the guitar and case for foreign objects, visitor badge. A uniformed guard led us through a series of doors, steel and thick glass. Then, out into the yard, surrounded by high fences topped with razor wire.

We made our way to the rec hall. But when we arrived we were shown, not to the classroom, but to the large community room with a tall wooden stage. There, a couple inmates were preparing the sound system. They asked if I was ready to do a sound check.

I ran though some songs while they checked the system. As we did, the room began to fill with men. They poured into the large, plain, linoleum-floored room. In waves they came, talking, laughing, pointing, like students let out of school at the end of the day. By the time they ceased to pour in, the room was filled with 250 milling, gazing inmates. They were there for the night's activity. It was me.

Ok! Inwardly I adjusted. "Ok. Ok. This is really gonna be great." How much better to reach 250 men instead of just 25!

It was 6:58 and we were set to start at 7. I closed my eyes and prayed to feel God's presence with us, His love for all these men, and that they would feel it in my songs. When I opened my eyes one of the inmates, the sound guy, gave me a thumbs up and with a smile said, "Ok, we're good to go until 9:30."

I asked him what he meant. "The rec time—7-9:30 PM. You're on!" He jumped off the stage and disappeared into the audience.

The men were settling in and quieting down. The room looked to me expectantly.

"Ok..." I resolved again, "Here we go!" I would need to play more like 30 songs—way more than I had prepared. But it was time to go. Who knew what they would be? I'd play the set list I'd prepared and then just... think of more. It would be fine.

I launched into the set and the men watched with wide eyes. I wanted them to feel me. I knew these songs were true, whether you're a suburban kid or a gang-banger—God is the same. My experiences of God were real.

There can be a temptation to try to show that I'm tough, or that somehow I relate to the experiences of these men in prison. The truth is, I'm not, and I don't. I'm not tough, and I've never had to steal. I don't know what poverty feels like and I haven't ever committed a crime.

But I have been on my knees in need. I have longed for forgiveness. I have felt the joy of answered prayer. I've stuck with prayer while it humiliated my pride and made me humble enough to listen. I've been terrified and out of ideas and felt the grace of God come to my rescue. I've felt the endless compassion of Love and that no one is beyond the reach of God.

The answer is never to pretend. It is always to get naked. The safe place is in telling the truth. That means being honest about what I have seen and felt of God, never pretending it didn't happen. It means being confident of the spirituality of my story, trusting that its spirituality speaks in terms that they can feel too—because they are spiritual. I let go and fell into the soulfulness of the songs, trusting that they would speak to this room full of men.

A few songs in we did the first sing-along. Its chorus is a simple prayer we sing together—"Let love rule in me." Before I taught it to them I looked out at their faces. They were all looking to me. They were Hispanic, black, white, Asian. They were 18 years old and 70 years old and everything in between. I loved them. I imagined them singing these words, "Let love rule in me." I knew it was what we all wanted. These men are good. No matter what they've done, or what someone might say. Each one of them, in their innermost place wants to live love. I loved them for it.

The song is easy to learn. It's a real simple one-note melody while the chords change underneath. I sang it to them: "This is what we're gonna sing. Let love rule in me." I told them, this is a prayer we can all sing together, asking

God to let us feel more love, live more love." Many of the men nodded their understanding. I said, "Now don't be shy. This is for real. We're praying to God here. We're gonna ask God to let us love more. Don't be afraid to sing out loud."

I sang it for them, "Let love rule in me!"

We sang it together, "Let love rule in me!"

The room was slowly easing into motion. We sang it together again. I saw their mouths opening, letting out the words. We sang it again. And again. Let love rule in me. More and more of the men were joining in. I knew, once we were singing it together, it would be easier for more of them to join in. I watched them. We continued to sing it. Many of the men closed their eyes, feeling the prayer.

I launched into the song, singing the verses. Then, we came to the refrain. I called out, "Here we go!" and like a sea, they lifted up their voices, "Let love rule in me!" they sang. They all sang. The room was filled with the innocent prayer of 250 men in prison scrubs, asking God to help them be ruled by love.

Over the four minutes of the song we sang the refrain together several times. By the end, everyone had it down and sang with feeling. The last chord rang out as we finished the last line, "…rule in meeeeee!" It felt as though the whole room breathed out a great sigh of feeling. The men cheered loud, as audience members always do after joining in on a sing-along. I thanked them and let them know how beautiful their singing had been.

The room was changed. We had sung together. We had gotten a little bit more naked. We had all shown that we did want to love. We had let our guard down, even if only a little.

A voice from the crowd, "Give us your testimony!"

"Uh, what do you mean?" I stumbled.

"Give us your testimony, man!"

A chance to get that much more naked—to reveal more of what God had done for me, and how I've seen prayer work. At the speed of thought I reached into myself. "What can I say that will be most useful? Which of my stories of healing and prayer can I tell that will be meaningful to them?" I listened.

I told of being depressed and afraid for years. I walked them through my experience of disciplining my thoughts, learning to yearn for God's love, ceasing to complain within myself. I spoke of gaining momentum in my faith, learning to expect to hear inspirations and listen more to God and less to my fears. I revealed how much I had come to need and love the Bible and go to it for guidance and examples of spiritual power. I let them know how it spoke to me like a living friend. Finally, I shared that after those years of waiting, listening and labor, the fear and depression not only disappeared, but were vanquished. I was a changed man, transformed in a way I could never have achieved or even known was possible.

"Tell us another one!" leapt from one of the many mouths.

I rejoiced. *It's happening!* I gloried in my thoughts. *It's all happening right now!* I could feel the room waiting for me—waiting for the next thought that would come from my mouth.

I figured, *I've told them a story of being pulled out of misery. Now let me tell about God doing something beautiful...*

I opened up about my year of prayer and feeling lost in my life. I let them know that I had always wanted to make beautiful songs and pictures and that I received the instruction to spend four hours every day only to be creative. I told them about listening, ever listening with all my heart for God's guidance, receiving songs, and filling my book with them. I detailed every step of my journey to become a musician, creating albums, going on concert tours, reaching people in concerts just like this one. I gave glory to God for the way he had led me in a way I could not have found without that divine guidance and inspiration. Finally, I thanked God for bringing me to sing with them tonight, the current expression of God's love for me, and for them.

By this time, the room was mine. I had laid it on the line and they trusted me for it. They watched me reveal myself, my weakness and need turned into strength and supply by the grace and power of God. They were with me, and we could proceed with the concert.

And in we plunged. For another hour and a half we sang together, going over all kinds of different spiritual ideas in the songs—forgiveness, confidence, safety, trust, love. We all drank in the riches.

By the end I was drenched in sweat, exhausted, and in heaven. I bowed and thanked them. They cheered and whistled like I was someone famous. I unplugged my guitar and went to put it back in the case. But as I did, I saw a line, 50, 60, 70 men in length, setting itself up at the front of the stage.

I walked over and greeted the first man. He thanked me and shook my hand. "God bless you!" he chirped as he unclasped my hand. Man after man, they approached me, as I sat on the front of the stage. So many hands, clasped, held in appreciation. Each one thanked me for coming, some mentioning songs that had touched them, or that they loved singing together. So many humble, grateful faces, all framed in the tan prison scrubs.

When we walked out of there, my guitar back in its case, the steel doors crashing closed behind us, I thanked God, "This is one of the best days of my life."

LOVE'S ENDLESS VIGOR—THE GREAT SNOW OF 2015

In the spring of 2015 I had been dating Marcy for a little over a year. (Now she's my wife!) She got my jokes, I got her jokes. We were having a good time and I cared about her a lot.

As things got more serious, we began to talk about more practical subjects—money being one of them. I'd noticed that Marcy was laboring under the weight of her seemingly endless college loans. For some 20 years she'd been faithfully making her payments each month. The going was slow. It was clear that she was despondent about it. The towering debt hung over her like a dreary cloud. With many thousands of dollars left to pay, the end was a distant dream.

One day I was thinking about Marcy, loving her, and wishing she could be free of that burden. I asked myself how I could help. Over the years I'd built up some savings I felt proud of. I thought, "I could just pay the whole thing off." It would be a wonderful gift. But, though I could do it, it didn't feel right. The debt would be gone, but it seemed possible that there might be other negative outcomes that I couldn't foresee.

Taking it out of the realm of my own abilities, I prayed. "How can I be helpful to Marcy? How can I help her put this burden behind her?"

As I let ideas come and go, a few things became clear. It would be absolutely wrong for me to simply pay it off. I let go of that as an option. Then, a really specific idea felt very right. I thought, "If I get a job, something totally different than my normal work as an artist, I can feel free to use any money I make towards paying off Marcy's loans." I could get a job for the express purpose of helping Marcy with her loan debt. I loved the idea!

I knew too that I wanted to keep it secret. How wonderful it would be to surprise Marcy with a few hundred dollars I might make on some side job. I wondered what I might do. I remembered an architect friend of mine who'd gotten a side job stocking milk at the local grocery store to pay child support. He'd done that job for a few years and squirreled away the weekly pay. Over time it added up to enough to meet the need. I considered the patience of secretly, silently working a part-time job, and letting the small dollars gradually add up over time. I thought of all the manual jobs I'd had years before, gardening, construction, maintenance crews, mowing lawns. In recent years my whole focus had been on getting work as an artist so I wouldn't have to do other kinds of work! It felt strange to actively seek non-art work.

I didn't know where to start. So I prayed again. The thought that came was "Do what you always do—put it out there. Ask questions. Tell people your need." So, I sat down to craft an email. As I considered my friends, church community, and neighborhood connections six or seven people came to mind who might be in a position to have some helpful ideas. Some were friends, others more peripheral connections.

Putting the plan into motion, almost on cue, there were the usual suspects—doubt, fear, and embarrassment—knocking on the door of my thoughts. The usual complaints, "It'll never work! Why are you asking people? No one is going to have any ideas for you. In fact, they're going to be annoyed at you for even asking." I rolled my eyes and wrote the email.

I was between mural jobs. In fact, it was a slow month in a slow year. I had free time.

To my delight, within a few days I'd heard back from a few of the folks I wrote to. One of them, an older gentleman I knew of through church, mentioned that in the complex where he lived there was a need for someone to shovel snow off peoples' porches.

I thought, "Snow shoveling sounds bad. Maybe I won't follow up on that one." But on the heels of that idea, "If you pray and get an answer, if you ask and get a reply, it's your job to take the next step." So, I called.

It was March. Boston was in the midst of what would go on to be the highest annual snowfall on record. There had been blizzard after blizzard, every week since January. The snow was piling up around the city in incredible amounts. When I shoveled out my own car I often had to walk several car lengths away with each shovel-full of snow, just to find a place to put it.

I soon was on the phone with the maintenance director of the condo complex that had been recommended to me. I learned that it was a bit of an upscale place and people were feeling concerned that the weight of the snow might damage the balconies that looked out from each unit. With all the snow the usual maintenance crew wasn't able to keep up with the demand. They were weeks behind and getting more calls daily. He was amazed and happy to have someone coming to him out of the blue to help when their need was so great. He let me know that there was work available and I could jump right in.

The door opened and I walked through. The maintenance director made it clear that I wouldn't be working for him. I could just talk to residents and work it out with them. It got real when he gave me a list of names and numbers to call.

It had been over 20 years since the last time I had tried to get someone to pay me to shovel their driveway. Just before we got off the phone, in my ignorance I asked, "What's the going rate? What should I be charging?" I really had no idea.

"Oh, 60, 70 dollars an hour," he guessed. I was surprised at that number, but decided to trust that he knew the place better than I did.

I soon had a full schedule of snow-shoveling jobs at $70/hour. I started that day.

I was overjoyed! I kept imagining giving Marcy the money I was going to make. It would be the best! She would freak out! I drank in the feeling of doing something truly helpful. I could feel the joy coursing through me.

I arrived at the first location and got down to work. The snow was up to my knees in some places and up to my thighs in others. It was heavy, covering every surface. I leapt into the work.

Without meaning to, I kept thinking about Marcy. The moment of giving her this money. My wonderful secret! I was here shoveling and she had no idea.

I finished the first job and went to the second. I reveled in my secret plan.

At the next job the door was so blocked with ice and snow, the balcony could not be accessed from inside. The apartment was on the second floor. We found an extension ladder and I carried it out into the back yard, covered with hip-deep, untouched snow. I slogged through in the quilted coveralls I'd found in the basement of my old apartment on Green Street. Climbing the ladder with the shovel on my shoulder, I felt vigorous and strong. It was late morning, cold and healthy, wind and snow blowing in squalls around me. Somehow my life had brought me to this moment—climbing up a ladder behind the house of stranger, hefting myself over the railing into three feet of driven snow.

In that moment I understood what was happening. My joy at helping Marcy made me strong. The great happiness that came from secretly doing good, living for the good of another, filled me up and wouldn't let me go.

I worked all day until it was dark. Finishing one job I went directly to the next, somewhere else in the same building or across the parking lot. Each new job was like taking a bite of a delicious meal. My desire to help Marcy made me hungry for the work. With each of the hundreds of shovels of snow I threw that day, I could feel that I was doing something useful. By the time the winter sky was deep blue and too dark to work anymore, I'd completed five jobs. Each one had taken about two hours. At the end of 10 hours of shoveling wet, heavy snow I had $700 in my hand.

I marveled. First of all, where previously there had been only a wish, now there was $700. The other marvel was that *I wasn't tired.* I was only happy. I'd had a joyful day, laboring for the good of another.

The next several days I went back. Each morning they had a new list of names and numbers of folks who were waiting to have their expansive balconies shoveled. And each day I was filled to the brim with delight at the life I'd found for myself. The desire to help, combined with answered prayer, put me in a position to give a truly spectacular gift. The lightness of this fact burned in me like a candle. Each day I shoveled multiple locations, worked for hours, feeling unhindered and strong.

This doesn't mean the work was easy. It was hard, athletic labor. But somehow because it was for the good of someone else, because the doors had been opened by answered prayer, I knew I was part of something so much bigger than myself. In fact, like an athlete, rather than being depleting, it was energizing to pour all my strength into it. Each shovel-full of snow, each hour of labor only felt like a joyful challenge, to be met with the endless strength of Love. Not my love, exactly, but the Love that seemed to fill the day, my body, my muscles and desire. I hadn't known it would be this way. But I did know that Love could do that. I went with it. I gave in and let the strength of Love be mine.

Each day I went to new locations, met the owners, and did the work. After a few hours, the snow and ice cleared, I left with a check or a wad of cash in my hand. I joyfully stuffed them in my bag, aware of the swiftly growing total.

Several days into the project, I found myself waist deep in snow in a cut-away around a submerged basement door. I had to throw the snow up and out of the 7-foot-deep hole, just to get it away from the door, back to ground level. But Love made it easy to revel in the challenge.

That morning as I worked, Marcy called me. I picked up my phone and saw her name. What would I say? These many days I hadn't mentioned a thing about the shoveling. But I'd been spending so much time shoveling I'd been missing calls from her. I had the feeling she was worrying that I was avoiding her.

My body steaming in the endless snow, I took the call. My shovel protruded from where I had tossed it into a nearby snowbank. Marcy asked what I was up to. "Oh, not much…" I lamely, joyfully responded.

Marcy *loves* secrets. At Christmastime she loves to play the game where I say, "I have a gift for you!" And she, playing her role, with mock surprise, says "For me? What is it?" I reply, "It's a secret! You'll find out on Christmas morning!" Then we go through rounds and rounds of her saying, "Give me a clue!" or "What letter does it start with?" both of us knowing darn well that my clues will be lies and the letters I provide will be incorrect because we both want the secret to remain secret until Christmas morning. So, with that in mind, I had no intention of letting her in on what was really happening. My mind raced. I also didn't want to tell an actual lie! Finally, I found a compromise. I told her I was doing something very secret. I promised her she would find out soon and that she was going to love it. She was uncertain. I assured her again, "You're going to *love* it."

That set us free to play the game.

"What have you been spending all your time doing?"

"I can't tell you that! It's a secret!"

"Gimme a clue…"

Finally, a week or two later, the time came. I'd cashed all the checks and changed all the bills to 20s so it would be a nice big, fat wad of cash. At a cute little shop in the neighborhood I bought a fancy little decorated purse to hold the money.

I sat next to Marcy, hiding the envelope in my lap. The secret had been kept to perfection. She had no idea what she was about to hear. She had no idea how good it actually was. I was like a pot of bubbling water, about to spill over. I handed her the purse.

In a moment as surreal as it was joyful, Marcy pulled $2400 out of the purse and gaped. She looked confused, and amazed, then shocked, then confused again. The pot boiled over and I let loose with the whole story—the idea, the prayer, the shoveling, the joy. She melted.

It was one of the best moments of my life. A feeling of overflowing abundance rained over us that night and for days after.

I had several more jobs and a little while later added another $900 to the total. The total debt went down by about 20%.

Months later, Marcy intimated to me that she was inspired and invigorated by seeing the amount she owed go down by so much all at once. She saw that the end *would* come. She began to feel that she could be debt-free. It would be real and it could be soon. She started leaning into paying it off faster. She let me know that she began to triple her usual monthly payment. What had been a lifeless, drudging necessity, became an active effort, making consistent progress. She paid off the whole debt within a couple of years.

I thanked God for each moment along the way. The inspiring thought that I could help. The open-minded response from my friend who knew about the need at his complex. The surprising hourly wage! And with humble gratitude, the joy I felt as the strength of Love coursed through me, making the labor into happiness. The endless strength of Love made the countless hours feel like deep, colorful living rather than back-breaking drudgery.

THE GIANT

The next year, in February 2016 I was working on a mural of a giant. It was a poetic image I'd wanted to make for some time. The image had been coming to me for years, working its way into my sketchbooks and my understanding. I felt this giant. He was quiet, gentle, and enormously strong. He was serious. He had a calm, slow, sadness about him. Tiny birds lit on his enormous shoulders and hands. They knew instinctively that they were safe with him. I knew he meant something. I was delighted to have the chance to bring him to life on a public wall in Boston.

Up to this point I had never drawn him on a wall. And now, with room to open up, he towered over me and everyone walking by. He crouched humbly

on the floor, his knees by his chin, his eyes reverently closed. Seated this way he was 12 feet tall. I imagined him slowly climbing to his feet, his long slow arms and enormous hands rising up with him into the air above us.

One day while I was working on him, deep in the process, bringing him to life, I received a phone call from a dear friend. In her moment of fear she called me. I took the call, laid down my brushes and listened. She told me that when she had been a teenager, she had been sexually abused by the family dentist, and now, and for her whole life, she had hated to go to the dentist. Her teeth were hurting her and she was scared to get them fixed. A thousand hurts, past and present, were threatening her now, making her feel small, trapped and horrible.

For some time we talked, and I tried my best to comfort her, validate her, defend and encourage her. I wanted so much to ease her pain, her mind, her suffering as I stood there on the sidewalk, across a busy traffic-filled street from my half-finished mural. I paced up and down the sidewalk, listening and taking her part. After some time it seemed she was feeling better and more courageous to meet the needs of the day. We got off the phone and I stood there looking at the giant half-painted man on my wall. I looked at him and loved him. I began to realize that he is the silent, calm, patient voice of Love, the Christ. He is waiting, ever longing for us to give him our suffering, share with him our tears, and let him take away our pain. He just cares, and cares, and endlessly cares. Though he and I were thousands of miles from my sweet friend, I knew he was with her. If he could announce his good, slow, unremitting energy to me, she could feel it too. I realized what he, and this mural, were all about.

Shortly after that I wrote a song, "The Giant." The first verse goes:

ALEX COOK 2016
STONEBALANCER.COM
YOUARELOVEDMURALS.COM

DEJAME TUS CARGAS Y TUS LAGRIMAS
LEAVE ME YOUR BURDENS AND YOUR TEARS
ERES AMADO · YOU ARE LOVED

In the quiet of night, the silent giant arrives
With his eyes closed and his hands folded
He walks to and fro in our lives

His lips ever are closed, and he murmurs never a sound
But he sings a song that fills the sky
Lay your suffering down

Leave me your burdens and leave me your tears
Give me your terrors and devouring fears
Leave me the reasons you've learned through the years
To be frightened, troubled, and sad

In the lower right hand corner of the mural I wrote, in Spanish and English, the words "Leave me your burdens and your tears—you are loved." I thought of all the people in this neighborhood—their burdens, tragedies, gnawing guilts and fears. I longed for them to see those words and feel His invitation to hand them over. I prayed that each one of them would see his gentle, sad, patient face and feel that invitation from this Love, so caring, so serious on their behalf.

YOU ARE LOVED

In 2013 I received an idea that would become the leading thought in my artistic and spiritual mission for years to come. I was on the road seven months out of that year. There was one five-month stretch where I only saw my home for a couple weekends. That fall I recorded and immediately released an album, *Songs of Deliverance*. The moment I had it in my hands, I was on a 25-show East Coast tour. Everything was working on all cylinders and it was all I wanted. Not infrequently, people would compassionately assert, "I bet you can't wait to sleep in your own bed. You must be exhausted from all this traveling!" The first time I heard it I was genuinely surprised. The thought hadn't occurred to me. I wasn't tired, and I didn't miss my own bed. I loved the road. I loved performing, meeting people, working. There was nothing I'd rather be doing.

Beginning in 2009 I wrote and recorded an album every year for five years. It became what I did, the normal thing. In times when I wasn't traveling I was writing, putting into words and chords the things I was learning about God, prayer, and spiritual living. The songs came easily and joyfully, work and play occupying the same space. I became a much better songwriter, simply from the practice of doing it so much. At church each Sunday there was a need for a song. Often I gave myself the enjoyable challenge of creating a song to fit with the Sunday sermon, beginning the Thursday before. Songs became like days— some are real keepers, some aren't great, but there's always another one coming.

During those five years my business was performing and selling CDs. It's what paid the rent and satisfied my soul. I got better at creating and organizing a tour. The process of recording an album was no longer a wilderness and a revelation. It was a normal, healthy project like making a painting or creating a mural.

I felt an enormous satisfaction looking at the albums I'd created. Every so often I received emails or letters from people around the country telling me how a particular song had helped them, or that their family listened to it as the kids brushed their teeth, or that they'd prayed with a song and found healing. Each one was precious beyond explaining. I loved to think of people driving in their cars, walking to work, or just living their lives at home, listening to my songs, my babies.

An artist's work is always developing. We make good work when we continue to explore. So every year or so I would check in with myself, "Is the work good? Am I learning new things?" In each case, the faucet was still on, the ideas were flowing. With each new album I was learning and it was coming out in my songs and the performances. The material, the themes and musical styles were changing from project to project.

In December 2013 I returned home from those five months on the road. It had included a performance trip to England, the recording of *Songs of Deliver-*

ance, and the subsequent tour. I was happy to see my own bed. After a few days of relaxing I began to think about what my work would be in the upcoming year. Another tour? Another album?

I looked inside myself to my artistic intuition. What would I make? What ideas were bubbling? Doing this for just a few days I was met with a surprise. There would be no new album.

I sensed, as real as anything, that the faucet had done its work. It was slowing down. I could feel, clearly, that if I made an album the next year, it would be going over ground I had already covered. I knew I could make another album. Writings songs was easy. But if I did, it would be the mind of little Alex that was doing it, not the deep creativity—not God. And with that I knew, I wouldn't do it. I want the real thing.

After years of trusting this process, I wasn't afraid. I knew it was what I was supposed to do. God, the real thing, is in charge. But all I knew was what I wasn't going to do. So, just like that, my calendar, my life, were open.

In the last week of my tour I had played a concert in New Orleans, Louisiana. There was about a week between that show and the next one in Mobile, Alabama. Amy, my contact at the church in New Orleans, was the principal at a local elementary school. With an open week between shows I offered to paint a mural at her school to fill the time. She happily accepted.

She mentioned to me that they were making special efforts to help the kids feel more safe at school. She asked if the mural could help. I didn't know, but I was delighted at the challenge.

I took it very seriously. Could I make a picture that would help these hundreds of kids feel safer? It got very real as I thought of these little children going through the world feeling unsafe. There was a need. I, and art, had been asked to help. I longed to see my mural succeed. I knew a mural could do this work if it was sincere, plain, brave. If it could take the problem seriously and pour in the qualities of the solution—safety, peace, harmony.

The mural would be an undulating pattern of colored squares, designed to feel like a huge, wall-sized hug. The kids would walk past it every day on their way to lunch. I hoped they would feel my intention—a warm, safe embrace. As I worked I continued to think about helping these kids feel safe. I didn't want to just say that's what this mural was supposed to do. I wanted it to do it. I kept pressing, asking God, "How do you make a work of art that a child will feel? That will make her actually feel safer as she goes through her day?"

I listened for an answer. A day or two into the process a question arrived in my thought, cutting through the mist. It said, "Why are you trying to be subtle? Why are you beating around the bush? Why don't you just say what you mean?" And what we mean, what we want each child to feel is, "We love you! You're great! We want you to succeed and flourish! We're taking care of you!"

The idea crystallized. "What if I just write it? What if I just write the words "You are loved" right there in the mural? It was an exciting thought. But can you just tell someone you love them in a public place? Permanently? On a wall? Isn't there some kind of rule against that? If there isn't, why don't we do it all the time? My eyes widened. I hoped we could!

I asked Amy what she thought. She was for it! We made a list of the things we would say. You are loved, you are important, you are special, you are needed, and you can do it. Amy added, you are a thinker. Our list was set.

I went back to the wall and, in six of the 8"x16" cinder blocks, I wrote the six messages. I felt like I was crossing some sort of boundary or border, putting those tender, bright, loving words on a wall. Just minutes after I put down the brush, a group of eight 4th grade girls came through the door into the hallway. They instantly saw the words and began to read them out loud, all together, in unison. Slowly, and methodically, in the thoughtful way of children learning to read, they recited them. The words filled the hall. The words came from their mouths. In just a moment, it was no longer a thing I was saying, or Amy was saying—the girls themselves were saying it. Words of love were on their tongues, natural and plain as fact.

Driving back up to Boston, finishing the tour, it stuck with me. It had felt amazing to write "You are loved" on a wall in a public place. It was like leaving school in the middle of the day, or leaping in the air and simply flying into the sky. It felt like something you weren't supposed to do, but doing it anyway. And once I saw that it could be done, I wanted to do it again, bigger.

When I got home I began to make sketches for murals where the entire content would be the words "YOU ARE LOVED." I dreamed. What if you could do it in a downtown intersection where thousands of cars and pedestrians passed daily? What if the letters could be 12-feet high, towering over the people, asserting themselves by their sheer size? What if you could just declare love, confidently, defiantly, beautifully, right there in front of everyone?

Back in Boston when I learned that I would not be making a new album the next year, I simply moved ahead with the idea in front of me. I took it out of my thoughts and put it on paper. I did everything I could think of it give it legs, to prepare for it to be real.

My central thought was that I wanted to make murals that directly say the very messages we most need to hear when we're suffering. These same messages would build up and support the community in general. They would support a warmer, more assured community. I thought back to my own hardest times. What were the messages that would have saved me suffering if I had known them and felt them in my bones? What had my greatest fears been? I had wondered if I was worth anything. If I was good enough. If I mattered. If I was capable of doing the things I needed to do. Uncertainty over those things had cost me endless pangs of worry and fear. I began to make a list of the hard-fought certainties I had gained. They were these: YOU ARE LOVED. YOU ARE NEEDED. YOU ARE IMPORTANT. YOU ARE BEAUTIFUL. YOU CAN DO IT. I dreamed of these messages written out beautifully in murals all over the country.

I looked at my list. It was all muscle. Each statement was true. I could faithfully stand with each one. A voice in me said they were cheesy and saccharine, and would be seen that way by others. People would laugh and mock these messages. They would disregard them and roll their eyes. I said to myself what I always say when I hear that threat—it's only cheesy if you don't mean it. But I did mean it. I meant it with all my heart. I'd seen in my own life, in the jail, in the resolutions of my hardest problems, that the simple fact of feeling loved is more important than anything else. When someone feels worthless, what they need to feel is that they are needed. When someone feels ugly, what they need to feel is that they are beautiful. I knew there would be as many reactions as there are people. But if one person was comforted, that was worth another who rolled their eyes.

I knew these murals would start conversations. Some people would see the words and drink it right in. But others would have questions. Who says I'm loved? How do they know? What do they mean? All those questions are good. I loved to imagine the inner conversations people would be having with themselves, maybe fighting it out over time. I loved to think of the outward conversations that would come from them. Maybe one person would roll their eyes, but another, maybe a friend of theirs, would feel it. They would disagree and talk it through. Thought would be moving, and the conversations would be about love. Are we worth anything? Is everyone worth something?

Along with the idea for the murals themselves came ideas for how to create them in the world. One of the project's strengths was its positivity and community warmth. I imagined scenarios in which businesses, faith groups, and community organizations would give these murals as a gift to their neighborhood or a local facility. The community would receive the mural and the sponsoring organization would benefit from warm, photogenic press. The message of the murals could be demonstrated in the process of creating it.

For years I had delighted in inviting people who didn't consider themselves to be artists to join in the painting process. Like writing YOU ARE LOVED on a wall, this too felt like crossing a tacit boundary. It was wonderful to break through invisible social barriers with a warm, friendly invitation to join in a successful creative project. This would be the ultimate. Volunteers, church congregants, students, and strangers could paint together, filling in the words. Every aspect, from the sponsorship to the design, to the painting itself, would express love.

At this point in my creative career, after ABC, after all these murals and albums and tours, it felt normal to be starting a new project, again. The joy of expression, the new idea, pulls me on. It has arrived, like an animal emerging from the woods. I've witnessed it and I'm in love. I want to see how it will turn out. I want to see it become real in the world. I want others to see it. The desire is strong, thank God. I submit to it and do what's necessary.

I sent out proposals to everyone I knew. Everyone I could think of who might have an interest in the idea or know someone who would. What once was a terrifying act of faith and vulnerability, was this time, a simple, hopeful creative act. I knew the idea was good.

From the hundreds of proposals I sent out, one of the first responses was from my sister, a mother of three in rural New Mexico. I had never known her to be much of a joiner or community player, so I was moved to see how touched she was by the idea. I'd never seen her leap into action as she did, making connections with the principals at her children's schools and exploring the community for paint donations.

When you put something out into the world. you never know what will come from it. In this case, it was my usually shy sister, stepping way out of her comfort zone, to bring my idea to her community. The project required enthusiasm from others. There was no way I could do it on my own. It lived or died on community support—people loving the message, wanting it to speak to their community. With the door opening in little Socorro, New Mexico I was happy to do the whole thing for free and simply step through the door.

Just like that, in March of 2014, I flew out to New Mexico and created the first two YOU ARE LOVED murals. My initial feeling of freedom only grew. I soared inwardly as I sketched out the words in the cafeteria of my nephew's elementary school. The message, the wonderful, tender, true thing, would be seen! During the week, kids and teachers passed by while I worked. More than once I heard a teacher gasp at the size and authority of the message and the color. I witnessed those same teachers expressing a kind of amazed relief. I came to understand that this was an enormous validation of the work they do every day. Implicit in the teachers' labors is a love for their students. Everything they do, every little patience, every detail, expresses a general, unspoken love

for their students, and children in general. When the teachers saw the mural, 10 feet tall in the cafeteria, it was as though they and their countless labors had been seen and recognized.

The principal and the teachers took the project under their wing. While I was painting, classes of children were writing poems about what it feels like to be loved. They were drawing love pictures and discussing how we express love in our lives. At the end of the week there was a ribbon cutting with the students presenting their poems. The cafeteria was filled with parents and teachers, all thinking about love.

Artistically, the YOU ARE LOVED project was different than anything I'd ever done. For these two decades my pictures and murals had been representational. I'd always been a storyteller. The pictures that came to me naturally were landscapes and narratives. There were characters, figures and symbolism. And somehow, my new idea had none of those things. Three months into creating the YOU ARE LOVED project, I began to feel a terrible fear that I was going to hate doing it. No pictures? The same words, over and over again? Am I going to be so bored? I felt seriously worried.

I fought back. In a basic way I felt that God, my deepest creative sense, brought me this idea. If so, it can be done right, with heart and soul. I also knew that God has infinite ideas and inspiration. In this faith I promised myself that each YOU ARE LOVED mural would be different. I would use the unchanging motif as a way to explore every other element of the murals—color, design, texture, font, and whatever else I found. I promised myself that I would learn from each mural and use what I'd learned in the next and the next. I would not stand still. I would not allow myself to be bored or stagnant.

In fact, the further along I got, the more I understood that in order for the message to be communicated successfully, these murals had to be painted with great authority and soulfulness. It was easy to see that the message, no matter how much I meant it, was easy to blow off. What was it that had the power to make someone take the meaning seriously? It was the art. The painting. The color choices and design. I began to understand that in addition to the size of the letters, the success of the communication largely depended on being able to paint it in a way that wouldn't allow people to dismiss the message.

That puts a lot of responsibility on the shoulders of the creative side of things. And that's how I wanted it. I loved the challenge of creating designs that wouldn't let people off the hook. What if you roll your eyes at the words, but the painting is so good you can't look away? I wanted every facet of the works themselves to be so strong that if it couldn't get you one way, it got you the other way.

By the end of 2014 I'd created five YOU ARE LOVED murals. I began to feel that I was standing for the message. When I arrived to do a project, I carried the message with me. When we painted together, I found that I was not only in charge of facilitating an event, I was also the messenger. I was not just myself anymore. I was a representative of the message.

Because of my work at the Nashua Street Jail, I was on the email list for State of Massachusetts Department of Corrections volunteers. That spring there was a request for a mural at Bridgewater State Hospital, a facility that's part prison, part mental hospital. My heart burned. This was just the kind of thing I most wanted to do with the YOU ARE LOVED project. I wanted to take this message and its warm, inclusive painting process into the darkest places. That was the real heart of this project. There is virtually endless suffering happening and it is Love that can go to the hardest places and make them softer. Love can go directly to the middle of the darkness and make it lighter. Yes, the murals were beautiful, but they are about saving lives. Love could handle it.

I responded and within a month or so the project was happening. I drove up to the facility and saw the slicing curls of razor wire at the top of every fence and wall. Entering, I felt the familiar combination of sadness and joy, thinking of all the suffering, knowing I was there to witness Love. The crushing metal doors clanged closed behind me and I walked into a grassy yard between the buildings.

My guide, the volunteer coordinator, walked me through the halls and pointed out several guards and officers who would need to know I was there. I was shown to the hall where the mural would be. He brought me the paint I would be using and went back to his office.

As soon as he was gone I felt the task that was ahead of me. I began to see what I had taken on. I am standing in a deeply tragic place. The inmates here are convicted of committing terrible crimes. On top of that, they are mentally ill, suffering in ways I can't imagine. There is every kind of debasement, cruelty, and loss in this building. There is fear and confusion and misunderstanding of what is real and unreal. And I've come here to write on the wall that these people are loved.

I gazed down the hall to the gate where the nearest guard was. I wondered what he thought of this. I thought of the officers who come here every day. They are the ones that respond when there's a fight, someone has a mental breakdown, or tries to kill himself. They deal with the hard, hard realities of being here day in and day out. I thought of the guards I knew at Nashua Street. Some were warm. Many were grouchy and surly.

I boggled, "What have I gotten myself into?" I looked at my blank wall. I hesitated to begin. The moment I write these words out I am exposed. Every-one will know what I'm doing. I imagined the guards shaking their heads in disbelief. Dumbfounded, they ask each other, "What is he doing? Who is this moron? Where does he think he is, the playground?" I thought they might be right. Now, I'd spent a lot of time in at the Nashua Street Jail. But then I was having conversations, reading the Bible, a well-understood activity. It was a different thing to splash paints on the wall, and assert this unequivocal mes-sage. It could be truly insulting to them to have a know-nothing artist waltz in the door and paint some Pollyanna garbage on the wall and leave. It felt awful.

I returned to myself. I would proceed. But I had to do it right. I prayed. Quickly, I thought, "Is it true or isn't it?"

Thoughtfully, and comforted, "It's true." I remembered that it's true and there's nothing anyone can do about it. Everyone in this facility is loved—including the guards, the administrators, and myself. If they mocked me, it was ok. If they hated and despised me for my brazenness in this tragic place, it was alright. There wasn't even anything *I* could do about it. It was just true. I gave up and started painting.

I worked there for four days. A couple of the days I was joined by three inmates specially chosen for the project. I became friendly with several of the guards. One of them came and sat with us while we worked and popped some classic rock CDs in an old boom box. We sang along, making jokes here and there. It was brotherhood, right there in the mental hospital.

The mural, across the hall from the cafeteria was seen by lots of guys every day. I listened to them talking about it. "I know I'm loved," I heard one of them say. There were lots of questions from the inmates, as well as thanks and gratitude.

There is joy in deciding to witness goodness in the midst of the worst. The men I worked with were sweet, gentle, and talented. It was clear that painting on the wall was a deep joy for them. We talked about the message and how it would speak to men in this facility for years to come. We talked about all the hard things people are dealing with and that our work would be a comfort to countless guys who come through this hall, suffering. Right there in the pit of darkness, working together expresses respect. Being friendly and making a joke instead of being afraid—that too expresses respect. When people are respected (especially people who are more used to being disrespected) it brings love right to the surface. We felt a warm love for each other, talking over how to paint the mural. I gave some simple instructions and left them to do their best. They had their own good ideas and asked questions like the most motivated students. How deeply they wanted to do a good job. And they did. When it was over it was painful to leave. I loved them. I could tell they loved me.

This was a turning point in the YOU ARE LOVED Mural Project. It could go anywhere. The message was true. I'd been tested on it, and saw that it was the truth of the message that was strong. It wasn't going to change. The response had shown me that when I was confident about it, when I could get myself out of the way and present the message without apology, it could succeed. It didn't matter if they were mentally ill or dismissive and stolid, the message would land with some, and maybe many.

The previous summer I'd told my friend Ben about the project. He'd been floored by the unapologetic expressiveness of the assertion. He was about to move across country and hired me to paint messages on his car. During his road trip he posted pictures on social media of the YOU ARE LOVED car in various locations around the U.S. It was impossible to miss his ebullient joy at being a LOVE ambassador.

Later that year he'd sold the car to another free spirit who'd driven it to LA. After that we lost tabs on it. Around Christmas 2015 I received this email:

"My life isn't where I wish it would be, financially or emotionally. I screwed up so many times and had let people down, and I was contemplating making a seriously bad decision that would affect a whole lot of people. It would have been a selfish decision, and ultimately my final decision. I felt like going away would solve a temporary problem. And I didn't feel like I mattered anymore.

I said a quick prayer asking God to help me and shed a little light. Afterwards I took a walk and saw this [YOU ARE LOVED] van. I felt like it was a personal message to me. I almost started to cry in the middle of the parking lot. It greatly lifted my heart.

And for that, I wanted to say thank you. Thank you so much."

It was perhaps the greatest email I ever received in my life. I sat there staring at my computer in stunned, humble gratitude. Things were really, truly working together. Life-sustaining, healing things are happening and it was beyond the scope of my personal efforts. Ben had been inspired to have the car painted. The woman who bought the car from Ben had her own relationship with the messages. All those things folded together, had landed the car in a parking lot in L.A. where a suffering soul found it. It spoke directly to him. And that person saw the website written in little letters on the bumper of the car and felt grateful enough to email me.

I had to think of God. God gives ideas that grow us and bless others. God's ideas become actions and relationships that go out into the world and make wonders happen. The notion of being useful to God is the definition of humbling. I thanked God for his messages and letting me be part of the massive, precious whole.

Over the next years the project grew. The network of supporters that had grown out of my nationwide travels for my music began to show interest in YOU ARE LOVED murals. Individuals and organizations began to take me

up on my invitation to give the murals as gifts. A church in Oregon gave one to a nearby correctional facility for teen girls. A supporter in Texas sponsored two murals in local high schools. An individual in Southern California did a crowdfunding campaign to raise the money to give one to a jail in her community. A friend shared the project website on her Facebook page and it was seen by a woman at the State of Vermont U.S. Attorney's Office. And in turn the U.S. Attorney's Office commissioned a YOU ARE LOVED mural to publicize their work in support of victims of human trafficking. It has become one of the most visited works of public art in Burlington, VT.

As it turns out, the commitment to make each mural different from the last has been more exciting than I could have imagined. Over seven years the style of the murals has changed and changed again. One can follow the almost linear unfolding of different aesthetic elements and ideas as I explored them, learned their lessons, and made them part of my toolkit. There have been phases that were simple, and others that were intricate. Some have been angular and geometric while others are marked by curves and soft colors.

Perhaps the most interesting idea that came along was recognizing that the more the letters could be reduced to shapes, the more the paintings would read as purely abstract paintings. I turned the A into a simple triangle. I treated the V similarly. The O's became circles, with no hole in the middle. All the letters became shapes. And with that, the murals ceased to feel like text on a background, and instead, felt more like abstract paintings that one can read.

I found endless opportunities to connect the diagonals of the Y, A, V, and R. And then, more ways to relate the curves of the O's and the U. I could feel my understanding transforming. After making several murals this way, I saw

connections I hadn't seen before. The spaces between the letters became as interesting and important as the letters themselves. What would happen if the contrast was low from one shape to the next? Could you still read it? What if all the letters are versions of the same color, changing only in value? As if I had new eyes, I could see that the YOU ARE LOVED motif provided infinite opportunities to explore all the most fascinating elements of painting—color, texture, form, contrast, depth, pattern—on and on. Sometimes I challenged myself to make the murals as abstract as possible, where at first glance you might not even recognize the letters. It was almost laughable that I had felt concerned that I might be bored because of the unchanging content. Now I know there could be hundreds more and I wouldn't run out of interesting experiments.

Over the years what began as an idea became a nationwide project. I stopped wondering if it was going to work, and began thinking about how it could grow and work better. How could it reach more people? How could it be more effective? As of this writing (March 2021) there are 73 YOU ARE

LOVED murals in 13 states and 2 countries. Over the seven years that the project has existed, my relationship with it has only deepened. I see more promise and potential now than I did at the beginning. It continues to find willing hearts and hands who see its value and its special ability to bring healing, supporting messages to public places. I've been moved to be at the center of an artistic idea that exists not just as an aesthetic or visual creation, but which acts as a vehicle of healing to pressing problems like suicide, mental health, and bullying. I've been gratified to see organizations using the project as a tool to address those issues in their communities. There is no substitute for seeing one's work be useful to others.

I have high hopes that in coming years we will see the number of YOU ARE LOVED murals grow to be expressed in hundreds rather than tens. The idea remains simple, indivisible, and necessary. It's true. It will always be true. And there are so many voices on the internet, in culture, and in our own thoughts that argue for its opposite, that its message is ever needed.

As the body of YOU ARE LOVED murals grows, I'm excited as much for the statement made by the whole group of them as I am for each individual mural. There is something important in the repetition of the message. It doesn't work to say it just once. It's something that we humans forget too easily. I relish the opportunity to say it again, and again, and again. It's also deeply important to the message that the murals are in a diverse array of locations. They are in prisons and homeless shelters. But they are also in churches, schools, and business centers. They are in wealthy neighborhoods and poor. Each mural makes its clear, confident statement, but the group of them together makes another one. It shows how persistent and universal we need to be, and can be with this message. I strive to bring it to such a stunning variety of locations that people will be pressed to feel just how universal the message is. No one is left out.

I feel humble wonder to see that an idea is enough. An idea I put out into the world seven years ago now exists in reality, interacting with thousands of people. It also supports me in my daily life. Just like a hitchhiking trip 20 years ago, I don't know where the next steps will be. It makes itself up month by month and season by season. The idea gets shared, it speaks to individual hearts, and they take the steps to bring it to their communities. It's clear to me like never before that I am an individual part of a network of hearts, moved by the message of love, moved by beauty and an impulse towards a warm community embrace. This project simply cannot exist as the work of one artist. It needs the motivation and enthusiasm of others. It requires soft, caring hearts. It needs people so excited about the idea that they are willing to do exploring of their own—finding walls, talking to organizations and community leaders. I am in grateful awe that this happens, and there is always a next step.

ASKING

As I move forward I continue to listen for ideas, instructions, and guidance. I am resolved to remain as alive as ever (more!) to new projects, adventures, and ways to express the nature of God, right here on Earth. I know the direction I'm going, but I don't know what the specifics will be. I am ever reaching out, asking for more.

The Bible promises that God will give us what we ask for—*if* we ask. "Ask and you will receive. Seek and you will find. Knock, and the door will be opened to you." (Matt. 7:7) "If any of you lacks wisdom, he should ask God... and it will be given to him." (James 1:5)

Yet, we have all had the experience of asking God for something and not receiving it.

The Lord on high is mightier than the noise of many waters, yea, than the mighty waves of the sea

Over and over again the Bible counsels us to not simply communicate with God with words, but with our whole hearts. It turns out that asking, in the most serious sense, has very little to do with words—and everything to do with our lives—what we do, and cultivate in our deepest selves.

An interesting experiment is to ask, "If I could only communicate my desires to God with my life—no words—what would my life right now be asking for?" This is real asking. Another way to put it is that the language in which God hears is not so much words, as our lives. Our days, weeks and months, are the sentences we are speaking to God. What are they asking for? Are we asking God, Infinite Love, for things that She is likely to think are best?

Desire implies a longing for something we don't have. And, bringing God into the picture, desire implies a petition to God to fulfill that desire. "Your Father knows what you need before you ask him." (Matt 6:8) There is no way

to live a full, rich life without feeling a great longing to do it. Deep desire is absolutely necessary for healing, progress, and meaningful, joyful living. Mary Baker Eddy says, "In the quiet sanctuary of earnest longings, we must deny sin and plead God's allness…Such prayer is answered, in so far as we put our desires into practice." (*Science and Health*)

What are our longings? Where do they come from? The deep desires, the longing we feel in our hearts—we did not make up ourselves. Those desires are inklings toward God. When we pray, listening, we *discover* those desires in our hearts like gifts under the Christmas tree.

So, in essence, there must be no disconnect between our "earnest longings" and our actions. Our deep desires are telling us what we are to work for. A life lived this way, keeping our outward actions in harmony with our innermost longings, is constantly reaching out to God with the heart, wordlessly asking for the heart's desire.

It's wonderful—challenging and exacting—to pay attention to the deep desires that we truly feel. It requires giving up on things we think we *should* want. It means letting go of notions of who we think we should be. And, it means abandoning small, inhibiting, backward-facing desires. Having done all that, we can simply admit to ourselves what remains in our heart. These are the desires that we didn't create. We didn't decide to have them. They are just in us. They are sometimes surprising. But to admit them is always a relief. Then we're entering the path. We are admitting that we are not in control, but our true, deep desires tell us who we are and what we will live for.

The adventure begins when we strive to have the outward life reflect the inner longings. Why? First of all because we must learn to be silent and humble in order to hear and feel how God is guiding us with our desires. Sometimes we don't even know what our desires are. We're often so busy doing things because we think we should, or because others are doing them, that we don't even know what we really want. Other times, we're so distracted by easier, less demanding desires, that we entirely ignore the things that truly ignite our love. For our asking to be sincere, we have to let go of shallower desires, fears, and distractions. This letting-go effects real changes in our lives. Secondly, as we listen more closely, we find that our inner longings are spiritual and very often bid us to leave well-trodden, familiar paths. Instead, they call us to explore higher, purer territories, and to serve. Following the desires God has put in our hearts forces us to grow, learn, and expand. It puts us in situations where we have to overcome fear, pride, and other vices. But there's no replacing the joy and satisfaction that comes from living a life that's guided by deep, individual, God-given desires—the real thing.

Our days of labor, listening, and exploring are prayers. By living the longing we feel we are asking God for help. And it is given step by step. This process of asking, prayer, and action causes us to put our money where our mouth is. We're forced to let go of faults and self-interest that work against our larger desire. We may not know exactly where it will lead—but when we follow desire honestly, each step will be engaging. It will feel alive. We will long to grow into it more fully.

In short, the "asking" that matters is a function of the heart in which we humbly allow God to tell us what we most want, and then live in such a way as to see those desires be fulfilled. This kind of asking leaves no need for words.

ABOUT THE AUTHOR

Alex Cook has painted over 200 murals in the US and abroad. He has created 6 albums of original spiritual music and performed hundreds of concerts around the country. Since 2014 he has worked with schools, worship organizations, prisons, shelters, and more as the YOU ARE LOVED Mural Project. A longtime student of the Bible, Alex served for 7 years as a chaplain at the Nashua Street Jail in Boston, his hometown.

stonebalancer.com
youarelovedmurals.com
alexcookmusic.com

CPSIA information can be obtained
at www.ICGtesting.com
Printed in the USA
BVHW070534050921
615738BV00002B/3